L8.13
6.13

Paul Roberts

MODERN GRAMMAR

Harcourt, Brace & World, Inc.

New York / Chicago / San Francisco / Atlanta

PUBLISHER'S NOTE *Modern Grammar* is an abridgment for college use of *The Roberts English Series: Complete Course*, © 1967 by Harcourt, Brace & World, Inc.

ACKNOWLEDGMENTS For permission to reprint copyrighted material, grateful acknowledgment is made to the following:

Harcourt, Brace & World, Inc., and Faber and Faber, Ltd.: From "Anyone Lived in a Pretty How Town" from *Poems 1923–1954* by E. E. Cummings.

COVER PHOTO Susan McCartney.

Library of Congress Catalog Card Number: 68–22216

PRINTED IN THE UNITED STATES OF AMERICA

CONTENTS

CHAPTER 4

CHAPTER 5

CHAPTER 6

CHAPTER 7

Contents

CHAPTER 12

CHAPTER 13

CHAPTER 14

CHAPTER 15

CHAPTER 16

CHAPTER 17

CHAPTER 18

CHAPTER 19

CHAPTER 20

APPENDIX

INDEX   435

CHAPTER 1

The Sentence-producing Mechanism

What do we learn when we learn a language? One's first reply might be "Words, obviously." Of course it is true that learning a language is partly a matter of learning words and what they mean. When we learned our native language, we somehow got onto the meaning of all sorts of different words, from place names to prepositions. We learned that *stand* was different from *sit,* and *in* from *out,* and *brother* from *sister.*

But knowing words is not the only thing to knowing a language, nor even the most important. One might know the meaning of all the words in a large English dictionary and still be quite unable to speak English. One must also know how to assemble words in sentences and how to pronounce the sentences. Grammar is the particular knowledge that enables us to do this.

A language is in fact a very complicated mechanism for the production of sentences. As children, we learn the mechanism for the production of sentences in our native language — for the most part quite unconscious of the fact that we are doing so. At a very early age, we begin figuring out, from the random utterances that we hear, the rules of English grammar — how to ask questions, how to request things, how to say no, how to make past tenses and plurals, how to make certain ideas depend on others. To say that a person speaks English is to say that he has built into him, as it were, a set of rules that enable him to produce, or generate, English sentences as he needs them. The rules allow him to come out as occasion demands with just those sentences that will serve him — that will permit him to buy a bar of candy, tell a stranger how to get to Fifth and Main, plan a picnic, describe the causes of the Revolutionary War. They also enable him to understand the sentences of another person speaking the language.

When we talk to each other in our native language, we are not at all conscious of grammatical rules. We scarcely know that we have used here a subject, there a past tense, there a relative clause. Yet all the time we are working with a grammar, a set of rules for sentence production which we acquired simply by being born into an English-speaking community.

This is not to say that, having acquired a knowledge of the grammar in this unconscious way, we always conform to it in our speaking and writing. On the contrary, in our ordinary speech we are ungrammatical more often than not, and this is quite apart from the use of substandard forms, like "I seen him" for "I saw him," or failure to manage such niceties, or supposed niceties, as contrasts between *shall* and *will* or *can* and *may*. The ungrammaticality of the ordinary speaker lies largely in such matters as forgetting what the subject of the predicate was, dropping a syntactic thread at some point and starting a new one, putting things together that don't fit. All this usually goes unnoticed in general conversation because the hearer, who also knows the grammatical rules, unconsciously sifts and fills in and, as it were, rebuilds the speaker's sentences until they conform to the grammar.

A grammatical description of a language aims at presenting in a precise and explicit way those facts of the language that its speakers know instinctively but are hardly every conscious of and frequently fail to observe, at least in speaking.

Ungrammaticality is less marked in writing than it is in speech. When we talk, we rush along, filling the silence with words so that we can have our say before someone else butts in. When we write, we can take our time, reread, revise until we get the sentences in some sort of grammatical shape. Even so, most writers diverge now and then from the grammar, intentionally or unintentionally, and some diverge widely and often. The student may frequently have had the experience of concocting a sentence that didn't seem at all right, without being able to say just what was wrong with it. An explicit grammar aims at showing just what is wrong with such a sentence and how it can be put right.

The sentence-producing mechanism — the grammar — is what you will be mainly studying as you use this text. We will examine at least the skeleton of the English sentence and see in a general way how English sentences are made and what they are composed of. With this foundation, you should be able to confront more successfully other problems of language, such as those that relate to writing, reading, and the study of literature.

For some users, part of this material will be review; for others it may be entirely new. However, even those people to whom some of the matter is familiar will need to proceed carefully, working with pencil and paper, point by point. The grammar is extended here in many sectors, and confusion will follow inattention.

Kinds of Ungrammaticality

There are at least seven different ways in which language can diverge from some specified grammar. The following sentences illustrate these different kinds of ungrammaticality. They are not all ungrammatical in respect to *all* possible grammars of English. It is possible to conceive of grammars that would encompass the first five, and maybe the sixth. (There is no grammar that would describe the seventh.) But all are ungrammatical in respect to a grammar describing the present-day usage of educated American adults who are native speakers of English. (We will use the asterisk throughout this text to mark sentences or phrases that are ungrammatical in this sense.)

1. *He have always buy good suit.
2. *We saw some mans today.
3. *Stand not upon the order of your going.
4. *He looked rather a fool.
5. *Me and Jim got throwed off the horse.
6. *Flying low, a herd of cows was seen.
7. *Anyone lived in a pretty how town, with up so floating many bells down.

Let us consider these in order.

1. The first sentence illustrates the kind of ungrammaticality likely to be produced by someone who is learning English as a foreign language. In addition to the visible mistakes — *have* for *has*, *buy* for *bought*, *suit* for *suits* — there would no doubt be mistakes in pronunciation. For example, *good* might be pronounced to rhyme with *booed* rather than with *could*. Pronunciation difficulties are part of the same problem — the failure of the foreigner to master fully the rules of English.

However, there is very likely some pattern to the mistakes. Probably they are not just random errors but are induced by the learner's habits in speaking his native language. For example, in the native language there may be nothing like our *have/has* contrast; the speaker may be used to employing the same form of his equivalent of *have*, whatever the subject, and may be carrying over this habit into English. He may be used to a simple form of the verb in what corresponds to our participle position. In his language, the word for *suit* may be a noncount noun, like our *material,* and so he makes *suit* noncount in English and doesn't pluralize it. His language may have no vowel sound like that in our *good,* and so he substitutes the nearest thing to it, from his point of view, the vowel of *booed* or *food.*

Now it might happen that a whole population will learn a new language on top of its native language. All will learn it imperfectly, with more or less predictable imperfections. In time, they will in effect create a new language, with new grammatical rules, a language similar to but not identical with the original one and perhaps divergent enough so as not to be understandable by the original speakers of the language. This has actually happened in historical times. The ancient Gauls learned Latin from their Roman conquerors, failed to master it altogether, but failed in similar ways, and eventually produced French. More recently, millions of people in India learned English but again learned it imperfectly. What they evolved was what we might call Indian English, a language similar to our English but not always intelligible to Americans or Englishmen, though perfectly serviceable for Indians using it among themselves. Of course it has a grammar, though the grammar is not precisely ours.

Try to think of other examples, like * "He have always buy good suit," which illustrate the foreign learner's failure to master completely the grammar of American English.

2. The second example, * "We saw some mans today," illustrates a different sort of ungrammaticality. This is the failure of the child, learning English as his first language, to manage all its ins and outs. He has either not noticed or has forgotten that there is a special rule for pluralizing *man:* **man + plural** → *men.* Still, in saying **mans* he shows that he has already figured out the *general* rule for noun plurals. Presumably nobody taught him to say **mans.* On the analogy of *pans, toes, pigs,* etc. he has arrived at **mans* — no small intellectual feat, when you stop to think about it. He just hasn't yet absorbed the fact that there is here a special overriding rule.

The mistakes of the child are not the same as those of the foreign learner, but like the latter they are more or less predictable. They are predictable enough that one might write a grammar of, say, a three-year-old's English. The rules of such a grammar would be very similar to yours and mine but would diverge in some respects. For example, the grammar might have the rule **man + plural* → *mans.* Or, if the child uses both forms, it might state the choice:

$$\textbf{man + plural} \rightarrow \begin{Bmatrix} mans \\ men \end{Bmatrix}$$

By the time he is five or six, the tot will have removed most of these childish differences and will be using a grammar pretty much like that of the adult.

If you have an opportunity to observe the speech of children of the age of two, three, or four, report on some of the ways in which it differs grammatically from adult speech.

3. The third example — *"Stand not upon the order of your going" — is a case of ungrammaticality on the time dimension. It is a line from Shakespeare's *Macbeth*. Lady Macbeth, wishing to speed the parting guests, tells them to push on out and not worry about who goes first. From our point of view the line is ungrammatical. We would have to say "Do not stand upon . . . ." or, more likely, "Don't insist on . . . ."

In saying that the line is ungrammatical, we are of course not asserting that Shakespeare didn't write good English. His was simply English of a rather different sort from ours, with different grammatical rules. With the passage of generations and centuries, grammatical rules change.

Open to any page in a Shakespeare play and find a half-dozen expressions that are ungrammatical in respect to the grammar of present-day English.

4. The sentence *"He looked rather a fool" is for us ungrammatical on the space dimension. It is a sentence formed according to the rules of British grammar, not American grammar, quite appropriate in London, somewhat odd in Chicago. An American would say "He looked rather foolish."

Some Americans have at times felt a little inferior about their use of English. They have felt that wherever there was a difference between American and British English, the British were probably "right" and we were "wrong." There is no reason for this modest opinion. British English is no better than American English, and no worse. It just operates on a slightly different grammar. When peoples are separated geographically for centuries, they naturally drift apart a bit in their ways of saying things — in their ways of naming places and in many other ways. It is not only American English and British English that differ, but also Canadian English, Australian English, New Zealand English, Irish English. Even in a single country there will be remarkable differences resulting from geographical separation. Alabama English, Illinois English, Vermont English are all very noticeably different — have, in fact, different grammars.

Find or think of other examples of differences between American and British English. Give any examples you can to illustrate differences in English in different areas of the United States.

5. A sentence like *"Me and Jim got throwed off the horse" comes closer to the layman's notion of ungrammaticality. Something like this is what people usually mean when they say, "So-and-so uses bad grammar." But it should be clear by now that this is just one kind of ungrammaticality. It is bad grammar in respect to a specified grammar — that of educated American adults.

However, it must be stressed that there is nothing *absolutely* wrong with *"Me and Jim got throwed off the horse." It is just that "Jim and I were thrown off the horse" is shaped according to the grammatical rules used by educated people.

The point is that we are not dealing with universal rules of some kind of supergrammar. There is no particular reason why verbs in *-ow* should have participles in *-own*, and, as a matter of fact, not all of them do. We don't say *"The river had formerly flown by their house." Neither is there any particular reason why *I* and not *me* should be the subject form of this personal pronoun. It just is, in the English of educated Americans.

One might think that one was on firmer ground in insisting that the speaker, from politeness, name himself last, saying, at the very least, "Jim and me got throwed off the horse." But even this is not a universal rule. There are some languages whose rules require that the speaker, however polite he is, name himself first.

The ungrammaticality of *"Me and Jim got throwed off the horse" resides solely in the fact that these are not the forms that educated speakers would use in such a sentence. Naturally, a person wanting to appear educated and move among educated people must adapt to their forms, if necessary altering grammatical rules that had formerly governed his use of the language.

Cite other examples of this type of ungrammaticality.

6. All of the types illustrated so far, though they do not conform to the grammar of present-day educated speakers of American English who are adults and who learned English as their first language, do conform to other grammars. Certainly there are grammars of the English of the uneducated — just as complex, just as rigorous in their rules, just as predictive as the grammar of the educated. The rules are simply different rules.

It is not so easy to think of a grammar that would predict *"Flying low, a herd of cows was seen." The structure is not uncommon; in fact, it occurs rather frequently in the work of good writers of the past. However, it is now generally felt to be an error and one that occurs because the writer or speaker gets involved in a somewhat complicated sentence and loses sight of the base, or kernel, sentences that underlie it. It is the sort of error to which the native speaker of

English who is trying to improve his writing is prone, and one which he must work to eradicate. It is mostly this kind of error that we will be dealing with in the latter part of this book.

There is a rule in English — or at least in modern English — that when two sentences are put together in such a way that a phrase like *flying low* modifies what follows, the two kernel sentences must have the same subject:

John was flying low. $\Big\}\rightarrow$
John saw a herd of cows.
   Flying low, John saw a herd of cows.

But the structure in our example, to be grammatical, must then have the following underlying forms:

A herd of cows was flying low. $\Big\}\rightarrow$
A herd of cows was seen.
   *Flying low, a herd of cows was seen.

But since the first sentence was not what was intended, the complex sentence has been wrongly put together and is ungrammatical. It is also a bad sentence.

7. However, we have not said that all ungrammatical sentences are bad. We have studiously avoided equating *grammatical* with *good* and *ungrammatical* with *bad*. A quite grammatical sentence might be bad in a variety of ways. It might be insipid or in poor taste. It might be nonsense or a lie. Conversely, an ungrammatical sentence might be very good — might, indeed, be good precisely because it is ungrammatical.

Our last example is a case in point:

anyone lived in a pretty how town
(with up so floating many bells down)

This is the beginning of a famous poem by the late E. E. Cummings. Of course it is ungrammatical in various ways. It uses the indefinite pronoun *anyone* as if it were a proper noun, like *Smith*. There is no such grammatical sequence as "pretty how town." The second line is quite ungrammatical in its word order and collocations. The lines might be paraphrased thus:

An ordinary person lived in a quite ordinary town,
in which there were many bells which swung up and down.

But in restoring the grammar, we have removed the poetry. Cummings was departing from the grammar not because he was careless or because he didn't know any better, but quite deliberately in order to obtain certain poetic effects.

All poets do this, though some, like Cummings, do it more than others. They use the grammar as a point of departure and move out from it, straining it, experimenting with it in the attempt to achieve more effective ways of saying things.

In this text we shall try to single out the main features of the ordinary grammar of ordinary English sentences. This foundation should help you not only in conforming to the grammar when conformity is necessary, but also in knowing how to depart from it when reasons for departure are good and sufficient. It should also give you a better understanding of the nature of and reasons for the departures in the literature that you read.

Read "Anyone Lived in a Pretty How Town," or any other poem by Cummings, and cite other departures from the grammar. Explain as precisely as you can the specific ways in which the sentences fail to conform to the grammar of English.

The Divisions of Grammar

There are three general grammatical questions that we can ask about any particular sentence:

1. What parts does it have?
2. How is it pronounced?
3. What does it mean?

These questions reflect the three chief divisions, or components, of the grammar: (1) the syntactic component, (2) the phonological component, (3) the semantic component. We shall be concerned with all three of these.

The syntactic component describes the parts of sentences and the order in which they are arranged. It sets forth various agreements that are required, such as that between subject and predicate. Its basic unit is the *morpheme*, which may be a word, as in *man*, or a part of a word, like the *–ly* in *manly* which may be added to a noun like *man* to form an adjective. Thus *manly* has two morphemes: **man** and **ly**. When all syntactic rules have been applied for any particular sentence, the result will be a sequence, or string, of morphemes, such as this one:

 # the # boy + plural # fight + past # like # very # man + ly # chap + plural #

This string represents the sentence "The boys fought like very manly chaps." The symbol # marks the beginning or end of a word and will be used from time to time later in this book.

The rules of the syntax, however, tell simply what morphemes compose a sentence, not how the sentence is pronounced. We must, for example, have a rule that tells us how to pronounce **boy + plural.** We must have a rule that tells us that **fight + past** is not **fighted* or **fit* but *fought.* A rule must tell us that before a consonant sound the word *the* is pronounced /th̶ə/, not /th̶ē/. Other rules will tell us just how certain consonant and vowel sounds are produced in particular situations. All rules of this sort belong to the phonological component of the grammar.

The last component is the semantic one, which tells what sentences mean. This is the part of the grammar about which it is most difficult to say anything with precision. It is the part which relates the grammatical forms to the real world in which the language is used, and the real world is so very complicated that it is impossible, at least at the present time, to set forth the relationship in any sure and ready way. Thus, while it is not difficult to list the tenses of English and show what forms they have and how they are attached to verbs and other words, it is sometimes quite hard to outline the meanings conveyed by these tenses or to distinguish the meanings one from another. *Tense* is relatively simple. *Time* is exceedingly complicated.

Nevertheless, there are some things we can say about meaning. The sentence "The boys fought like very manly chaps" doesn't tell us whether the fighting took place this morning or last year, but it certainly informs us that it is not going on now. It doesn't tell us that it will happen tomorrow. It tells us who the actors are — the boys — and what the action is — fighting. It tells us how they fought — like manly chaps. Such things we can discuss in the semantic component of the grammar.

The Kernel Sentence

Grammar is essentially about sentences. There are some grammatical features — such as reference of pronouns — that cross sentence boundaries. But at least at the beginning we must confine our attention to the sentence and in particular to the very simple sentences that form the foundation of the more complicated sentences we generally use.

These simple sentences we call *kernel* sentences. This is a technical term. There are technical reasons why it is best to consider one type of sentence a kernel sentence and another — which may *seem* every bit as simple — not a kernel sentence.

A sentence that is not a kernel sentence is called a *transform*. Transforms are made by making changes on the structure of kernel sentences, reworking them, or combining them.

A kernel sentence is not necessarily, or even usually, a common or frequent sentence. "Lions growl" is a kernel sentence, but it is a sentence that hardly ever occurs. One rarely if ever has occasion to say it. Yet clearly if one wishes to understand the structure of something like "The growling of lions was heard in the night," one must begin with the more simple, though less common, "Lions growl." We shall spend quite a lot of time on simple sentences of this sort — those in which native speakers, at least, seldom make errors — before going on to their transforms, in which errors are more likely to occur.

The First Rule of the Syntax

A kernel sentence is made up of two main parts: a *nucleus* and an *intonation pattern*. The nucleus is a word or, more commonly, a group of words. The intonation pattern is a musical tone with which the nucleus is uttered. This is a combination of *stress* (the loudness with which syllables are uttered) and *pitch* (the speed of the vibrations with which syllables are uttered and which imparts to them a "high" or "low" quality).

Any kernel sentence has one syllable which predominates over all the rest and which is said to have the first or *principal* stress. This syllable is usually the last word in the sentence, or falls within the last word, as in the following:

> He saw a cát.
> She is his móther.
> The gardener procrástinated.

Copy the following, and use the mark ′ to show the syllable which has principal stress. Put the mark over the vowel of the syllable.

1. He has a kitten.
2. They watched the parade.
3. The plane landed.

If, however, the last word is a personal pronoun, a word before it takes the principal stress in a kernel sentence:

We sáw him.
They resénted it.
I recáptured them.

Copy the following and mark the principal stress.

4. He likes her.
5. John helped them.
6. Mabel found me.

If the kernel sentence ends in a prepositional phrase in which a personal pronoun is the object of the preposition, the principal stress comes before the prepositional phrase:

He gave the bóok to me.
He wálked with her.
I insísted on it.

Copy these and mark the principal stress.

7. I argued with him.
8. He stepped on it.
9. They fought over it.

The pitch is linked with the stress. English has three main pitch levels — high, medium, and low. It is usual to refer to these with numbers: 3 for high, 2 for medium, and 1 for low. In speaking a kernel sentence, which is just an ordinary sentence with no special emphasis, we begin on 2, the medium pitch level, rise to 3 on the syllable with primary stress, and fall to the lowest level — 1 — between the beginning of the syllable with primary stress and the end of the sentence:

$$^2\text{He had }^3\text{bought it.}^1$$

At the beginning of what word in that sentence does the pitch rise to level 3?

The intonation pattern may be shown graphically by a series of lines. A line just below the letters means level 2, a line just above means level 3, and a line well below means level 1:

He saw a cat.   They procrastinated.

Copy the following, and indicate the intonation pattern by drawing lines.

10. They have found it.
11. She may hesitate.
12. They fought over them.
13. You might like it.
14. He did very well.

This intonation pattern — with the pitch beginning on 2, rising to 3 on the syllable with principal stress, and falling to 1 somewhere between the rise and the end of the sentence — is the pattern of the kernel sentence. We will refer to it simply as "2-3-1." There are various other intonation patterns that we use in transforms, but 2-3-1 is the kernel pattern.

We may now write the first rule of the grammar, the rule that gives the two main ingredients of the kernel sentence:

$$S \rightarrow \text{nucleus} + 2\text{-}3\text{-}1$$

We will generally use abbreviations when it is convenient to do so in order to save space. What does S stand for in the first rule of the grammar?

The items to the right of the arrow define, at a certain level, the item to the left. This rule says that a kernel sentence consists of a nucleus plus a 2-3-1. We still haven't said what a nucleus is, except that it consists of one or more (usually more) words. We know what a 2-3-1 is only because we have discussed the matter. If we had just the rule to go by, we would have this still to find out.

The Second Rule of the Syntax

The following rule is the second rule of the grammar. It tells what a *nucleus* may be.

$$\text{nucleus} \rightarrow \begin{Bmatrix} \text{interjection} \\ \text{NP} + \text{VP} \end{Bmatrix}$$

This says that the nucleus (which will be pronounced with the intonation pattern 2-3-1) may be either of two things. We will regularly use braces to indicate a choice of this sort. The rule defines *nucleus* by saying that a nucleus may be either an interjection or the sequence NP + VP. It doesn't say what an interjection is or what NP + VP signifies. These terms must be defined by rules of their own.

We define *interjection* by simply giving examples of interjections:

$$\text{interjection} \rightarrow \text{gosh, heavens to Betsy, alas} \ldots$$

Note the three dots at the end of the list which indicate that the list is not complete. There are many more interjections than these three. Give three others. Interjections are special phonologically in that sometimes they are made with noises not used in other sentences of the language. How, for example, do you make the interjection usually written "tsk-tsk"? Otherwise, interjections are not very interesting syntactically, having no particular grammatical form. We put interjections at the top of the grammar, as the first part of this rule for nucleus, and from now on we need say no more about them so far as the syntax goes.

The Semantics of Interjections

Though rather dull syntactically, interjections may be lively enough semantically. We use them to express our joy, anguish, or despair. Any noise of pleasure and alarm is an interjection, and we differ a good bit on the particular expressions we use.

One kind of interjection is the swear word; among the most common is the verbal appeal to the Deity. Such expressions are often softened by the use of something that sounds like a word for the Deity but isn't quite — *gosh, golly, gee.* Such expressions are called *euphemisms.* Similarly, instead of saying "Damn!" one might use the softer interjection *darn. Heck* for *hell* is another frequently used euphemism.

Usage changes for interjections as it does for other features of language. Although you may occasionally hear the once popular expressions "Pshaw!" and "Gee whilikins!" for example, these are no longer in common use. In Shakespeare's time "'Ods bodkins!" was a rapping good interjection. It meant "God's little body," and it conveyed also the idea that the interjector was a pretty tough swaggering fellow. Leaf through a Shakespeare play and find other examples of interjections now fallen into disuse.

Syntax
Noun Phrase + Verb Phrase

So far as syntax goes, the interesting type of nucleus is not the interjection but the second possibility, NP + VP, and it is this type that will occupy us from now on. The letters NP stand for *noun phrase* and the letters VP for *verb phrase.* In saying this, we are not defining NP and VP but are merely telling what the abbreviations stand for. The structures must be defined by their own defining rules.

The word *structure* is also a technical term. It means a word or a group of words without reference to its use in a sentence. We indicate the use by stating the *function* of a structure. A nucleus (if it is not an interjection) consists of a noun phrase followed by a verb phrase. The noun phrase functions as the *subject* of the kernel sentence; the verb phrase functions as its *predicate*. Thus in the sentence "The cat swallowed the mouse," the structure that functions as subject is the noun phrase *the cat*. The structure that functions as predicate is the verb phrase *swallowed the mouse*.

Tell what noun phrase functions as subject and what verb phrase functions as predicate in these kernel sentences.

1. The mouse ran away.
2. The man beat the donkey.
3. A messenger brought the telegram.
4. Some porters carried the suitcase.
5. The nurse bandaged it.
6. A swallow flew by.
7. Her heart beat fast.
8. The guide led the way.
9. The lions growled fiercely.
10. Some villagers found it.

Semantics

The Meaning Relationship of Subject-Predicate

If all sentences were like 1–10 above, we could describe their semantics fairly easily. We could say that the subject names an actor — like *the mouse* in Sentence 1. The predicate tells of an action — like *ran away* in the same sentence. What are the actors and the actions of Sentences 6, 7, and 9?

Even in this group of sentences, however, there are some complications. Some name not only an actor and an action but also a receiver of the action. Thus in Sentence 2, the subject *the man* is the actor and *beating* is the action. But there is also a receiver — *the donkey*. The donkey gets beaten. What is the receiver of the action in Sentence 4?

The distinction between simple actor-action and actor-action-receiver will appear more formally later on when we discuss intransitive and transitive verbs. We shall see, however, and may note immediately, that meanings here as elsewhere are slippery. We may say that *the donkey* receives the action in 2 and *the suitcase* in 4, and yet feel that the donkey is a good deal more a receiver than the suitcase is. And we might want to balk entirely at calling *the way* a receiver in Sentence 8.

Furthermore, we shall consider many sentences in which there is no action at all and therefore no actor. In "The animal is a donkey," no action is alluded to, and therefore the subject *the animal* cannot be called the actor. Sometimes the whole meaning relationship is turned around. In "The donkey was beaten by the man," the subject is not the actor but the receiver of the action.

We shall note what we can of such shifts in meaning as we take up the different kinds of subjects and predicates in kernel sentences and transforms.

Syntax

The Noun Phrase

Recall the rule that tells what the main parts of a kernel sentence are. What is the rule for *nucleus?* What graphic device is used to show that something may be either of two things? How is *interjection* defined? What do the letters NP and VP stand for? Does the term *noun phrase* name a structure or a function? Does the term *subject* name a structure or a function?

We now define NP in the manner we have used previously, by showing the different things that a noun phrase may be:

$$NP \rightarrow \begin{Bmatrix} \text{proper noun} \\ \text{personal pronoun} \\ \text{indefinite pronoun} \\ \text{Det} + \text{N} \end{Bmatrix}$$

The braces again indicate a choice. They show that a noun phrase may be any one of the four things listed. These terms — *proper noun, personal pronoun, indefinite pronoun,* and Det + N — are also terms for structures, more particular ones than noun phrase.

We define each of the first three items by giving examples or complete lists of the structures that can occur in each category. Here is the rule for *proper noun:*

proper noun → David, Eleanor, Mexico, Sandy Hook, Mt. Shasta, Sycamore Street, the United States . . .

What do the three dots at the end mean? Give other examples.

The following is the rule for *personal pronoun:*

personal pronoun → I, he, she, it, we, you, they

This time there are no dots at the end, which means that the list is complete. If we were describing the English of an earlier period, we would add an eighth personal pronoun: *thou.* But in present-day English, *thou* is not worth bothering about.

Of course, all of the personal pronouns have other forms. For example, *I* has the object form *me* and the possessive forms *my* and *mine.* These will be introduced when we come to objects and possessives.

The third type of noun phrase is the *indefinite pronoun:*

indefinite pronoun → everyone, everybody, everything; someone, somebody, something; no one, nobody, nothing; anyone, anybody, anything

Is this list complete or not? How many indefinite pronouns are there? Of what four first parts and three second parts are they composed? Which one is spelled as two words?

Notice that we are using the term *phrase* in a technical way to include single words as well as groups of words. *David, she, everyone* are single words, but they all come under the general structure *noun phrase.* We have encountered some noun phrases, such as *the United States,* which are groups of words, and we shall see many more.

The noun phrase functioning as subject in each of the following sentences is a proper noun, a personal pronoun, or an indefinite pronoun. Tell which.

1. Everyone agreed.
2. They packed a lunch.
3. Angela gave her report.
4. Mr. Sinsheimer was reelected.
5. Nothing had changed.
6. I objected rather strongly.
7. Portugal abstained from the vote.
8. Something had disturbed Trudy.
9. You should have known better.
10. The Netherlands is a small country.
11. She wore a ring on her finger.
12. Miss Whimple dropped the ice cubes.

Semantics

The Meaning of Proper Nouns

Leaving aside, for the moment, Det + N, we may consider the meaning of the other noun phrases given by the rule, beginning with proper nouns.

Philosophers have tried for centuries to determine just what is and what is not a proper noun, and we can't expect to come any nearer the truth than they have. Actually, though we don't have much trouble in most cases, the concept of proper noun is a rather slippery one. Obviously we can't find out which nouns are proper ones by just noting which nouns are capitalized in the material that we read. Even if we could rely on an author's correctness in capitalization, we should still have to ask ourselves how he knows which nouns to capitalize and which not.

Proper nouns may be described briefly as those which name particular persons, places, and things. Thus *John* is a proper noun, and *boy* is not. This is true even though a million boys may have the name *John*. In any particular use of the word, it applies only to some particular person of that name. Similarly, *Omaha* is a proper noun, being the name of a particular place, but *city* is not. The *Department of Agriculture* is a proper noun, but *government department* is not.

Most proper nouns are not used with the articles *the, a,* or *some.* We don't say *the England or *a Jean or **some Omahas.* The word *the* does occur in some proper nouns like *the United States* or *the Netherlands* or *the Mississippi River,* but it is probably best to consider this *the* a part of the proper noun, not a separate article. It is something we learn when we learn the proper noun.

The names of the days of the week, the months of the year, and holidays like Christmas and Easter are usually considered proper nouns and are regularly capitalized. However, it is clear that they differ somewhat in meaning from the names of people and places. *Sunday* isn't a particular time in the same way that *Omaha* is a particular place. Sunday keeps disappearing and coming around again, but Omaha doesn't. Also *Sunday,* unlike *Omaha,* can form a plural: "He works on Sundays."

There are some words that are proper nouns by any definition a person can devise, but which are not capitalized. If *Satan* is a proper noun, then *the devil* must be too, but we don't usually capitalize *the devil.* If *Mars* is a proper noun, so is *the moon,* but we don't capitalize *the moon.*

Which of the following should be capitalized? Which do you think

are proper nouns? (There are right and wrong answers for the first
question, but not always for the second.)

mr. field	tuesday	winter
the sun	time	the atlantic ocean
the dictionary	cape cod	annabelle
hatred	water	the robinsons

Semantics

The Meaning of Personal Pronouns

The personal pronouns may be classified in two ways — according
to number (singular or plural) and according to person (first, second,
third). These are not just classifications based on meaning, because
the number and person of the pronoun may decide the form of the
verb or *be* used in the predicate. Thus we say *I am, you are, he is.*

The first person pronouns are those that refer to the person or persons speaking: *I* and *we.* The second person *you* refers to the person
or persons spoken to. The third person pronouns — *he, she, it, they* —
refer to some person or thing other than the speaker or the person
spoken to.

As for number, *I, he, she,* and *it* are singular in meaning, and *we*
and *they* are plural. *You* is a plural form, but it is either singular or
plural in meaning; that is, it may be used to mean one person or
more than one.

Give the number and person of each pronoun subject of the following sentences — that is, say "first person singular," "third person
plural," etc.

1. She did it herself.
2. We did it ourselves.
3. I did it myself.
4. They did it themselves.
5. It did it itself.
6. You did it yourselves.
7. You did it yourself.

As usual, the meaning here is a little more complicated than the
form. For example, though we call *we* a first person plural pronoun,
it doesn't actually refer to a group of speakers. If someone says
"We're going," just one person is speaking, unless the sentence is
shouted in chorus. *We* means "I and my associates."

We has a number of special meanings in addition to this usual one. It is used by kings and popes in referring to themselves, even though the meaning is singular. This is what is called the "royal we." An editorial writer on a newspaper may also use *we* with singular meaning, referring to himself. *We* is sometimes used with the normal meaning of *you*, particularly by adults in wheedling children: "We're going to drink our nice milk, aren't we, so that we'll grow up to be big and strong."

The pronoun *you* serves in English for both singular and plural. This is a recent development, having come about only in the last thousand years or so. Formerly *thou/thee* were the singular second person forms, and *ye/you* were the plural. The use of *you* (which eventually came to be used as subject in place of *ye*) to refer to a single person seems to be related to the royal use of *we*. Since kings saw fit to refer to themselves in the plural with *we*, it seemed only proper to address them in the plural with *you*. This usage was then extended to other royal people, to people who were noble but not royal, to people who were rich though not noble, and so on until eventually everyone was addressed as *you*, and *thou* went out of use. In some parts of the United States a new plural, *you-all*, has been introduced. In these areas, *you* by itself may be thought of as a singular form.

The pronouns *you* and *they* are often used not to mean the person addressed or specific other people, but just people in general: "You never know," "They say he did it." This is often called vague reference and sometimes disapproved of, but it is a very common usage.

The pronoun *it* may refer to a specific thing, as in "He spotted the car and followed it." But it has many purely syntactic usages in English, in which it is impossible to point out any particular thing that the *it* stands for: "It's raining," "It's getting dark," "It's time to move on," "Get with it."

Point out the difference in meaning of the pronouns repeated in the following pairs of sentences.

8. We go to the movies sometimes.
   We have ourself observed it.
9. You're a fool, Carruthers.
   You then add a spoonful of lemon juice and stir.
10. They confessed to the crime.
    They make children go to bed early in France.
11. It had a long tail.
    It should be getting light in an hour.
12. You'd think Jenny would know better.
    You are the one who borrowed my pen.

13. It was hard to see anything in the alley.
    It climbed the wall and got away.
14. They should pass a law against puns.
    They took the bus an hour ago.

Semantics

The Meaning of Indefinite Pronouns

One thing that you have probably learned before now is that the name of a grammatical category is no sure clue to the items in the category. One might reasonably think that an indefinite pronoun is simply any pronoun that is indefinite, but this is not so. *Indefinite pronoun* is a technical term meaning any of the twelve words that can be made by putting together *every–, some–, any–, no–* with *–one, –body, –thing.* Other pronouns may be semantically indefinite; we have seen that the personal pronouns *you* and *they* sometimes are. On the other hand, it is not always easy to see indefinite meaning in the indefinite pronouns. We might agree that the subject of "Someone agreed" is indefinite but argue a long time over whether the subject of "Everyone agreed" is. This simply makes again the point that semantics is much more slippery than syntax.

Perhaps the most important point to bear in mind about the indefinite pronouns is that, though they are often semantically plural, they are always syntactically singular, at least in conservative usage. That is, when they are subjects they are followed by *is, was, has, likes,* not *are, were, have, like.* It is hard to think of anything more plural in meaning than *everyone,* but of course we don't say * "Everyone are here" or * "Everyone like Sally" but "Everyone is here" and "Everyone likes Sally." The tendency for the meaning to dominate is strongest in the use of *they (them, their)* in reference to an indefinite pronoun: "Everyone averted their eyes." Conservative usage prefers "Everyone averted his (or her) eyes." It's a niggling point but one on which many people niggle.

SUMMARY OF RULES

A summary of rules is given at the end of each chapter. If, with reference to the summary of rules, you can complete the test and answer the questions rather easily, particularly those having to do with syntax, you should be able to proceed without trouble. If not, it would be best to review the explanations in the chapter. Only con-

fusion will ensue if you press on without a pretty good grip on what
has gone before.

These are the rules presented in Chapter 1:

S → nucleus + 2-3-1

nucleus → $\begin{Bmatrix} \text{interjection} \\ \text{NP + VP} \end{Bmatrix}$

interjection → gosh, heavens to Betsy, alas . . .

NP → $\begin{Bmatrix} \text{proper noun} \\ \text{personal pronoun} \\ \text{indefinite pronoun} \\ \text{Det + N} \end{Bmatrix}$

proper noun → David, Eleanor, Mexico, Sandy Hook . . .

personal pronoun → I, he, she, it, we, you, they

indefinite pronoun → everyone, everybody, everything; someone,
    somebody, something; no one, nobody, nothing; anyone, anybody,
    anything

TEST

1. Write three examples of interjections. Do not use those given
in the summary of rules above.

2. Give examples of three different kinds of proper nouns. Do not
use those given in the summary of rules.

3. Write the names of the three different persons, and under each
write the pronouns of that person.

4. One of the personal pronouns may be either singular or plural
in meaning. Which pronoun is it?

5. Copy the noun phrases that function as subjects in the following sentences. Tell of each whether it is a proper noun, a personal
pronoun, or an indefinite pronoun.

   a. George Williams rang the bell.
   b. It was a great surprise.
   c. Nobody was prepared for it.
   d. Las Vegas welcomed the delegates.
   e. Anything might happen.
   f. They renewed their acquaintance.
   g. The moon was at the full.
   h. You never can tell about Harry.

6. Each of the following sentences is ungrammatical in one of the

seven ways illustrated on page 3. Write the letter of the sentence, and tell the way in which it is ungrammatical.

    a. *Rides the King hence tonight?

    b. *He seen his duty and he done it.

    c. *He felt a complete idiot.

    d. *She good customer but no pay bill.

    e. *There is a ragged beside the who limps man crying silence.

    f. *My feets are cold.

    g. *He was very hard-working but who had no particular ambition.

7. Copy each of the following three times, filling the blank space successively with a proper noun, a personal pronoun, and an indefinite pronoun.

    a. —————— likes peanuts.

    b. —————— is very large.

    c. I think it was ——————.

    d. —————— would be all right.

REVIEW QUESTIONS

1. Where are Spanish names most likely to be found in the United States? Why?

2. In what way does the ungrammaticality of *"We buyed some things" differ from that of *"He are seeming very intelligent person"?

3. In what sense is *"They knowed it was wrong, but they done it anyways" ungrammatical?

4. In what circumstance might ungrammaticality be intentional and useful?

5. In what ways is the native speaker of a language likely to be ungrammatical in his ordinary talking?

6. Why is ungrammaticality less likely in writing than it is in speech?

7. What does S stand for in the first rule of the grammar?

8. What is meant by a 2-3-1 intonation pattern? On what syllable of the kernel sentence does the pitch rise to level 3?

9. One possibility for the nucleus is NP + VP. What is the other?

10. What words do the letters NP and VP stand for?

11. What do three dots at the end of a list mean?

12. What is a *euphemism?* Give an example of an interjection that is a euphemism.

13. The rule for NP gives four kinds of noun phrases. What are they?

14. So far as meaning goes, why is *Wednesday* less obviously a proper noun than *Chicago*?

15. Give three proper nouns that start with the word *the*.

16. Cite a proper noun that is not usually capitalized.

17. What are the seven personal pronouns of English?

18. What is meant by the "number" of a personal pronoun?

19. What is meant by the "royal we"?

20. What is meant by "person"?

21. What pronoun may be either singular or plural in meaning?

22. Indefinite pronouns are made up of four different first parts and three different second parts. What are they? How many indefinite pronouns are there in all?

23. Indefinite pronouns are singular in syntax but sometimes plural semantically. How does this conflict explain an expression like *"Everybody brought their own lunch"?

CHAPTER 2

Syntax

Determiner + Noun

This is the rule we have given for the noun phrase:

$$NP \rightarrow \begin{Bmatrix} \text{proper noun} \\ \text{personal pronoun} \\ \text{indefinite pronoun} \\ \text{Det + N} \end{Bmatrix}$$

We have considered the first three of the four possible choices. The fourth, Det + N, is more complicated and interesting.

The abbreviation Det stands for the word *determiner.* As the rule indicates, a determiner is a kernel structure that comes before an N in any noun phrase that is not a proper noun, a personal pronoun, or an indefinite pronoun. N stands for *common noun* — which means any noun that is not a proper noun. It means a word like *boy, salt, floor, love,* but not something like *David, Mount Whitney, the Netherlands.*

The rule for Det is complicated, and we shall give only the beginning of it in this chapter. Every determiner must contain an *article,* though, as we shall see later, it *may* contain other structures as well. We show this required part of the determiner in this way:

$$\text{Det} \rightarrow \text{Art}$$

An article may be either definite or nondefinite. As usual, we use braces to indicate the choice:

$$\text{Art} \rightarrow \begin{Bmatrix} \text{Def} \\ \text{Nondef} \end{Bmatrix}$$

If the article is definite, it is the word *the:*

$$\text{Def} \rightarrow \text{the}$$

24

If the article is nondefinite, it is one of three things:

$$\text{Nondef} \rightarrow \begin{Bmatrix} \text{a} \\ \text{some} \\ \text{null} \end{Bmatrix}$$

The word *a* in the rule for Nondef includes the form *an*. By a phonological rule *a* becomes *an* in certain situations: *a boy, a child, a mother*, but *an angel, an uncle, an hour*. Under what circumstances does the nondefinite article *a* have the form *an?*

The nondefinite article *some* occurs in such noun phrases as *some boys, some aunts, some meat, some love*. We shall see in more detail presently in just what circumstances *some* may be used.

Before some common nouns, we use no word at all. Thus we can say either "Some boys were playing in the yard" or "Boys were playing in the yard." Since the subjects of these sentences are quite similar, it is convenient to be able to say that they are the same kind of noun phrase and specifically that both are cases of Det + N. We can do this by saying that in "Boys were playing in the yard," the Det is a *null* article. That is, the article here consists of *the absence of a word*.

It remains to decide what kind of article the null article is — whether definite or nondefinite. Compare these sentences:

1. The boys were playing in the yard.
2. Some boys were playing in the yard.
3. Boys were playing in the yard.

Clearly only the first of these is definite. There is some difference in meaning between 2 and 3, but they are much closer to each other than either is to 1. Therefore, it is plausible as well as convenient to list *null* as a nondefinite article along with *a* and *some*.

Tell what the article is in each of the following noun phrases and whether it is definite or nondefinite.

some grapes	the fire	mutton
the dishes	a lady	some oatmeal
books	the doctor	candy

Common nouns can be subdivided in a variety of ways, but the most important subdivision is the following:

$$\text{N} \rightarrow \begin{Bmatrix} \text{count + (plural)} \\ \text{noncount} \end{Bmatrix}$$

A *count noun* is one that can form a plural — that is, can be counted. *Boy* is a count noun, because one can say "one boy, two boys, three boys," and so on. *Table, angel, disturbance* are count nouns: *five tables, ten angels, several disturbances.*

We indicate that count nouns can be plural, though of course they don't have to be, by putting the word *plural* in parentheses after *count.* The parentheses mean that the item doesn't have to occur.

But many nouns do not form plurals — or at least do not do so usually. *Information* doesn't. We don't say **three informations,* and therefore we don't say *one information or **an information.* Other examples of nouns that can't be counted — or aren't counted in ordinary language — are *furniture, laziness, indignation, wheat, salt, bread.*

Tell whether the noun in the noun phrase subject of each of the following sentences is count or noncount. If the noun phrase is plural, mention this fact also.

1. Sarcasm causes resentment.
2. Geese flew in ragged formation toward the marshes.
3. An accident caused the electrical failure.
4. The responsibility was too much for Harold.
5. Some nutmeg on the pie improved the flavor.
6. The mistake tied up the bookkeepers for hours.
7. Some explosions were heard at the fireworks factory.
8. Gravity exerts force on orbiting space vehicles.
9. Terror was visible in every move she made.
10. A riot broke out on campus.
11. Persuasion was tried, but it failed.
12. Catcalls followed the mayor's speech.

The definite article *the* can be used whether the N is a count noun or a noncount noun and, if it is a count noun, whether it is singular or plural:

the boy   the boys   the information

The nondefinite articles do not have this freedom. *A* is used only when the N is a singular count noun: "A boy spoke up." We can't say *a boys or **an information.*

Some and *null* are used only with plural count nouns and with noncount nouns:

Some boys spoke up.   Boys spoke up.
Some information was needed.   Information was needed.

We can't use *null* with a singular count noun: *"Boy spoke up." It is true that we can use a word *some:* "Some boy spoke up." But this *some*, which is pronounced with a heavier stress than the *some* of "Some information was needed," is in fact a different word, not the nondefinite article. We shall return to it later on.

Tell of each subject of the following sentences what kind of noun phrase it is — proper noun, personal pronoun, indefinite pronoun, Det + N. If it is Det + N, tell whether the determiner is a definite or a nondefinite article. Tell whether the N is a count noun or a noncount noun. If it is a count noun, tell whether it is singular or plural.

13. The band played on.
14. Gonzales trained the mare.
15. We weren't even invited.
16. Gazelles roamed in the meadow.
17. Some roosters were fighting in the pen.
18. No one had heard of the book.
19. Belgium signed the treaty.
20. A bee had got into the car.
21. Birds were twittering in the treetops.
22. Dorothy had another helping.
23. Everybody liked Williamson.
24. Some furniture had been moved in.
25. The chairman read the report.
26. Nutmeg should have been added.
27. They shoveled the snow off the walk.

Semantics

The Meaning of the Articles

The articles are actually quite complicated and give a good deal of trouble to those who are not native speakers of English. People learning English as a foreign language often never quite get the hang of them.

Essentially, the definite article signifies that the noun it goes with has been fully identified in some way. If someone says *the boy*, we know just what boy he means. The identification may have been made in a previous sentence:

We saw a boy and a dog. The boy was whistling. The dog was carrying a stick.

Or we may just know from the situation the particular reference of the noun:

"How's the team this year?"

"Well, the quarterback looks pretty good."

We know that *the quarterback* refers to that player on the team in question.

The identification is often established by a modifying phrase of some sort:

The man upstairs . . .

The dog that was carrying the stick . . .

In this kind of structure even proper nouns can have the definite article: "The John Keats that I mean runs a hotdog stand in Omaha." These, however, are transforms, not kernel structures.

Not all languages use the definite article in quite this way, which accounts for the mistakes foreign learners are prone to. The following sentences might be uttered, in the process of learning English, by people with certain language backgrounds. Rewrite them and correct them by adding or omitting definite articles.

1. *My oculist is the Dr. Witherspoon.
2. *They live on the Cape Cod.
3. *Please hand me monkey wrench.
4. *He smokes the cigarettes too much.
5. *Mr. Jones is in back room.

Some of our uses of the definite article follow no logical pattern. We say "He's in the office" but "He's in school." There is no particular reason why *office* should require the article here and *school* not. In this area, there are some differences between American and British English. Where we would say "We went to the hospital," the British would say "He went to hospital." Our *in the future* is their *in future*.

The nondefinite article *a(n)* is a form of the Old English word for *one,* and it still has much the meaning of *one.* The difference between "I saw a boy" and "I saw one boy" is that the first sentence merely assumes the singularity, and the second emphasizes it. As we have seen, *some* is plausibly taken as the plural counterpart of *a:*

a boy/some boys   an orange/some oranges

The word *a* in "He comes twice a week" is historically a form of the preposition *on,* not of *one,* though we would consider it now just another use of the nondefinite article. It is the same *a* that occurs in the archaic expression "They went a-hunting."

As explained earlier, *null*, the absence of a word, is best considered a nondefinite article, because it fills out the syntactic pattern with count and noncount nouns:

Some men were waiting.   Some information was needed.
Men were waiting.   Information was needed.

However, *null* is not always semantically like *some*. "Men are waiting" means about the same as "Some men are waiting," but "Men are mortal" doesn't have at all the same meaning as "Some men are mortal." "Men are mortal" means that all men are, whereas "Some men are mortal" suggests that there are others who are immortal. In other words, *null* can mean all members of a class, can express totality, whereas *some* can only refer to a portion of a class. Tell in the following sentences which subjects express totality and which do not.

6. Cats like milk.
7. Clouds drifted by.
8. Water flows downhill.
9. People were phoning in to complain.
10. Life is too short.

The complexity of our nondefinite articles, like that of the definite, is reflected by the mistakes foreign learners make. Sometimes they use the definite where we require nondefinite, and vice versa. Rewrite the following, making them grammatical.

11. *All the people hoped for the peace.
12. *When he was little, he was afraid of dark.
13. *He studies the music with Professor Katz.
14. *You have the good heart.
15. *We met young man at the game.

Semantics

The Meaning of Nouns

Nouns are usually said to be words that refer to persons, places, and things, and they usually do, but of course that is not how we know that they are nouns. It is rather the other way about. We recognize certain words as nouns from the way in which they are used in sentences, and thus know that they refer to persons, places, or things.

You can prove to yourself that one can recognize words as nouns without knowing what the words mean by pointing out the nouns in the following passage:

> The young rath was eating strubs in the strippin behind the mam-well when a princh came by. Seeing the princh, the rath naturally headed for a nearby quigwire, but a large gollytap barred the way. Dodging the gollytap, the rath stumbled into a whamble, where the princh caught him and ate him up.

The syntax tells us that *strubs* are things that can be eaten, or, at least, that can be eaten by raths. A *princh* is presumably an animal, one that preys on raths, and so on.

So we can with some truth say that nouns name persons, places, and things, and that the syntax tells us which words are nouns and do this. We have to take the word *thing* in a very broad sense, however, for nouns name not only tangible objects, like sticks and stones, quigwires and gollytaps, but also such items as leisure, time, ignorance, angel, unhappiness, future. Frame a sentence for each of these words, using the word as a noun.

We have seen that common nouns can be divided into two main subtypes — count and noncount. Count nouns — those that can be counted — are most commonly tangible. That is, they refer to things that can be seen and touched. *Boy, desk, church, street* are count nouns of this sort. Not all count nouns refer to tangible persons, places, or objects, however. *Angel* is a count noun, because we can say *five angels*, but few people have seen or touched an angel. *Nuisance* is a count noun, because we say "That's a nuisance," but it doesn't refer to any tangible thing.

Noncount nouns are of two main types: (1) those that name masses or materials and (2) those that name qualities, states of mind, and the like. Examples of the first sort are *dirt, bread, grease, water.* Give five more examples. Examples of the second are *enthusiasm, quietness, dignity, seclusion.* Give five more.

Most words that commonly are used as noncount nouns may also occur as count nouns. That is, they may be pluralized or used with the nondefinite article *a: a bread, breads.* There is always at least a slight change in meaning, sometimes not so slight:

NONCOUNT: He bought paper.
COUNT: He bought a paper.

What is the meaning of *paper* in each sentence?

It is not really difficult to think of a situation in which *bread* might be used as a count noun:

Mrs. Popperwill tried several different breads before she found a
bread she really liked.

Make two sentences for each of the following nouns. Use the noun
as a noncount noun in the first sentence and as a count noun in the
second.

meat   material   root beer   sand

Noncount nouns of the other group — the *enthusiasm* type — may
sometimes occur as count nouns also:

NONCOUNT: He has trouble.
COUNT: He has troubles.
NONCOUNT: Mabel was notable for kindness.
COUNT: Mabel was notable for her little kindnesses.

Use each of the following first as a count noun and second as a
noncount noun:

energy   anxiety   sin   pleasure

While most words commonly thought of as being in the noncount
group may also occur as count nouns, the reverse is not true. The
great group of count nouns cannot become noncount. *Table* is simply
a count noun, and if we put it in a noncount structure, the result is
an ungrammatical sentence: *"He bought table," *"He bought some
table."

Semantics

Concrete and Abstract Nouns

Nouns are sometimes spoken of as being either *concrete* or *abstract*.
Roughly, a concrete noun is one that refers to something tangible
or perceivable — like *boy, pig, table*. An abstract noun is one that
refers to a quality or idea — like *mankind, courage, truth*. This is a
semantic classification, and it does not run parallel with the structural
one of count/noncount. A count noun may be either concrete or
abstract, and so may a noncount noun.

Once again we may note the great complexity of semantics as
compared with syntax. We can easily tell whether a noun is count or
noncount by noting the way in which it is used with the nondefinite
articles, but we might argue a good deal about whether certain nouns
are concrete or abstract without finding any way to resolve the argu-

ment. Thus, is *truths* count or noncount in "He learned some hard truths"? Is it concrete or abstract?

It is also true that there are degrees of abstraction. *Pig* is less abstract than *mammal*, which is less abstract than *animal*, which is less abstract than *living being*. We would arrange these from most abstract to most concrete this way:

living being   animal   mammal   pig

Reorder the following groups, arranging them similarly:

furniture	object	refrigerator	kitchen appliance
George	male	boy	human being
book	novel	*Tom Sawyer*	American Literature

Syntax

The Verb Phrase

The rule for nucleus gives a choice between interjection and NP + VP. What additional feature will be present, whichever the nucleus is?

We have looked at some (though by no means all) of the characteristics of the NP of NP + VP. This is the noun phrase that functions as the subject of the kernel sentence. We shall see that a noun phrase may function in other ways too; it may function in various ways *within* the verb phrase. But the NP of NP + VP functions as the subject.

The VP functions as the predicate of the kernel sentence. This is the rule for the *verb phrase:*

$$VP \rightarrow Aux + \left\{ \begin{array}{l} be + \left\{ \begin{array}{l} NP \\ Adj \\ Adv\text{-}p \end{array} \right\} \\ verbal \end{array} \right\}$$

The rule says that the verb phrase of the kernel sentence must first of all contain an Aux, whatever that is. (The abbreviation stands for the word *auxiliary,* but this term remains to be defined, and we will define it later on.) After the Aux come braces, which mean as usual that we have a choice of things to come next. One is the word *be.* What is the other?

Again, what is meant precisely by *verbal* will be explained in due course. The point now is that the choice after Aux must be either a form of the word *be* or a verbal. Nothing follows verbal, so it is clear that a VP may be made up simply of Aux + verbal. But other items follow *be*. This means that if we have *be* instead of verbal in the kernel sentence, we must have something else too. What we will have is shown by the inner set of braces. What do braces signify? How many choices do we have of items to follow *be* in the kernel verb phrase?

The preceding rule shows that the following are the four possible general structures of the verb phrase:

$$\text{Aux} + \text{be} + \text{NP}$$
$$\text{Aux} + \text{be} + \text{Adj}$$
$$\text{Aux} + \text{be} + \text{Adv-p}$$
$$\text{Aux} + \text{verbal}$$

What element occurs in all four? What occurs in three?

Syntax

be + NP

Let us now consider more closely the structures that occur after *be*. One is NP, which we have already partially examined. What do the letters NP stand for? What four kinds of NP's are there?

We have said that the NP of NP + VP functions as a subject. We say that the NP of *be* + NP functions as a *complement*. Such an NP completes the meaning of a particular kind of verb phrase — one in which we have *be* instead of a verbal.

The following sentence patterns contain two noun phrases each. Tell which functions as subject and which as complement, and tell what kind of noun phrase each one is.

1. John + Aux + be + the winner
2. everyone + Aux + be + a servant
3. it + Aux + be + she
4. the chairman + Aux + be + Mr. McKay
5. they + Aux + be + the actors
6. Mr. Stone + Aux + be + a cook
7. the author + Aux + be + he
8. the city + Aux + be + Cincinnati

It will probably have occurred to you that Aux + *be* is going to turn out as something like *is, was, could be, must have been,* etc., so that 1 above will represent such sentences as "John is the winner,"

"John must have been the winner," and so on. However, we will postpone detailed examination of the part played by Aux until we have looked at the other structures that come after it.

Syntax

be + Adj

The second choice for what may follow *be* in the kernel sentence is Adj, which is of course an abbreviation of *adjective*. We define Adj as we did interjection, count noun, proper noun, by simply giving examples:

$$\text{Adj} \rightarrow \text{warm, neat, repulsive, rambunctious . . .}$$

There will be much more to say about adjectives as we proceed into the grammar. One helpful rule can be given now:

$$\text{Adj} \rightarrow \text{(very)} + \text{Adj}$$

This means that the word *very* may precede an adjective. We can have expressions like *very warm* and *very repulsive*. However, the significance of the parentheses around *very* is that *very* doesn't have to occur with an adjective. This will be the regular meaning of parentheses in these rules: the item within them may occur but doesn't have to in order to make the expression grammatical. "He is very repulsive," in which *very* occurs before the adjective, is grammatical, but so is "He is repulsive," in which it doesn't.

Very is a partial test for adjectives. A word before which *very* cannot be used is by definition not an adjective, though the presence of *very* does not prove that the following word *is* an adjective, since *very* occurs with another word class too — the adverbial of manner, as in *very repulsively*. It doesn't come before noun phrases, however, and so it distinguishes adjectives from noun phrases. The following are all ungrammatical:

* It was very Richard.   * It was very someone.
* It was very she.   * It was very information.

We shall see a number of different uses for adjectives, but they appear in kernel sentences only in the verb phrase — after *be* and as part of certain verbals. "A repulsive person spoke to us" is not a kernel sentence but a transform.

Semantics

The Meaning of Adjectives

We might say in general that adjectives denote qualities that nouns have. They don't exactly name qualities; nouns corresponding to them do that. Thus in "The boy was courageous," *courageous* denotes the quality that we would name with the corresponding noun *courage*. In "The boy was strong," the adjective *strong* indicates the quality for which the noun is *strength*. What nouns name the qualities indicated by the adjectives *insolent, long, tender, young, desperate*? Would you say these nouns are generally concrete or abstract?

The *very* rule distinguishes adjectives from words that occur in positions like those in which adjectives occur, and from other words that have forms similar to adjective forms. For example, we can't take *asleep* as an adjective in "The boy was asleep," because we wouldn't also say *"The boy was very asleep." *Asleep* also has a different semantic relationship to *the boy* than, say, *strong* has in "The boy was strong." It doesn't indicate any quality that he has but tells what he's doing, if sleeping can be thought of as doing something. This difference is again reflected in structure in that we can have *the strong boy* but not *the asleep boy*.

Apply the *very* test to the following to tell whether the word after the form of *be* is an adjective or not.

1. The boat was adrift.
2. Bert is uneasy.
3. The girls were afraid.
4. The room was alight.
5. The men were alert.

Thus it will be seen that the *very* rule defines the adjective group in a quite narrow way, cutting out a number of similar words which behave somewhat differently and have somewhat different meanings in relation to nouns. We could call such words *semi-adjectives* or *partial adjectives,* or of course one could think up some brand new term for them. We will just note that they exist.

Sometimes an adjectivelike word will be clearly an adjective in one expression and not in another. Consider *a musical person* and *a musical instrument.* According to the *very* test, which phrase contains the adjective? Note also that we say "The person is musical" but not *"The instrument is musical," and also that in *a musical instrument,* the word *musical* does not indicate a quality that the instrument has but tells what it is used for, like *eye* in *eye medicine*. It thus differs semantically as well as structurally from the *musical* of *a musical person*.

There are some words which logic would seem to bar from use with *very*, though it doesn't always do so. These are words which indicate that something is something or isn't something, with no in-between possibilities. An example is *absent*, as in "The boy was absent." We would probably want to reject *"The boy was very absent" as ungrammatical and therefore say that *absent* isn't altogether an adjective, even though *the absent boy* is quite grammatical.

Use each of the following in a sentence. Then see if you can use it in another in which it is preceded by *very*.

> federal   inaugural   structural   annual

A more controversial example is *unique*. If this word means "the only one of its kind," it cannot be used with *very*, and therefore it isn't an adjective. Many people do, however, use it with *very*, as in sentences like "The book was very unique." But now it can no longer mean "the only one of its kind." Taking the *very*, it moves right into the adjective class, and its meaning changes to something like *strange* or *unusual*. Other similar words are *universal, horizontal, perfect*. Many well-educated people would use *very* with these words — that is, would use them as adjectives — whereas others would not. This is a point on which the grammars of even the educated differ a bit.

Sometimes we pop one of these marginal words into the adjective class just for the fun or shock of it: "The corpse was very dead indeed." This should probably be called an ungrammaticality of the literary type, frequently used by poets.

Syntax

Adv-p

The third choice after *be* in the kernel verb phrase is Adv-p, which means *adverbial of place*. Adverbials of place are words or phrases with a *where* meaning:

> Adv-p → there, upstairs, in the garage, near me . . .

As this rule indicates, there are two main types — single words like *outside* and *here* and prepositional phrases like *under the sofa* and *in South America*.

Single-word adverbials of place may be called simply *adverbs of place.* There are not a great many of them. Some of the more common are *here, there, inside, outside, upstairs, downstairs, away, yonder, underneath, beyond.* Some of these occur also in other word classes.

Prepositional phrases consist of prepositions plus noun phrases. You already know what noun phrases are. Prepositions are such words as *on, in, by, around, with, under, over, beyond, next to.* What word on this list occurs also on the list for simple adverbs of place? It is a preposition if it makes a unit with a following noun phrase, an adverb of place if it doesn't:

ADVERB OF PLACE: It is beyond.
PREPOSITION: It is beyond the moon.

There are several such words which may occur in either category.

Make a prepositional phrase with each of the prepositions listed above by using a noun phrase after it. For instance, for *on* you could have *on the desk, on the sea, on the road.*

Tell of each structure after Aux + *be* in the following whether it is an NP, an Adj, or an Adv-p.

1. John + Aux + be + in the house
2. Edna + Aux + be + friendly
3. they + Aux + be + grapes
4. his cousin + Aux + be + James Russell
5. the cat + Aux + be + outside
6. she + Aux + be + unhappy
7. the girls + Aux + be + persistent
8. the moon + Aux + be + behind a tree
9. it + Aux + be + I
10. the group + Aux + be + nervous

Syntax, Phonology

Objects of Prepositions

The inclusion of prepositional phrases gives us a third function of the noun phrase. A noun phrase following a preposition is said to function as the *object* of the preposition.

With the exception of personal pronouns, noun phrases do not have different forms for different functions. However, five of the personal pronouns have special object forms. When they are objects of prepositions (and also objects of verbs) they change to the object form. Therefore, a person speaking or writing English must know whether a personal pronoun is an object, and if so, how to change it.

Let the symbol o stand for *object*. Then whenever in a sequence of morphemes we have a personal pronoun in an object function, we write o after it, in this fashion:

Jim + Aux + be + beside + I + o

Now we observe the following *phonological* rules, which tell us how to pronounce combinations like *I* + o:

I + o → me	he + o → him	she + o → her
it + o → it	we + o → us	you + o → you
	they + o → them	

On which of the seven personal pronouns does o have no effect?

Write the actual prepositional phrases represented by the following.

1. toward + he + o
2. around + they + o
3. near + we + o
4. by + she + o
5. on + I + o

This device permits us to go on saying that there are just seven personal pronouns but displays the actual forms that they have in the object function. Phonological rules of this sort are quite different from the syntactic rules that we have been studying so far. The phonological rule tells how something is pronounced; the syntactic rule tells what something consists of or may consist of. Notice that there are two items to the left of the arrow in these phonological rules, only one in the type of syntactic rule we have considered so far.

The object forms of the personal pronouns commonly occur also when the pronouns function as verb phrase complements — e.g., "It's me" rather than "It's I." This text illustrates only the *I, he, she, we, they* forms in the complement function, but rather from a wish to simplify the description than to condemn "It's me," "It was them," etc. as ungrammatical.

Identify the noun phrases in the following sentences, and tell the function of each.

6. The policeman was on a motorcycle.
7. Randolph was the secretary.
8. She was in church.
9. They were next to me.
10. Nothing was underneath it.
11. The losers were they.

12. They were with us.
13. The sword was above him.
14. Everything was beyond our reach.

Syntax

Verbals

Look again at the rule for *verb phrase:*

$$VP \rightarrow Aux + \left\{ \begin{array}{l} be + \left\{ \begin{array}{l} NP \\ Adj \\ Adv\text{-}p \end{array} \right\} \\ \\ verbal \end{array} \right\}$$

What must come first in the verb phrase of a kernel sentence?
What choice is indicated by the outer braces? What choice is indicated by the inner ones?

We have examined the structures that occur when *be* instead of
verbal is involved. Let us look now at the structures summed up as
verbal. This is the rule:

$$verbal \rightarrow \left\{ \begin{array}{l} \left. \begin{array}{l} \left\{ \begin{array}{l} V_I \\ V_T + NP \end{array} \right\} + (Adv\text{-}m) \end{array} \right. \\ V_s + Adj \\ V_b + \left\{ \begin{array}{l} NP \\ Adj \end{array} \right\} \\ V\text{-}mid + NP \end{array} \right\}$$

It will be seen that verbal can be any of five different structures.
Each of them begins with, or consists of, a V of some sort. The symbol V stands here for *verb*, and a verb is a word like *occur, repel, look,
remain, have.* These examples illustrate several different kinds of
verbs, and, in fact, the rule for verbal shows that a number of different kinds exist. How many?

Syntax

V_I and V_T

The symbol V_I stands for *verb intransitive.* Most English verbs
belong to either the intransitive or the transitive group. *Transitive*
is a word borrowed from Latin, and it means "going across." The

notion is that a transitive verb expresses the idea of an action passing across from the subject to an object. An intransitive verb expresses the idea of an action that does not so pass across. This is a rather primitive — or perhaps a rather poetic — grammatical notion, but there is some basis to it, and it is given here to explain the origin of the terms *intransitive* and *transitive*.

A V_I may be a verb like *occur, rain, depart, wait, play.* Some of these occur in other verb categories also. The rules tell us that we may have sentences with structures like the following:

$$\text{something} + \text{Aux} + \text{occur}$$
$$\text{it} + \text{Aux} + \text{rain}$$

These stand for such actual sentences as "Something occurred," "It may rain," and various others.

The V_I is the only type of verbal that may consist of a verb alone. In all the others, the verbal must be followed, in the kernel sentence, by some other structure. What structure follows the verb in the second type of verbal, in which the verb is a V_T?

The symbol V_T stands for *verb transitive.* A transitive verb is one like *throw, polish, mail, dislike, inspect.* The rule says that we can have such structures as these:

$$\text{the pitcher} + \text{Aux} + \text{throw} + \text{the ball}$$
$$\text{Henry} + \text{Aux} + \text{shove} + \text{William}$$

These stand for such sentences as "The pitcher should have thrown the ball" and "Henry shoved William." What noun phrases come after the transitive verbs?

A noun phrase following a transitive verb in a kernel sentence is said to function as the object of the verb. This gives us a fourth function of the noun phrase. What are the other three? The object forms of personal pronouns are used when the pronouns function as objects of verbs, just as they are when they function as objects of prepositions. What pronouns have special object forms, and what are the forms?

The rule for *verbal* specifies that both a V_I and a V_T + NP may be followed by an Adv-m. What is the significance of the parentheses around Adv-m before the rule? The abbreviation Adv-m stands for *adverbial of manner.* This is the second kind of adverbial introduced. What was the first?

An adverbial of manner indicates *how* something happens. Like an adverbial of place, it may be a single-word adverb or a preposi-tional phrase, but it is much more likely to be a single-word adverb. Adverbs of manner are generally made by adding the ending –ly to adjectives: *repulsively, prettily, strangely, happily.* What are the ad-jectives underlying the adverbs in these examples? A few words are used either as adjectives or adverbs of manner without change of form: *fast, straight, hard, high.* They are adjectives, in kernel sen-tences, when they occur after *be,* and they are adverbs of manner when they occur after a V$_I$ or a V$_T$ + NP.

Examine the following structures. Tell whether the verbal is a V$_I$ or a V$_T$ + NP. In the latter case, tell what the NP is. Point out any adverbials of manner.

1. the boys + Aux + work
2. Mark + Aux + break the window
3. Sheila + Aux + reply insolently
4. he + Aux + drive recklessly
5. the store + Aux + require a deposit
6. someone + Aux + hurt the child cruelly
7. the soldier + Aux + shoot straight
8. he + Aux + open the entrance with a pick
9. you + Aux + shock + I + o
10. they + Aux + address + we + o + in a friendly way
11. everybody + Aux + like + she + o
12. Mr. Edson + Aux + walk with a cane
13. a swallow + Aux + build a nest quickly
14. she + Aux + see + he + o
15. the turtle + Aux + crawl slowly
16. an antelope + Aux + eat sagebrush
17. Chicago + Aux + welcome the D.A.R. Convention
18. some peddlers + Aux + open the gate
19. actors + Aux + speak distinctly
20. we + Aux + sing like nightingales

In which four of the structures above is there an adverbial of man-ner in the form of a prepositional phrase? In which one is there an adverb of manner which would have the same form if used as an adjective?

What is the significance of the symbol o in Sentences 9, 10, 11, and 14? What words are represented by **I** + **o** and **we** + **o**? What kind of rule tells this?

Syntax

The Other Verb Categories

Here again is the rule for *verbal:*

$$
\text{verbal} \rightarrow
\left\{
\begin{array}{l}
\left(
\begin{array}{l}
\left\{
\begin{array}{l}
V_I \\
V_T + NP
\end{array}
\right\} + (\text{Adv-m})
\end{array}
\right) \\
V_s + \text{Adj} \\
V_b + \left\{
\begin{array}{l}
NP \\
\text{Adj}
\end{array}
\right\} \\
V\text{-mid} + NP
\end{array}
\right\}
$$

The symbol V_s stands for a "verb of the *seem* class." What, according to the rule, follows a verb of the *seem* class? The verb *seem* occurs in such sentences as "It seems safe" or "She seems friendly," in which it is followed by adjectives. A verb that occurs in such a structure is sometimes called a "linking verb," but we will more simply call it a verb like *seem,* or a verb of the *seem* class.

The class is not a very large one, nowhere near as large as the intransitive and transitive verb classes. Other common verbs that belong to this class — that is, that may be followed by adjectives — are *look, appear, feel, sound, taste, smell.* Use each of these in a sentence with an adjective following. Some verbs occur in this class in special contexts, such as *ring* in "It rang true."

It is characteristic of English that words often occur in different classes or subclasses without change of form. Thus *board* is a noun in "They needed a board," but a verb in "They ought to board it up." Many verbs occur now in one sort of verbal, now in another. The verb *grow* is a V_I in "John is growing," a V_s in "John grew tall," a V_T in "John grows roses."

There are a few verbs that may be followed by either an adjective or a noun phrase. The most common one is *become:*

> John became a friend.
> John became friendly.

We call this category "verbs of the *become* class," and indicate it with the symbol V_b. In American English the only V_b other than *become* that has a wide range of occurrence is *remain:*

> He remained a friend.
> He remained friendly.

Some other verbs operate in the V_b class in special contexts. *Seem* does in "It seemed a shame."

The abbreviation V-mid stands for *middle verb*. It is middle in the sense that it is something between an intransitive and a transitive verb. Like an intransitive verb, it is not followed by an object; like a transitive verb, it is followed by a noun phrase.

An example of a V-mid is *cost* in "It costs a dollar." This structure looks rather like the transitive verb structure, as in "He found a dollar." Yet we feel that the relationship of the verb to the following NP is not the same in both sentences. This feeling is based on the fact that the sentence with *find* can be altered in ways in which the sentence with *cost* cannot. For example, the *find* sentence can be transformed into a passive: "A dollar was found by him." But "It costs a dollar" cannot be similarly changed into * "A dollar was cost by it." The transitive verb construction can be followed by an adverbial of manner: "He found a dollar quickly." The V-mid construction cannot be followed by an adverbial of manner; we don't say * "It costs a dollar quickly."

Other words that are, or may be, middle verbs are *weigh* ("He weighs two hundred pounds"), *total* ("It totalled five hundred dollars"), *amount to* ("It only amounts to sixty cents").

In this category we list also the very common verb *have*, which is followed by a noun phrase but doesn't form a passive or take an adverbial of manner. "He has a bicycle" does not become * "A bicycle is had by him."

See if you can identify the verbals in the following structures as (1) V_I, (2) V_T + NP, (3) V_s + Adj, (4) V_b + NP or Adj, or (5) V-mid + NP. Remember that the first two may be followed by adverbials of manner.

1. John + Aux + help the butcher
2. the wheat + Aux + weigh a ton
3. Julia + Aux + look sick
4. he + Aux + become a minister
5. she + Aux + sing beautifully
6. his father + Aux + have a car
7. George + Aux + collect stamps zealously
8. they + Aux + appear calm
9. Mr. Montrose + Aux + repair the motor
10. it + Aux + cost a fortune
11. they + Aux + leave
12. Sylvia + Aux + remain a friend
13. the story + Aux + ring true
14. the parents + Aux + wait helplessly
15. she + Aux + seem cross

16. we + Aux + grow impatient
17. you + Aux + grow vegetables
18. the baby + Aux + grow rapidly
19. the story + Aux + sound plausible
20. she + Aux + scream in a terrified way
21. the bill + Aux + amount to three dollars
22. the soup + Aux + smell heavenly

SUMMARY OF RULES

$$NP \rightarrow \begin{cases} \text{proper noun} \\ \text{personal pronoun} \\ \text{indefinite pronoun} \\ \text{Det + N} \end{cases}$$

Det → Art (This is a partial rule. Other features
of the determiner will be added later.)

$$Art \rightarrow \begin{cases} \text{Def} \\ \text{Nondef} \end{cases}$$

Def → the

$$Nondef \rightarrow \begin{cases} a \\ \text{some} \\ \text{null} \end{cases}$$

$$N \rightarrow \begin{cases} \text{count + (plural)} \\ \text{noncount} \end{cases}$$

$$VP \rightarrow Aux + \begin{cases} be + \begin{cases} NP \\ Adj \\ Adv\text{-}p \end{cases} \\ \text{verbal} \end{cases}$$

Adj → warm, quiet, repulsive, rambunctious . . .

Adv-p → there, upstairs, in the garage, near me . . .

$$verbal \rightarrow \begin{cases} \begin{cases} V_I \\ V_T + NP \end{cases} + (Adv\text{-}m) \\ V_s + Adj \\ V_b + \begin{cases} NP \\ Adj \end{cases} \\ V\text{-mid} + NP \end{cases}$$

V_I → occur, arrive, sing, wait, procrastinate . . .

V_T → send, help, train, remind, beat . . .

$V_s \rightarrow$ seem, look, taste, smell, sound . . .

$V_b \rightarrow$ become, remain . . .

V-mid $\rightarrow$ cost, weigh, total, have . . .

Adv-m $\rightarrow$ quickly, happily, rambunctiously, fast . . .

TEST

1. Identify the noun phrases that function as subjects. Tell of each whether it is a proper noun, a personal pronoun, an indefinite pronoun, or a Det + N. If it is a Det + N, tell whether the N is a count noun or a noncount noun, and whether Det is a definite or a nondefinite article.

    a. Some ducks were swimming in the pond.
    b. Murphy will see about it.
    c. Acorns covered the ground beneath the trees.
    d. Somebody should have unhooked it.
    e. The farmers weren't very happy.
    f. A duck drowned in the pond.
    g. She answered sulkily.
    h. Sarcasm will get you nowhere.

2. Tell of the structure following *be* in each of the following whether it is (1) an NP, (2) an Adj, or (3) an Adv-p.

    a. John + Aux + be + hungry
    b. John + Aux + be + here
    c. they + Aux + be + sisters
    d. Edwards + Aux + be + behind the pigpen
    e. it + Aux + be + he

3. Tell of each verbal in the following sentence structures whether it consists of (1) a V_I, (2) a V_T + NP, (3) a V_s + Adj, (4) a V_b + NP or Adj, or (5) a V-mid + NP. Remember that some verbals can include adverbials of manner.

    a. they + Aux + strengthen the foundation
    b. she + Aux + seem sweet
    c. Mark + Aux + have a ticket
    d. they + Aux + breathe deeply
    e. his brother + Aux + become a dentist
    f. they + Aux + grow old
    g. we + Aux + remain contented

4. Copy each noun phrase in the following sentences and write a numeral after it to tell whether it functions (1) as subject, (2) as complement, (3) as object of a preposition, or (4) as object of a transitive verb.

    a. Mr. Wilkins brought the letters.
    b. We live in the town.
    c. The caller was Mr. Thackeray.
    d. Maxwell polished the brass.
    e. She is a winner.

REVIEW QUESTIONS

    1. What are the four kinds of noun phrases?
    2. What structure must every determiner contain?
    3. What two forms are meant when we speak of the nondefinite article *a*?
    4. What do we call the nondefinite article when it is expressed by the absence of a word?
    5. What are count and noncount nouns? Give examples of each.
    6. What do we mean by concrete and abstract nouns? Is this a syntactic classification or a semantic one?
    7. What must the nondefinite article be if the N is a singular count noun? What nondefinite articles occur with plural count nouns and with noncount nouns?
    8. What meaning may the *null* article have that the article *some* does not have?
    9. What structure occurs in every verb phrase and comes first in it?
    10. If we have *be* in the verb phrase of a kernel sentence, some other structure must follow it. One possibility is a noun phrase. What are the other two?
    11. What is the significance of a pair of parentheses enclosing an item in a rule?
    12. What word may, but need not, occur with any adjective?
    13. What corresponding nouns name the qualities indicated by the adjectives *courageous, violent, strong*?
    14. Why might we want to call the words *asleep, musical,* and *absent* semi-adjectives instead of, simply, adjectives?
    15. What are the two common kinds of adverbials of place? Give examples of each.
    16. What noun phrases undergo a change of form when they function as objects?

17. What are the literal meanings of the words *transitive* and *intransitive?*

18. What structure must follow a V_T?

19. What does the symbol V_s mean, and what follows a V_s?

20. What does V_b mean, and what may follow a V_b?

21. In what ways is a structure containing a V-mid different from one containing a V_T?

22. What verbals may ordinarily be followed by adverbials of manner?

CHAPTER 3

Syntax

The Auxiliary

Here once again is the rule for the *verb phrase:*

$$VP \rightarrow Aux + \left\{ \begin{matrix} be + \left\{ \begin{matrix} NP \\ Adj \\ Adv\text{-}p \end{matrix} \right\} \\ \\ verbal \end{matrix} \right\}$$

We have discussed all of the structures given in this rule except the all-important Aux, which must occur in every verb phrase. To this we now turn.

This is the rule for the *auxiliary:*

$$Aux \rightarrow tense + (M) + (have + part.) + (be + ing)$$

Notice that the rule specifies a sequence of four items, but that three of them are in parentheses. What do parentheses signify? Which item is not in parentheses?

Since *tense* is not in parentheses, the rule says that every auxiliary, and therefore every verb phrase in a kernel sentence, must contain tense. It may, as the rule shows, contain other structures too, but it *must* contain tense.

English has two tenses, *present* and *past*. Naturally it has ways of showing many more distinctions in time, but present and past are the only grammatical tenses. We express this fact in a rule as follows:

$$tense \rightarrow \left\{ \begin{matrix} present \\ past \end{matrix} \right\}$$

The rules that have been given will now produce all of the morphemes (units of meaning) of certain kernel sentences. For example, they will produce the following sequence of morphemes:

John + present + be + here + 2-3-1

This stands of course for the actual sentence "John is here." But, having noted that, let us look more closely at the structures that "John is here" consists of.

First, *John* is a proper noun and, besides that, a noun phrase. Then of course it is just itself — just John. It can therefore be identified by three different terms, in descending order of generality, from most general to least general: noun phrase, proper noun, John.

The word *is* is made up of two morphemes: **present** and **be**. Of these, **present** is a tense and also an Aux. **Be** is just *be*. It doesn't derive from some more general category but is simply one of the possible items provided for in the rule for verb phrase. The word *here* is an Adv-p. What does this abbreviation stand for? What does 2-3-1 mean?

The sequence **present** + **be** + **here** makes up the verb phrase that functions as the predicate of the sentence "John is here."

We can show all of this structure — not only the morphemes themselves but also the more general categories of which some of them are a part — by a kind of diagram called a *tree of derivation*. This is a tree in the sense that it has branches, and it is a tree of derivation because it shows what general categories more particular items derive from.

Here is a tree of derivation for the sentence "John is here."

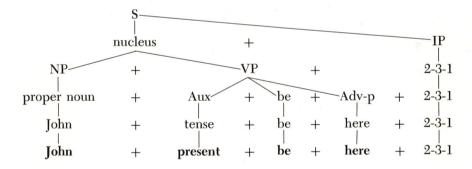

This diagram permits us to take any morpheme on the last line and trace it back to see what it comes from. For example, **John** comes from *proper noun*. It is one of the proper nouns of English. What does *proper noun* come from? **Present** comes from *tense*. It is a kind of tense. What does *tense* come from? What does **here** come from?

Notice that, while we can say that *John* is a kind of proper noun and *proper noun* is a kind of NP, we cannot say that NP is a kind of nucleus. The noun phrase is not the nucleus but only part of the nucleus. This is shown in the fact that there are two lines going off from *nucleus*. One leads to NP. Where does the other lead?

Neither can we say that a nucleus is a kind of sentence. It is only a part of the sentence. What is the other part? Neither is *be* a kind of VP. What other elements are joined by lines to the VP?

Notice that we run out of rules earlier for some items than for others. We carry these items down repeatedly until all syntactic rules have been applied. Thus there is no rule which will turn *John* into something more particular. But when the level *John* has been reached, there is still one item in the diagram for which another rule must be applied. What is it? So we write *John* again on the next line while we complete the development of the auxiliary. And so with *be* and *here*. What item is simply repeated five times?

The last line of a tree of derivation is called a *K-terminal string*. It is a *string* because it is a sequence, or string, of morphemes — minimal units of meaning. It is *terminal* because it is the end of something — the set of *kernel* rules of the syntax for a particular sentence. Hence, with K standing for *kernel*, it is a K-terminal string.

A K-terminal string presents not the words of a sentence but the morphemes. Sometimes morphemes are also words. Thus **John** is a morpheme and also a word. However, **present** is a morpheme but not a word. **Be** is a word in some sentences, but not in this one. Instead, it goes with **present** to make a word. What word?

Another thing to notice is that the K-terminal string presents all of the morphemes of a sentence but not all in the order in which they occur in the actual sentence. The most obvious example in this sentence of a morpheme whose actual placement is not shown is the pitch pattern 2-3-1. Naturally we don't say the words of the sentence and then add the pitch pattern. Instead, the pitch pattern extends clear across the sentence.

Let us have another example of a tree of derivation leading to a K-terminal string, this time for "He ate a sandwich."

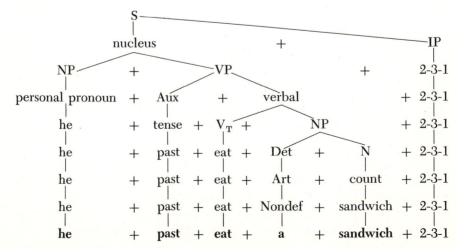

Study the diagram, tracing back the items in the K-terminal string. What does **he** come from immediately? What is **he** besides being *he* and a personal pronoun? What is **past** besides being *past?* What kind of verb is *eat?* What two items make up *verbal?* What is the verb of the verbal? What two items make up VP? What two make up *nucleus?* What two make up S?

In the actual sentence for this tree of derivation, "He ate a sandwich," **past** and **eat** go together to make up the word *ate.* **Past** in the K-terminal string means whatever we do to the following word to make it a past tense. Usually, we just add a sound spelled *–ed,* as in *walked* or *waited.* Sometimes we make irregular changes, as in *ate* or *drove.* The rules which specify how to make past tenses of *walk, wait, eat, drive,* and other verbs are phonological rules, not syntactic ones. We shall be considering such rules presently.

The best way to grasp the nature of the tree of derivation is to try making a few. Try first with the sentence "Jane was inside." The K-terminal string for this is **Jane + past + be + inside +** 2-3-1. The task is to draw the lines leading from S to **Jane + past + be + inside +** 2-3-1. The structure is similar to that of "John is here," so you can use that tree of derivation for that sentence as a guide.

Now try drawing a tree for "We found a knife," which has the K-terminal string **we + past + find + a + knife +** 2-3-1. The structure is similar to that of "He ate a sandwich."

If you got along all right with those trees, you may try the following, which are harder because they differ at several points from the models given. However, the principles are the same, and the rules which produce all of the items have been given. Check the rules if necessary. Draw lines leading to the following K-terminal strings.

1. **nobody + past + smile +** 2-3-1
2. **the + child + past + be + happy +** 2-3-1
3. **the + box + present + weigh + a + ton +** 2-3-1
4. **she + present + seem + neat +** 2-3-1
5. **Mr. Davis + past + be + a + clerk +** 2-3-1
6. **Donald + past + start + the + motor + fast +** 2-3-1

Morphology

Kinds of Morphemes

The study of morphemes, *morphology,* has a bearing on all three main branches of grammar: syntax, phonology, semantics.

A K-terminal string may contain three different kinds of morphemes: *base words, inflectional affixes,* and *derivational affixes.* Every string that has the NP + VP structure contains the first two of these. A string may or may not contain the third.

The word *affix* is a general term that means either *prefix* or *suffix*. Most affixes in English are suffixes rather than prefixes. We might call English a suffixing language, because it chiefly alters words by changing or adding to their endings rather than their beginnings. However, a number of the derivational affixes are prefixes.

Inflectional affixes are those that express ideas like tense, number, or comparison. Some languages have a lot of them and others only a few. English has just eight: *plural, possessive, present, past, participle, ing, comparative, superlative.* The first two of these apply to nouns, the next four to verbs, and the last two to adjectives.

Derivational affixes change words from one word class or subclass to another. For instance the affix *–ness* added to the adjective *good* makes the noun *goodness.* Other examples of derivational affixes are *–ful (hopeful), –ion (action), –ous (dangerous), be– (becalm).* There are many more.

Here is a partial tree of derivation leading to a K-terminal string that illustrates all three types of morphemes. Notice that this tree begins with the nucleus of the kernel sentence and omits the pitch pattern. Since the 2-3-1 pitch pattern applies to all kernel sentences, we will omit it in most of the trees of derivation for kernel sentences from now on, but you should remember that these trees are incomplete without it.

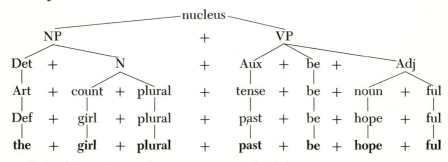

This string of morphemes contains the following units:

BASE WORDS:	**the, girl, be, hope**
INFLECTIONAL AFFIXES:	**plural, past**
DERIVATIONAL AFFIX:	**ful**

What will **girl + plural** go together to form in the actual sentence? What will **past + be** form? What word will **hope + ful** make? What is the actual sentence?

See if you can draw a tree of derivation leading to the following string of morphemes. You may begin with *nucleus,* omitting S and the pitch pattern.

the + gun + plural + past + be + danger + ous

What kind of word is *danger* — noun, verb, or adjective? What kind is *dangerous?* Check with the previous example to find out how to show this information in the tree.

Phonology

Noun Plurals

We have seen that we may have such combinations in the K-terminal string as **girl + plural** or **gun + plural.** The effect of the inflectional affix *plural* is here to change *girl* to *girls* and *gun* to *guns.* The rules which tell precisely what the changes consist of are phonological rules. They belong to that part of the grammar which tells not what parts sentences have but how sentences are pronounced. Then spelling rules may be applied to tell how the changes are written.

Phonological rules are either *regular* or *irregular.* For example, we have a general, or regular, rule for making nouns plural. This rule applies to the great majority of the nouns in the language and to all new nouns added to the language. Such nouns as *boy, tree, garden,* come under the regular rule. What are the plurals of these nouns?

Certain nouns, however, have a special, or irregular, rule. The plural of *foot* is not **foots,* as it would be if the regular rule applied, but *feet.* Other nouns with irregular rules for the plural are *man, child, sheep, knife.* What are the plurals?

When we learn our language, in early childhood, we quickly get onto the regular rule for pluralizing nouns. We apply this rule — quite unconsciously, usually — as we speak English. We don't have to learn the rule for each particular noun that we use. Having noticed that **pan + plural** is *pans* and **bun + plural** is *buns,* we jump correctly to the conclusion that **gun + plural** is *guns,* and we can use this form even if we have never seen or heard it before.

A child or a non-native speaker of English may feel that the plural of *man* ought to be **mans.* He has to learn separately the fact that it's *men.* And so with all of the irregular rules of the language. Each is a separate item that must be learned by itself. But since most irregular words are quite common, we learn their forms easily because we hear them often. We know most of these irregular rules before we even start school.

Here are some examples of the different kinds of irregular rules for the pluralizing of nouns.

1. man + plural → men

We form the plural of *man* by changing the vowel sound, not by adding an ending. Can you think of any other nouns which are made plural by changing the vowel sound? There are about half a dozen.

2. ox + plural → oxen

Formerly a large number of English nouns formed the plural by adding a sound spelled *–en* and pronounced /ən/. *Ox* is the only simple example left, though *child* is similar. How is the plural of *child* similar to but different from that of *ox?* What is the noun of which *brethren* is a plural form?

3. sheep + plural → sheep

For some nouns, plural is null; that is, there is no change at all. We say "He saw a sheep" and "He saw three sheep." Similarly, we say "He shot some quail." Think of other words like these. They are mostly nouns referring to animals being hunted.

4. knife + plural → knives

A number of nouns ending in the sound /f/ change the /f/ to /v/ and add the sound /z/ to make the plural. The sounds /vz/ are spelled *–ves* of course. How many other words in this group can you think of? There are about a dozen.

5. memorandum + plural → memoranda

English has borrowed most of its words from other languages, and sometimes it has borrowed plural forms too. This is particularly true of words borrowed from Latin or Greek. The tendency is for these words to follow the general rule — for example, for *memorandum* to take the plural *memorandums* instead of *memoranda*. For *memorandum* this is still considered bad form, but other words may pluralize either in the foreign way or in the regular English way; thus one may use either *appendixes* or *appendices* as the plural of *appendix*.

Use a dictionary to find the plural forms of the following words. Some have two possible plurals. Note the meaning of any that are unfamiliar to you.

alumnus	criterion	thesis	phenomenon
focus	stigma	dictum	stimulus

Phonology

The Regular Rule for Noun Plurals

When all of the irregular noun plurals have been noted, we can take care of all of the other nouns in the language with the regular rule below. Read it, and then study it with the aid of the explanation and questions that follow.

N + plural → N + /əz/ when the N ends in one of the sounds /s/,
/z/, /sh/, /zh/, /ch/, /j/
N + plural → N + /s/ when the N ends in one of the sounds /p/,
/t/, /k/, /f/ /th/
N + plural → N + /z/ in all other cases

N of course means *noun* — or, more precisely, *count noun*, since
only count nouns form plurals. Notice that the rule is based on sound,
not spelling. The letters between diagonal lines refer to sounds.
Sometimes these sounds are spelled in normal writing with the same
letters, but sometimes they are not. You are probably familiar with
these ways of representing sounds from earlier study or from the
respellings used by dictionaries, but if not, you will find an account
of the symbols used for sounds in this book in the Appendix.

The sounds named in the first part of the rule can be illustrated
with the words *kiss* (/s/ at the end), *quiz* (/z/), *crash* (/sh/), *rouge*
(/zh/), *church* (/ch/), *cage* (/j/). When the regular noun ends with
any one of these sounds, we make it plural by adding the extra
syllable /əz/. The vowel sound represented by the symbol /ə/ is
called *schwa*. It is the vowel sound that occurs in any syllable that
has the weakest degree of stress. It is most commonly spelled with
the letter *e*, though the other vowel letters are often used to spell it
too. Each of the following words normally has the sound /ə/ in the
second syllable: *letter, total, pencil, doctor, murmur.*

In our normal spelling, we ordinarily represent the syllable /əz/
with the letters *es: match/matches.* Write the plurals of the following, and then pronounce them and identify the sound /əz/: *church,
rush, hiss, buzz, bus.* Give five other nouns that form plurals by adding the sound /əz/.

Many nouns ending with one of the sounds /s/, /z/, /sh/, /zh/,
/ch/, or /j/ are spelled with the letter *e* at the end. For example, *face*
ends with the sound /s/, which is spelled with the letters *ce*. In making *face* plural, we of course add just the letter *s* in spelling (*faces*),
not *es* (**facees*). Nevertheless, in pronunciation a whole extra syllable,
/əz/, is added. *Face* has one syllable; *faces* has two. Say the plurals
of the following and note the extra syllable: *place, price, judge, badge,
breeze.* Give five other nouns ending in *e* that add the syllable /əz/
in the plural.

The second part of the rule tells how plurals are formed when the
noun ends in one of the sounds /p/, /t/, /k/, /f/, or /th/. These are
what are called *voiceless* sounds. When the breath with which sounds
are made comes from the lungs, it passes through an opening in
the throat called the *glottis*. The muscles in the glottis can be either

relaxed or tense. If they are tense, the sound is made to vibrate, and this vibration is what is called *voice*. A sound with voice is a *voiced* sound. If the muscles are relaxed, the sound is voiceless.

Say the words *thin* and *then,* and put your hands over your ears as you do so. Draw out the first sound in each word as you say it. You should hear a buzzing sound with the first part of *then* but not with *thin*. This buzz is voicing. *Then* begins with a voiced consonant, *thin* with a voiceless one. Try it again with *Sue* and *zoo*. Which begins with a voiced consonant?

The voiceless consonants of English are /p/, /t/, /k/, /ch/, /f/, /th/, /s/, and /sh/. Three of these have been named in the first part of the regular rule for plurals, and therefore the second part doesn't apply to them. Which three? When a noun ends with one of the other voiceless consonants, the plural is made by adding the sound /s/, which is regularly spelled with the letter *s*. Here are examples of such nouns: *pipe* (/p/ at the end), *hat* (/t/), *rock* (/k/), *giraffe* (/f/), *oath* (/th/). Pronounce the plural of each of those words and listen for the /s/ sound. Give five more words which form the plural by simply adding an /s/ sound. (You can't include *thief* in your list, even though it ends in the sound /f/. Why not? Can you include the word *sheaf* in your list?)

The last part of the rule is what might be called an "in all other cases" statement. If the noun is not irregular and if it does not come under either of the first two parts of the general rule, then it forms its plural by simply adding the sound /z/. The plural is usually spelled with the letter *s*, but you should be able to hear the /z/ sound pretty easily when you say the plural form. Pronounce the following pairs: *caps/cabs, knacks/nags, lice/lies*. Which words end with the /s/ sound and which with /z/?

Pronounce the plurals of the following words, and listen for the /z/ sound with which the plural is formed:

tub	goad	rug	cave
war	rule	fly	lady
toe	ring	pan	tree

Which two plurals of the words on the list above are not spelled by simply adding the letter *s*? Notice, however, that this spelling complication doesn't make them irregular, either in spelling or in pronunciation. They are regular in pronunciation because they simply add the /z/ sound. They are regular in spelling because they change *y* to *i* and add *–es* according to the general rule for words ending in the letter *y* with a consonant letter before it. Give another example of such a word. Give five other examples of nouns that form plurals by simply adding a /z/ sound.

Syntax

A Transformational Rule

Look at this K-terminal string:

the + girl + plural + past + mind + the + baby + plural

There are three inflectional morphemes in the string. What are they? What actual sentence does the string stand for?

There is something a little untidy about the arrangement of morphemes in the string. The plural morphemes come after the words to which they attach — *girl* and *baby*. This is reasonable, because these morphemes are expressed as suffixes at the end of the words *girls* and *babies*, not as prefixes. But the inflectional morpheme **past** comes before the word to which it attaches — *mind* — and this is not so reasonable, for **past** also is generally a suffix, not a prefix. **Past +** **mind** is *minded*, not **edmind*. So one may ask what has gone wrong.

Well, nothing has gone wrong really. The position of **past** is a necessary consequence of the rule for verb phrase, in which the Aux comes before everything else, and there is no other way of writing that rule. Suppose we put Aux after verbal. This would work only when the verbal is a single word, like the intransitive verb *smile*. We would then get a string like **he + smile + past.** But suppose the verbal is something like **watch + the + game.** Then putting the verbal before the auxiliary would give us strings like **he + watch +** **the + game + past,** which suggests that **past** applies to **game** and that the sentence is something like **"He watch the gamed."*

All of the rules that have been studied so far in this book have been kernel rules, which simply tell what various categories consist of or may consist of. *Transformational rules*, in contrast, tell how items in strings may be switched about or which items may be added to the string or which dropped out.

For this first transformational rule, we need two special symbols:

Let AF (for the word *affix*) mean any tense morpheme or the participle or the *ing* morpheme.

Let v mean any modal, *have, be,* or verb.

Then the rule is simply this:

$$AF + v \rightrightarrows v + Af$$

The rule is here stated in full, though we have not yet considered some of the items to which it applies — specifically, *participle, ing, modal,* and *have.* We will here illustrate it with just those that we have examined — present and past tense (affixes) and *be* and verbs (v's). We will regularly use, as here, a double arrow for transformational rules, thus distinguishing them from the single-arrow kernel rules. We will call this transformation the *affix transformation* and refer to it as T-affix.

Here again is our original string, to which the rule may be applied:

the + girl + plural + past + mind + the + baby + plural

The rule says to change any sequence of Af + v to v + Af. Now **past** is a tense and therefore, as defined, an Af. The word *mind* is a verb, and a v is, among other things, any verb or any occurrence of the word *be*. **Past + mind** is consequently a sequence of Af + v and must be changed to **mind + past**:

the + girl + plural + mind + past + the + baby + plural

This is, of course, quite a lot of trouble to go to just to get **past** and **mind** switched around, but it tidies the string.

T-affix puts the affixes that come from the auxiliary in the same position in relation to their words as other affixes are to theirs, demonstrating more clearly the nature of English as a suffixing language. We shall see that it applies widely to underlying strings of English sentences.

Apply T-affix to the following strings. Identify the sequences of Af (any present or past tense) + v (any *be* or verb) and rewrite the strings, switching these.

1. John + present + be + here
2. Ruth + past + smile
3. nobody + past + answer + the + phone
4. the + boy + plural + past + be + happy
5. the + box + present + weigh + a + ton
6. she + past + be + in + the + kitchen
7. they + present + be + neighbor + plural
8. everybody + past + work + hard
9. Mrs. Johnson + present + design + dress + plural
10. some + fox + plural + past + bark + on + the + hill
11. thief + plural + past + loot + the + store
12. the + boy + plural + past + be + the + champion + plural

Syntax

Word Boundary

One further step must be taken to complete the syntactic description of any particular sentence. We must show which morphemes or groups of morphemes are words and which are not. This is quite simply done. As shown on pages 8–9, we let the symbol # stand as a marker of the beginning or end of a word. Then we rewrite the string, replacing + with #, except where the plus sign comes before an inflectional or derivational affix:

the + girl + plural + mind + past + the + baby + plural →
the # girl + plural # mind + past # the # baby + plural

What three sets of two morphemes each are now identified as making up single words?

We attain the same result in strings that contain derivational suffixes:

she + be + past + hope + ful →
she # be + past # hope + ful

Which affix above is inflectional and which derivational?

Rewrite the following, replacing + with # except where + comes before an affix.

1. everybody + like + past + Jim
2. the + child + plural + wait + past + patient + ly
3. Mr. Young + seem + present + friend + ly
4. I + be + past + there
5. the + man + plural + be + past + care + ful
6. the + boy + plural + chase + past + the + goose + plural
7. rose + plural + grow + present + in + clay + soil
8. bus + plural + take + present + child + plural + to + school
9. the + market + sell + present + vegetable + plural
10. the + man + plural + row + past + down + the + lake
11. a + cat + get + past + the + goldfish
12. Mrs. Hand + knit + present + sock + plural

The strings that you have just written represent the end of the syntactic description for these particular sentences. There are no more syntactic rules — either kernel or transformational — that can be applied to them. Since they are the result of the second set of syntactic rules, the transformational rules, they may be called T-terminal strings.

Of course, the strings do not complete the grammar. There are two other questions still to be answered beyond the T-terminal string: (1) How is the sentence pronounced? and (2) What does the sentence mean? As has been pointed out, the first of these is the concern of the phonological component of the grammar, the second of the semantic component.

Phonology

The Phonological Rules for *be* + tense

In its formation of tenses, as in most of its other behavior, *be* is quite special. The forms must be learned individually by the child learning the language. As with the irregular plurals of nouns, the learning is quick and painless because *be* occurs so often in the sentences we hear.

This is the rule for forming **be** + **present** in standard English:

be + present → *am* when the subject is *I*
be + present → *is* when the subject is *he, she, it,* a proper noun, an indefinite pronoun, or a common noun not accompanied by plural
be + present → *are* in all other cases

There are a few situations in which proper nouns are followed by *are,* as in such a sentence as "The Smiths are our friends," but for the most part the rule holds, even when the proper noun *looks* plural. Thus we say "The United States is a country" not *"The United States are a country."

Write the actual sentences represented by the following T-terminal strings.

1. # I # be + present # hungry #
2. # Jack # be + present # upstairs #
3. # the # tree + plural # be + present # bare #
4. # the # grass # be + present # wet #
5. # no one # be + present # angry #
6. # you # be + present # a # hero #
7. # he # be + present # in # the # house #
8. # they # be + present # the # choirboy + plural #
9. # the # sheep + plural # be + present # black #
10. # everybody # be + present # asleep #
11. # we # be + present # the # loser + plural #
12. # she # be + present # with # the # other + plural #

Unlike verbs, *be* has two past tense forms. Like the present tense forms, the choice depends on the subject. This is the rule:

be + past → *was* when the subject is *I, he, she, it,* a proper noun, an indefinite pronoun, or a common noun not accompanied by plural
be + past → *were* in all other cases

Write the actual sentences represented by the following T-terminal strings. In some of them tense is **present** and in some it is **past**.

13. # **George** # **be** + **past** # **a** # **sailor** #
14. # **the** # **visitor** + **plural** # **be** + **present** # **in** # **the** # **office** #
15. # **they** # **be** + **past** # **here** #
16. # **everyone** # **be** + **past** # **tired** #
17. # **I** # **be** + **present** # **the** # **secretary** #
18. # **it** # **be** + **past** # **pleasant** #
19. # **he** # **be** + **past** # **at** # **home** #
20. # **Miss Parsons** # **be** + **past** # **a** # **teacher** #
21. # **the** # **match** + **plural** # **be** + **past** # **wet** #
22. # **the** # **gift** + **plural** # **be** + **past** # **in** # **box** + **plural** #

Phonology

The Present Tense of Verbs

As you know, verbs have two present tense forms, depending on the subject. One is the null form, like *work* or *seem* in "They work" or "The children seem tired." In these, no ending is added to the verb in the present tense. The other form is what we will call the *s* form, because it is normally spelled *–s* or *–es*, though, as we shall see, these letters may represent different sounds. *Works* and *seems* are *s* forms in "He works" and "The child seems tired."

The rule telling when to use the null form and when the *s* form may be stated as follows:

verb + present → verb + s when the subject is *he, she, it,* a proper noun, an indefinite pronoun, or a common noun not accompanied by plural

verb + present → verb + null in all other cases

Check this rule by writing the sentences represented by the following T-terminal strings:

1. # **he** # **work** + **present** # **hard** #
2. # **Mabel** # **cry** + **present** # **often** #
3. # **everybody** # **like** + **present** # **George** #
4. # **the** # **boy** # **look** + **present** # **angry** #
5. # **the** # **boy** + **plural** # **look** + **present** # **angry** #
6. # **I** # **hear** + **present** # **it** #
7. # **they** # **weigh** + **present** # **the** # **box** + **plural** #
8. # **the** # **team** # **try** + **present** # **hard** #

The rule that tells just how *s* forms are pronounced is a little more complicated. First there are three irregular verbs to list. To show their precise sounds, we will give them in respellings, between diagonal lines. All the regular verbs can then be summed up in a three-pronged rule which is, in fact, the same as the regular rule for noun plurals.

Here is the phonological rule for *s* forms of the present tense of verbs:

> have + s → /haz/
> do + s → /duz/
> say + s → /sez/
> verb + s → verb + /əz/ when the verb ends in one of the sounds /s/, /z/, /sh/, /zh/, /ch/, /j/
> verb + s → verb + /s/ when the verb ends in one of the sounds /p/, /t/, /k/, /f/, /th/
> verb + s → verb + /z/ in all other cases

First let us be clear on the nature of the irregularity of the three irregular verbs. If they were regular, they would come under the "all other cases" line, since they do not end in any of the sounds specified in the two lines above. That means that they would simply add the sound /z/. *Have + s* would thus be pronounced */havz/, rhyming with *calves*. *Does* would be pronounced to rhyme with *ooze* and *says* to rhyme with *gaze*.

The word *goes* is regular so far as the phonological rule is concerned. It comes under "all other cases" and simply adds the sound /z/. This is spelled –*es* as it is in a number of noun plurals in which the noun ends in the letter *o: hero/heroes, tomato/tomatoes.*

The fourth and fifth lines of the rule take care of those verbs ending in an "s-like" sound. The technical name for "s-like" sound is *sibilant.* Verbs which end in sibilants make the *s* form by adding the extra syllable /əs/, which is spelled –*es* or –*s*. Make the *s* forms of the following and note the nature of the sound you add: *pass, buzz, crash, watch, budge.* Give five other words that make the *s* form this way.

The sixth and seventh lines of the rule say that if the verb ends in a voiceless consonant (other than a sibilant), the *s* form has the sound /s/. Make the *s* form of the following and note the sound: *rip, swat, knock, laugh, sheath.* Give five other verbs whose *s* forms end in the sound /s/.

Pronounce these pairs and tell which words end in the sound /s/ and which in /z/: *lops/lobs, tags/tacks, pats/pads.*

Here are some examples of the "all other cases" verbs that make the *s* form with the sound /z/. Pronounce them and listen for the /z/ sound.

cares	loves	brags	robs	hides	stays
calls	breathes	hums	runs	sings	sighs

Give five other words in which the *s* form has the /z/ sound.

Semantics

The Meaning of the Present Tense of Verbs

A point that the student of grammar must keep firmly in mind is that tense is not the same thing as time. *Tense* is a term that we use to identify certain forms that we meet in the syntactic component of the grammar. *Time,* which we talk about in the semantic component, is the way we think about the progression of existence. *Tense* is a relatively simple matter; *time* is very complex. We can show only a few of the relationships between tense and time.

One might think that the *present tense* is so called because it indicates that something happens at the present time. It does, sometimes, but it usually has more complicated meanings, or indeed quite different ones. A case of present tense representing present time in a rather simple way is the verb *seem* in "John seems happy." Here the reference is to "now," with no large complications.

If, however, we say "John works hard," the time meaning of *works,* though it also is a present tense form, is quite different. Here the present tense doesn't mean "now" so much as "all the time," and we could indeed say "John works hard all the time." It would be ungrammatical, in reply to a question like "What is John doing at this moment?" to say *"He studies his mathematics." What would one say instead?

Present tense forms are not infrequently used in sentences with future meanings rather than present meanings. An example is "John leaves tomorrow." Can you give another illustration of such usage?

In the writing of fiction and, for some people, in conversation, the present tense is used to describe actions which took place in the past. This usage is sometimes called the *historical present.*

John looks at Mary and sighs, then turns sadly away and boards the plane.

In conversation, this usage frequently imparts a lively slangy tone to the discourse:

John walks up to me and for no reason at all that I can see calls me a big baboon.

Concoct another example of the present tense used to report a past action.

Phonology

The Past Tense Form of Verbs

The vast majority of English verbs form the past tense in a regular way, adding sounds spelled *–d*, as in *hoped,* or *–ed,* as in *walked.* However, quite a large number are irregular, and this particular patch of irregularity in the grammar gives speakers of English quite a lot of trouble. There are two reasons why.

One difficulty is that the irregular rules are not the same in all varieties of English. One may, for example, grow up in a community in which the rule for **sing + past** is *sung:* "She sung beautifully." The rule in standard English, however, is *sang.* A child who learned *sung* at his mother's knee will ordinarily have to change to *sang* to avoid making a fool of himself in college or business circles, and may have to change his rules for a large number of other verbs as well.

The other reason why we have trouble with verb forms is that there are so many irregular ones, many more than there are irregular noun plurals. So, no matter what kind of English we learned in childhood, we may not have the rule built in deeply enough for instant unconscious use. This is particularly true of verbs that we don't use very often. What, for example, is the past tense of *swing?* And if you have passed that, what's the past tense of *slink?* And if that gave you no trouble, what's your feeling about *awake?*

Sometimes our trouble with irregular verbs resides in the fact that two verbs have very similar forms. The most obvious example is *lie* and *lay. Lay* is a transitive verb; you don't just lay — you lay something. This verb has the regular past tense *laid:* "He laid the book on the table." *Lie* is an intransitive verb; you don't lie anything — you just lie. The past tense of *lie* is *lay,* which, unfortunately, is the same as the base form of *lay:* "He lay in the hammock." This similarity makes many people so nervous that they avoid using either verb altogether and say instead "He put the book on the table" or "He rested in the hammock."

We can examine the general nature of verb past tense forms much as we did the plurals of nouns. We first list different kinds of irregularities with examples. We then go on to the general rule, which is again three-pronged and ends with an "in all other cases" line.

1. drive + past → drove

A number of verbs, like *drive*, form the past tense by changing the vowel sound, much as nouns like *man* form the plural. Other verbs in this group are *sing, eat, fall, swim, come*. What are the past tenses of these verbs? List as many more like them as you can — verbs that form the past tense with a change of the vowel sound and no other sound change.

2. bring + past → brought

Some verbs change the vowel sound and make other changes too. We can see what happens to *bring* more clearly if we write the rule with phonetic symbols: /bring/ + **past** → /braut/. The past tense has only two sounds in common with the base form. Which two? Another example is *catch*: /kach/ (or /kech/) + **past** → /kaut/. What sound do the base form and the past tense share? Other words in this group are *teach, buy, fight, think, seek, beseech*. What are the past tenses of these?

3. bend + past → bent

Some verbs change only a *d* to a *t* to form the past tense. What are the past tense forms of *send, build, spend, gird?* A number of verbs have two possible past tense forms, both of them proper. *Gird* is one. What may its past tense be instead of *girt?*

4. put + past → put

Quite a few verbs have a null form of the past tense morpheme, just as *sheep* and *deer* have a null form of the plural morpheme. Other examples are *cost* and *hit*. Can you think of any others? The verb *read* looks as if it should belong to this group, but in fact it doesn't. Why not? Which group does it belong to?

5. go + past → went

The very common verb *go* uses an entirely different word to express the past tense. *Went* is an old past tense of the verb *wend*, as in "He wends his way." What verbs discussed above was *wend* like in the formation of the past tense? What is now the past tense of *wend?*

Write the sentences represented by the following.

1. # John # take + past # a # aspirin #
2. # we # leave + past # early #
3. # they # have + past # a # car #
4. # the # mother + plural # go + past # home #
5. # Mr. Whitners # fall + past # from # the # tree #
6. # Jack # build + past # a # house #

   7. # nobody # hear + past # it #
   8. # a # youngster # see + past # the # accident #
   9. # you # go + past # to # the # party + plural #
  10. # somebody # send + past # a # cake #
  11. # she # give + past # some # penny + plural #
  12. # the # man + plural # bring + past # flower + plural #

Phonology

The Rule for Regular Past Tenses

The foregoing discussion doesn't give all the irregular verbs in English, or even all the types. Verbs we use frequently usually give us no trouble, provided we are accustomed to the standard variety of English. We can resolve particular uncertainties that confront us when we write by using the dictionary.

The rule for regular verbs goes like this:

verb + past → verb + /əd/ when the verb ends in a /t/ or /d/
    sound
verb + past → verb + /t/ when the verb ends in a voiceless con-
    sonant
verb + past → verb + /d/ in all other cases

Just as we form plurals and *s* forms with an extra syllable in certain circumstances, so do we with the past tense form of verbs — specifically when the base form ends in the sound /d/ or /t/. Make the past tense forms of the following and listen to the added /əd/ sound: *end, wait, pad, hate, report.* Give five other verbs to which this part of the rule applies.

The next part applies to verbs ending in voiceless consonants — other than /t/, of course, which has been taken care of in the first part of the rule. Thus *walk*, since it ends in the voiceless consonant /k/, forms the past by adding /t/: /wɑʊk/ + **past** → /wɑʊkt/. The regular spelling, *walked*, somewhat obscures the fact of the sound, making it look as if an extra syllable had been added, but in fact just /t/ is added. Similarly with the past tense of *miss: missed* is identical in sound with the noun *mist*.

Pronounce the past tenses of the following, and note the /t/ sound: *pass, bake, hope, laugh, rush.* Give five other verbs whose past tenses have the /t/ form of the morpheme **past.**

In all other cases the form of the past tense morpheme is the sound /d/. Here are some examples of verbs with the sound /d/. Pronounce them and identify the /d/ sound.

| robbed | smiled | lagged | roved | tried | judged |
| rammed | phased | lined | banged | flowed | cheered |

Pronounce the following pairs and tell which words end in a /t/ sound and which in a /d/ sound:

roped/robed   leagued/leaked
surged/searched   faced/fazed

Give five verbs not mentioned above whose past tense is formed with the sound /d/.

Semantics

The Meaning of the Past Tense of Verbs

Semantically, the past tense of verbs is simpler than the present tense. At least it generally refers to something that happened in the past and doesn't wander through time the way the present tense does. The relative semantic simplicity of *past* in contrast with the complexity of *present* has led some grammarians to use the terms *past* and *non-past* instead of the more traditional *past* and *present*.

Still, *past of verb* is not the only way of expressing past time, and it has a meaning somewhat different from that of other forms. Most simply, the past tense of a verb indicates an action that took place at some specific time in the past. If we say "John shot Bill," we imply that this happened at a particular past time. We may or may not know just what time. If we do, we may tell it: "John shot Bill at 2:53 in the morning of December 1, 1927." But even if we don't know it, the implication is that it happened at some particular past time, if the verb is one like *shoot, strike, eat, find, smile.*

If the verb is, however, one like *seem, know, feel, think,* the semantic application is a little fuzzier. The sentence "John seemed courageous" doesn't indicate a specific point in time but rather a condition that extends over an indefinite period of past time. *Seemed* is still a past tense form, but the meaning is somewhat different.

Tell which of the following suggest a specific moment of past time and which an indefinite period in the past.

1. Albert liked music.
2. Angela replied courteously.
3. Agnes looked sick.
4. Alfred opened the door.
5. Ada removed the tooth.

6. Alexander remained quiet.
7. The clock struck the hour.
8. Time passed slowly.
9. Alice cooked breakfast.
10. Hubert traveled a lot.
11. The leaves changed color.
12. A flock of geese flew overhead.
13. The sun went down.
14. The surf pounded the beach.
15. The party began promptly.

SUMMARY OF RULES

Syntactic Rules

$$VP \rightarrow Aux + \left\{ \begin{array}{l} be + \left\{ \begin{array}{l} NP \\ Adj \\ Adv\text{-}p \end{array} \right\} \\ \\ verbal \end{array} \right\}$$

$$Aux \rightarrow tense + (M) + (have + part.) + (be + ing)$$

$$tense \rightarrow \left\{ \begin{array}{l} present \\ past \end{array} \right\}$$

$$N \rightarrow \left\{ \begin{array}{l} count + (plural) \\ noncount \end{array} \right\}$$

Phonological Rules for plural

man + plural → men
ox + plural → oxen
sheep + plural → sheep
knife + plural → knives
memorandum + plural → memoranda

N + plural → N + /əz/ when the N ends in one of the sounds /s/,
  /z/, /sh/, /zh/, /ch/, /j/
N + plural → N + /s/ when the N ends in one of the sounds /p/,
  /t/, /k/, /f/, /th/
N + plural → N + /z/ in all other cases

Phonological Rules for *be* + tense

be + present → *am* when the subject is *I*
be + present → *is* when the subject is *he, she, it,* a proper noun, an
  indefinite pronoun, or a common noun not accompanied by plural
be + present → *are* in all other cases

be + past → *was* when the subject is *I, he, she, it,* a proper noun, an indefinite pronoun, or a common noun not accompanied by plural

be + past → *were* in all other cases

Phonological Rules for Tenses of Verbs

verb + present → verb + s when the subject is *he, she, it,* a proper noun, an indefinite pronoun, or a common noun not accompanied by plural

verb + present → verb + null in all other cases

have + s → /haz/

do + s → /duz/

say + s → /sez/

verb + s → verb + /əz/ when the verb ends in one of the sounds /s/, /z/, /sh/, /zh/, /ch/, /j/

verb + s → verb + /s/ when the verb ends in one of the sounds /p/, /t/, /k/, /f/, /th/

verb + s → verb + /z/ in all other cases

drive + past → drove

bring + past → brought

bend + past → bent

put + past → put

go + past → went

verb + past → verb + /əd/ when the verb ends in a /t/ or /d/ sound

verb + past → verb + /t/ when the verb ends in a voiceless consonant

verb + past → verb + /d/ in all other cases

Affix Transformation

$$\text{T-Affix: Af} + \text{v} \rightrightarrows \text{v} + \text{Af}$$

Where Af means any tense, participle, or *ing,* and v means any modal, *have, be,* or verb.

Word Boundary

After the application of T-affix, replace all plus signs with word boundary signs (#) except when the plus sign comes before an affix.

TEST

1. Rewrite each of the following strings twice. First apply T-affix, the affix transformation. Then replace each + with #, except when the + comes before an affix.

a. June + present + be + here
b. he + past + be + a + soldier
c. the + dentist + past + be + angry
d. Judith + past + smile
e. the + animal + plural + past + seem + danger + ous
f. it + present + remain + a + problem
g. nobody + past + have + the + answer + plural

2. Write trees of derivation leading to the following K-terminal strings.
a. Sam + past + be + upstairs
b. he + present + like + candy
c. everybody + past + want + a + chance

3. Write the actual sentences represented by the following T-terminal strings.
a. # they # be + past # foolish #
b. # Jones # take + past # a # bite #
c. # the # tree + plural # be + present # bare #
d. # the # bird + plural # go + past # south #
e. # he # find + past # the # woman + plural #
f. # everyone # have + past # a # complaint #
g. # Nelson # hit + past # a # single #
h. # they # seem + past # hope + ful #

4. Give an example of each of the following.
a. a noun that forms the plural by changing the vowel sound
b. a noun that forms the plural by changing /f/ to /vz/
c. a noun that forms the plural by adding the sound /əz/
d. a noun that forms the plural by adding the sound /s/
e. a noun that forms the plural by adding the sound /z/
f. a noun that forms the plural with null
g. a verb that forms the past by simply changing the vowel sound
h. a verb that forms the past by changing the vowel sound and making some other change as well
i. a verb that forms the past by changing /d/ to /t/
j. a verb that forms the past with null
k. a verb that forms the past by adding the sound /əd/
l. a verb that forms the past by adding the sound /t/
m. a verb that forms the past by adding the sound /d/

REVIEW QUESTIONS

1. What structure comes first in every verb phrase of a kernel sentence?

2. What structure *must* occur in every auxiliary?

3. What are the two tenses of English?

4. What is meant by *tree* and by *derivation* in the term *tree of derivation?*

5. Why is a K-terminal string K, why is it terminal, and in what sense is it a string?

6. Give one example of a morpheme that is a word and one of a morpheme that is not a word.

7. What are the three main kinds of morphemes?

8. How many inflectional morphemes does English have? Name as many as you can and tell what word classes they go with.

9. What is meant by the term *affix?*

10. How do derivational affixes differ from inflectional ones? Give examples of derivational affixes.

11. Why does *tense* have to come before the item that it applies to in the verb phrase, even though in the actual sentence it will be a suffix and not a prefix?

12. When is + *not* replaced by # in the word boundary rule?

13. Why is a T-terminal string so called?

14. What examples can you think of in which nouns form the plural by simply changing the vowel sound?

15. What word is the only case of a noun forming the plural by simply adding the ending spelled *–en?*

16. Under what circumstances do regular nouns and regular verbs make the plural and the *s* form by adding the syllable /əz/?

17. What three verbs have irregular *s* forms?

18. What is the difference between a voiced and a voiceless sound?

19. What is a sibilant sound?

20. When is **be** + **present** *is?* When is it *am?*

21. How many past tense forms does *be* have? How many do verbs have?

22. What are some of the time meanings that the present tense can have? What is meant by the "historical present"?

23. What are two reasons why the irregular verbs give speakers of English quite a lot of trouble?

24. Under what circumstances is the past tense of regular verbs formed with the syllable /əd/?

CHAPTER 4

Syntax

Modals

The rule for Aux contains four segments, only one of which, tense, we have discussed so far:

$$\text{Aux} \rightarrow \text{tense} + (M) + (\text{have} + \text{part.}) + (\text{be} + \text{ing})$$

Tense is not in parentheses, and so it is obligatory. That is, we must have it in each auxiliary. The other items are in parentheses, and therefore they are *optional*.

The first optional item is M. This stands for the word *modal*. Modals are words that modify the meaning of the verb phrase, usually giving it a future meaning as well as other meanings. There are five common modals in English, which we list in their present tense forms:

$$M \rightarrow \text{can, may, will, shall, must}$$

With the addition of M, we can draw a tree of derivation for such a sentence as "John may refuse." Once more, S and the pitch pattern 2-3-1 are omitted from this partial tree:

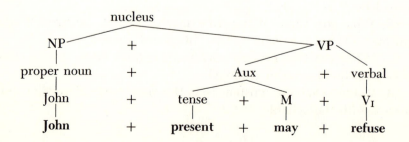

Present is the tense in this structure, but *tense* is not the Aux. It is only part of the Aux. What is the other part? What kind of verb is *refuse?*

Recall now the affix transformation: Af + v $\Rightarrow$ v + Af. Af, we said, stands for any tense, participle, or *ing*. Small v stands for any modal, *have, be,* or verb. **Present** is a tense and hence an Af; **may** is a modal and hence a v. Therefore **present** + **may** is a case of Af + v, and the affix transformation applies to produce the following:

$$\textbf{John} + \textbf{may} + \textbf{present} + \textbf{refuse}$$

Now we can apply the word boundary rule, replacing + with # except where + comes before an affix, in this case **present**:

$$\textbf{\# John \# may} + \textbf{present \# refuse \#}$$

What kind of a string is this last line?

We saw that in the T-terminal string **# John # be + present # here #** the morpheme **present** has the effect of turning **be** into the word *is*. If the subject had been *I*, it would have turned it into *am*, and if *they*, into *are*. Similarly, the tense **past** converts a **be** into *was* or *were*, depending on the subject. Into what are *eat, run, think* changed by **past?**

We saw also, however, that *tense* does not always effect a form change on the word to which it is attached by the plus sign. The string **# he # put + past # it # away #** comes out "He put it away," with **put** unchanged. The past tense form of *put* is null — no addition, no change. The string **# he # know + present # it #** stands for the sentence "He knows it." But **# they # know + present # it #** stands for "They know it," in which the **know** comes out unchanged.

The effect of *tense* on the modals is a little different from that on verbs and *be*. Present tense produces no change of form in any of the modals. So **can** + **present** is *can*, **will** + **present** is *will*, etc. This is true no matter what the subject is. However, past tense can apply to four of the modals:

can + **past** → *could*	**shall** + **past** → *should*
will + **past** → *would*	**may** + **past** → *might*

The modal *must* has no past tense. Whenever *must* is used, tense must be present.

Remember that the grammatical concept *tense* has to do with form, not with meaning. Most of the modals, including the past tense ones, usually convey a future meaning. Thus *should* does in a sentence like "John should go tomorrow." But *should* is in form the past tense of *shall*, and we are talking just now about form. Meaning is more complicated.

Here is the partial tree of "They might know it":

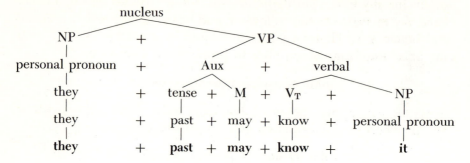

The last line of the tree of derivation is this K-terminal string:

they + past + may + know + it

What structures are **they** and **it** besides being *they* and *it?* What does Aux come from and what does it develop into?

The K-terminal string contains one sequence of Af + v. What is it? Apply the affix transformation and the word boundary rule.

Write the trees leading to the following K-terminal strings, and then convert them into T-terminal strings with word boundary marked.

1. **Mary + past + shall + leave**
2. **the + child + present + must + hate + it**

Semantics

The Meanings of Modals

Relatively simple in form, the modals are quite complex in meanings. First of all, they all may express the meaning of future time, as can be seen from the following:

> John can do it tomorrow.
> John may do it tomorrow.
> John will do it tomorrow.
> John shall do it tomorrow.
> John must do it tomorrow.
> John could do it tomorrow.
> John might do it tomorrow.

John would do it tomorrow.
John should do it tomorrow.

The modal *could,* the past tense of *can,* can also refer to past time: "John could recite the poem yesterday (but he can't today)." In the present tense, *can* may have a general time meaning, like the present tense of verbs. The following mean about the same thing:

John can play the violin well.
John plays the violin well.

Neither sentence says that he's playing it right now.

Would sometimes refers to actions that took place from time to time in the past: "John would sometimes swim in the mornings last summer."

Point out the modals in the following sentences and tell whether the time reference is to the past, the future, or to past, present, and future all together. Tell whether the form of the modal is present or past.

1. You may see David at the game.
2. You could ask him.
3. He would often tell about his experiences.
4. At that time a person could drive for miles without seeing a house.
5. Mr. Perkins will be here at six.
6. Maxwell can speak Portuguese.

Although all the modals may convey the meaning of future time, *will* and *shall* always do, and they don't convey much of any other sort of meaning. For this reason, many grammarians have called phrases like *will go* and *shall arrive* the "future tense" of English. Most modern English grammarians, however, restrict the concept of *tense* in English to the morphemes **present** and **past,** as we have here, and simply point out that the meaning of future can be expressed in a variety of ways, of which the use of the modals *will* and *shall* is one. From this point of view, *will* and *shall* are present tense forms, contrasting with the past tense forms *would* and *should.*

There has been a great deal of to-do about when one should use *will* and when *shall,* and many people have believed that *shall* should be used with first person subjects (*I* and *we*) and *will* after other subjects. Actually, it doesn't matter much, at least in statements. There is no difference in meaning between "I will see him" and "I shall see him." *Will* is much more common than *shall* for all three persons, occurring, in conversation, generally in the contracted form *I'll* or *we'll.* The student will not go far wrong in using either form.

The other modals, though they usually express future time, have other meanings as well. *Can* has a meaning like that of *be able to:* "John can speak Portuguese." It often also has the meaning *have permission to:* "Mother says that I can go." *May* also has this meaning ("Mother says that I may go") and some people feel that it is more proper to use *may* in such a sentence than *can.* In many sentences *may* expresses the meaning of possibility: "It may rain."

The modal *must* conveys the idea that something has got to happen: "He must report at once." This drifts off a bit into a use of *must* to suggest an explanation of some sort of puzzle or problem: "He must be mad," "He must like bananas."

Should, the past tense of *shall,* has a meaning similar to that of *must:* "He should report at once." However, where *must* in such a sentence says that something has got to happen, *should* suggests that it ought to but maybe won't. *Should* may also have the meaning of probability: "The team should win the game on Friday." When the subject is *I* or *we* and the predicate contains expressions like *be glad, like, hope,* the modal *should* is sometimes used: "I should like to see him." This is probably more British than American. In American English, *would* is more likely to occur: "I would like to see him."

In addition to the usage just noted, *would* may be used to express actions repeated in the past: "In the summer he would swim every day." It is also used to express disapproval of past actions:

> He got hit by a car.
> Well, he *would* cross the street without looking.

Would has various other meanings, but they mostly occur in transforms, not in kernel sentences.

We noted that *may* expresses two meanings: permission and possibility. The past tense, *might,* expresses the second of these also, with very little difference from *may.* "It may rain" and "It might rain" mean about the same thing, except that *might* perhaps suggests that the rain is a little less likely. Both *may* and *might* occur with *as well,* again with little difference in meaning: "I may as well do it," "I might as well do it."

Could is in form the past tense of *can,* and it often is in meaning as well:

> He can do it now.
> He could do it then.

Could also expresses a possibility, like *might:*

> You might ask him.
> You could ask him.

Fill the blanks in the following sentences with as many of the nine modal forms as will grammatically fit. In some all nine will fit. Describe the meanings, including the time meanings, expressed by the different modals.

7. I _____ go to Springfield tomorrow.
8. Joan _____ play the piano.
9. We _____ as well try it.
10. He _____ be crazy.
11. Henry _____ be wise not to ask.

Syntax

have + participle

The second optional item in the auxiliary is *have* + part.:

$$\text{Aux} \rightarrow \text{tense} + (M) + (\text{have} + \text{part.}) + (\text{be} + \text{ing})$$

The order of the rule shows that *have* + part. must come after the modal, if there is one, and in any case after tense. The coupling of *have* + part. in a single pair of parentheses means that we must take them together. If we have a *have* as an item from the auxiliary, we must also have a part., and vice versa.

The symbol part. is an abbreviation of *participle,* and it means whatever we do to a verb or *be* to make it into the participle form, just as *past* means whatever we do to something to make it past tense. The participle form is the form used after *have* in such expressions as "They have seen it."

Here is a partial tree of derivation in which both tense and *have* + part. are used from the auxiliary.

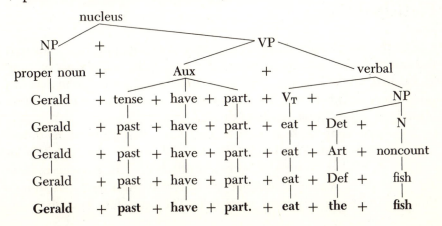

Our setup for the affix transformation was this:

Af = any tense, part., or ing
v = any modal, have, be, or verb
T-affix: Af + v $\rightrightarrows$ v + Af

In the K-terminal string on page 77 there are two sequences of
Af + v: **past + have** and **part. + eat**. These will therefore reverse:

Gerald + have + past + eat + part. + the + fish

Now we indicate word boundary:

 # Gerald # have + past # eat + part. # the # fish #

What actual sentence is represented by this T-terminal string?
    What would be the actual sentence for this T-terminal string if
tense were **present** instead of **past?**

 # Gerald # have + past # eat + part. # the # fish #

What would be the actual sentence for the T-terminal string above
if the tense were **past** and the transitive verb were *see?* What would
it be if tense were **past** and *have* + part. were omitted from the
auxiliary? What would it be if the tense were **past** but the modal
shall were used instead of *have* + part.?
    Draw partial trees of derivation like the one on page 77 leading
to the following K-terminal strings. Then apply T-affix to the strings
and mark word boundary.

1. **John + past + have + part. + hear + it**
2. **we + present + have + part. + invite + Alice**

Phonology

Participle Forms

For the overwhelming majority of verbs, the participle form is
the same as the past tense form. We say "John walked away" and
"John had walked away," "John invited Mary" and "John had invited Mary." This is true even of most irregular verbs. We say "John
brought it" and "John has brought it."
    There are some verbs, however, that have participle forms differ-
ent from their past tense forms. We say "John ate it" but not * "John
had ate it." What do we say instead of the latter? It is because there
are some verbs whose participles are different from their past tenses
that we must use the term *participle*. They are few enough, how-

ever, that they can be listed. The following are the principal verbs that have participle forms which are different from their past tense forms. Give the participle and past tense form of each.

rise	drive	ride	fly
bear	swear	tear	wear
break	freeze	speak	steal
weave	bite	choose	lie
blow	grow	know	throw
shake	take	forbid	draw
eat	fall	give	see
slay	begin	drink	ring
shrink	sing	sink	spring
stink	swim	come	run

Semantics

The Meaning of *have* + part.

The construction resulting when the optional *have* + part. from the auxiliary is used is sometimes called a "perfect" construction. It is "present perfect" when the tense, which applies to *have*, is present, "past perfect" when the tense is past.

When *have* is present, the verb phrase expresses the meaning that something happened in the past which is, however, in some sense linked up with the present. This contrasts with the past tense of verbs and *be*, which ordinarily tell of things that happened in the past, period. Compare these:

> John watered the horses.
> John has watered the horses.

The first sentence simply names an action in the past. The second suggests a connection with the present and might be continued in such a way as this: "John has watered the horses and now we can ride."

Another distinction is that the past tense commonly has a definite time meaning, whereas the *have* + part., with *have* present tense, doesn't. Thus we can say "John watered the horses at one o'clock" but not *"John has watered the horses at one o'clock." *Has watered* leaves indefinite the time that he watered them.

When the *have* of *have* + part. is past tense, the general meaning is of a time before some other past time:

John had watered the horses (before the posse arrived).
He had seen the show the day before.

Sometimes we use the past of *have* + part. before a past tense verb and sometimes we use just a past tense verb, but there is a slight difference in meaning. Compare these:

When I had seen the television show, I called the police.
When I saw the television show, I called the police.

The second of these suggests that there is a connection between my seeing the show and calling the police; perhaps I want to complain about something. The first merely relates the two actions in time without suggesting any cause and effect.

Discuss the difference in meaning between the members of the following pairs.

1. Edwin drove the car.
   Edwin has driven the car.
2. Bernice was there.
   Bernice has been there.
3. The police have searched the apartment.
   The police had searched the apartment.
4. When we had seen what was happening, we went home.
   When we saw what was happening, we went home.
5. They investigated.
   They have investigated.
6. They investigated.
   They had investigated.
7. They have investigated.
   They had investigated.

Syntax

be + ing

We have considered all of the parts of the rule for the auxiliary except the last:

Aux → tense + (M) + (have + part.) + (be + ing)

In addition to tense, which it must contain, the auxiliary may contain a modal or *have* plus the participle morpheme. Or it may contain the word *be* plus the morpheme **ing**. The morpheme **ing** is simply that which makes *eat* into *eating*, *shoot* into *shooting*, etc.

This is the second rule that has introduced the word *be*. What was the other?

Here is a partial tree of derivation for the sentence "They were shooting rabbits," which contains the auxiliary elements tense and *be + ing*.

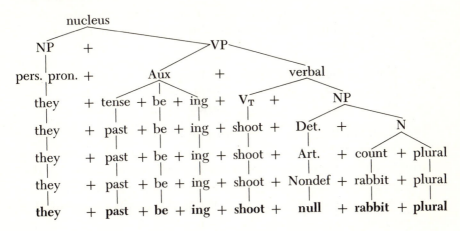

We have now encountered all of the elements that play a part in the affix transformation:

$$Af = \text{any tense, part., or ing}$$
$$v = \text{any M, have, be, or verb}$$
$$\text{T-affix: } Af + v \Rightarrow v + Af$$

In the K-terminal string above there are two sequences of Af + v. **Past + be** is one, and **ing + shoot** is the other. These now reverse by the affix transformation:

they + be + past + shoot + ing + null + rabbit + plural

We then put in word boundary except before the affixes:

 # they # be + past # shoot + ing # null # rabbit + plural #

What word will **be + past** be in the actual sentence? What will **shoot + ing** be? What will **rabbit + plural** be? What nondefinite article might have been used instead of *null?*

Draw partial trees of derivation leading to the following K-terminal strings. Then apply the affix transformation and indicate word boundary.

1. **David + past + be + ing + watch + them**
2. **he + present + be + ing + help + Gerald**
3. **nobody + past + be + ing + smile**

Phonology

The *ing* Form

The morpheme **ing** provides us with one of those rare and pleasant things in language — a rule to which there are no exceptions, no irregularities. We add **ing** to a verb or *be* or *have* (it doesn't occur with modals) by simply suffixing a syllable spelled *ing* and pronounced either /ing/ or /in/:

shoot + **ing** → *shooting*	**write** + **ing** → *writing*
have + **ing** → *having*	**be** + **ing** → *being*
run + **ing** → *running*	**study** + **ing** → *studying*

The usual spelling rules concerning affixes beginning with a vowel apply of course: a final *e* (if there is one) in the base word drops (*writing*), and a final consonant with a single vowel before it doubles if the syllable has principal stress (*running*). The letter *y* before –*ing* does not drop or change to *i*. Write the words represented by the following:

hope + **ing**	**plan** + **ing**	**marry** + **ing**
nod + **ing**	**hurry** + **ing**	**drive** + **ing**

In pronunciation, **ing** sometimes comes out /ng/, where /ng/ represents the sound spelled *ng* in *sing*, and sometimes /in/, with the final sound of *sin*. The sounds /ng/ and /n/ are both nasal sounds, made by stopping the breath in the mouth and letting it come out through the nose. The difference is that for /ng/ the breath is stopped at about the point where /k/ and /g/ are made and for /n/ it is stopped farther forward in the mouth, where /t/ and /d/ are made. Thus if you say /shootin'/ you don't drop the g so far as pronunciation is concerned. You just end the syllable spelled –*ing* with a different nasal sound.

Semantics

The Meaning of *be* + *ing*

Constructions containing *be* + *ing* from the auxiliary are sometimes called "progressive" forms. If *be* is in the present tense, they are "present progressive"; if *be* is in the past, they are "past progressive."

We have already noted that the present tense of verbs does not commonly tell of actions presently underway. "John writes letters" doesn't mean that that is what he is doing at the time of speaking. It means that this is one of his regular activities. To express the actual present meaning, we use the present progressive: "John is writing letters."

However, the *be* + *ing* does not simply pinpoint an action in the present moment. Rather it expresses an action continuing through the present moment, beginning before it and going on after it. The present tense of verbs, in contrast, generally suggests a series of occurrences in past, present, and future. The two might be represented thus:

PAST   PRESENT   FUTURE

 # verb + pres. #   · · · · · · · · · · · ·

 # be + pres. # verb + ing #   —————

The dots might represent the different occasions of letter writing in "John writes letters" and the line the duration of the action in "John is writing letters."

Some verbs do not, or do not usually, take the *be* + *ing* form. We would hardly say * "He is knowing it." Examples of other verbs for which this form is not used or is rare are *seem, hear, realize, understand, hate.*

The "past progressive," in which the *be* is a past tense form, usually describes an action in progress in the past when some other action occurred:

Murphy was blowing soap bubbles when the coach came in.

The blowing of soap bubbles was in progress when the coach arrived and may have continued after.

Compare these:

Murphy was laughing when the coach came in.
Murphy laughed when the coach came in.

In the second the laughing didn't begin before the arrival of the coach. It coincided with it.

Discuss the different meanings expressed by the members of the following pairs.

1. Alice eats a large breakfast.
   Alice is eating a large breakfast.
2. They watch birds.
   They are watching birds.
3. Steinmetz was taking a bath when the lights went out.
   Steinmetz took a bath when the lights went out.

4. Sodbury works in the garage.
   Sodbury is working in the garage.

Are there situations in which the two sentences in 4 above would be about the same in meaning?

Syntax

Combinations from the Auxiliary

We can not only have in a verb phrase any of the three optional choices given in the rule for auxiliary, but we can have any combination of them provided that they occur in the order given:

Aux → tense + (M) + (have + part.) + (be + ing)

A modal must come before a *have* + part. or a *be* + *ing*. A *have* + part. must come before a *be* + *ing*.

Let us start with this K-terminal string, omitting 2-3-1:

John + past + watch + them

What element of the auxiliary does this contain? What would the actual sentence be after the affix transformation?

The string can be expanded as follows:

John + past + may + watch + them

What element of the auxiliary has been added? What is the actual sentence now?

Instead of **John + past + may + watch + them,** we can have the following:

John + past + have + part. + watch + them

Now what are the auxiliary elements? To what do **past** and **part.** apply? What is the actual sentence?

Or we can have this:

John + past + be + ing + watch + them

What do **past** and **ing** apply to? What is the sentence?

So much we have illustrated earlier. Now let us add combinations of the optional elements of the auxiliary:

John + past + may + have + part. + watch + them

What four morphemes in this string come from the auxiliary? What do **past** and **part.** apply to? What is the sentence?

We could keep the modal but have **be + ing** in place of **have + part.**:

   John + past + may + be + ing + watch + them

What is the actual sentence?

   We could have no modal but both **have + part.** and **be + ing:**

   John + past + have + part. + be + ing + watch + them

What will **past, part.,** and **ing** apply to after the affix transformation?
What is the sentence?

   Or we can have all of the elements of the auxiliary, taking them
in the order given by the rule:

John + past + may + have + part. + be + ing + watch + them

How many morphemes in this string come from the auxiliary? What
is the sentence?

   In summary, with the NP subject *John,* the verbal *watch them,* the
tense *past,* and the modal *may,* eight different sentences are possible
through variations in the auxiliary:

John watched them.   (tense alone)
John might watch them.   (tense + M)
John had watched them.   (tense + have + part.)
John was watching them.   (tense + be + ing)
John might have watched them.   (tense + M + have + part.)
John might be watching them.   (tense + M + be + ing)
John had been watching them.   (tense + have + part. + be + ing)
John might have been watching them.   (tense + M + have
                                       + part. + be + ing)

   Of course we could use other modals, present instead of past, and
other subjects and other verbals.

   Here is the partial tree of derivation for "John might have been
watching them":

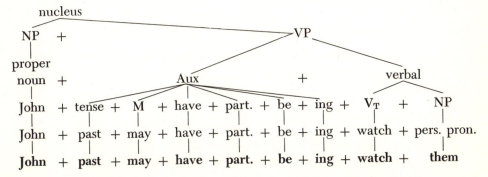

nucleus

NP   +   VP

proper
noun +   Aux   +   verbal

John + tense + M + have + part. + be + ing + V_T + NP

John + past + may + have + part. + be + ing + watch + pers. pron.

John + past + may + have + part. + be + ing + watch + them

There are three sequences of Af + v in this K-terminal string. What are they? Rewrite the string applying the affix transformation and reversing these sequences. Then write the string again, indicating word boundary.

Write a tree of derivation for **Sally + past + shall + have + part. + be + ing + work.** Apply the affix transformation to the result and show word boundary.

Syntax

Application of the Auxiliary Rule

In theory, all of the different combinations permitted by the rule for Aux can be applied to any of the several structures that may follow Aux in the verb phrase. Here again is the rule for *verb phrase:*

$$VP \rightarrow Aux + \left\{ \begin{array}{l} be + \left\{ \begin{array}{l} NP \\ Adj \\ Adv\text{-}p \end{array} \right\} \\ \\ verbal \end{array} \right\}$$

Recall also the rule for *verbal:*

$$verbal \rightarrow \left\{ \begin{array}{l} \left\{ \begin{array}{l} V_I \\ V_T + NP \end{array} \right\} + (Adv\text{-}m) \\ V_s + Adj \\ V_b + \left\{ \begin{array}{l} NP \\ Adj \end{array} \right\} \\ V\text{-mid} + NP \end{array} \right\}$$

The rules for VP and verbal give us nine basic patterns in the verb phrase, as follows:

be + NP   (John is a nuisance.)
be + Adj   (John is silly.)
be + Adv·p   (John is at the door.)
V_I (John joked.)
V_T + NP   (John watched them.)
V_s + Adj   (John looked strange.)
V_b + NP   (John became a soldier.)
V_b + Adj   (John became resentful.)
V-mid   (John had a good time.)

These examples are given with just tense — present or past — used from the auxiliary. But in theory, and often also in practice, each one could be varied into seven more sentences through optional choices of Aux. We have already shown how to do this with "John watched them." We can do it also with "John is a nuisance":

John is a nuisance.   (tense alone)
John must be a nuisance.   (tense + M)
John has been a nuisance.   (tense + have + part.)
John is being a nuisance.   (tense + be + ing)
John must have been a nuisance.   (tense + M + have + part.)
John must be being a nuisance.   (tense + M + be + ing)
John has been being a nuisance.   (tense + have + part. + be + ing)
John must have been being a nuisance.   (tense + M + have +
                                             part. + be + ing)

Make seven similar sentences for "John is silly."

In practice, not all of the theoretical possibilities can be cited in actual English usage. We have seen that verbals with such verbs as *know* and *understand* do not readily admit the *be + ing*. Neither do structures consisting of *be* and an adverbial of place. Thus we can have "John must be at the door," "John has been at the door," "John must have been at the door," but hardly "John is being at the door," "John must be being at the door," "John has been being at the door," or "John must have been being at the door." One might wish to go so far as to call these last four ungrammatical.

When *be* is followed by a noun phrase or an adjective, the admissibility of *be + ing* depends to some extent on the particular noun phrase or adjective. The sentence "John was being a nuisance" is a good deal more likely than "John was being a teacher." The sentence "John was being silly" is more likely than "John was being healthy."

The point is, however, that if the circumstances of living and speaking should somehow make it useful to say "John was being a teacher" or "John was being healthy" or "John was being at the door," the grammatical machinery is available and one would apply it with hardly a second thought.

Make seven other sentences from each of the following by changing the content of the auxiliary, as shown for "John is a nuisance" above. Use either the present or the past tense.

  1. Sally waited.
  2. Edna became impatient.
  3. Randolph had a good time.

Notice in the last sentence that when you add *have* + part. you get two *have*'s in the verb phrase. For convenience and brevity only the morphemes that figure significantly in the changes are bold or marked to show word boundaries here.

Randolph + **past** + **have** + **part.** + **have** + a good time $\Rightarrow$
Randolph + **have** + **past** + **have** + **part.** + a good time $\rightarrow$
Randolph # **have** + **past** # **have** + **part.** # a good time
Randolph had had a good time.

The first **have** is from the auxiliary in the *have* + part. element. The second **have** is a middle verb. We shall see that this distinction makes a difference in the formation of questions and other kinds of sentences.

Syntax

Two Semi-Modals

It is characteristic of modals (1) that, unlike verbs, they do not have an *s* form and (2) that they are not followed by the word *to*. Thus we say "He knows it" but not *"He mays know it." **May** + **present** is always *may*, no matter what the subject is. Similarly, we can say "He came to know it" but not *"He may to know it."

There are two words in English, however, that vacillate between the modal class and the verb class. Sometimes they behave like modals and sometimes like verbs. These are the words *dare* and *need*.

The word *need* is used as a modal in the sentence "He need wait." What characteristics make it a modal in this sentence? "He need wait" by itself is quite an unlikely sentence, but if we add the word *only* the sentence becomes familiar enough: "He need only wait." However, *need* is more commonly used as a verb. Then it takes the *s* form after subjects that require that form with verbs, and is used with *to* before other verbs, as in "He needs to improve his manners."

Dare is used as a modal even less commonly than *need*. We would probably be merely confused by a sentence like "He dare talk back." We would expect the verb usage: "He dares to talk back," or possibly only part of this usage — the *s* form, *dares*, but not the *to*: "He dares talk back." As a pure modal, *dare* is sometimes used in questions and negatives: "Dare he do it?" "He dare not do it." This is probably felt as a little old-fashioned, however.

Tell in which of the following *dare* and *need* are used as modals.

1. We hardly need wait until they come.
2. They need to understand it better.
3. He dared to answer me back.
4. She dare not think about it.

Syntax

ought to, have to, be to, be going to

Various other forms occur as auxiliaries in the verb phrase, some of them with meanings similar to those of modals. For example, *ought to* means approximately *should*.

Like the modals, *ought to* can occur before *have* + part. or *be* + *ing* or both of them:

> He ought to have helped.
> He ought to be helping.
> He ought to have been helping.

Make three similar sentences from "They ought to watch it." The structure *have to* has much the meaning of *must*:

> I must leave.
> I have to leave.

Have to will also occur before *be* + *ing:* "I have to be going." However, it will not generally occur before *have* + part. We would not ordinarily say "I have to have gone."

Another modal-like structure is *be to.* This occurs before verbals and also before verb phrase structures with *be:*

> He is to help us.
> He is to be here later.

This will occur sometimes before *have* + part.: "He is to have finished it by nine," or "They were to have been here by nine." It does not generally occur before *be* + *ing.* We would hardly say "He is to be doing it later" or "He is to have been finishing it by now."

A very common structure for expressing the meaning "future time" is *be going to.* This occurs before all verbals and also before constructions with *be:*

> He is going to be a teacher.   (be + NP)
> He is going to be silly.   (be + Adj)
> He is going to be at the party.   (be + Adv-p)

He is going to finish it.   (V_T + NP)
He is going to feel foolish.   (V_s + Adj)

The *be going to* will also occur before *have* + part. and before *be* + *ing*, though the resulting structures may sometimes strike us as odd and only marginally grammatical. What do you think of the following? Would you say that they are grammatical or not?

1. He was going to have finished it.
2. He is going to be working when they come.
3. He was going to have been working when they came.
4. He is going to have started before we get there.

Which of the sentences above contain *have* + part. and which contain *be* + *ing*?

It will be seen that we cannot simply list *ought to, have to, be to, be going to* as modals, because they don't behave quite as modals do. If we added them to the modal list, the grammar would generate ungrammatical sentences, like *"He had to have been thinking." It is true that, so far as we have explored the matter, *ought to* and perhaps *be going to* would fit in the modal group, since they will occur both before *have* + part. and *be* + *ing*. But there are other parts of the grammar in which *ought to* behaves differently from modals. For example, "He should go" becomes the question "Should he go?" but "He ought to go" does not become *"Ought to he go?"

In order to incorporate *ought to, have to, be to, be going to* in the grammar, we must add extra lines to the rule for Aux.

This is the expanded rule for the auxiliary:

$$\text{Aux} \rightarrow \text{tense} + \begin{cases} \text{(M)} + \text{(have + part.)} + \text{(be + ing)} \\ \left.\begin{matrix} \text{(ought to)} \\ \text{(be going to)} \end{matrix}\right\} + \text{(have + part.)} + \text{(be + ing)} \\ \text{(be to)} + \text{(have + part.)} \\ \text{(have to)} + \text{(be + ing)} \end{cases}$$

Look at this K-terminal string:

he + present + ought to + have + part. + be + ing + pay + attention

Present and **ought to** will come out as *ought to*, just as **present** and **must** come out *must*. (Like *must, ought to* has no past tense.) To what do **part.** and **ing** apply in the string above? What is the actual sentence?

Look at this:

he + past + have to + watch + them

To what will the tense apply? What is the sentence?

Draw trees of derivation leading to the following K-terminal strings. Derive **have to, be to,** and **be going to** from Aux.

5. **Bert + past + have to + smile**
6. **he + past + be to + have + part. + finish + it**
7. **he + past + be going to + have + part. + finish + it**

Phonology

A Point of Pronunciation

Historically, the three *have's* of "They have a car," "They have gone," and "They have to study" come from the same word. But as English has developed, they have become sharply distinct in the ways in which they are used. Only one of them is a verb. Which one?

The *have* of "They have to study" differs from the other two also in pronunciation, though the spelling hides this fact. Pronounce the following sentences at normal speed:

> They have two names for it.
> They have to name it.

In one of these, the *have* ends with an /f/ sound and in the other with a /v/ sound. Which has /f/ and which /v/?

> Now pronounce these:

> George has two objections.
> George has to object.

Which *has* ends with an /s/ sound and which with a /z/ sound?

SUMMARY OF RULES

Syntactic Rules

$$\text{Aux} \rightarrow \text{tense} + \begin{cases} \text{(M) + (have + part.) + (be + ing)} \\ \begin{Bmatrix} \text{(ought to)} \\ \text{(be going to)} \end{Bmatrix} + \text{(have + part.) + (be + ing)} \\ \text{(be to) + (have + part.)} \\ \text{(have to) + (be + ing)} \end{cases}$$

M → can, may, will, shall, must

(*Dare* and *need* also behave as modals in some sentences.)

Phonological Rules for the Participle Morpheme

Except for about forty verbs, the participle is formed exactly as the past tense is. All regular verbs and many irregular ones have identical past tenses and participles. The forty have special rules for participle, such as these:

drive + part. → driven   eat + part. → eaten

(The list of common verbs with special rules for participle is given on page 79. *Be* has the participle form *been*.)

Phonological Rules for *ing*

All verbs and *be* make the *ing* form by adding a syllable spelled –*ing* and pronounced /ing/, or, sometimes, /in/.

TEST

1. Write trees of derivation leading to the following K-terminal strings. (The pitch pattern 2-3-1 is omitted.)
   a. **June + past + be + there**
   b. **she + present + like + George**
   c. **Arnold + past + find + a + purse**
   d. **they + past + shall + know + it**
   e. **they + past + have + part. + eat + it**
   f. **he + present + have + part. + be + here**
   g. **Bill + past + be + ing + loaf**
   h. **I + past + shall + have + part. + see + it**
   i. **Billy + past + may + have + part. + be + ing + loaf**

2. Apply the affix transformation to the following K-terminal strings, and replace the plus signs with the word boundary symbol in the proper places. Then write the actual sentences represented by the strings.
   a. **we + past + lose + it**
   b. **George + present + may + find + it**
   c. **Mabel + present + have + part. + be + there**
   d. **they + present + be + ing + leave**
   e. **Mr. Wilkins + past + shall + feel + good**
   f. **Martin + past + have + part. + be + ing + wait**
   g. **he + present + may + have + part. + be + ing + be + funny**

3. Make three sentences from "He ought to try." In the first, use

ought to before *have* + part., in the second before *be* + *ing*, and in the third before both *have* + part. and *be* + *ing*.

4. Write a numeral for each sentence below to tell whether *be going to* occurs before (1) *be* + NP, (2) V_I + Adv-m, (3) *be* + Adv-p, (4) V_T + NP.

    a. He was going to drive slowly.
    b. He was going to be the catcher.
    c. He was going to buy some milk.
    d. He was going to be at home.

REVIEW QUESTIONS

1. In the rule for Aux, what term does M stand for?
2. What four of the common modals have past tense forms, and what are the forms?
3. What is **will** + **present**?
4. What sort of time meaning do the modals usually convey?
5. Which of the modals *must, should, could* sometimes express past time?
6. *Can* and *may* are both used to express the meaning of permission. What meaning does *can* sometimes have that *may* doesn't, and what meaning does *may* have that *can* doesn't?
7. What is the difference in meaning between *must* and *should*?
8. If the morpheme **part.** is used as an item from the auxiliary, what else must also be used?
9. How does the "present perfect" — that is, # **have** + **present** # **verb** + **part.** # — differ in meaning from # **verb** + **past** #?
10. What time relationship does "past perfect" show?
11. Discuss the difference in meaning between the members of the following pairs.

    a. Bernard struck the policeman.
       Bernard had struck the policeman.
    b. Erin saw the movie.
       Erin has seen the movie.
    c. The men have finished the job.
       The men had finished the job.
    d. We were there.
       We have been there.
    e. Henry walks by the lake.
       Henry is walking by the lake.

f. Albert was milking the cows when the electricity failed.
Albert milked the cows when the electricity failed.
g. They play football.
They are playing football.

12. How many morphemes come from the auxiliary in the following K-terminal string, and what are they? **the + boy + past + shall + have + part. + be + ing + write + the + letter**

13. In that string, to what are **past, part.,** and **ing** attached after the affix transformation?

14. How many sentences can be made with the morphemes **John, past,** and **leave** by varying the content of the auxiliary? Suppose that the modal, when it occurs, is always *may*.

15. How many basic verb phrase patterns are provided for by the rules for VP and verbal? List the patterns — *be* + NP, etc.

16. What different sources do the two **have**'s come from in the following T-terminal string: **# John # have + past # have + part. # a # bicycle #** What is the actual sentence?

17. What are the modal characteristics of *need* in "He need only ask"?

18. What part of the auxiliary sometimes follows *be to?*

19. What part of the auxiliary is not ordinarily used with verbs like *know* and *understand?*

20. What simple modal does *have to* resemble in meaning?

21. How does the pronunciation of *has* differ in "He has to" and "He has two"?

22. What parts of the auxiliary may follow *ought to?*

CHAPTER 5

Other Structures in the Determiner

The rule for *noun phrase* gives us four possible kinds:

$$NP \rightarrow \begin{Bmatrix} \text{proper noun} \\ \text{personal pronoun} \\ \text{indefinite pronoun} \\ \text{Det} + \text{N} \end{Bmatrix}$$

These are the rules for Det + N as given so far:

$$\text{Det} \rightarrow \text{Art}$$

$$\text{Art} \rightarrow \begin{Bmatrix} \text{Def} \\ \text{Nondef} \end{Bmatrix}$$

$$\text{Def} \rightarrow \text{the}$$

$$\text{Nondef} \rightarrow \begin{Bmatrix} \text{a} \\ \text{some} \\ \text{null} \end{Bmatrix}$$

$$\text{N} \rightarrow \begin{Bmatrix} \text{count} + \text{(plural)} \\ \text{noncount} \end{Bmatrix}$$

What words do the abbreviations Art, Def, and Nondef stand for? What do *count* and *noncount* mean? What are the two forms of the nondefinite article *a?* What article is used with both count and noncount nouns? Which nondefinite article is used with singular count nouns? Which articles are used both with plural count nouns and with noncount nouns?

The determiner must contain *article*, but it may optionally contain a number of other features too. One is a set of structures called *pre-articles*. Others are elements called *demonstration* and *number*.

Syntax

Pre-Articles

The set of structures called *pre-articles*, which may optionally be contained in the determiner, are so called because they occur before articles. Here are the rules for them:

> Det → (pre-article) + Art
> pre-article → several of, many of, much of, one of, two of . . .

The pre-articles add to the noun phrase a meaning of number or quantity. There are quite a few pre-articles. In addition to those listed, we have others such as *both of, a lot of, a few of, few of, most of, half of, none of.* All of the cardinal numbers team with *of* to form pre-articles: *one of, two of, eight of,* etc.

When a pre-article is used, it controls the number — singular or plural — of the noun phrase and determines the form of the *be* or verb in the verb phrase. Compare these sentences:

Several of the boys know it.

One of the boys knows it.

The noun *boys* is plural in both sentences, but the noun phrase is plural in only one of them. Which one?

Here is a partial tree of derivation showing the structure of the noun phrase *several of the boys:*

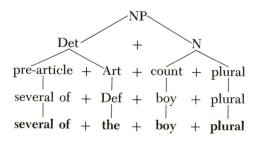

Draw a similar tree for *many of the girls.*

When the obligatory article of the determiner is nondefinite rather than definite, certain changes take place. Usually the nondefinite article must be *null,* not *a* or *some,* and the *of* of most pre-articles must be dropped in the finished sentence. Thus we can have a tree of derivation like the following:

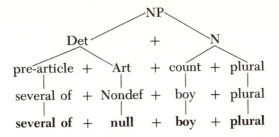

Since *several of boys* is of course ungrammatical, a phonological rule must now drop the *of* in this position, so that the noun phrase will come out *several boys*.

Draw a similar tree for *many girls*.

There are certain conditions, however, in which these changes do not take place — in particular when the noun is what is called a *collective* noun. This is a noun referring to a group of people or things, like *group, team, family*. These are still count nouns, because they form plurals: *groups, teams, families*. With these we may have the nondefinite article *a* and retain the *of* of the pre-article:

several of a group

one of a family

Here is the tree for *several of a group:*

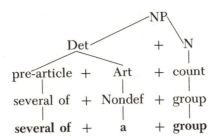

Draw the tree for *one of a family.*

The pre-article *a lot of* does not drop the *of* even before the null nondefinite article. Thus we say "a lot of boys," not * "a lot boys." What is the nondefinite article in "a lot of boys"?

Write the actual noun phrases represented by the following.

1. many of + the + house + plural
2. most of + the + man + plural
3. much of + the + meat
4. all of + the + information
5. some of + null + child + plural

6. much of + null + furniture
7. many of + null + door + plural
8. two of + a + kind
9. a lot of + null + coin + plural
10. several of + null + spectator + plural
11. a few of + null + egg + plural
12. one of + the + winner + plural
13. a dozen of + null + orange + plural
14. half of + a + apple
15. none of + the + syrup
16. both of + null + horse + plural

Syntax

Demonstration

Other features can occur after the obligatory article of the determiner. One of these is an element that we call *demonstration*. This is not itself a word or group of words. Rather it combines with the preceding article to form words. We add it to the rule for determiner as follows:

$$\text{Det} \rightarrow \text{(pre-article)} + \text{Art} + \text{(demonstration)}$$

Demonstration will ultimately produce the words *this, these, that,* and *those,* and two other expressions. But we can't say that it *is* these words, because then, since article must occur and demonstration may, we would produce such ungrammatical noun phrases as **the these people.*

Instead, we incorporate the notion of demonstration in the rules as follows. We first say that there are two kinds of demonstration, which we will arbitrarily call D_1 and D_2:

$$\text{demonstration} \rightarrow \begin{Bmatrix} D_1 \\ D_2 \end{Bmatrix}$$

Then we include the following rules in the phonological component of the grammar:

$$\text{Def} + D_1 \rightarrow \begin{Bmatrix} \text{this} \\ \text{these} \end{Bmatrix} \quad \text{Def} + D_2 \rightarrow \begin{Bmatrix} \text{that} \\ \text{those} \end{Bmatrix}$$

The choice depends obviously on whether the following noun is singular or plural. $\text{Def} + D_1$ is *this* if the noun is singular, *these* if the noun is plural. $\text{Def} + D_2$ is *that* with singular nouns, *those* with plural ones.

We may now have such a tree of derivation as this:

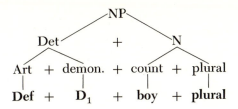

This will stand for the noun phrase *these boys*, since **Def + D₁** will become *these* and **boy + plural** will become *boys* by phonological rules.

Draw a tree of derivation for *those girls*.

The rule now says that a determiner must contain *article* but may optionally have *pre-article* before it and *demonstration* after it. Therefore, we may have such a structure as this:

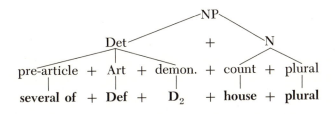

What noun phrase does this string of morphemes stand for? Draw a similar tree for *many of those streets*.

This, these, that, those combine the semantic notions of definiteness and demonstration, or pointing out. Furthermore, *this* and *these* are linked in the idea of nearness, while *that* and *those* share the idea of farness. All of this is summed up in the phonological rules for Def + D₁ and Def + D₂.

Since the definite article in combination with D₁ and D₂ takes care of the very important words *this, these, that,* and *those*, we could now say that when *demonstration* occurs, *article* must be *definite*, not *nondefinite*. But it is simpler to let Nondef occur too before D₁ and D₂, because by doing so we can incorporate in the grammar two other expressions that are nondefinite but have something of the semantic quality of demonstration: *a certain* and *some*. We add these rules to the phonology:

$$\text{Nondef} + D_1 \rightarrow \text{a certain}$$
$$\text{Nondef} + D_2 \rightarrow \text{sôme}$$

The mark ῀ over the *o* in *some* means that *some* is pronounced with second stress — not weak stress like the *some* of *some pie*.

Thus we can have such a tree of derivation as the following:

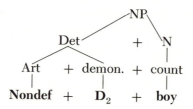

What actual noun phrase does the last line stand for? Draw a similar tree of derivation for *a certain man*.

Instead of **Nondef + D₁ + house**, we could have this:

$$\begin{array}{c} \text{NP} \\ \text{Det} \qquad + \qquad \text{N} \\ \text{Art} \quad + \quad \text{demon.} \quad + \quad \text{count} \\ \textbf{Nondef} \; + \quad \textbf{D}_2 \quad + \quad \textbf{boy} \end{array}$$

This string stands for the noun phrase *some boy*. This *some* is clearly different from the *some* listed as one of the nondefinite articles. In the first place, it occurs with singular count nouns, whereas the other *some* occurs only with plural count nouns and noncount nouns. In the second place, this *some* is pronounced with louder stress than the simple nondefinite article is. Say the following, and note the difference:

> Some boys were playing in the yard.
> Some boy was playing in the yard.

Normally one would pronounce the first *some*, the nondefinite article, with weak stress and the vowel sound schwa, the vowel sound of *a* in *a boy*. One would pronounce the second, the product of Nondef + D₂, with secondary stress and the vowel sound of *u* in *dumb boy*.

We can see a similar stress contrast between the simple definite article and Def + demonstration:

> The boys were playing in the yard.
> Those boys were playing in the yard.

The word *the* in the first sentence is pronounced with weak stress and the vowel sound schwa. But *those* in the second is pronounced with secondary stress. This similarity in the stress patterning is another reason for associating *this, these, that,* and *those* with *a certain* and *some*, both containing the element demonstration, but the first group being definite and the second nondefinite.

Draw a tree of derivation for the noun phrase *some dog*. Then use the noun phrase as subject of a sentence.

Apply T-affix and write actual sentences for the following. Tell which *some* is pronounced with second stress.

1. **Nondef + D$_2$ + dog + plural + present + can + hunt**
2. **some + dog + plural + present + be + ing + hunt**

Syntax

Number

We will note one other optional element that may occur in the determiner of the noun phrase. This is *number:*

Det → (pre-article) + Art + (demonstration) + (number)

As the rule shows, number occurs after D$_1$ or D$_2$, if they occur, and in any case after article.

Number is of two sorts:

$$\text{number} \rightarrow \begin{Bmatrix} \text{cardinal} \\ \text{ordinal} \end{Bmatrix}$$

cardinal → one, two, three, four, five . . .
ordinal → first, second, third, fourth, fifth . . .

With the inclusion of number, we can account in the grammar for noun phrases of the sort shown in the following:

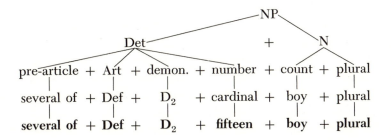

What will **Def + D$_2$** become when the following noun is plural? What is the actual noun phrase represented by the K-terminal string?

Draw a tree for the noun phrase *many of these twenty girls.*

Since number may be ordinal instead of cardinal, we may also have a structure such as the following:

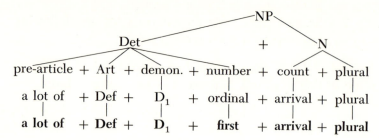

What noun phrase is represented by the K-terminal string? Draw a similar diagram for *most of those second floors.*

Write the noun phrase represented by each of the following.

1. **the + child + plural**
2. **many of + the + child + plural**
3. **many of + null + child + plural**
4. **Def + D$_1$ + child**
5. **Nondef + D$_1$ + child**
6. **Nondef + D$_2$ + child**
7. **the + first + child + plural**
8. **Def + D$_2$ + first + child + plural**
9. **many of + Def + D$_1$ + hundred + card + plural**
10. **most of + Def + D$_2$ + fifth + group**

In certain contexts, *number* can occur after a nondefinite article: *one of a third team.* It most often occurs, however, after the definite article, with or without demonstration.

These rules account for a large variety of the structures possible in the English noun phrase but by no means for all of them. A foreigner learning English would have still a number of special rules to learn in his effort to master the English determiner — such, for example, as the fact that the *of* of the pre-articles *both of, all of,* and *half of* can be optionally dropped before *the.* We can say either "both of the boys" or "both the boys" and mean the same thing. But this is not true of the other pre-articles. We can say only "several of the boys," not *"several the boys."

All of these small features of the kernel sentence the native manages automatically, without being aware, usually, that there is much of anything to manage. There is quite a lot, actually, and the rules given show at least some of the complexity.

Syntax

Adverbials of Place

We have so far talked about two kinds of adverbials — those of place and those of manner. In what rule have adverbials of place been mentioned? What two structures are used as adverbials of place? After what kinds of verbals do adverbials of manner occur? Are they optional or obligatory?

Adverbials of manner do not ordinarily occur after *be* constructions. We do not say * "He was angry slowly" or * "He was outside indignantly." However, adverbials of place do occur after verbals as well as after *be*. They occur after intransitive verbs ("The professor stood by the frame") and after transitive verbs and their objects ("Churchill attended school in England"). We shall have quite a bit more to say about the occurrence of adverbials of place in such constructions later on, but for the moment we shall pass over them.

Adverbials of place occur also after the other verbal types:

V_s + Adj: He got sick on the train.
V_b + NP: He became a teacher in Detroit.
V_b + Adj: He became violent upstairs.
V-mid + NP: He has a cave under the cliff.

What are the adverbials of place in these examples?

We can show the possibility of such an occurrence by expanding the rule for *verbal* as follows:

$$\text{verbal} \rightarrow \left\{ \begin{array}{l} \left. \begin{array}{l} \left\{ \begin{array}{l} V_I \\ V_T + NP \end{array} \right\} + (\text{Adv-m}) \\ \left. \begin{array}{l} V_s + \text{Adj} \\ V_b \left\{ \begin{array}{l} NP \\ Adj \end{array} \right\} \\ V\text{-mid} + NP \end{array} \right\} + (\text{Adv-p}) \end{array} \right. \end{array} \right\}$$

The Adv-p is in parentheses because it is optional in these constructions. "He has a cave under the cliff" is grammatical, but so is "He has a cave," with the adverbial of place omitted. In the VP rule, the Adv-p is not in parentheses after *be*, because it is not optional. If it is omitted, we are not left with a grammatical kernel sentence. "He is under the cliff" is grammatical, but * "He is" is not, at least not as a kernel sentence. "He is" can occur only in response to a question: "Who's under the cliff?" "He is." Here it is not a kernel sentence, but a transform.

Identify the adverbials of place in the following sentences and tell whether they follow (1) *be*, (2) V_s + Adj, (3) V_b + $\begin{Bmatrix} NP \\ Adj \end{Bmatrix}$, or (4) V-mid + NP.

1. A haircut costs three dollars in Cheyenne.
2. The axe was in the woodshed.
3. Gabriel felt uneasy in that house.
4. Myrtle has an apartment over the store.
5. Uncle Frank remained an outsider on the trip.
6. The dress looked good on Gertie.
7. The boy became sleepy on the train.
8. Bacon smells better outdoors.
9. The gloves were on the shelf.

Syntax

Adverbials of Frequency

Certain adverbials tell how often something happens. They may be single-word adverbs like *often, frequently, sometimes, seldom.* Or they may be phrases like *now and then, every day.* Such adverbials are called *adverbials of frequency:*

Adv-f → usually, often, every day, once in a while . . .

In kernel sentences, adverbials of frequency occur both after *be* constructions and after verbals. They are optional in both cases, since they are not needed to make the verb phrase grammatical. We indicate them for the *be* constructions as follows:

$$VP \rightarrow Aux + \begin{Bmatrix} be + \begin{Bmatrix} NP \\ Adj \\ Adv\text{-}p \end{Bmatrix} + (Adv\text{-}f) \\ \\ verbal \end{Bmatrix}$$

What does Adv-f stand for?

Point out the Adv-f's in the following sentences.

1. Howard was sulky sometimes.
2. They were partners once in a while.
3. Susan is very angelic occasionally.
4. Mr. Stoddard is in the office now and then.
5. She had been sick frequently.

Adverbials of frequency can also occur optionally after any type of verbal. We show this as follows:

$$
\text{verbal} \rightarrow \left\{ \begin{array}{l} \left\{ \begin{array}{l} V_I \\ V_T + NP \end{array} \right\} + (Adv\text{-}m) \\ \left. \begin{array}{l} V_s + Adj \\ V_b + \left\{ \begin{array}{l} NP \\ Adj \end{array} \right\} \\ V\text{-}mid + NP \end{array} \right\} + (Adv\text{-}p) \end{array} \right\} + (Adv\text{-}f)
$$

This rule has now become pretty complicated, so study it carefully. What does Adv-m stand for and what verbal types may it follow? What types may it not follow? What is an Adv-p, and what, so far as this rule goes, may it follow? What may an adverbial of frequency follow? If an Adv-m and an Adv-f occur in the same verb phrase, which comes first?

Point out all of the adverbials in the following. Tell of each whether it is an adverbial of place, of manner, or of frequency.

6. A haircut costs three dollars in Cheyenne sometimes.
7. Susan smiles occasionally.
8. Nelson hit the ball hard most of the time.
9. He became a nuisance at parties frequently.
10. George has a cold often.
11. She studied industriously every day.
12. She was sick on the plane usually.
13. We saw them seldom.
14. A plane leaves for Paris every day.

Syntax

Adverbials of Time

We shall consider one other type of adverbial — the *adverbial of time*. Like other adverbials, adverbials of time may be of several sorts. They may be single words: *then, yesterday*. They may be prepositional phrases: *in a moment, after the dance*. Or they may be noun phrases: *this morning, next week*.

Adv-t → then, yesterday, last week, in the morning . . .

Adverbials of time tell when — not how often — something happened or happens. Adverbials of frequency have something to do with time also, of course, but they differ in that their function is to indicate the frequency of an occurrence, not the actual time when it happened. Compare these sentences:

> She studies on Tuesdays.
> She was studying on Tuesday.

In the first sentence *on Tuesdays* is an adverbial of frequency; it tells when the studying usually takes place. In the second sentence, *on Tuesday* is an adverbial of time; it tells when a particular bout of studying was going on.

Adverbials of frequency and time differ also in their positioning in sentences. Normally, adverbials of time come after any other adverbials in the sentence, including adverbials of frequency. We add them to the rules for VP and verbal as follows:

$$VP \rightarrow Aux + \begin{cases} be + \begin{cases} NP \\ Adj \\ Adv\text{-}p \end{cases} + (Adv\text{-}f) + (Adv\text{-}t) \\ verbal \end{cases}$$

$$verbal \rightarrow \begin{cases} \begin{cases} V_I \\ V_T + NP \end{cases} + (Adv\text{-}m) \\ V_s + Adj \\ V_b + \begin{cases} NP \\ Adj \end{cases} \\ V\text{-}mid + NP \end{cases} + (Adv\text{-}p) \end{cases} + (Adv\text{-}f) + (Adv\text{-}t)$$

Study these rules. According to the VP rule, how many adverbials may occur in one sentence after *be?* If all are used, in what order do they occur? What adverbials may occur after an intransitive verb? In what order? What adverbials may occur after a V-mid + NP and in what order?

This is as far as we shall go with the elaboration of the rules for VP and verbal, so far as kernel sentences are concerned. This is by no means to say that the rules will account for all the structures in all English kernel sentences. You can probably easily think of quite normal sentences not covered by the rules. The sentence "He was sick on the train sometimes" is one. This has the *be* followed by an adjective, an adverbial of place, and an adverbial of frequency. Can you explain why the VP rule does not account for this?

Similarly, one can think of sentences in which adverbials of manner occur with verbals other than the intransitive and transitive verb ones. One might say "He got sick intentionally," which is a case of

V_s + Adj + Adv-m, though the rule for verbal makes no allowance for an Adv-m following V_s + Adj.

However, we must call a halt somewhere in the elaboration of the rules for VP and verbal, just as we had to in the rule for determiner. As stated, the rules show the *general* structure of English kernel sentences, and enough of it to enable us to see how the kernel is changed by transformation into the sentences that we more habitually use.

Identify the adverbials in the following sentences, and tell what kind of adverbial each is.

1. John was sulky frequently last month.
2. Edna should study hard every day.
3. Bert felt ill in class yesterday.
4. Mary was late to class every day last year.
5. Buck brushed his teeth carefully each morning before breakfast.
6. Jean works diligently sometimes.
7. Rick was in the lab every morning at seven.
8. Anne had an argument in the gym last week.
9. Fred is going to go to New York next month.
10. Beth caught the bus usually at five o'clock.

Fill out the following sentences by supplying an adverbial or adverbials of the kind indicated.

11. The children crossed the street + Adv-m.
12. Several of the students were + Adv-p.
13. We were + Adv-p + Adv-t.
14. Angelo had a cold + Adv-f.
15. Miss Wilkins got sick + Adv-p.
16. She works + Adv-m + Adv-f.
17. The policeman is + Adv-p + Adv-f.
18. Mary Lou is + Adv-p + Adv-f + Adv-t.
19. Burgess played + Adv-m + Adv-f + Adv-t.
20. A haircut cost a dollar + Adv-p + Adv-f + Adv-t.

Syntax

Another Transformational Rule

We have already discussed one transformation: T-affix. This is the rule which produces a T-terminal string by putting the morphemes in the proper order, switching the positions of any tense, part., or *ing* preceding an M, *have, be,* or verb.

However, between the K-terminal string and the T-terminal string, any of a number of other transformations may occur to turn kernel sentences into the more complicated structures that we ordinarily make use of in writing and speaking. It is these transformations that we will be concerned with from now on. The kernel rules set forth all of the basic grammatical relationships of the language — such relationships as subject to verb, verb to object, subject to *be* to adverbial of place. These relationships persist no matter how the structures are turned around or complicated. Thus the relationship of *lion* to *roar* is just the same in *the roaring lion* as it is in "The lion roars." It is the lion that does the roaring in both expressions. *The man* and *in the house* have the same relationship in *the man in the house* as they do in "The man was in the house."

Transformational rules alter kernel structures by switching things around, leaving things out, putting things in, or, most commonly, putting two or more structures together. But they do not alter the kernel relationships. If we want to understand the relationships of structures in a transform, we have only to look at them in the kernel from which the transform was made.

We will start with a simple transformation which alters the position of adverbs of frequency. We have seen that adverbials of frequency may occur in kernel sentences with *be* or with verbals.

Adverbs of frequency (not usually prepositional phrases or noun phrases of frequency) commonly shift to a position after *be* or before a verb:

He is in the office *seldom.* ⇾ He is *seldom* in the office.
He works hard *sometimes.* ⇾ He *sometimes* works hard.

We can state the general rule for *be* constructions as follows:

$$NP + Aux + be + X + adverb\text{-}f + Y \Rrightarrow$$
$$NP + Aux + be + adverb\text{-}f + X + Y$$

Let us study this rule carefully. If you learn to read it easily, you won't have any trouble with the many similar rules that follow. In the first place, the items between plus signs mean any structure of the sort indicated. The NP here means any noun phrase subject: *Bill* or *they* or *the dog* or *several of those eleven children.* Similarly Aux can be just tense or tense + M or tense + M + *have* + part. + *be* + *ing.*

Now the X and Y are position markers. Here X means anything that occurs between *be* and an adverb of frequency. Y means anything occurring after the adverb of frequency. X and Y can also mean nothing, when nothing occurs in the position they mark. This cannot happen for the X in this particular rule, but it can for the Y, as we shall see. This use of X and Y simply shows that it doesn't matter what occurs, or whether nothing occurs, in the places indicated. Between *be* and the adverb of frequency we may have an NP, an adjective, an adverbial of place or various other structures. It doesn't matter. The transformation will work just the same, and the result will be a grammatical sentence.

We use a double arrow to distinguish transformational rules from the kernel rules we have been dealing with so far. In the line after the double arrow we indicate the reshuffle that the transformation calls for. The italicized items are those that shift position. Here the rule is very simple: the adverb of frequency just changes places with the X.

Here is an example, with the structures specified in the rule separated by plus signs:

some of the boys (NP) + past (Aux) + be (be) + here (X) + *usually (adverb-f)* + early (Y)

If we applied the affix transformation immediately to this, we would get the kernel sentence "Some of the boys were here usually early." Instead, we can apply the adverb of frequency transformation first and switch the adverb-f to a position after *be* and before X, as shown by the item in color that follows:

some of the boys (NP) + past (Aux) + be (be) + *usually (adverb-f)* + here (X) + early (Y)

This gives the transform "Some of the boys were usually here early."

Notice that the transform is actually more common, more "right-sounding," than the kernel sentence. This is often true. Indeed, we shall find cases in which the kernel structure is downright ungrammatical and can be made grammatical only by application of the transformational rule. In such cases we say that the transformational rule is obligatory.

Here is an example in which the Y is nothing, or null:

She is sick *seldom.* ⇉ She is *seldom* sick.

The parts specified in the rule are as follows:

she (NP) + present (Aux) + be (be) + sick (X) + *seldom (adverb-f)* + null (Y) ⇉
she (NP) + present (Aux) + be (be) + *seldom (adverb-f)* + sick (X) + null (Y)

Point out the X, the adverb of frequency, and the Y in the following sentences. In some of them the Y is null. Apply the transformational rule by switching the X and the adverb-f.

1. David was happy seldom then.
2. Mabel was at home rarely at that time.
3. Mr. Warbanks was a winner frequently.
4. Mrs. Schofield is in the hospital always.
5. The grass is wet sometimes in the morning.
6. Lunch is ready occasionally by twelve-fifteen.
7. They were in the park often.
8. We were there commonly before nine.
9. I am in class usually by then.
10. Wilkins was funny always.

In most of Items 1–10, the transform sounds more natural than the kernel sentence. Are there any for which the kernel sounds just as good?

The rule could be made more general if we were to write Adv-f instead of adverb-f between X and Y, thus letting the rule apply to any adverbial of frequency and not just to single-word adverbs. This would work for many phrasal adverbials:

He is at home *now and then* in the morning. ⇉
He is *now and then* at home in the morning.

However, it would also produce some rather odd sentences, like "He is every day in class in the morning." This is at best only marginally grammatical.

There are some kernel structures for which this transformation *must* be applied in order to produce a grammatical sentence. One of the adverbs of frequency is the word *never*, which clearly belongs in this group along with *always, sometimes*, etc. The choice of *never* as the adverbial of frequency will give such a K-terminal string as this one:

she + past + be + happy + never

If we make this into a sentence directly, the result will be the ungrammatical *"She was happy never." Instead, when the adverbial is *never*, the adverb of frequency transformation is obligatorily applied to give this:

she + past + be + never + happy

What actual sentence does this stand for?

Apply the transformation to these. Write just the strings.

11. **John + present + be + at home + never**
12. **the house + past + be + vacant + never + in the summer**
13. **the teacher + past + be + the headmaster + never**

Syntax

T-adverb of frequency Applied to Verbal Structures

We will continue the practice of referring to the various transformations by using the letter T, for *transformation,* followed by something that identifies the transformation.

T-adverb of frequency applies to structures containing verbals as well as to those containing *be,* but in a slightly different way. The adverb of frequency is shifted to a position immediately *after be,* but *before* a verb and its auxiliary:

$$NP + Aux + verb + X + adverb\text{-}f + Y \Rrightarrow$$
$$NP + adverb\text{-}f + Aux + verb + X + Y$$

Here is an example:

Jim (NP) + past (Aux) + have (verb) + a cold (X) + *often* (*adverb-f*) + last year (Y) $\Rrightarrow$
Jim (NP) + *often* (*adverb-f*) + past (Aux) + have (verb) + a cold (X) + last year (Y)

What actual sentence is represented by the kernel structure? What by the transform?

In the following example, Y is null:

Alex (NP) + past (Aux) + see (verb) + Edith (X) + *occasionally* (*adverb-f*) + null (Y) $\Rrightarrow$
Alex (NP) + *occasionally* (*adverb-f*) + past (Aux) + see (verb) + Edith (X) + null (Y)

What actual sentences are represented by the kernel structure and the transform?

When a verbal instead of *be* is involved in this transformation, both X and Y may be null, as in the following:

Trudy smiles *seldom* $\Rrightarrow$ Trudy *seldom* smiles.

Here the kernel structure is Trudy (NP) + present (Aux) + smile (verb) + null (X) + seldom (adverb-f) + null (Y). Write the structure of the transform, showing the elements between plus signs.

Never must be switched with verbals as with *be* from the kernel position. *"Tom had a good time never" is ungrammatical. What do we say instead?

Write the sentences resulting from the application of T-adverb of frequency to the following.

1. Judy bakes a cake usually.
2. He took the train sometimes last winter.
3. Bill yawned occasionally during the concert.
4. Margaret washed the dishes never after supper.
5. I eat an apple frequently in the afternoon.
6. Mr. Arnold stands by the window regularly.

For which of the sentences above is the transformation obligatory? For which of the others does the transform sound more natural than the kernel sentence?

Apply T-adverb of frequency to the following. Some of them are verb constructions, others *be*.

7. Margery was cross always in the morning.
8. Mervin bathes the baby seldom.
9. He catches the bus generally at five.
10. John is home never before six.
11. Elsie seems cheerful always.
12. The children were in the way sometimes.
13. The children got in the way sometimes.
14. Jennifer was polite usually to old people.
15. He practices the violin rarely these days.
16. Jack takes a shower never before dinner.
17. The coach raises his voice angrily seldom.
18. The spectators disturbed the golfers often.

SUMMARY OF RULES

Syntactic Rules for the Kernel Noun Phrase

Det → (pre-article) + Art + (demonstration) + (number)

pre-article → several of, much of, a lot of, three of . . .

demonstration → $\begin{Bmatrix} D_1 \\ D_2 \end{Bmatrix}$

number → $\begin{Bmatrix} \text{cardinal} \\ \text{ordinal} \end{Bmatrix}$

cardinal → one, two, three, four, five . . .

ordinal → first, second, third, fourth, fifth . . .

Phonological Rules for the Kernel Noun Phrase

Certain phonological rules operate in the production of the actual sentence represented by the K-terminal string.

The *of* of most pre-articles is dropped before the null nondefinite article:

$$\textbf{several of} + \textbf{null} + \textbf{boy} + \textbf{plural} \rightarrow \textit{several boys}$$

Also:

Def + $D_1 \rightarrow$ this, these
Def + $D_2 \rightarrow$ that, those
Nondef + $D_1 \rightarrow$ a certain
Nondef + $D_2 \rightarrow$ some   (with secondary stress)

These rules complete the account of the kernel noun phrase given in this text.

Syntactic Rules for VP and verbal

$$\text{VP} \rightarrow \text{Aux} + \left\{ \begin{array}{l} \text{be} + \left\{ \begin{array}{l} \text{NP} \\ \text{Adj} \\ \text{Adv-p} \end{array} \right\} + (\text{Adv-f}) + (\text{Adv-t}) \\ \\ \text{verbal} \end{array} \right\}$$

$$\text{verbal} \rightarrow \left\{ \begin{array}{l} \left. \begin{array}{l} \left\{ \begin{array}{l} V_I \\ V_T + \text{NP} \end{array} \right\} + (\text{Adv-m}) \\ \left\{ \begin{array}{l} V_s + \text{Adj} \\ V_b + \left\{ \begin{array}{l} \text{NP} \\ \text{Adj} \end{array} \right\} + (\text{Adv-p}) \\ \text{V-mid} + \text{NP} \end{array} \right\} \end{array} \right\} + (\text{Adv-f}) + (\text{Adv-t}) \end{array} \right\}$$

Adv-f $\rightarrow$ usually, often, every day, once in a while . . .

Adv-t $\rightarrow$ then, yesterday, last week, in the morning . . .

The rules for VP and verbal as elaborated above are now, for our purposes, completed.

T-adverb of frequency

a. NP + Aux + be + X + adverb-f + Y $\Rrightarrow$
  NP + Aux + be + adverb-f + X + Y
b. NP + Aux + verb + X + adverb-f + Y $\Rrightarrow$
  NP + adverb-f + Aux + verb + X + Y

This transformation is optional except when the adverb of frequency is *never*, in which case it is obligatory. It can be applied to some adverbials other than single-word adverbs, but with some phrasal adverbials it will produce ungrammatical sentences.

TEST

1. Draw trees of derivation for the following noun phrases.
a. the cat
b. those cats
c. several cats
d. many of the cats
e. most of these cats
f. a lot of those twenty cats

2. Write the noun phrases represented by the following.
a. **the + woman + plural**
b. **a + olive**
c. **Def + D$_1$ + horse + plural**
d. **a few of + null + coin + plural**
e. **Def + D$_2$ + fifth + post**
f. **Nondef + D$_1$ + freshman + class**
g. **all of + the + six + chicken + plural**
h. **most of + Def + D$_2$ + thirty + lobster + plural**

3. Identify the adverbials in the following, and tell of each what kind it is — place, manner, frequency, or time.
a. Dick was there often.
b. Mr. Hall has a cabin in the mountains.
c. Williams spoke eloquently last night.
d. The class was lively yesterday.
e. He followed the trail successfully until nightfall.

4. Complete the following sentences by supplying an adverbial or adverbials of the type indicated.
a. They stalked the moose + Adv-m.
b. Some of the books were + Adv-p.
c. They were + Adv-p + Adv-t.
d. Max + is + Adv-f + Adv-p.
e. They had an argument + Adv-p + Adv-t.
f. I felt fine + Adv-t.
g. She sang + Adv-m + Adv-t.
h. She + Adv-f + sang + Adv-m.
i. They + Adv-f + argued + Adv-m + Adv-t.
j. George got sick + Adv-p + Adv-f + Adv-t.

5. Rewrite the following sentences applying T-adverb of frequency. The new position of the adverb-f will depend on whether the verb phrase is a *be* construction or a verbal one.

a. She spoke softly always.
b. Buck was kind occasionally.
c. Mr. McMasters was on television sometimes last year.
d. Angela typed the letters carefully usually.
e. Mr. Burbank smoked never before dinner.
f. Peter was a pest constantly yesterday.
g. He is there seldom in the morning.
h. We had heard the noise rarely at night.
i. Jaspar worked hard frequently last week.
j. They are in class generally by this time.

REVIEW QUESTIONS

1. What part of the determiner is obligatory?
2. Are pre-articles obligatory or optional in the determiner?
3. What word occurs in each pre-article?
4. What effect does the pre-article have on the number — singular or plural — of the noun phrase?
5. What part of the pre-article is generally dropped when the pre-article occurs with Nondef? What is the nondefinite article in this case?
6. In what way is the pre-article *a lot of* different from *several of, many of,* or *much of?*
7. When *demonstration* occurs as part of the determiner, what is its position in relation to *article?*
8. Into what two parts is *demonstration* divided?
9. What is Def + D_2? What are Nondef + D_1 and Nondef + D_2?
10. How does the word *some* in "Some man was here" differ from the simple nondefinite article *some?*
11. What is the stress difference between the determiner parts of *the boys* and *these boys?*
12. What is the position of *number* in relation to other parts of the determiner?
13. What are the two kinds of *number?*
14. In which rule — VP or verbal — does adverbial of manner appear? After what structures can it be used, according to the rule?
15. After what constructions does the rule for *verbal* provide for adverbials of place?
16. From what kernel structure can an adverbial of place not be omitted?
17. What do Adv-f and Adv-t stand for? What is the difference between Adv-f and adverb-f?

18. If adverbials of frequency, manner, and time occur in a kernel structure, in what order do they occur?

19. If adverbials of frequency, place, and time occur in a kernel *be* structure, in what order do they occur?

20. Give an example of a noun phrase that might be used as an adverbial of time.

21. What is the difference between the adverbials in "She studies on Tuesdays" and "She was studying on Tuesday"?

22. Explain why the VP rule as given will not account for the sentence "She was sick on the train sometimes."

23. A sentence resulting directly from kernel rules plus the affix transformation is called a kernel sentence. What is a sentence involving other transformations called?

24. Give a sentence that fits the description NP + Aux + be + X + adverb-f + Y.

25. How would T-adverb of frequency change the order of the items given in 24?

26. Give a sentence that fits the description NP + Aux + verb + X + adverb-p + Y.

27. What do the symbols X and Y stand for in rules like T-adverb of frequency?

CHAPTER 6

Questions, Negatives, Reassertions

It probably never occurs to the native speaker of English that "Did you see it?" is a rather peculiar way of asking a question. It is, though. What is the *did* for, and what does it mean? What is the grammatical relationship of the question to the corresponding statement "You saw it"? What is its relationship to the negative sentence "You didn't see it," where the *did* appears again?

Our peculiar English mechanism for asking questions, negating statements, making reassertions ("You did too see it") has grown over a period of several hundred years. In Shakespeare's time it was coming into being, though it had not yet assumed the form it has now. We will consider it with some care, because it is highly characteristic of English, and because it plays an important role in many structures of the language in addition to simple questions, negatives, and reassertions.

The transformations that produce these structures, like T-adverb of frequency, are called *single-base* transformations, because they involve just one underlying string of morphemes. The string is simply changed in some way — morphemes switched about, taken out, or put in. Later we will come to *double-base* transformations in which morphemes from two underlying strings are put together.

Syntax

T-yes/no

There are two main kinds of questions: those that can be answered by saying yes or no and those that cannot be. For instance, "Did you see it?" can be answered by "Yes, I did" or "No, I didn't." But "What

117

did you see?" cannot be answered in this way. We must answer "What did you see?" by uttering some other structure, usually a noun phrase: *a horse, Bill, an accident.*

We call questions that can be answered yes or no *yes/no questions.* We call those that cannot be so answered *wh questions,* because most of them are introduced by words with the initial letters *wh.* The transformation that changes kernel strings into the strings of yes/no questions is called the *yes/no question transformation,* or, more simply, *T-yes/no.*

Let us start with these examples of statements changed into questions:

John should wait. ⇉ Should John wait?
John had waited. ⇉ Had John waited?
John was waiting. ⇉ Was John waiting?
John waited. ⇉ Did John wait?

Obviously the first three changes differ markedly from the fourth. In the first three, the NP subject *John* changes places with the following word — *should, had, was.* But in the fourth there is no such switch. Instead, *waited* becomes *wait,* and the word *did* appears at the beginning of the sentence.

We will take the first three first. Here is the tree of derivation leading to the K-terminal string of "John should wait."

Notice that we show here the complete tree of derivation including the pitch pattern, which was generally omitted when we were dealing only with kernel sentences. Transforms may have different pitch patterns than the 2-3-1 pattern of the kernel sentence, and when this is true, pitch patterns will be included.

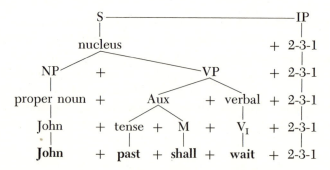

What word will be made up of **past** and **shall** in the final sentence? What does "2-3-1" mean?

This is the string for the question "Should John wait?":

past + shall + John + wait + 2-3-3

What two morphemes have changed places with the subject in the formation of the question string?

Another change is that the pitch pattern 2-3-1 has been replaced by 2-3-3. The typical yes/no question in English has a pitch pattern somewhat different from that of the typical statement. It begins in the same way on the middle level, rises in the same way to the high level 3 on the syllable with primary stress, but then, instead of falling to 1, stays high to the end, with the final little upturn. The patterns contrast in this way:

John should|wait.

Should John|wait?

Say the two sentences and try to perceive the difference in the pitch patterns.

The following rule sums up all of this. It is the first part of T-yes/no, the part that shows how statements containing modals in the verb phrase are turned into yes/no questions.

NP + tense-M + X + 2-3-1 $\Rrightarrow$ tense-M + NP + X + 2-3-3

What changes position with the subject, according to the rule? What other change takes place? The X means whatever comes between the modal and the 2-3-1 in the K-terminal string. It means that it doesn't matter what occurs in that position. The modal can be followed by a verb, as in our example, or by a *have* or a *be*. The transformation is the same:

John should have waited. $\Rrightarrow$ Should John have waited?

John should be taking his medicine every day. $\Rrightarrow$
Should John be taking his medicine every day?

When tense is followed not by a modal but by the word *have*, the transformation is very similar. Here is the transformation for "John had waited."

John + **past** + **have** + **wait** + 2-3-1 $\Rrightarrow$
past + **have** + **John** + **wait** + 2-3-3

What two morphemes change places with **John**? What other change takes place? Thus we add another line to the general rule for T-yes/no:

NP + tense-M   + X + 2-3-1 ⇒ tense-M   + NP + X + 2-3-3
NP + tense-have + X + 2-3-1 ⇒ tense-have + NP + X + 2-3-3

What changes places with the NP according to the new line? What is the significance of the X?

Kernels with *be* are transformed according to the same general plan. Here is the change for "John was waiting":

John + past + be + ing + wait + 2-3-1 ⇒
past + be + John + ing + wait + 2-3-3

Notice that **be + ing,** which came into the kernel as a unit from the auxiliary, is now separated by **John.** What will **past + be** become in the actual sentence?

We now add a third line to T-yes/no:

NP + tense-M   + X + 2-3-1 ⇒ tense-M   + NP + X + 2-3-3
NP + tense-have + X + 2-3-1 ⇒ tense-have + NP + X + 2-3-3
NP + tense-be   + X + 2-3-1 ⇒ tense-be   + NP + X + 2-3-3

Convert these into yes/no questions, and tell whether each change involves a tense-M, a tense-*have*, or a tense-*be*.

1. The girls are waiting.
2. Mr. Carson has left a message.
3. We must finish it by tomorrow.
4. They have had time to think it over.
5. She's a cheerleader.
6. I can get the book.
7. They were friendly.
8. Williams could do it next week.
9. He's forgotten about it.
10. He might have the flu.

Syntax

T-do

Let us now consider the transformation of the statement "John waited" into the yes/no question "Did John wait?" Here are the strings underlying both sentences:

John + past + wait + 2-3-1 ⇒ do + past + John + wait + 2-3-3

Forget about the *do* for the moment. What morpheme of the statement string has changed places with the NP subject in the formation of the question?

When the tense of the statement string is followed by a verbal instead of a modal, a *have*, or a *be*, the tense alone reverses with the subject. Here is the complete rule for T-yes/no:

NP + tense-M   + X   + 2-3-1 $\Rightarrow$ tense-M   + NP + X   + 2-3-3
NP + tense-have + X   + 2-3-1 $\Rightarrow$ tense-have + NP + X   + 2-3-3
NP + tense-be   + X   + 2-3-1 $\Rightarrow$ tense-be   + NP + X   + 2-3-3
NP + tense   + verbal + 2-3-1 $\Rightarrow$ tense   + NP + verbal + 2-3-3

Look again at the string **John + past + wait + 2-3-1**. Here the tense is followed not by a modal, a *have*, or a *be* but by a verbal — the intransitive verb *wait*. Therefore the fourth line of the rule applies, and this change takes place:

John + past + wait + 2-3-1 $\Rightarrow$ **past + John + wait + 2-3-3**

But now we have a peculiar situation in the string to the right of the double arrow. We have a tense with nothing next to it for which it can be a tense. Tense — past or present — can be expressed by a modal, a *have*, a *be*, or a verb, but not by a noun phrase like *John*. Whenever this happens — and, as we shall see, it happens often in English — a special transformation becomes obligatory. To any floating tense — one not adjoining a modal, *have*, *be*, or verb — there must be added the word *do* in order to express the tense:

$$\text{tense} \Rightarrow \text{do} + \text{tense}$$

We label this transformation T-do. It will provide for the following change:

past + John + wait + 2-3-3 $\Rightarrow$ **do + past + John + wait + 2-3-3**

Notice that we put in the *do* before the tense, not after it. We could put it in after and then make the affix transformation apply also to **past + do,** but this would be a useless complication requiring an extra step in the explanation of the sentence.

By a morphological rule, **do + past** becomes the word *did*. **Do + present** becomes *does* or *do*, depending on the subject. This *do* has no meaning in the usual sense. It serves only to express tense — present or past — and to introduce the question.

Here is another example of the successive application of T-yes/no and T-do:

Garry + present + help + them + 2-3-1 $\Rightarrow$ *(by T-yes/no)*
present + Garry + help + them + 2-3-3 $\Rightarrow$ *(by T-do)*
do + present + Garry + help + them + 2-3-3

What is the actual sentence represented by the final line?

Apply T-yes/no and T-do similarly to the following strings.

1. **he + past + dream + it + 2-3-1**
2. **the + child + present + seem + ill + 2-3-1**
3. **Mr. Sluter + past + make + a + speech + 2-3-1**
4. **the + teacher + plural + present + agree + 2-3-1**
5. **most + of + the + guest + plural + past + leave + 2-3-1**
6. **Daniel + past + become + truculent + 2-3-1**
7. **the + dandelion + plural + past + ruin + the + lawn + 2-3-1**
8. **a + train + present + stop + here + 2-3-1**

Change the following into yes/no questions. Simply write the finished questions, not the strings of morphemes.

9. Jack could have done it.
10. Jack had done it.
11. Jack was doing it.
12. Jack did it.
13. Somebody should have stopped them.
14. They were very happy.
15. A haircut costs three dollars in Cheyenne.
16. Several people objected strongly.
17. They have wired it for sound.
18. Biff got hurt in the accident.

Syntax

T-negative

If the yes/no question were all there was to it, it probably wouldn't pay us to go this deeply into the mechanism of questions. We might just say that you make a question by switching the subject with the modal, *have*, or *be* if there is one, and put in a *do, does,* or *did* if there isn't. But the yes/no question is by no means all there is to it. We shall see this machinery working in many parts of the grammar. If you have understood it as it operates in yes/no questions, you will have little trouble understanding its operation elsewhere.

We find it, for example, in the transformation by which kernel sentences are made negative. How do we negate a sentence like "John should wait"? Obviously by inserting the word *not* after the tense-modal:

John should wait. $\Rightarrow$ John should not wait.

Most commonly, of course, we say or write the contraction: "John shouldn't wait." Here the apostrophe is used to mark the omission of *o* in the contracted form.

The change in the string of morphemes is the following:

John + past + shall + wait + 2-3-1 $\Rightarrow$
John + past + shall + not + wait + 2-3-1

We can form this as part of the general rule as follows:

NP + tense-M + X $\Rightarrow$ NP + tense-M + not + X

Notice that here we do not have to mention the pitch pattern, because the pitch doesn't change in this transformation. The X stands for everything occurring after the modal, including the 2-3-1 at the end. Otherwise the structure indicated at the left of the arrow is just what it is for the first line of T-yes/no.

Kernels with *have* are changed in a similar way, as shown by the following:

John had waited. $\Rightarrow$ John hadn't waited.

Here is the change shown in the morpheme strings:

John + past + have + part. + wait + 2-3-1 $\Rightarrow$
John + past + have + not + part. + wait + 2-3-1

Notice that the **have + part.**, which came in together from the auxiliary, are now separated by **not.**

We can now enlarge the general rule as follows:

NP + tense-M   + X $\Rightarrow$ NP + tense-M   + not + X
NP + tense-have + X $\Rightarrow$ NP + tense-have + not + X

Kernels with *be* behave in a parallel way:

John was waiting. $\Rightarrow$ John wasn't waiting.

The change in the morpheme strings is as follows:

John + past + be + ing + wait + 2-3-1 $\Rightarrow$
John + past + be + not + ing + wait + 2-3-1

This gives us the third line of the rule:

NP + tense-M   + X $\Rightarrow$ NP + tense-M   + not + X
NP + tense-have + X $\Rightarrow$ NP + tense-have + not + X
NP + tense-be   + X $\Rightarrow$ NP + tense-be   + not + X

Now here is the fourth line, which covers the kernels in which tense is followed not by a modal, *have,* or *be* but by a verbal:

NP + tense + verbal ⇉ NP + tense + not + verbal

Let us apply this to the string **John + past + wait + 2-3-1,** which represents the kernel sentence "John waited." Since here the tense is followed by a verbal — the intransitive verb *wait* — it fits the fourth line of the rule, and we insert the word *not* between **past** and the verbal:

John + past + not + wait + 2-3-1

But again we have a floating tense, since **past** cannot be expressed by either of the morphemes adjacent to it — **John** and **not.** So the *do* transformation (tense ⇉ do + tense) applies automatically:

John + past + not + wait + 2-3-1 ⇉
John + do + past + not + wait + 2-3-1

The sequence **do + past + not** will of course come out *did not* or *didn't,* and the string represents the sentence "John didn't wait."

Here is another example showing the successive application of T-negative and T-do:

Ellen + present + like + Bill + 2-3-1 ⇉ *(by T-negative)*
Ellen + present + not + like + Bill + 2-3-1 ⇉ *(by T-do)*
Ellen + do + present + not + like + Bill + 2-3-1

What actual sentence is represented by the last line?

In similar fashion, apply T-negative and T-do successively to the following strings.

1. **George + present + work + hard + 2-3-1**
2. **the + nurse + past + give + the + injection + 2-3-1**
3. **he + past + smile + 2-3-1**
4. **they + present + look + well + 2-3-1**
5. **Mrs. Melanzano + past + agree + 2-3-1**
6. **it + past + please + him + 2-3-1**
7. **the + team + past + win + 2-3-1**

Make the following sentences negative. Write just the actual sentences, not the strings of morphemes.

8. Pinkerwell has written the letter.
9. Mothergood arrived in time.
10. Brandenson will help us.
11. Andersmith pruned the roses.
12. Brucelette is attending church.
13. Carronfeld understood.
14. Marklefish is a scientist.

15. Antonucci had agreed to it.
16. Hepplewhite marked the spot.
17. Witherwood has a chance.

Syntax

The Double Nature of *have*

In doing Number 17 in the exercise above, you could have come out with either of two sentences, both permitted by the rule for the negative transformation. Look again at the rule:

NP + tense-M   + X $\Rightarrow$ NP + tense-M   + not + X
NP + tense-have + X $\Rightarrow$ NP + tense-have + not + X
NP + tense-be   + X $\Rightarrow$ NP + tense-be   + not + X
NP + tense   + verbal $\Rightarrow$ NP + tense   + not + verbal

Now the sentence "Witherwood has a chance" is composed of the following string of morphemes:

Witherwood + present + have + a + chance + 2-3-1

This is a case of NP + tense-*have* + X, so it fits the second line of the description in the rule. Therefore we can add *not* after the tense-*have:*

Witherwood + present + have + not + a + chance + 2-3-1

This will give us the actual sentence "Witherwood has not a chance," or, more likely, "Witherwood hasn't a chance."

But the kernel string also fits the fourth line of the description, for *have* in this sentence is not only a *have* — that is, itself — but also a verb, and *have a chance* is a verbal, a case of V-mid + NP. Therefore we can transform it according to the fourth line and apply T-do to get the following:

Witherwood + present + not + have + a + chance + 2-3-1 $\Rightarrow$
     Witherwood + do + present + not + have + a + chance
     + 2-3-1

This represents the sentence "Witherwood does not have a chance," or "Witherwood doesn't have a chance."

This double possibility of *have* serves to mark a distinction between American English and British English. Americans tend to take the *have* in such a sentence as a verb and to transform according to the fourth line: "Witherwood doesn't have a chance." Englishmen tend to construe *have* as just a *have* and to transform according to the second line: "Witherwood hasn't a chance." Similarly, the American is more likely to say "He doesn't have a car," the Englishman "He hasn't a car" (or "He hasn't got a car").

Write two negative sentences for each of the following, treating *have* as just a *have* in the first and as a verb in the second.

1. Bruce has time.
2. Rudy has the book.
3. Anne had the nerve.
4. Connie had a dime.
5. The children have a home.

The double possibility shows up also in T-yes/no. "Witherwood has a chance" can be transformed as follows, with **have** taken as just a *have:*

> **Witherwood + present + have + a + chance + 2-3-1** $\Rightarrow$
> **present + have + Witherwood + a + chance + 2-3-3**

What would the actual sentence be?
But if **have** is taken as a verb, the process is as follows:

> **Witherwood + present + have + a + chance + 2-3-1** $\Rightarrow$
> **present + Witherwood + have + a + chance + 2-3-3** $\Rightarrow$
> **do + present + Witherwood + have + a + chance + 2-3-3**

What is the actual question?
Write two questions from each of the following, taking the *have* as a *have* in the first and as a verb in the second.

6. We have time.
7. They had a head start.
8. Andrew has a cold.
9. The housekeeper had the key.

Now look at this string:

> **Murchison + present + have + part. + finish + it + 2-3-1**

We can take **have** as a *have* and make the string negative thus:

> **Murchison + present + have + not + part. + finish + it + 2-3-1**

What actual sentence would this give us?
But suppose we here take **have** as a verb. Then we would get the following:

> **Murchison + present + have + part. + finish + it + 2-3-1** $\Rightarrow$

Murchison + present + not + have + part. + finish + it +
  2-3-1 ⇛
Murchison + do + present + not + have + part. + finish + it +
  2-3-1

But this would produce the ungrammatical sentence *"Murchison
doesn't have finished it." However, the rules will not in fact permit
this development. In **Murchison + present + have + part. + finish
+ it + 2-3-1, have** is not a verb and has never been identified as a
verb. It is just a member of the **have + part.** element derived from
the auxiliary. **Have + part. + finish + it** is therefore not a verbal,
and the fourth line of T-negative does not apply to this construction.
Only the second line does.

Similarly, the following is not a possible development of the sentence "Jones is a soldier":

> Jones + present + be + a + soldier + 2-3-1 ⇛
> Jones + present + not + be + a + soldier + 2-3-1 ⇛
> Jones + do + present + not + be + a + soldier + 2-3-1

This, in which **be** is taken as a verb and **be + a + soldier** as a verbal,
would give us the ungrammatical sentence *"Jones doesn't be a
soldier." But of course *be* has never been identified as a verb, and
this is one of many reasons why it hasn't been. If we put it in with
the verbs, the grammatical machinery would simply generate a large
number of ungrammatical sentences.

Have is sometimes both a *have* and a verb and sometimes just a
have (when it comes from the auxiliary). But *be* is always just a *be*,
no matter where it comes from.

Syntax

T-reassertion

We will look at one more example of this modal-*have*-*be*-verbal
mechanism. Consider the sentence "John can finish it." In the normal
kernel way of pronouncing this, the primary stress will be on the
first syllable of *finish,* and *can* will be pronounced with weak stress
and the vowel sound schwa: /kən/. However, if someone has said
that John can't finish it, and we want to affirm or reassert that he
can, we put the primary stress on *can* and pronounce it with the
vowel /a/: /kan/.

John CAN finish it.

Similarly we have these contrasts:

> John has finished it. $\Rightarrow$ John HAS finished it.
> John is finishing it. $\Rightarrow$ John IS finishing it.
> John finished it. $\Rightarrow$ John DID finish it.

These contrasts result from the application of the *reassertion transformation,* which we will call T-reassertion. T-reassertion describes the process by which we make sentences that affirm, or reassert, that something someone has said "is not so" or "is too so."

It can be shown that the same machinery is working in T-reassertion that produces T-yes/no and T-negative transforms. At this point we will introduce a new symbol, R, and assign to it this meaning: "Put the primary stress on the word preceding this symbol." We take the letter R from the word reassertion. Notice how the symbol is used in T-reassertion:

NP + tense-M	+ X	$\Rightarrow$ NP + tense-M	+ R + X
NP + tense-have	+ X	$\Rightarrow$ NP + tense-have	+ R + X
NP + tense-be	+ X	$\Rightarrow$ NP + tense-be	+ R + X
NP + tense	+ verbal	$\Rightarrow$ NP + tense	+ R + verbal

If we reassert, for example, that "He was trying," we transform it in this way, according to the third line of the rule:

> **he + past + be + ing + try + 2-3-1** $\Rightarrow$
> **he + past + be + R + ing + try + 2-3-1**

The **R** puts the primary stress on the word preceding it. Since **past + be** is *was,* the actual sentence will be "He WAS trying."

Now suppose we begin with "He tried." Here we have a case of NP + tense + verbal, so the fourth line of the rule applies:

> **he + past + try + 2-3-1** $\Rightarrow$
> **he + past + R + try + 2-3-1**

But now **past** is a floating tense, since it is separated from the verb **try** by the **R.** Therefore T-do must apply.

Applying T-do, we have the following:

> **he + past + R + try + 2-3-1** $\Rightarrow$
> **he + do + past + R + try + 2-3-1**

The **R** will put the primary stress on the preceding word. Since **do + past** is *did,* the preceding word will now be *did,* and the sentence will be "He DID try."

Say the following aloud, applying T-reassertion:

1. Wanda will be there.
2. Ida is sick.
3. Theda washed the dishes.
4. Helen has memorized the poem.
5. Edith looked guilty.
6. Roberta is typing the letter.
7. Wendy arrived on time.
8. Olive had seen the accident.
9. Orinda answered politely.
10. Dorothy did the work well.

Notice that in the last sentence you came out with two *do*'s. The first is the *do* of T-do. The second is a transitive verb.

The double possibility of *have* appears again in T-reassertion:

Witherwood + present + have + a + chance + 2-3-1 $\Rightarrow$
Witherwood + present + have + R + a + chance + 2-3-1

Here **have** is taken as a *have*. How is the actual sentence pronounced? But we can also in this sentence take *have* as a verb:

Witherwood + present + have + a + chance + 2-3-1 $\Rightarrow$
Witherwood + present + R + have + a + chance + 2-3-1 $\Rightarrow$
Witherwood + do + present + R + have + a + chance + 2-3-1

What is the actual sentence?

Explain why, according to the rules that have been given, "John has opened it" and "Martha is the secretary" cannot become *"John does have opened it" and *"Martha does be the secretary."

Semantics

The Meaning of the Reassertion Structure

In its simplest use, a reassertion transform contradicts a previous statement and asserts the contrary:

> "John can't come with us."
> "Yes, he CAN come with us." (Or "Yes, he CAN.")
> "Martha didn't do the dishes."
> "Yes, she DID do the dishes." (Or "Yes, she DID.")

However, there isn't always, or perhaps even often, a correspondence in the structures used in the verb phrases. That is, a modal doesn't always echo a modal, a *have* a *have*, a *be* a *be*. We might, for example, have this:

> "Martha didn't do the dishes."
> "Well, she SHOULD have done them."
>   *or:*
> "Martha shouldn't have done the dishes."
> "Well, she DID do them."

The construction is used also, rather commonly, in situations in which no contradiction is involved. For example, a television reporter describing an aborted launching might say this:

> The motors HAVE shut down.

Nobody said they hadn't, but the reassertion form is used anyway. Similarly, we might hear this in the description of a football game:

> The Bears ARE going to try for the first down.

Again, nobody said they weren't. What is meant by such usage is the resolution of an uncertainty. We rather thought that the Bears would try for the first down but weren't sure that they wouldn't punt instead. The ARE confirms that our (or the announcer's) previous guess is in accord with the facts.

The next time you listen to a reported event on television, note any occurrence of this use of the reassertion structure.

Notice that there is a difference between what we have called reassertion and simple emphasis. Just about any word in a sentence can be emphasized by being pronounced with primary stress. The result of this will be to contrast the word with some other word that might have been used in its place. For example, the following are all possible ways of saying the sentence "My brother read the book":

> MY brother read the book.   (not Sam's brother)
> My BROTHER read the book.   (not my sister)
> My brother READ the book.   (didn't just skim it)
> My brother read THE book.   (not just some book)

In the kernel form, *book* would have primary stress, but we can make a contrast by giving *book* an extra heavy primary stress:

> My brother read the BOOK.   (not the magazine)

All of these are different from the reassertion construction "My brother DID read the book," which means something like "Why do you deny it?" or "Didn't you know that he read it?"

Syntax

Other Uses of the Mechanism

We have now discussed three transformations — T-yes/no, T/negative, and T-reassertion — that all involve a highly similar use of modals, *have, be,* and verbals. Presumably this similarity or relationship has an important bearing on the way we learn our language. We don't learn these separately, as if they had no connection with one another. Instead we learn the mechanism — unconsciously, of course — and then apply it in a number of ways in the generation of sentences.

The three transformations we have studied are by no means the only ones in which this machinery is used. We will notice a few more, without stopping to work out the details, since these are essentially the same as those of the transformations we have examined. Look at this series:

> Can John go with them?
> Has John gone with them?
> Is John going with them?
> Did John go with them?

Now finish the following by copying and completing them. The first sentence in each group is completed for you.

1. John can go with them, can't he?
   John has gone with them . . .
   John is going with them . . .
   John went with them . . .
2. John may accept, and so may Mary.
   John has accepted, and so . . .
   John is accepting, and so . . .
   John accepted, and so . . .
3. John will refuse, and Mary will too.
   John has refused, and Mary . . .
   John is refusing, and Mary . . .
   John refused, and Mary . . .
4. John won't help us, nor will Mary.
   John hasn't helped us, nor . . .
   John isn't helping us, nor . . .
   John didn't help us, nor . . .

SUMMARY OF RULES

T-yes/no

NP + tense-M   + X   + 2-3-1 ⇉ tense-M   + NP + X   + 2-3-3
NP + tense-have + X   + 2-3-1 ⇉ tense-have + NP + X   + 2-3-3
NP + tense-be   + X   + 2-3-1 ⇉ tense-be   + NP + X   + 2-3-3
NP + tense   + verbal + 2-3-1 ⇉ tense   + NP + verbal + 2-3-3

T-negative

NP + tense-M   + X   ⇉ NP + tense-M   + not + X
NP + tense-have + X   ⇉ NP + tense-have + not + X
NP + tense-be   + X   ⇉ NP + tense-be   + not + X
NP + tense   + verbal ⇉ NP + tense   + not + verbal

T-reassertion

NP + tense-M   + X   ⇉ NP + tense-M   + R + X
NP + tense-have + X   ⇉ NP + tense-have + R + X
NP + tense-be   + X   ⇉ NP + tense-be   + R + X
NP + tense   + verbal ⇉ NP + tense   + R + verbal

The symbol R, which stands for *reassertion*, means "the primary stress goes on the preceding word."

T-do

$$\text{tense} \rightrightarrows \text{do} + \text{tense}$$

This transformation is obligatory whenever the tense is "floating" — that is, when it is not adjacent to something for which it can be a tense — i.e., a modal, a *have*, a *be*, or a verb. This situation will occur whenever the development of the sentence proceeds according to the fourth lines of T-yes/no, T-negative, T-reassertion, and in various other parts of the grammar.

TEST

1. Make two yes/no questions of each of the following. In the first take *have* as simply a *have*. In the second, take it as a verb.
   a. He has a car.
   b. They had a problem.
   c. Ronald has objections.
   d. We have plenty of time.
   e. She had the nerve.

2. For each of the following, write the corresponding yes/no question, negative, and reassertion. In the reassertion sentences, underline the word that has primary stress.
   a. Agnes should answer the letter.
   b. They opened the package.
   c. We are leaving before dawn.
   d. Stewart has asked Douglas about it.
   e. Rumblehold became a dentist.

3. Complete the following sets.
   a. John will wait, won't he?
      John has waited . . .
      John is waiting . . .
      John waited . . .
   b. Steve must take the examination, and Ralph must too.
      Steve has taken the examination, and Ralph . . .
      Steve is taking the examination, and Ralph . . .
      Steve took the examination, and Ralph . . .

4. Rewrite each of the following strings, applying T-yes/no. For example, for **the + boy + present + be + here +** 2-3-1, you would write **present + be + the + boy + here +** 2-3-3. If a floating tense results, write the string again, applying T-do.
   a. **Jack + present + have + part. + do + the + problem +** 2-3-1
   b. **he + past + solve + it +** 2-3-1
   c. **they + present + be + friend + plural +** 2-3-1
   d. **we + present + can + go + now +** 2-3-1

5. Rewrite each of the following strings, applying T-negative. If a floating tense results, write the string again, applying T-do. (The intonation pattern is omitted from these, since it doesn't change.)
   a. **he + present + must + be + in + class**
   b. **Randy + past + enjoy + it**
   c. **it + past + be + a + ghost**
   d. **they + past + have + part. + forget + it**

6. Rewrite each of the following strings, applying T-reassertion. If a floating tense results, write the string again, applying T-do.
   a. **the + child + plural + present + be + ing + behave**
   b. **Mathews + present + have + part. + write + poetry**
   c. **Clara + past + marry + Mr. Winters**
   d. **nobody + present + can + explain + it**
   e. **the + boy + plural + past + find + the + treasure**

REVIEW QUESTIONS

1. What are the two main kinds of questions? Give an example of each.

2. What is the short term for the yes/no question transformation?

3. What reverses with the subject to form a yes/no question when the verb phrase contains a modal, a *have,* or a *be?*

4. What does the pitch pattern 2-3-1 change to in the yes/no transformation?

5. What reverses with the subject when the verb phrase does not contain a modal, *have,* or *be?*

6. What does X stand for in the description NP + tense-*be* + X + 2-3-1?

7. What is the *do* transformation, and when is it obligatory?

8. What is the function of the word *do* in a yes/no question?

9. Where does the word *not* occur in a negative statement if the verb phrase contains a modal, *have,* or *be?* Where does *not* occur when the verb phrase contains a verbal?

10. Why can two negative sentences result from the application of T-negative to the sentence "John has time"?

11. Why can't the ungrammatical sentence *"John doesn't be here" result from the rules?

12. What two things are unmodern about "And we did think it writ down in our duty to let you know of it"?

13. In NP + tense-M + R + X, R stands for the word reassertion. What does it mean?

14. What must be done to the string he + past + R + read + the + book + 2-3-1?

15. What is the probable meaning of the reassertion construction in such a sentence as "The Bears ARE going to try for the first down"?

CHAPTER 7

wh Questions

We have seen that there are two general kinds of questions — those that can be answered by yes or no and those that can't be. The latter we call *wh* questions because most of them begin with an interrogative word, such as *who, what, where, why, when,* that starts with the letters *wh.*

All *wh* questions, like all yes/no questions, are transforms that relate to kernel sentences. Thus a question like "Where is John?" obviously has some connection with a sentence like "John is there" or "John is in the house." A question like "What did he buy?" has some connection in form with a statement like "He bought a canary."

However, it also turns out that *wh* questions have many formal characteristics in common with yes/no questions. In particular, we find in *wh* questions much the same behavior of modals, *have,* and *be,* and much the same use of *do* with verbals, that we found in yes/no questions. In order to tie up all of this structure and show the inner relationships, we proceed as follows.

First, we say that the *wh* question transformations apply to strings of morphemes that result from T-yes/no. They thus have built into them the structure of yes/no questions. Then we show that in each *wh* question an interrogative word replaces some sort of structure from the kernel string. The particular kind of structure depends on the particular kind of *wh* question.

T-wh, adverbial of place

We will begin with the kind of structure in which the interrogative word *where* replaces an adverbial of place. We will call this T-wh, adverbial of place.

This is the rule for T-wh, adverbial of place:

$$X + Adv\text{-}p + Y + 2\text{-}3\text{-}3 \Rrightarrow$$
$$where + X + Y + 2\text{-}3\text{-}1$$

What is the significance of the symbols X and Y in rules of this sort? What happens to the intonation pattern?

Let us begin with the kernel string representing the sentence "John was here this morning":

John + **past** + **be** + **here** + **this** + **morning** + 2-3-1

First we must apply T-yes/no to this:

past + **be** + **John** + **here** + **this** + **morning** + 2-3-3

Now we have a string to which T-wh, adverbial of place can apply, since the string is a result of T-yes/no and also contains an adverbial of place. What is the adverbial of place?

Look again at the rule for the *wh* transformation, T-wh, adverbial of place. If we apply this rule to **past** + **be** + **John** + **here** + **this** + **morning** + 2-3-3, in which Adv-p is **here**, what morphemes constitute the X and Y?

Applying the rule, we write first *where:*

where

Then the X:

where + **past** + **be** + **John**

Then the Y and the 2-3-1:

where + **past** + **be** + **John** + **this** + **morning** + 2-3-1

What will the actual question be?

The rule shows that *wh* questions, unlike yes/no questions, have the falling 2-3-1 intonation pattern of the kernel sentence.

Here is an example in which Y is null:

the + **bull** + **present** + **be** + **in** + **the** + **barn** + 2-3-1 $\Rrightarrow$
present + **be** + **the** + **bull** + **in** + **the** + **barn** + 2-3-3 $\Rrightarrow$
where + **present** + **be** + **the** + **bull** + 2-3-1

What morphemes in the second line are replaced by **where** in the third line?

Here is one with a verbal:

Nancy + **past** + **have** + **a** + **nosebleed** + **on** + **the** + **train** + 2-3-1 $\Rrightarrow$

past + Nancy + have + a + nosebleed + on + the + train +
  2-3-3 ⇒
where + past + Nancy + have + a + nosebleed + 2-3-1

In the first transformation — T-yes/no — was the **have** taken as just
a *have* or as a verb? What further transformation must be applied
to the third line? What will the actual question be?

Transform each of the following strings twice, applying first
T-yes/no and then T-wh, adverbial of place.

1. **June + present + be + upstairs + 2-3-1**
2. **the + ship + past + shall + be + at + Naples + by +
   tomorrow + 2-3-1**
3. **a + haircut + present + cost + three + dollar + plural
   + in + Cheyenne + 2-3-1**
4. **they + past + be + in + Boston + yesterday + 2-3-1**
5. **she + past + get + sick + at + home + 2-3-1**

Without writing the strings of morphemes, write two actual questions for each of the following. First write the yes/no question for
it, and then the *where* question.

6. Andrew was at the game yesterday.
7. Barney should be in Boston now.
8. Clarice has the money in a suitcase.
9. Daniel was upstairs at the time.
10. Evelyn was in the back room when the bomb exploded.
11. Mack went to Kansas City.
12. Debby traveled to New Orleans last winter.
13. Alice can knit in the dark.
14. Jeremy hit the ball into left field.
15. Madelaine fainted in the back seat.
16. Joe was at the movies last night.
17. Edith stood in the rain for two hours.

Syntax

T-wh, adverbial of time

If you have understood the mechanism of T-wh, adverbial of place,
you won't have much trouble with that of other *wh* questions. The
principle is the same for all of them, the difference being that interrogatives other than *where* are substituted for structures other than
adverbials of place. Here is the rule for T-wh, adverbial of time, in
which the interrogative *when* substitutes for an adverbial of time:

$$X + Adv\text{-}t + Y + 2\text{-}3\text{-}3 \Rightarrow$$
$$when + X + Y + 2\text{-}3\text{-}1$$

In order to get the intonation pattern 2-3-3, we must first transform a kernel sentence by T-yes/no. Suppose we begin again with
"John was here this morning," which is composed of this string:

John + **past** + **be** + **here** + **this** + **morning** + 2-3-1

T-yes/no will change the string thus:

past + **be** + **John** + **here** + **this** + **morning** + 2-3-3

This would represent the yes/no question "Was John here this morning?" But it is also a string to which T-wh, adverbial of time can
apply, since it is a result of T-yes/no and also contains an adverbial
of time. What is the adverbial of time? What is the X of X + Adv-t
+ Y + 2-3-3? What is the Y?

Applying the rule, when + X + Y + 2-3-1, we first write *when:*

when

Then the X:

when   + **past** + **be** + **John** + **here**

The Y is null, so we now merely add the intonation pattern:

when + **past** + **be** + **John** + **here**   + 2-3-1

Like other *wh* questions, a *when* question normally has the falling
pattern of the kernel sentence. What is the actual question represented by the string above? What would it have been if T-wh, adverbial of place had been applied instead of T-wh, adverbial of time?

Here is an example of T-wh, adverbial of time with a verbal:

Henry + **past** + **shoot** + **the** + **moose** + **yesterday** + 2-3-1 $\Rightarrow$
past + **Henry** + **shoot** + **the** + **moose** + **yesterday** + 2-3-3 $\Rightarrow$
when + **past** + **Henry** + **shoot** + **the** + **moose** + 2-3-1

What further transformation must now be applied to the last line?
Why? What is the actual question?

Transform the following strings similarly. Apply first T-yes/no and
then T-wh, adverbial of time. Then apply T-do if the tense is floating. In all of these strings Y is null.

   1. **Bennie** + **past** + **be** + **here** + **this** + **morning** + 2-3-1
   2. **Barbara** + **past** + **leave** + **at** + **eight** + **o'clock** + 2-3-1
   3. **Bernice** + **past** + **shall** + **have** + **part.** + **go** + **last** +
     year + 2-3-1

4. **Bert + present + want + the + report + at + once +** 2-3-1
5. **Bob + present + come + at + six + 2-3-1**
6. **Jennie + present + make + candy + on + Sunday + 2-3-1**
7. **Arthur + past + break + his + arm + yesterday + 2-3-1**
8. **Nellie + past + be + there + by + seven + 2-3-1**

Without writing the strings of morphemes, write two actual questions for each of the following. First write the yes/no question needed as a basis for the *when* question. Then write the *when* question.

9. The toastmaster showed up before dinner.
10. A signal was heard afterwards.
11. He lived in Florida in 1966.
12. Margaret was here the day before yesterday.
13. We will be in Stamford by five.
14. The ship went on the rocks at midnight.
15. The weather improved last week.
16. Mr. Edwards should have written long ago.
17. Washington was in an uproar last night.

Syntax

T-wh, adverbial of manner

We make *wh* questions from strings with adverbials of manner by substituting the interrogative *how* (one of the interrogatives that does *not* begin with the letters *wh*) for the adverbial of manner. This is the rule:

$$X + Adv\text{-}m + Y + 2\text{-}3\text{-}3 \Rightarrow$$
$$how + X + Y + 2\text{-}3\text{-}1$$

You will recall that adverbials of manner normally occur optionally after verbals with intransitive or transitive verbs. Let us begin with the string for "Julius spoke forcefully yesterday":

Julius + past + speak + forcefully + yesterday + 2-3-1

What is the adverbial of manner in the string?

We must first apply T-yes/no in order to get the 2-3-3 and the proper position of the tense:

Julius + past + speak + forcefully + yesterday + 2-3-1 $\Rightarrow$
past + Julius + speak + forcefully + yesterday + 2-3-3

What is the Adv-m of X + Adv-m + Y + 2-3-3? What is the X?

What is the Y?

Now we can apply T-wh, adverbial of manner. First, *how:*

how

Then the X:

how   + past + Julius + speak

Then the Y:

how + past + Julius + speak   + yesterday

Then the intonation pattern:

how + past + Julius + speak + yesterday   + 2-3-1

Now the tense is floating, so T-do must apply:

how + do + past + Julius + speak + yesterday + 2-3-1

What is the actual sentence?

Here is an example in which Y is null:

Barbara + past + seal + the + package + with + tape + 2-3-1 ⇶
past + Barbara + seal + the + package + with + tape + 2-3-3 ⇶
how + past + Barbara + seal + the + package + 2-3-1 ⇶
how + do + past + Barbara + seal + the + package + 2-3-1

What intonation pattern does the original kernel sentence have? What transformation was applied to the string for that sentence to get the intonation pattern 2-3-3? What transformation was applied next to get a *how* question from the yes/no question? What was done to the string to eliminate the floating tense? What is the actual question?

Transform the following similarly into *how* questions. Apply T-do at the end whenever the tense is floating:

1. **Howard + past + reply + angrily + 2-3-1**
2. **Ernest + past + shall + have + part. + speak + politely + 2-3-1**
3. **Edwin + present + will + study + hard + now + 2-3-1**
4. **Florence + past + consider + the + idea + carefully + 2-3-1**
5. **Hilda + past + serve + the + meal + beautifully + yesterday + 2-3-1**

Without writing the strings of morphemes, write two actual questions for each of the following. First write the yes/no question needed as a basis for the *how* question. Then write the *how* question.

6. The police carried the boy on a stretcher.
7. We will travel by plane to Detroit.
8. He spoke nervously on the television program.
9. The doctor bandaged the wound with tape.
10. They issued the warning through the newspaper.
11. Patsy won handily.
12. The parson sang with a quavering tenor.
13. Upsala beat Long Island with ease.
14. Mr. Crockett killed the bear with a knife.
15. Mark should have been working hard.
16. Mabel whistled softly while she studied.

Syntax

T-wh, adverbial of frequency

Kernel structures with adverbials of frequency may be made into *wh* questions, through T-yes/no, by the substitution of the interrogative *how often* for the adverbial of frequency:

$$\text{X + Adv-f + Y + 2-3-3} \Rightarrow$$
$$\text{how often + X + Y + 2-3-1}$$

Take the string underlying the kernel sentence "Howie came to class every day last year":

Howie + **past** + **come** + **to** + **class** + **every** + **day** + **last** + **year** + 2-3-1 $\Rightarrow$
past + **Howie** + **come** + **to** + **class** + **every** + **day** + **last** + **year** + 2-3-3

What is the adverbial of frequency in the last string? What morphemes make up the X of X + Adv-f + Y + 2-3-3? What make up the Y?

We transform **past** + **Howie** + **come** + **to** + **class** + **every** + **day** + **last** + **year** + 2-3-3 just as we did the others, beginning with the interrogative:

how often

Then the X:

how often + **past** + **Howie** + **come** + **to** + **class**

Then the Y:

how often + **past** + **Howie** + **come** + **to** + **class** + **last** + **year**

Then the change back to the kernel intonation pattern:

> **how often + past + Howie + come + to + class + last + year + 2-3-1**

Then, since the tense is floating, T-do must apply:

> **how often + do + past + Howie + come + to + class + last + year + 2-3-1**

Here is another example, one in which Y is null:

> **Mabel + present + cook + dinner + occasionally + 2-3-1 ⇒**
> **present + Mabel + cook + dinner + occasionally + 2-3-3 ⇒**
> **how often + present + Mabel + cook + dinner + 2-3-1 ⇒**
> **how often + do + present + Mabel + cook + dinner + 2-3-1**

What is the actual sentence represented by the last line?

Transform the following strings, applying first T-yes/no and then T-wh, adverbial of frequency. In some you will also have to apply T-do.

1. **Williams + present + swim + frequently + in + the + summer + 2-3-1**
2. **Burbank + past + be + there + often + 2-3-1**
3. **Simpson + past + shall + report + every + day + 2-3-1**
4. **Edgell + present + come + here + now + and + then + in + the + afternoon + 2-3-1**
5. **Joe + present + have + part. + see + it + seldom + 2-3-1**

Without writing the strings of morphemes, write two actual questions for each of the following. First write the yes/no question needed, and then write the *how often* question.

6. He is in the office occasionally.
7. Bernice mows the lawn every Saturday.
8. The mailman comes twice a day.
9. He must report to the parole board every week next year.
10. They have open house on Thursdays in the wintertime.
11. They shifted his duties every other week.

Syntax

T-wh, noun phrase

There are other types of *wh* questions like those we have been considering, such as "Why did James do it?" But these have the same basic structure as those with the interrogatives *where, when, how, how often.* We will look now at some questions that are slightly different — those questions in which an interrogative replaces a noun phrase. Here is the rule for T-wh, noun phrase:

$$X + NP + Y + 2\text{-}3\text{-}3 \Rrightarrow$$
$$\begin{Bmatrix} who \\ what \end{Bmatrix} + X + Y + 2\text{-}3\text{-}1$$

In this transformation we have a choice of interrogatives. This choice is shown in the rule by the bracketing of *who* and *what* after the arrows. The general rule is that we take *who* as the interrogative if the replaced NP refers to a person and we take *what* if it does not.

Let us take as the first example the sentence "John found a bracelet in the drawer":

John + past + find + a + bracelet + in + the + drawer + 2-3-1

This must first be transformed into a yes/no question string:

past + John + find + a + bracelet + in + the + drawer + 2-3-3

This now qualifies for T-wh, noun phrase. In fact, it qualifies for three such transformations, since it contains three different noun phrases. What are they?

Suppose we focus on *John* as the NP of X + NP + Y + 2-3-3. Then what is the X in **past + John + find + a + bracelet + in + the + drawer + 2-3-3?** What morphemes make up the Y?

Since *John* refers to a person, we begin the *wh* string with *who* rather than *what:*

who

Then the X:

who   + past

Then the Y:

who + past   + find + a + bracelet + in + the + drawer

Then the intonation pattern:

who + past + find + a + bracelet + in + the + drawer   + 2-3-1

Notice that the transformation in this case has put the tense back with the verb *find.* Therefore the tense no longer floats, and T-do doesn't apply. What is the actual question?

Transform the following strings in the same way, applying first

T-yes/no and then T-wh, noun phrase. Take the subject of each sentence as the NP of X + NP + Y + 2-3-3.

1. **Maurice** + **past** + **eat** + **the** + **cake** + 2-3-1
2. **Annie** + **past** + **feed** + **the** + **cat** + 2-3-1
3. **the** + **child** + **plural** + **present** + **do** + **the** + **dish** + **plural** + 2-3-1
4. **the** + **mailman** + **past** + **be** + **at** + **the** + **door** + 2-3-1
5. **Mr. Webb** + **past** + **answer** + **the** + **phone** + 2-3-1

Now look again at the example we started with:

John + **past** + **find** + **a** + **bracelet** + **in** + **the** + **drawer** + 2-3-1 $\Rightarrow$
  past + **John** + **find** + **a** + **bracelet** + **in** + **the** + **drawer** + 2-3-3

This has the noun phrases *a bracelet* and *the drawer*, in addition to *John*. Suppose we take *a bracelet* as the NP of X + NP + Y + 2-3-3. What is now the X? What is the Y?

If we take *a bracelet*, we must start with *what*, since this noun phrase does not refer to a person:

what

Then the X:

what + **past** + **John** + **find**

Then the Y and the intonation pattern:

what + **past** + **John** + **find** + **in** + **the** + **drawer** + 2-3-1

What further transformation must now be applied?

Transform the following through T-yes/no and T-wh, noun phrase, taking the italicized noun phrase as the NP of X + NP + Y + 2-3-3.

6. **Maurice** + **past** + **eat** + *the* + *cake* + 2-3-1
7. **Donald** + **past** + **have** + *a* + *mouse* + **in** + **the** + **desk** + 2-3-1
8. **they** + **past** + **see** + *a* + *movie* + **last** + **night** + 2-3-1
9. **the** + **child** + **plural** + **present** + **drink** + *milk* + 2-3-1
10. **everybody** + **present** + **want** + *a* + *job* + 2-3-1

Phonology

T-object: *who* and *whom*

Suppose now that we transform the string underlying "John found Bill in the closet" through T-yes/no and T-wh, noun phrase, taking *Bill* as the NP to focus on.

Here are the strings showing these transformations:

John + past + find + Bill + in + the + closet + 2-3-1 $\Rightarrow$
past + John + find + Bill + in + the + closet + 2-3-3 $\Rightarrow$
who + past + John + find + in + the + closet + 2-3-1

If *Bill* is the NP of X + NP + Y + 2-3-3, what is the X? What is the Y? Will the *do* transformation apply to the last string?

Now if nothing more is done to the string, the actual sentence will be "Who did John find in the closet?" But, one may ask, is it not better to say "Whom did John find in the closet?" It depends somewhat on whom one is speaking to, or writing to. It would be quite normal in most speech situations to say "Who did John find in the closet?" This is common usage of educated and uneducated people alike. However, in serious writing a further transformation generally takes place to convert *who* into *whom*.

We have already mentioned a transformation that changes the form of certain noun phrases when they are objects. This is called the *object transformation* and is abbreviated as T-object. We can now state this transformation more formally.

$$X + \begin{Bmatrix} V_T \\ \text{V-mid} \\ \text{Prep} \end{Bmatrix} + NP + Y \Rightarrow X + \begin{Bmatrix} V_T \\ \text{V-mid} \\ \text{Prep} \end{Bmatrix} + NP + o + Y$$

This transformation applies obligatorily to five personal pronouns, the words *I, he, she, we,* and *they.* These are the phonological rules:

$$\text{I} + \text{o} \rightarrow \text{me} \quad \text{he} + \text{o} \rightarrow \text{him} \quad \text{she} + \text{o} \rightarrow \text{her}$$
$$\text{we} + \text{o} \rightarrow \text{us} \quad \text{they} + \text{o} \rightarrow \text{them}$$

This is obvious. Nobody says *"He came with I" or *"He has they" or *"I saw she." Clearly when these personal pronouns are used after transitive verbs, middle verbs, or prepositions the form must change. We must say "He came with me," "He has them," and "I saw her."

But with *who* it is not so obvious. You can say "Who did you see?" without, probably, anyone thinking that you're being ungrammatical. Nevertheless, the more conservative, serious, formal usage would require the object transformation here, too, so that *who* is converted to *whom* and the sentence becomes "Whom did you see?"

Apply T-object to the following, substituting *whom* for the objects in the kernel sentences. Thus "John saw Bill" is transformed into "Did John see Bill," and this into "Who did John see?" and finally, by means of T-object, into "Whom did John see?"

Write just the final sentences with *whom.*

1. David helped Shirley.
2. The police questioned Mr. Westerman.

3. The explosion injured the boy.
4. He assisted the secretary.
5. They guarded the children.
6. He saw somebody.
7. Mr. Porterfield interrogated her.
8. They asked them about it.

Phonology

T-object, preposition

Let us now make the transformation T-wh, noun phrase, focusing on the third NP in the kernel sentence "John found a bracelet in the drawer":

> **John + past + find + a + bracelet + in + the + drawer +**
> 2-3-1 ⇉
> **past + John + find + a + bracelet + in + the + drawer +**
> 2-3-3

If we focus on **the drawer**, then the X of X + NP + Y + 2-3-3 is **past + John + find + a + bracelet + in** and the Y is null. So we would write, in order, the following:

> **what**
> **what + past + John + find + a + bracelet + in**
> **what + past + John + find + a + bracelet + in + 2-3-1**

T-do will now apply, since the tense is floating. What will the actual sentence be?

The sentence "What did John find the bracelet in?" ends with the preposition *in*, and there are those who feel that an English sentence should not end with a preposition. There is no obvious reason why a sentence should not end so, and a very casual inspection of published writing will show that many of our best writers do use this structure, ending sentences now and then with prepositions. On the other hand, it is true that we have a feeling of somewhat greater formality and elegance in a sentence like "In what did John find the bracelet?"

This, however, is a more complicated sentence, and we need a more complicated rule for it. We now must not only put in the interrogative but also specify and shift the preposition:

$$X + Prep + NP + Y + 2\text{-}3\text{-}3 \Rightarrow$$
$$Prep + \begin{Bmatrix} who \\ what \end{Bmatrix} + X + Y + 2\text{-}3\text{-}1$$

We can work this out on the same example:

> John + past + find + the + bracelet + in + the + drawer +
> 2-3-1 $\Rightarrow$
> past + John + find + the + bracelet + in + the + drawer +
> 2-3-3

Now the NP under consideration is **the drawer,** Prep is **in,** X is everything before **in,** and Y is null. The application of the rule unfolds as
follows:

> in
> in + what
> in + what + past + John + find + the + bracelet
> in + what + past + John + find + the + bracelet + 2-3-1

T-do must of course apply to change **past** to **do + past,** and we will
have the sentence "In what did John find the bracelet?"

If one is adamantly opposed to having sentences end with prepositions, he simply says that the preposition-shifting rule is obligatory
in a structure of this sort. If one doesn't care, he says the rule is
optional. If one *wants* sentences to end with prepositions he says the
rule does not apply.

Let's now apply T-wh, noun phrase to the sentence "John spoke
to Clarice."

> John + past + speak + to + Clarice + 2-3-1 $\Rightarrow$
> past + John + speak + to + Clarice + 2-3-3 $\Rightarrow$
> who + past + John + speak + to + 2-3-1

After T-do, this will give us "Who did John speak to?" Or, if we are
being a little more elegant, we may apply T-object and get "Whom
did John speak to?"

But here we might also shift the preposition from the end of the
string to the beginning of it:

> past + John + speak + to + Clarice + 2-3-3 $\Rightarrow$
> to + who + past + John + speak + 2-3-1

But now T-object is obligatory. Nobody says *"To who did John
speak?" If the preposition shifts, the *who* must be converted to *whom.*
Therefore, the actual sentence would have to be "To whom did John
speak?"

For practice, transform the following sentences into *wh* questions
in which the preposition shifts. Write the actual final sentences, not
the strings of morphemes. Use *whom* if the NP after the preposition

refers to a person, *what* if it doesn't. Thus, given "John spoke to Clarice," you would write, "To whom did John speak?" Given "John sat on a tack," you would write, "On what did John sit?"

1. Allen was walking with Mildred.
2. Alice arrived in a Ford.
3. Agnes lives with her mother.
4. Adams reports to the captain.
5. Beryl rode on a horse.
6. Billy climbed up a rope.
7. Bixby left the will with an aunt.
8. Cathy tied the goat to a tree.
9. Cindy ate the spaghetti with a fork.
10. Clark brought the message from Mr. Anderson.

Do 1–10 again, this time applying the simple NP rule:

$$X + NP + Y + 2\text{-}3\text{-}3 \Rightarrow \begin{Bmatrix} who \\ what \end{Bmatrix} + X + Y + 2\text{-}3\text{-}1$$

Take the noun phrase after the preposition as the NP, and use either *who* or *whom* for persons, whichever sounds better to you.

Syntax

An Adjective-making Transformation

Compare the following sentences:

Mary is working.   Mary is interesting.

On the surface, these appear to be exactly alike, each consisting of NP + be + present + verb + ing. However, *interesting* doesn't seem to be a verb in the way that *working* does; it seems more like an adjective. This view is reinforced when we try using the word *very*, which goes optionally with adjectives according to the rule Adj → (very) + Adj. We can quite grammatically say "Mary is very interesting." But *"Mary is very working" is clearly ungrammatical. We might therefore conclude that there are words ending in *ing* that are not verbs but adjectives. We would be right. But they are not kernel structures. They result from a transformation.

There is a set of transitive verbs, like *interest*, which take as their objects noun phrases referring to people:

Mary interests John.

Now these can add *be + ing* to produce sentences like this one:

Mary is interesting to John.

Then the prepositional phrase at the end drops off:

Mary is interesting.

Now the word *interesting* behaves like any adjective. For example, it can be used with *very*. This is the rule:

$$NP_1 + Aux + V_T + NP_2 \Rrightarrow$$
$$NP_1 + Aux + be + ing + V_T + to + NP_2 \Rrightarrow$$
$$NP_1 + Aux + be + ing + V_T$$

Let us apply this step by step to "Mary interests John." This is composed of the following string of morphemes:

Mary + present + interest + John

In reference to the rule, what is the NP_1 of this string? What is the NP_2? What is the Aux? What is the V_T?

Now we just add the morphemes called for by the second line of the rule:

Mary + present + be + ing + interest + to + John

What will **present** now apply to? What will **ing** apply to? Now the prepositional phrase may be deleted:

Mary + present + be + ing + interest

Apply this transformation to the following strings, first inserting **be + ing** and **to,** and then deleting the prepositional phrase. Write the strings, not the sentences.

1. **Evelyn + past + charm + Montrose**
2. **the + story + past + move + Mrs. Wilson**
3. **the + news + present + terrify + us**
4. **he + present + amuse + the + class**
5. **this + present + will + please + you**
6. **she + past + love + the + child**
7. **the + announcement + past + stun + Murchison**
8. **it + past + bewilder + me**
9. **the + victory + present + cheer + the + team**
10. **the + friendship + past + warm + Clarence**
11. **the + explosion + past + frighten + him**
12. **the + loss + past + discourage + the + team**
13. **the + odor + present + sicken + me**

14. your + speech + past + amaze + Harrison
15. the + music + present + soothe + her

The following sentences are transforms. For each one, write a kernel sentence which might underlie it. There will be many possibilities. For example, "Mary is very interesting" could relate to "Mary interests John," "Mary interests the class," "Mary interests me," etc. Keep the tense the same.

16. The news was very alarming.
17. Jackson was very threatening.
18. That is very galling.
19. The wind is very chilling.
20. That movie was very thrilling.
21. The problem is very baffling.
22. A space launch is very exciting.
23. The music was very enchanting.
24. The trip was very rewarding.
25. The tale was very haunting.
26. The soup was very nourishing.
27. Her mother is very forgiving.
28. The show was very entertaining.
29. The fire was very comforting.
30. The reporter was very worrying.

Make two sentences with each of the following words. In the first, use the word as a transitive verb with its object. In the second, use it as an adjective with *very*. For instance, if the word were *interest,* you might write "Ernestine interests people" for the first and "Ernestine is a very interesting young lady" for the second.

disgust	forgive	astound	encourage
oblige	bewitch	nourish	shock
convince	embarrass	distress	fascinate

Syntax

The *there* Transformation

Such a sentence as "A mouse is in the cupboard" is a kernel sentence and a perfectly good one. But like many kernel sentences, it is of rather rare occurrence. We would be much more likely to express its meaning with a transform: "There's a mouse in the cupboard." Similarly, instead of saying "Several Norwegians are on the football team," we would most likely transform with *there* and say "There are several Norwegians on the football team." Let us now consider the nature of this T-there.

Note the structure of both "A mouse is in the cupboard" and "Several Norwegians are on the football team." Both consist of noun phrase subjects. What are they? Both have forms of *be*, rather than verbals, in the verb phrase. What are the forms of *be?* What follows the form of *be* in each sentence — a noun phrase, an adjective, or an adverbial of place?

Note further the nature of the noun phrase subjects. What is the article in *a mouse?* Is it definite or nondefinite?

The noun phrase *several Norwegians* also contains a nondefinite article in the determiner. You may remember that in a structure like **several of + definite + Norwegian + plural, definite** will be the word *the,* and the **of** will stay: *several of the Norwegians.* But in **several of + nondefinite + Norwegian + plural, nondefinite** will be null, and the **of** will drop: *several Norwegians.* What actual noun phrase is represented by **many of + nondefinite + Dane + plural?** What is represented by **much of + nondefinite + milk?** When the pre-article is *a lot of,* the *of* doesn't drop. What is represented by **a lot of + nondefinite + boy + plural?**

We can now state the conditions under which the *there* transformation is generally applicable. It applies if the subject is a case of determiner plus noun; and if the determiner contains a nondefinite article — *a, some,* or *null;* and if the predicate has a form of *be* instead of a verbal; and if the *be* is followed by an adverbial of place. Then we can transform this into a sentence beginning with the word *there,* followed by the form of *be,* followed by the original subject, followed by the adverbial of place:

A mouse is in the cupboard. ⇉
There is a mouse in the cupboard.

The rule can be stated as follows:

X + Nondef + Y + Aux + be + Adv-p ⇉
there + Aux + be + X + Nondef + Y + Adv-p

This rule specifies all of the crucial structures: a nondefinite article in the subject, a *be,* an adverbial of place after the *be.* The X and Y are position markers, as usual. The X means anything before the nondefinite article; the Y means anything between the nondefinite article and the auxiliary. Let us take as an example a case in which neither X nor Y is null:

a lot of + nondefinite + fellow + plural + present + be + here

Compare this with the part of the rule preceding the arrow. The X is what appears before **nondefinite.** It is a pre-article. What pre-article is it? **Nondefinite** will be null after the pre-article. The auxiliary is **present** tense in this sentence. What appears between nondefinite and the auxiliary and is therefore the Y? What is the adverbial of place?

So we apply the rule. First the word *there:*

there

Then Aux:

there   + present

Then *be:*

there + present   + be

Then X:

there + present + be   + a lot of

Then Nondef:

there + present + be + a lot of   + null

Then Y:

there + present + be + a lot of + null   + fellow + plural

Finally, Adv-p:

there + present + be + a lot of + null + fellow + plural   + here

The noun phrase **a lot of + null + fellow + plural** is still the subject, so what must **present + be** become? What is the sentence?

When there is no pre-article, X will be null:

a + man + present + be + outside

What is the nondefinite article? What is the Y, coming between Nondef and Aux? What is the adverb of place?

First we write *there.*

there

Then Aux:

there   + present

Then *be:*

there + present   + be

X is null, so next we write Nondef:

there + present + be   + a

Then Y:

there + present + be + a   + man

Then Adv-p:

there + present + be + a + man   + outside

What is the subject? Therefore, what will **present + be** become?
What is the adverb of place? What is the sentence?

Generally in speech and often in writing *there is* contracts to
there's: "There's a man outside."

Apply the *there* transformation similarly to the following kernel
structures. Write the strings, not the finished sentences.

1. **a + fly + present + be + in + the + milk**
2. **some + parent + plural + present + be + here**
3. **null + snow + past + be + on + the + street**
4. **a + trick + present + must + be + in + it**
5. **some + cookie + plural + past + may + be + in + the +
box**
6. **null + workman + plural + past + be + downstairs**
7. **a + fish + past + be + on + the + line**
8. **many of + null + child + plural + present + be + in +
the + pool**
9. **few of + null + motorist + plural + past + be + on + the +
road**
10. **much of + null + confusion + past + be + in + the +
office**

In the finished sentences of 8, 9, and 10, what part of the pre-article
would be dropped?

Apply the *there* transformation to the following kernel sentences.
Write the sentences, not the strings. Remember that the subject is
the same and that you will therefore have the same form of *be* in
the transform.

11. A policeman was on the bus.
12. Some frogs are in the desk.
13. Ice is outside.
14. A driver should be near the car.
15. An obstruction must have been in the gas line.
16. Spots were on the suit.

17. Some debris was behind the sofa.
18. Lots of troublemakers were on the team.
19. Three rings are on her fingers.
20. One shirt was in the drawer.
21. An egg was in the nest.
22. Logs were on the truck.
23. Some pickles are in that barrel.
24. People must be upstairs.
25. A plane is on the runway.
26. Many passengers are on the boat.

SUMMARY OF RULES

T-wh, adverbial of place

$$X + Adv\text{-}p + Y + 2\text{-}3\text{-}3 \Rightarrow where + X + Y + 2\text{-}3\text{-}1$$

T-wh, adverbial of time

$$X + Adv\text{-}t + Y + 2\text{-}3\text{-}3 \Rightarrow when + X + Y + 2\text{-}3\text{-}1$$

T-wh, adverbial of manner

$$X + Adv\text{-}m + Y + 2\text{-}3\text{-}3 \Rightarrow how + X + Y + 2\text{-}3\text{-}1$$

T-wh, adverbial of frequency

$$X + Adv\text{-}f + Y + 2\text{-}3\text{-}3 \Rightarrow how\ often + X + Y + 2\text{-}3\text{-}1$$

T-wh, noun phrase

$$X + NP + Y + 2\text{-}3\text{-}3 \Rightarrow \begin{Bmatrix} who \\ what \end{Bmatrix} + X + Y + 2\text{-}3\text{-}1$$

When the NP of X + NP + Y + 2-3-3 is the object of a preposition, a special rule may be applied to shift the preposition to the beginning of the *wh* question:

$$X + Prep + NP + Y + 2\text{-}3\text{-}3 \Rightarrow$$
$$Prep + \begin{Bmatrix} who \\ what \end{Bmatrix} + X + Y + 2\text{-}3\text{-}1$$

The source of the 2-3-3 intonation pattern is the yes/no transformation. This is an automatic consequence of the requirement that the *wh* transformations be applied only to strings that result from T-yes/no.

The *whom* Phonological Rule

$$\text{who} + \text{o} \rightarrow \text{whom}$$

This rule is generally felt as optional in speech, when the *who* functions as an object, but it is usually adhered to in writing. It is obligatory in either speech or writing whenever the preposition shifts: "To whom did John speak?"

T-ing, adjective

$$\text{NP}_1 + \text{Aux} + \text{V}_T + \text{NP}_2 \Rrightarrow$$
$$\text{NP}_1 + \text{Aux} + \text{be} + \text{ing} + \text{V}_T + \text{to} + \text{NP}_2 \Rrightarrow$$
$$\text{NP}_1 + \text{Aux} + \text{be} + (\text{very}) + \text{ing} + \text{V}_T$$

Ordinarily the NP_2 refers to an animate being and usually to a human being.

T-there

$$\text{X} + \text{Nondef} + \text{Y} + \text{Aux} + \text{be} + \text{Adv-p} \Rrightarrow$$
$$\text{there} + \text{Aux} + \text{be} + \text{X} + \text{Nondef} + \text{Y} + \text{Adv-p}$$

This rule accounts just for the transform in *be* constructions, such as "A man was waiting" $\Rrightarrow$ "There was a man waiting," not for sentences with verb phrases containing *be* + *ing* + verb.

TEST

1. Apply T-yes/no and then T-wh, adverbial of place to each of the following. Write the strings, not the sentences.
   a. **Bert + past + be + here + 2-3-1**
   b. **Mark + past + shall + be + in + Boston + now + 2-3-1**
   c. **Stan + present + have + a + home + in + Rye + 2-3-1**
   d. **Jane + past + faint + in + the + drugstore + 2-3-1**
   e. **we + past + be + outside + at + the + time + 2-3-1**

2. Apply T-yes/no and then T-wh, adverbial of time to each of the following. Write the strings, not the sentences.
   a. **Mark + past + shall + be + in + Boston + now + 2-3-1**
   b. **Mr. Samuels + past + live + there + last + year + 2-3-1**
   c. **you + past + be + there + in + February + 2-3-1**

3. Apply T-yes/no and T-wh, adverbial of manner to each of the following. Write the strings, not the sentences.
   a. **the + boy + plural + past + eat + hungrily + 2-3-1**

  b. **Mr. Grant** + **present** + **write** + **well** + 2-3-1

  c. **Nelson** + **past** + **hit** + **the** + **ball** + **hard** + 2-3-1

  4. Apply T-yes/no and T-wh, adverbial of frequency to each of the following. Write the strings, not the sentences.

  a. **Bristow** + **present** + **come** + **here** + **occasionally** + 2-3-1

  b. **she** + **present** + **swim** + **twice** + **a** + **week** + **in** + **the** + **summer** + 2-3-1

  c. **Bob** + **past** + **wash** + **the** + **car** + **every** + **day** + 2-3-1

  d. **she** + **past** + **visit** + **us** + **often** + **last** + **month** + 2-3-1

  5. Apply T-yes/no and T-wh, noun phrase to each of the following. Take the italicized noun as the NP of the formula, and write **who** + **o** if it refers to a person and functions as an object. Do not shift the preposition in *d*.

  a. *Mark* + **past** + **report** + **the** + **accident** + 2-3-1

  b. **Mark** + **past** + **report** + *the* + *accident* + 2-3-1

  c. **they** + **past** + **invite** + *Edwin* + 2-3-1

  d. **he** + **past** + **dig** + **the** + **hole** + **with** + *a* + *spoon* + 2-3-1

  6. Apply T-yes/no and T-wh, noun phrase to each of the following. Take the object of the preposition as the NP, and shift the preposition according to the rule X + Prep + NP + Y + 2-3-3 $\Rightarrow$ Prep + $\begin{Bmatrix} \text{who} \\ \text{what} \end{Bmatrix}$ + X + Y + 2-3-1. Write o when *who* is used.

  a. **she** + **present** + **go** + **with** + **Abe** + 2-3-1

  b. **he** + **past** + **dig** + **the** + **hole** + **with** + **a** + **spoon** + 2-3-1

  c. **the** + **fireman** + **past** + **speak** + **to** + **Tom** + 2-3-1

  d. **she** + **past** + **ride** + **in** + **a** + **chariot** + 2-3-1

  7. Make *wh* questions by substituting the proper interrogative word for the italicized structure. Write the sentences, not the strings.

  a. She waters the lawn thoroughly every day *in the summer*.

  b. She waters the lawn thoroughly *every day* in the summer.

  c. She waters the lawn *thoroughly* every day in the summer.

  d. She waters *the lawn* thoroughly every day in the summer.

  e. *She* waters the lawn thoroughly every day in the summer.

  f. Trudy brought *Albert* to the party.

  g. Trudy brought Albert *to the party*.

  8. Apply the *there* transformation to the following kernel structures. Write the strings, then the finished sentences.

  a. **null** + **woman** + **plural** + **present** + **be** + **outside**

b. some + syrup + past + be + in + it
c. few of + null + boy + plural + past + be + there
d. a + fire + present + be + in + the + stove

REVIEW QUESTIONS

1. Why are *wh* questions so called?

2. How is the structural relationship between yes/no questions and *wh* questions brought out in the rules for making the latter?

3. What interrogative replaces an adverbial of place in the making of a *wh* question? What interrogative replaces an adverbial of time?

4. What adverbials do *how* and *how often* replace?

5. What is the difference in intonation pattern between yes/no questions and *wh* questions?

6. What do X and Y stand for in a string like X + Adv-p + Y + 2-3-3?

7. In T-wh, noun phrase, what interrogatives may replace the NP of X + NP + Y + 2-3-3?

8. When may *who* become *whom* in T-wh, noun phrase? How do speech and writing differ in the use of *who* and *whom*?

9. So far as rules are concerned, why is "To whom did John speak?" a more complicated sentence than "Who did John speak to?" or "Whom did John speak to?"

10. What can be said about ending sentences with prepositions?

11. In what sort of *wh* question is it obligatory to use *whom* and not *who*?

12. Give a kernel sentence that might underlie "Edna was very fascinating."

13. What kind of article does the noun phrase of a sentence qualifying for the *there* transformation have to have?

14. What kind of adverbial does such a sentence have?

15. What is the article in "Several Norwegians are on the football team"?

16. What is the subject of "There are lions in the back yard"?

17. When can a sentence containing a verbal be transformed with *there*?

CHAPTER 8

Syntax

T-there with *be + ing*

T-there doesn't ordinarily work when the article is definite. "The mouse is in the cupboard" does not transform into "There is the mouse in the cupboard." It is true that such a sentence as "There is the mouse in the cupboard" may occur. It might be a way of pointing out the mouse, as the sentence "There's Joe" points out Joe. Or it might be a response to a question:

> What can we depend on to get rid of the cheese?
> Well, there's the mouse in the cupboard.

But clearly neither of these has the meaning of "The mouse is in the cupboard."

The *there* transformation does not occur either when tense is followed immediately by a verbal. "A girl smiled" does not become *"There smiled a girl." An exception is certain structures containing the verb *come*. "A time comes when we regret it" becomes "There comes a time when we regret it."

But when the auxiliary contains *be + ing* before a verbal, the *there* transformation takes place pretty much as it does in constructions with *be + Adv-p*:

> A man was waiting. ⇉
>   There was a man waiting.
> A girl was mopping the floor. ⇉
>   There was a girl mopping the floor.

Such transformations are not included in our rule for T-there, and we will not stop to complicate the rule so as to include them. Still you should be able to make *there* sentences of the following.

1. Some children were throwing stones.
2. A cowboy was leaning against the fence.
3. Women were crying.
4. A messenger must have been standing by.
5. A policeman should be directing traffic.
6. Some water may be leaking into the motor.
7. A storm could have been brewing.

Notice that in all of these the determiner is the nondefinite article. This part of the rule still holds.

Syntax

Deletion

A very important part of syntax, and one that we will be talking about more and more from now on, is *deletion*. Very often, in the sentences we speak and write, we just don't use that part of the structure that is repetitious or that can be easily understood from the context. For example, instead of saying "John smiled, and Mary smiled," we would ordinarily delete *smiled* and say "John and Mary smiled."

It is very common to delete — leave out — a noun following a determiner. For example, though we might say "This pie tastes good," we might also say "This tastes good," deleting the noun *pie*. If everyone at the table can see that it is pie that we are eating, there is no point in uttering the word in the sentence. So we delete it.

In certain noun phrases containing the nondefinite article, the noun following the determiner can be deleted. Instead of "Some boys were there," we may say "Some were there." Instead of "Several boys were outside," we may say "Several were outside." What is the nondefinite article in "Several boys were outside"?

These structures that remain after deletion transform with *there* in the same way that undeleted structures do:

> There were some there.
> There were several outside.

Transform the following with *there*. For each one, suggest a noun that might have been deleted.

1. Many were in the soup.
2. One was upstairs.
3. Some is on the way.

4. Fourteen are coming.
5. A few are in the glove compartment.
6. Several were underneath the sofa.

Syntax

The Passive Transformation

We are still working on single-base transformations — those in which we make transforms by simply switching morphemes of kernel structures around and putting in or taking out other morphemes. Another of these is the passive transformation.

The passive transformation applies only to kernel sentences which contain a transitive verb and its object. In this transformation, the object becomes subject and *be* and the participle morpheme are inserted before the verb. The subject optionally appears at the end after the preposition *by*:

Ronald signed the contract. $\Rightarrow$
The contract was signed by Ronald.

What is the subject of the kernel sentence? What is the object? What is the transitive verb?

We can state the rule in this way:

$$NP_1 + Aux + V_T + NP_2 \Rightarrow$$
$$NP_2 + Aux + be + part. + V_T + (by + NP_1)$$

The numerals 1 and 2 under the NP's simply identify the noun phrases and show what becomes of them in the transform. What is the function of the NP_1 in the kernel? What is the function of the NP_2? What does V_T stand for? What do the parentheses around *by* + NP_1 mean? Apart from *by*, what morphemes occur in the transform that do not occur in the kernel?

Here is a fairly simple example of a sentence structure that might be transformed by this rule:

John + past + watch + Bill

John is the NP_1 of this structure. What is the NP_2? What is the V_T? What is the Aux?

Applying the passive rule, we first write the NP_2:

Bill

Then Aux:

Bill + past

Then *be* + part.:

Bill + past   + **be** + part.

Then V_T:

Bill + past + **be** + part.   + watch

Finally, if we like, *by* + NP₁:

Bill + past + **be** + part. + watch   + by + John

Applying the affix transformation, we get this:

Bill + **be** + past + watch + part. + by + **Bill**

Be and **part.**, which were added together, are now separated. The insertion of word boundary will give us the T-terminal string:

 # Bill # be + past # watch + part. # by # John #

What will **be** + **past** be for this sentence? What will **watch** + **part.** be? What is the actual sentence?

Apply the passive transformation to the following strings. Check with the rule so that you don't get mixed up.

1. the + policeman + past + see + Ernest
2. **Margaret** + past + find + the + ring
3. the + child + plural + past + eat + the + cake
4. everyone + present + like + Mildred
5. a + company + present + sand + the + floor + plural
6. **Keats** + past + write + the + poem
7. the + teacher + past + punish + Archibald
8. **Millicent** + past + invite + Harold
9. he + past + do + it
10. null + woman + plural + present + gather + them

The fact that *by* + NP₁ is in parentheses in the rule means that it is optional. Often it is better style to omit it than to include it. Make the following sentences passives, but omit the *by* + NP₁. "John watched Bill," for example, would become "Bill was watched," not "Bill was watched by John." Write just the sentences. Don't change the tense.

11. A policeman saw Ernest.
12. Somebody insulted Ernestine.
13. The rain ruined the crops.

14. Mrs. Willoughby sang the national anthem.
15. They process the cloth.
16. Something reduces the danger.

In all of the examples you have had so far, the auxiliary has been simple tense — present or past. But the rule works just the same whatever the auxiliary is. Here is the rule again:

$$NP_1 + Aux + V_T + NP_2 \Rightarrow$$
$$NP_2 + Aux + be + part. + V_T + (by + NP_1)$$

Let us take the kernel sentence "John should have watched Bill."

John + past + shall + have + part. + watch + Bill

What four morphemes come from the auxiliary?
The process is exactly the same. First we write the NP_2:

Bill

Then the Aux:

Bill   + past + shall + have + part.

Then *be* + part.:

Bill + past + shall + have + part.   + be + part.

Then V_T:

Bill + past + shall + have + part. + be + part.   + watch

Then, optionally, *by* + NP_1:

Bill + past + shall + have + part. + be + part. + watch   + by + John

Notice that there are now two participle morphemes in the string. Tell which rule each comes from.
The affix transformation and the word boundary rule will produce a T-terminal string as follows:

BY T-AFFIX: **Bill + shall + past + have + be + part. + watch + part. + by + John**
BY BOUNDARY RULE: **# Bill # shall + past # have # be + part. # watch + part. # by # John #**

What is the actual sentence?
Apply T-passive to the following strings.

17. **Minnie + past + shall + return + the + money**
18. **Clancy + present + will + escort + Clara**
19. **the + monkey + past + have + part. + tease + the + donkey**
20. **Mabel + past + be + ing + clean + the + stable**
21. **Ben + present + must + have + part. + injure + the + wren**
22. **the + people + past + can + have + part. + donate + the + steeple**
23. **the + lady + past + be + ing + serve + O'Grady**

Transform the following, omitting the *by* + NP₁. Write the sentences, not the strings. Don't alter the auxiliary.

24. Somebody might have seen Desmond.
25. They should have finished the work.
26. The men ought to have collected the laundry.
27. Bill had to paint the garage.
28. Gonzales should be exercising the mare.

Style

Use of T-passive

In the single-base transformations we have studied up to this point, not much judgment is required on the part of the writer or speaker. You simply respond to the situation, making a statement if you want to impart information and a question if you want to get some.

The passive transformation is a little different. Here taste and judgment do enter in, and the careful writer will give a little thought to whether in a particular context it is better to say "John watched Bill" or "Bill was watched by John." How does he decide?

It is commonly said (or one could write "People commonly say") that when other things are equal the active kernel structure is better than the passive transform. It is a "stronger," more direct, more straightforward way of saying the thing, whereas the passive is roundabout, wordy, and weak. This is probably true so long as other things are equal, but they aren't always. "George admires Julia" may be a better sentence than "Julia is admired by George," and yet we may doubt whether "All admire Julia" is better than "Julia is admired by all."

The point to understand is that the existence of the passive serves some clear stylistic needs. It permits one to bring the object of a transitive verb into prominence, by making it the subject of the passive transform, and to subordinate the kernel subject either by putting it into the *by* phrase or by leaving it out altogether.

Suppose we have these three ingredients of a sentence: (1) an action — killing; (2) an actor — a disease; (3) a receiver of the action — Mr. Winthrop. We could express this in a kernel sentence, with subject, transitive verb, and object:

A disease killed Mr. Winthrop.

But most likely our interest will be much more in Mr. Winthrop than in the disease, and we will wish to give him the prominent position, as the passive permits us to do:

Mr. Winthrop was killed by a disease.

Or, more simply, "Mr. Winthrop was killed."

Similarly, "The accident was thoroughly investigated" is very probably a better sentence than "Investigators thoroughly investigated the accident." It is only if the investigator is important for some reason that the kernel structure would be preferable: "Patrolman Brodsky thoroughly investigated the accident."

Some of the following sentences are active and some are passive. Probably, in most contexts, all would be better turned around — the active made passive and the passive active. Reverse them in this way. Keep the tense the same and write the sentences, not the strings.

1. Mary is loved by John.
2. Everybody commonly says it.
3. A bullet struck Sergeant Noble.
4. Lightning hit the barn.
5. The cows were milked by Uncle George.
6. The facts are known by Mrs. Andrews.
7. Irrigation waters the land.
8. A rumor hurt Mr. Bicycles.
9. My teeth were brushed by me.
10. Miss Billingtree was married by Mr. Clump.
11. Some houses were wrecked by a hurricane.
12. A visitor broke the grandfather clock.
13. An accident crippled Aunt Susan.
14. The game was won by Central College.
15. Something annoyed Mr. Best.

Syntax

Adjectives That End in *-ed*

We have seen two ways of generating participles in the sentences we use. One is by the addition of *have* + part. from the auxiliary to a sentence such as "Ralph ate the fish": "Ralph had eaten the fish." The other is by the passive transformation:

Ralph ate the fish. ⇉

The fish was eaten by Ralph.

Now some participles produced in the second way become adjectives, much as some *ing* verbs become adjectives. *Eaten* doesn't. We don't say *"The fish was very eaten." Neither does the *watched* of "Bill was watched by John." We don't say *"Bill was very watched." But some participles do become adjectives.

Suppose we start with the verb *dumbfounded* in a sentence like "The news dumbfounded John." The passive transformation will change this sentence as follows:

the + news + past + dumbfound + John ⇉
   John + past + be + part. + dumbfound + by + the + news

What will the actual sentence be?

But now the participle *dumbfounded* has moved into adjective territory, because we can also say "John was very dumbfounded by the news" or "John was very dumbfounded" or "John was a very dumbfounded young man." Similarly:

Something misguided John. ⇉

John was misguided by something. ⇉

John was very misguided.

Write similar second and third sentences for the following.

1. Mabel hurried Albert.
2. The plan worried Annabelle.
3. The wind dishevelled her hair.
4. The accident deformed Mr. Willoughby.
5. The outcome chastened us.
6. The example inspired everyone.
7. The strike congested the traffic.
8. Dissipation degraded Uncle Horace.
9. Science advanced the country.
10. The announcement decided John.

The last sentence shows a bit of strain on the transformation. "The announcement decided John" is grammatical but a trifle strange. There are other participlelike words in –*ed* which we can't really derive from participles through the passive transformation. Such a one is *devoted* in a sentence like "Mrs. Green was a very devoted wife." There is a verb *devote,* as in "Mrs. Green devoted her time to her family." But there is no such kernel sentence as * "Something devoted Mrs. Green" and therefore no such passive sentence as * "Mrs. Green was devoted by something."

Another example of an –*ed* adjective built on a verb but not coming through the passive transformation is *detached* in "John was very detached." There is a verb *detach,* as in "I detached the button," but "John was very detached" cannot derive from "Something detached John."

Make adjectives ending in –*ed* from the following verbs, which cannot, or cannot obviously, go to the adjective use through the passive transformation.

dissipate	detail	determine	concern
elate	bedraggle	accustom	abandon

Some adjectives that end in –*ed* are formed with the aid of a negative prefix; *un–, in–,* or *dis–.* For example, *unconstrained* is made of the verb *constrain,* as in "The ruling constrained them," plus the –*ed* ending, plus the negative prefix *un–.* Though there is no verb *unconstrain,* we do have the word *unconstrained,* which can be used as an adjective with *very:* "It was a very unconstrained party."

Other examples of –*ed* adjectives are:

unlettered	unconcerned	unbridled
unqualified	uninterested	indisposed
undecided	disinterested	disorganized

In general, the prefix *un–* can be added to participles: *uneaten, unwatched.* We can say "Bill was unwatched." Usually this *un–* cannot appear in the kernel sentence. We don't say * "John unwatched Bill." Often it doesn't go into the adjective use either. We would hardly say * "Bill was very unwatched."

There is a difference of opinion among English-speaking people about whether some words in –*ed* can be used as true adjectives or not — that is, whether they can take *very.* An example is *surprised.* Should one say "John was very surprised" or is it more grammatical to say "John was very much surprised"? This book can make no recommendation on the point, simply because there is no agreement among well-educated people. It can merely report that many consider

"John was very much surprised" to be more elegant. Others in this group are *absorbed, offended, amused.*

There are a few words which are pronounced differently when they are adjectives than when they are participles (or past tenses of verbs). An example is *learned.* As a participle, this is pronounced as one syllable: /lərnd/; as an adjective it is pronounced as two: /lə́rnəd/. Pronounce the following sentences:

> John has learned a great deal.
> John is a very learned man.

Use each of the *–ed* words in the following as an adjective in another sentence with *very.* Pronounce the adjective as two syllables.

11. Tragedy dogged her.
12. He cursed his luck.
13. Nelda crabbed a lot.
14. The priest blessed the congregation.

Syntax

Adjectives That End in –ed Formed from Nouns

The ending *–ed* is used also to form adjectives from nouns. Very commonly these nouns refer to body parts — like *head, blood, ear, eye.* Usually the noun is modified by a qualifying word in front of it. Thus *hot + head + ed* gives us the adjective *hotheaded:* "Nancy is very hotheaded." Often the qualifying word that comes first is separated from the noun by a hyphen: "Mark is very hot-blooded." There is really no way to tell whether the hyphen is conventional in such words except by observing what one reads and using the dictionary.

Make sentences with the following adjectives:

long-legged	highhanded	one-eyed
dog-eared	able-bodied	pink-cheeked
onesided	openhearted	open-mouthed

See how many other such words you can make with the nouns *hand, head, heart, mouth.* For example, for *eye* you might suggest *two-eyed, dark-eyed, green-eyed, bleary-eyed.*

Other adjectives are made by adding *–ed* to nouns. These adjectives have the meaning "having the character or quality of the noun." For instance *bigot + ed → bigoted,* which means having the character of a bigot.

Make adjectives by adding *–ed* to the following nouns.

frenzy	cloister	disease	skill
conceit	talent	manner	point

Morphology

Derivational Morphemes

We have said that there are three kinds of morphemes in English: base words, inflectional morphemes, and derivational morphemes. The latter two are affixes — that is, either suffixes or prefixes. In English they are mostly suffixes. We have already considered six of the eight inflectional morphemes — those that attach to nouns and verbs. We will take up the other two — the comparative and superlative of adjectives — when we come to these structures in the syntax.

The derivational morphemes are forms that change words from one word class or one subclass to another. For example, the morpheme **ity** makes a noun like *finality* from the adjective *final*. The morpheme **hood** makes the abstract noun *priesthood* from the concrete noun *priest*.

Derivational morphemes are a very important part of the functioning of language. Essentially they permit us to make up and use a large number of words without having to learn them separately, one by one. They permit us to recognize words without having encountered them previously.

Suppose you come across the following sentence:

The recommender was John Jones, and the recommendee was Mary Smith.

It is quite unlikely that you ever saw the words *recommender* and *recommendee* before, since they are not at all common. However, if you know anything about the English derivational system, you know that a *recommender* is a person who recommends and that a *recommendee* is someone who gets recommended. You take them in your stride, probably without even noticing that they are new words for you. If, in your speaking or writing, you have need of such words, you simply make them up.

In this chapter we will review some of the common and simple derivational morphemes very quickly. All of these are no doubt quite familiar to you. In later chapters we will consider some that are less common or more complex or both.

Morphology

Some Noun-forming Morphemes

Five morphemes much used to make nouns are **er, ness, ful, man,** and **ment.** All of these are *active* morphemes. That is, they are used by present-day speakers and writers of English to make new words. All are rather simple in meaning, and all except **er** are simple in spelling.

The morpheme **er,** of course, means "one who does" or "something that does" and it makes nouns from verbs. A *writer* is one who writes, a *recommender* is one who recommends. What is a *multilither?* a *vibrator?*

The last item shows the spelling complication of the morpheme **er** — that it is sometimes spelled *–or* instead of *–er.* The more common spelling is *–er,* and most new words are made with this spelling.

Quite a large number of words, however, use the *–or* spelling for the morpheme **er.** Some common ones are *actor, governor, reflector, tormentor, editor, contributor, director.* These are all made from verbs borrowed from Latin. Verbs ending in *–ate,* which also come from Latin, like *agitate* and *investigate,* also form nouns in which the **er** morpheme is spelled *–or: agitator, investigator.*

Make nouns by adding the "one who does" morpheme to the following:

> educate   stimulate   anticipate   violate

The morpheme **ness** also makes nouns, but from adjectives rather than from verbs. The nouns made are abstract. Thus *quiet* + **ness** is *quietness* — the quality of being quiet. Make **ness** nouns from the following adjectives:

> lazy   helpful   sweet   imaginative

Some adjectives are themselves made from abstract nouns. *Angry* is made from the abstract noun *anger.* Ordinarily we do not add **ness** to such adjectives to make still another abstract noun. We don't say **angriness.* Tell which of the following would not be likely to add **ness** because they are already made from abstract nouns. Tell what the abstract noun is in each such case.

> kind   beautiful   gentle   courageous
> reluctant   hopeless   sordid   insistent

The morpheme **ful** makes nouns of measure from concrete nouns.

For example, *cup* + **ful** is *cupful; arm* + **ful** is *armful*. Make such nouns from each of the following, and use each one in a sentence:

car   church   hand   mouth   room

Occasionally nouns ending in *–ful* form the plural by adding the plural morpheme after the base noun: *armsful*. It's more common, however, to say *armfuls*. There's a difference in meaning between *two armfuls of books* and *two arms full of books*. What is it?

The morpheme **man** has the meaning "someone connected with whatever the base word means." Thus *clergyman* means a person connected with the clergy. A *swordsman* is a person skilled in using a sword. Mostly this morpheme is pronounced /mən/, with weak stress, not /man/, as in *a good man*.

Add **man** to the following and use the words in sentences:

ship   work   fire   sports   foot   post

The morpheme **ment** is added to verbs to make abstract nouns with the meaning of the verb. The verb *govern* adds **ment** to make *government. Achieve* adds **ment** to make *achievement*.

Make abstract nouns by adding **ment** to the following.

amend   advance   enforce   engage   bereave

Morphology

A Verb-forming Morpheme

There are not as many different morphemes for making verbs as there are for making nouns and adjectives, though some of those that do exist account for thousands of English words. One simple verb-making morpheme is **en**, which is added as a suffix to adjectives. *Sweet* + **en** is *sweeten*, to make sweet. Make verbs of the following by adding **en:**

fat   thick   soft   broad   short   weak

A few verbs with **en** are made from nouns rather than from adjectives. Make verbs of the following:

length   strength   height   heart

Morphology

Some Common Adjective-forming Morphemes

In addition to the noun-making **ful,** as in *armful,* there is a **ful** that makes adjectives from nouns. The adjective *beautiful,* for instance, is composed of *beauty* + **ful.** This morpheme means having the quality of the noun. Add **ful** to these nouns:

> pain   pity   power   doubt   deceit

The morpheme **y** is a very common adjective-making ending added to nouns. For example, *sand* + **y** is *sandy.* Make similar adjectives in y from the following:

> dirt   wind   peach   trick   murk
> milk   length   tooth   fish   bog

We have already noted one of the **en** morphemes — the one that makes verbs out of adjectives, as in *sweeten.* There is another that makes adjectives from nouns. An example is *oaken,* which means made of oak, or having the quality of oak. Make similar **en** adjectives of these, and use them in sentences:

> wood   gold   hemp   silk   flax

The last of the adjective-forming morphemes to be considered now is also the most complicated of the four — **able.** It is complicated because there are two ways of spelling it: *–able* and *–ible.* The *–able* spelling is easily the more common one, and it is the one we always use when making new words, which we do quite easily with this morpheme. We can make words like *trippable* or *knowable* with confidence, even if we have never seen or heard them before. Conversely, when we come across such words, we have no difficulty in understanding them.

Make words in **able,** with the spelling *–able,* from the following, and use each word in a sentence:

> catch   grow   find   smell   teach

The spelling *–ible* for the morpheme **able** occurs mostly with base verbs that have been borrowed from Latin. Make adjectives in **able** with the spelling *–ible* from the following:

> digest   coerce   reduce   reverse

Often such a verb undergoes a change in form when **able** is added.

For example *defend* + **able** is *defensible,* with the *d* changing to
s; admit + **able** is *admissible,* with the *t* changing to *ss.* Form adjectives
by adding the morpheme **able** to the following. The suffix is spelled
–ible in each word, and the form of the root changes.

divide + **able**   comprehend + **able**   respond + **able**

There are a number of pairs of **able** words in English, with the
spelling *–able* added to a native English word in one member and
–ible added to a Latin borrowing in the other. *Eatable* and *edible* is
such a pair. *Touchable* and *tangible* is another. Write the *–able* word
that corresponds to each of the following:

visible   legible   credible   frangible

Morphology

An Adverb-forming Morpheme

We add the morpheme **ward** to nouns and certain other kinds of
words to form adverbs of *direction: city* + **ward** is *cityward.* An adverb
of direction is something like an adverb of place. Both have to do
with space. But they are not quite the same. An adverb of place, as
we have seen, is one of the structures that occur after *be* in kernel
sentences: "He is inside." But adverbs of direction do not usually occur
there. We would hardly say *"He is cityward."

Adverbs of direction occur mostly in verbals after intransitive verbs
or transitive verbs and their objects:

He traveled cityward.
They pointed the spaceship earthward.

Make adverbs of direction by adding **ward** to the following nouns,
and use each adverb in a sentence:

home   wind   sea   bed   cafeteria

Cafeteriaward is certainly an unusual word. It may be that one
couldn't find it in regular speech or writing. However, if one saw it,
one would know what it meant, and if one needed it, one could make
it up. **Ward** is an active derivational morpheme.

Ward combines with words for compass directions to form *north-
ward, eastward, southward, westward.* It also combines with some
prepositions — like *up* and *in.* Make adverbs by adding **ward** to the
following, and use each word you make in a sentence:

out   for   down   back

Centuries ago, **ward** combined with *to* to form *toward*. This has become a regular preposition, as in "He walked toward the city," and it is pronounced as a single syllable.

The morpheme **ward** has also the form *–wards*, with no difference in meaning: "He traveled citywards." Mostly we can use *–wards* wherever we can use *–ward. Ward* is a little more common, however.

SUMMARY OF RULES

T-passive

$$NP_1 + Aux + V_T + NP_2 \Rightarrow$$
$$NP_2 + Aux + be + part. + V_T + (by + NP_1)$$

TEST

1. Apply T-there to the following kernel sentences. Write the sentences, not the strings of morphemes.
   a. A catch is in it.
   b. Some students were sitting in the room.
   c. Fish are in the brook.
   d. Some visitors were downstairs.
   e. A pigeon must have been nesting on the ledge.
   f. Many cars are on the road.
   g. One cookie is in the jar.
   h. Some relatives are visiting us.
   i. Several bystanders were watching.
   j. A truck driver was eating a sandwich inside.

2. Apply T-passive to the following strings. Write the morphemes, not the sentences. Include *by* + NP_1.
   a. the + cat + past + chase + the + rat
   b. **Mabel + past + invite + me**
   c. the + foreman + past + fire + Smithers
   d. it + present + delight + us
   e. the + group + past + approve + the + resolution
   f. the + police + present + want + Mr. Ferryteyl
   g. **Mrs. Tompkins + past + invent + it**

3. Transform the following into passive sentences. Write the

sentences, not the strings. Include the by + NP$_1$ or not, as you like. Don't change the auxiliary.

   a. Something worried Evangeline.
   b. The girls trample the grapes.
   c. I enclosed it.
   d. Saralyn had driven the car.
   e. He may see Tolliver.
   f. They should have paid the bill.
   g. Somebody ought to water the pigs.
   h. Gilroy had to clean the stables.

4. If the sentence is passive, change it to active. If it is active, change it to passive.

   a. Bob was beaten by Bert.
   b. The collision damaged the car.
   c. An idea struck Mr. Schiller.
   d. The pie was eaten by us.
   e. Everyone disliked her.
   f. The task was undertaken by Partridge.

5. Write two sentences for each of the following. Use the word as a transitive verb with an object in the first and as an adjective preceded by $very$ in the second.

   amuse   horrify   alarm   enchant   disarm

6. Use each of the verbs in the following sentences as an adjective with –ed. Use $very$ before the adjective. For example, for "The news worried Martha," you might write "Martha felt very worried."

   a. Albert hurried Mildred.
   b. The praise inspired him.
   c. Experience had biased Daniel.
   d. The reply chastened me.

7. Make an adjective with –ed from each of the following nouns, using a qualifying word before each noun. For example, for $hand$ you might write $highhanded$ or $heavy-handed$.

   heart   mouth   ear   eye   body

8. Make nouns from the following, and use them in sentences:

   educate + **er**   helpful + **ness**   find + **er**
   mouth + **ful**   engage + **ment**   clergy + **man**

9. Make adjectives from the following, and use them in sentences:

> bog + y   wool + en   pity + **ful**
> teach + **able**   care + **ful**   divide + **able**

10. Make adverbs of direction by adding **ward** to the following nouns. Use each adverb in a sentence.

> home   town   beach   wind

REVIEW QUESTIONS

1. Why might we be more likely in some circumstances to say "This is pretty" instead of "This dress is pretty"?

2. Is T-there a single-base or a double-base transformation?

3. What structure in a kernel sentence becomes the subject in a passive transform?

4. What kind of verb must a kernel sentence have in order for T-passive to apply?

5. How may the subject of the kernel sentence be expressed in the passive transform? Must it be expressed?

6. Apart from *by*, what new morphemes are added by the passive transformation?

7. Why may it be said that the passive transformation requires taste and judgment on the part of the writer? So far as emphasis goes, what does the passive transformation permit one to do?

8. Why might "Mr. Winthrop was killed by a disease" be a better sentence than "A disease killed Mr. Winthrop"?

9. What is the general function of derivational morphemes?

10. What is meant by an active morpheme?

11. What can be said in general about when **er** is spelled –*er* and when –*or*?

12. From what word class does **ness** form nouns?

13. Why is *angriness* an ungrammatical form?

14. From what word class does **ment** form nouns?

15. From what word class does **en** form verbs?

16. What kinds of words are formed by the two different morphemes spelled –*ful*?

17. What are the two spellings of the morpheme **able**? What can you say about the difference in their use?

18. What morpheme is used to form adverbs of direction?

19. How do adverbs of direction differ in their use from adverbs of place?

20. How does *devoted* in "She was a very devoted mother" differ from *worried* in "She was a very worried mother"?

21. What prefix can be added to most participles?

22. What question of proper usage arises in connection with a word like *surprised?*

23. What are the two different pronunciations of *learned,* and when is each used?

CHAPTER 9

The Relative Clause

The noun phrases that you have studied so far have all been generated by kernel rules. Of the four kinds of noun phrases, three — proper nouns, personal pronouns, and indefinite pronouns — are quite simple, being for the most part made up of single words. The fourth kind — Det + N — is more complicated, since the determiner can contain a variety of items. Thus the kernel rules will give us such noun phrases as *several of those thirty boys*. Still this consists only of the determiner *several of those thirty* and the noun *boys*.

But noun phrases can be much more complicated than this. The following is a noun phrase: *several of those thirty little boys who attend the nursery school which is located at the end of the street on which we live*. Here all the additions to *several of those thirty boys* have been added by transformational processes which we will now begin to consider. This structure, though it has several sentences embedded in it, is not itself a sentence. It is just a noun phrase. In order to make it a sentence, one would have to add to it the VP of NP + VP:

Several of those thirty little boys who attend the nursery school which is located at the end of the street on which we live *have the mumps*.

The most important structure in the enlargement and expansion of noun phrases like *several of those thirty boys* is what is called a *relative clause*, and this is what we will begin with. Relative clauses are structures like *who attend the nursery school* or *which is located at the end of the street* or *on which we live*. They resemble sentences because they have predicates, but they are not sentences. They are modifiers of noun phrases. They expand the information contained in the noun phrase to which they are attached.

Noun phrases are expanded by relative clauses in this way:

$$X + NP + Y \Rrightarrow NP + \begin{Bmatrix} who \\ that \\ which \end{Bmatrix} + X + Y$$

You may note that this rule is somewhat similar to T-wh, noun phrase, which makes *wh* questions from statements:

$$X + NP + Y \Rrightarrow \begin{Bmatrix} who \\ what \end{Bmatrix} + X + Y$$

There are several differences, however. One is that in the relative clause rule, the NP doesn't disappear as it does in T-wh, noun phrase. Another is in the words put in: *who* is put in in both, but how do the rules differ otherwise? A third difference is that the relative clause rule does not apply to strings resulting from T-yes/no.

This rule is only a part of the transformation T-relative. Here is an example of its operation. Take the sentence "The boys attend the nursery school." This has the following morphemes:

the + boy + plural + present + attend + the + nursery + school

If we take **the + boy + plural** as the NP of X + NP + Y, the X is null. What is the Y? Following the instructions to the right of the arrow, we write the NP first:

the + boy + plural

Then we must choose *who, that,* or *which.* These words are called *relative pronouns.* We may use *who* if the NP refers to a person or persons and *which* if it doesn't. We may use *that* no matter what the NP refers to. So what relative pronouns can we use in this case?

Let us choose *who:*

the + boy + plural   + who

Then X is null, so we have only the Y to add:

the + boy + plural + who   + present + attend + the + nursery + school

This will give us the expanded noun phrase *the boys who attend the nursery school.* This is not a sentence. It is only an expanded noun phrase, though the relative clause in the noun phrase was made from a sentence.

Take this one:

the + school + present + be + part. + locate + at + the +
  end + of + the + street

If T-af were applied, and this were made immediately into a sentence,
what would the sentence be?

If *the school* is the NP of X + NP + Y, what is the X and what
the Y? We write first the NP:

the + school

Which two of the three relative pronouns may we use here? Suppose
we use the relative pronoun *which:*

the + school   + which

X is null, so only the Y remains:

the + school + which   + present + be + part. + locate + at +
  the + end + of + the + street

Write similar transformations of the following. Take the subject of
each as the NP of X + NP + Y. Use *who* for persons and *which* for
nonpersons.

1. a + boy + present + live + here
2. everybody + present + know + Julia
3. the + train + past + go + to + Chicago
4. a + mouse + past + be + in + the + cupboard
5. the + man + present + collect + the + garbage

Write the actual noun phrases represented by the strings you wrote
for 1–5. Since they are just noun phrases, not sentences, don't use
initial capitals and closing periods.

Syntax

Relative Pronouns Replacing Objects of Verbs

Suppose we begin with the kernel sentence "The man collected
the garbage yesterday." This kernel sentence has the following K-
terminal string:

the + man + past + collect + the + garbage + yesterday

There are two noun phrases, either of which could be the NP of
X + NP + Y. Suppose we decide it will be *the garbage.* Then what
is the X; that is, what comes before **the + garbage?** What is the Y;
that is, what comes after the NP?

First we write the NP:

the + garbage

Then the relative pronoun, either *that* or *which:*

the + garbage   + that

Then the X:

the + garbage + that   + the + man + past + collect

Then the Y:

the + garbage + that + the + man + past + collect   + yesterday

What is the actual expanded noun phrase?
   Study this additional example:

> **we + past + meet + the + girl + yesterday** $\Rightarrow$
> **the + girl + that + we + past + meet + yesterday**

Which noun phrase was chosen as the NP of X + NP + Y? What
was the X? What was the Y? What is the actual expanded noun
phrase that the second string represents?
   Transform the following similarly. Use the relative pronoun *that* in
each, and take the italicized noun phrase as the NP of X + NP + Y.

1. **Gerald + past + buy + *a + car* + last + week**
2. **Mr. Wilson + present + own + *a + house***
3. **he + past + know + *a + girl* + in + school**
4. **Sammy + past + have + part. + lose + *a + book***
5. **we + past + like + *a + boy* + very + much**

We have seen that when the NP refers to a person, we may have
either *who* or *that* in the relative clause. Suppose we choose *who*
for Sentence 5 above. We would get this string:

> **a + boy + who + we + past + like + very + much**

If nothing more is done, this will give us the noun phrase * "a boy
who we liked very much." But, just as with the interrogative *who,*
the more formal usage will be *whom* because the relative pronoun
has replaced a noun phrase functioning as object. We can show this
in the string, as we did for the *wh* questions, by inserting the symbol
o for *object:*

> **a + boy + who + o + we + past + like + very + much**

Then the phonological rule already noted will convert **who + o** to
whom.

Transform the following, taking the italicized NP as the NP of X + NP + Y. Use *who* for persons and *which* for nonpersons. When *who* replaces a noun phrase functioning as object, write **who + o.**

6. he + past + save + *the + child*
7. *a + priest* + past + have + part. + enter + the + room
8. she + past + have + part. + admire + *a + dress*
9. Max + past + visit + *a + doctor* + yesterday
10. *people* + past + speak + Bulgarian
11. Sally + present + admire + *a + actor*
12. Gonzales + present + be + ing + train + *the + colt*
13. she + present + teach + *the + child + plural*
14. Jack + past + build + *the + garage*
15. *the + garage* + past + collapse

Write the actual noun phrases represented by the strings you produced for 6–15.

Whom occurs more frequently in *wh* questions than it does in relative clauses. We must say either "Who did you see?" or "Whom did you see?" and either way we may lose. If we use *who*, people may think we're uneducated, and if we use *whom*, they may think we're showing off our education. But it must be either *who* or *whom*, and if we want to meet the more formal standards, there is no alternative — it must be *whom*.

In relative clauses, on the other hand, there are innocent alternatives. One is the relative pronoun *that*. We can say "the man that you saw" and avoid the *who/whom* choice altogether. That is one reason why we are more likely to say "Whom did you see?" than "the man whom you saw."

But there is still another innocent alternative. When the NP of X + NP + Y functions as an object, we can omit the relative pronoun altogether:

> We saw the man. $\Rightarrow$ the man we saw
> He bought a house. $\Rightarrow$ a house he bought
> Gonzales trained a colt. $\Rightarrow$ a colt Gonzales trained

Transform each of the following three times, taking the object as the NP of X + NP + Y. Use *whom* or *which* in the first, depending on what kind of NP the object is. Use *that* in the second, and nothing in the third. Write just the actual phrases, not the strings.

16. She had bought a hat.
17. He married the girl.
18. I admired a lawyer.
19. We met a salesman yesterday.

20. George found a wallet on the sidewalk.
21. Eloise had known a boy in school.
22. Henry carried a sandwich in his pocket.

Syntax

Relative Pronouns Replacing Objects of Prepositions

Once again, this is the rule that changes sentences into noun phrases expanded by relative clauses:

$$X + NP + Y \Rightarrow NP + \begin{Bmatrix} who \\ that \\ which \end{Bmatrix} + X + Y$$

Suppose we apply this rule to the kernel sentence "John spoke to the girl yesterday." The sentence has the following K-terminal string:

John + past + speak + to + the + girl + yesterday

If we take **the + girl** as the NP, what is the X, and what is the Y? If we choose *who* as the relative pronoun, we will get **who + o**, since *who* replaces an object, and the transformation will run in this way:

the + girl
the + girl   + who + o
the + girl + who + o   + John + past + speak + to
the + girl + who + o + John + past + speak + to   + yesterday

What is the actual expanded noun phrase?

Transform the following similarly, taking the italicized noun phrase as the NP of X + NP + Y. Use *who* + o if the NP refers to a person and *which* if it doesn't.

1. **I + past + work + with + a +** *man* **+ last + week**
2. **Doug + past + find + the + ring + in +** *the + drawer*
3. **she + past + borrow + the + money + from + a +** *lawyer*
4. **Mary + past + appear + in + a +** *play* **+ last + month**
5. **we + past + live + near +** *some + Irishman + plural* **+ in + Chicago**

Here again we have alternatives. Instead of *who* + o or *which,* we may use *that* or nothing:

John spoke to the girl. $\Rightarrow$ the girl that John spoke to
John spoke to the girl. $\Rightarrow$ the girl John spoke to

Transform each of the following three times. Use *who* + o or *which* in the first transform, *that* in the second, and nothing in the third.

    6. Mr. Dennis lives in the house.
    7. Aunt Isabel works for a dentist.
    8. His sister rooms with an aunt.
    9. He left the money on the shelf.
  10. I told you about the lumberjack.

Write noun phrases expanded by relative clauses from the following sentences. Take the italicized noun phrase as the NP of X + NP + Y. Use any correct relative pronoun you like.

  11. *The lady* took the trip.
  12. The lady took *the trip*.
  13. A *farmer* found the child in the basket.
  14. A farmer found *the child* in the basket.
  15. A farmer found the child in *the basket*.
  16. He encountered *a bear* in the woods.
  17. He encountered a bear in *the woods*.
  18. *The dog* brought the ball to the umpire.
  19. The dog brought *the ball* to the umpire.
  20. The dog brought the ball to *the umpire*.

Syntax

A Variation with a Preposition Shift

The relative clause rule as given will generate a number of different types of relative clauses, including those in which the relative pronoun replaces the object of a preposition: *the girl whom John spoke to*. It will not, however, produce *the girl to whom John spoke*. This is more complicated, because the preposition shifts too, and the transformation — T-relative, preposition — requires a rule of its own:

$$X + Prep + NP + Y \Rightarrow NP + Prep + \begin{Bmatrix} who \\ which \end{Bmatrix} + X + Y$$

We can illustrate this with the example already given:

John + past + speak + to + the + girl

The noun phrase *the girl* is the NP in question. What is the preposition? What is the X? What is the Y?
    First we write the NP:

the + girl

Then the preposition:

the + girl   + to

Then, since the noun phrase refers to a person, we choose *who,* and since it is an object, we add the object marker:

the + girl + to   + who + o

Then the X:

the + girl + to + who + o   + John + past + speak

This is all, since Y is null. What is the actual noun phrase?
Here is an example with *which:*

I + past + wait + for + a + bus + yesterday

With *a bus* as the NP, what is the preposition? the X? the Y?
The transformation unfolds in the same way:

a + bus
a + bus   + for
a + bus + for   + which
a + bus + for + which   + I + past + wait
a + bus + for + which + I + past + wait   + yesterday

What is the actual expanded noun phrase?
Apply the rule to the following, writing the strings.

1. **Anne + past + be + ing + ride + in + a + car**
2. **we + past + be + ing + look + for + a + child**
3. **he + past + leave + the + paper + plural + on + a + desk**
4. **she + past + listen + to + a + speaker + last + night**
5. **Bill + past + work + with + a + man + on + Monday**

Write the actual noun phrases for 1–5.
You may have noticed another difference between this relative clause rule and the general one, apart from the shifting of the preposition: *that* is not given as a possible relative pronoun. We can say *a girl that John spoke to* but not **a girl to that John spoke.* Also there is now no possibility of omitting the relative clause altogether. We have *a girl John spoke to* but not **a girl to John spoke.* Also there is now nothing optional about the object marker. We might say *a girl who John spoke to* but we couldn't have **a girl to who John spoke.*
All of these complexities make the construction *a girl to whom John spoke* irregular in the sense that many features which apply to most relative clauses do not apply to it. This irregularity may account

for the fact that *the girl to whom John spoke* is not so common as *the girl John spoke to.*

Write expanded noun phrases from the following, shifting the preposition and using *whom* or *which.*

   6. The President signed the bill with the pen.
   7. I heard from a correspondent yesterday.
   8. Julian works in a bank.
   9. We had our picnic beside the stream.
   10. Everyone goes to the dentist.
   11. The planes flew over a factory.
   12. Renfrew lives near a banker.
   13. He had stirred the coffee with a spoon.
   14. We all felt small beside a soldier.
   15. Pearl went to a guidance counselor.

Syntax

Double-Base Transformations

The rules that produce relative clauses are only the first part of a transformation process. They do not produce sentences; they produce expanded noun phrases. This expanded noun phrase must now be used in some other sentence. Suppose we apply the rules to the sentence "The boys attend the nursery school," with the following results:

**the + boy + plural + present + attend + the + nursery school $\Rightarrow$
   the + boy + plural + who + present + attend + the + nursery
      school**

This gives us the expanded noun phrase *the boys who attend the nursery school.* This can now be inserted in any sentence in which the original noun phrase *the boys* can be used.

Like the original noun phrase *the boys,* the expanded noun phrase *the boys who attend the nursery school* can occur in any noun phrase function:

SUBJECT: The boys are young.
                  The boys who attend the nursery school are young.
COMPLEMENT: These are the boys.
                  These are the boys who attend the nursery school.
OBJECT OF A VERB: Mrs. Flox spanked the boys.
                  Mrs. Flox spanked the boys who attend the
                     nursery school.

OBJECT OF A PREPOSITION: I waved at the boys.

I waved at the boys who attend the nursery school.

It is clear that two base sentences are involved in the making of a transform like "The boys who attend the nursery school are young." One is the sentence from which the relative clause is made: "The boys attend the nursery school." The other is the structure into which the expanded noun phrase is inserted: "The boys are young." We call the first sentence the *insert* sentence, because it provides material to be inserted in another sentence. We call the second sentence the *matrix* sentence. A matrix is a mold or form in which something is shaped. The matrix sentence provides the fundamental form of the finished sentence. We call the finished transform the *result* sentence, because it results from the insertion of material from the insert sentence into the matrix.

INSERT: The boys attend the nursery school.⎤ ⇒
MATRIX: The boys are young.   ⎦
RESULT: The boys who attend the nursery school are young.

Write similar result sentences from the following, and tell what the function of the repeated noun phrase is in the insert and the matrix sentences.

1. INSERT: The girl spoke to you.
   MATRIX: The girl is Sally Andrews.
2. INSERT: The house burned down.
   MATRIX: The house is the old Mulligan place.
3. INSERT: The dentist pulled the tooth.
   MATRIX: The dentist is Harry's father.

In all of these examples, the noun phrase which is expanded happens to have the same function — subject — in both insert and matrix. But of course this doesn't have to be true. Tell the function of the repeated noun phrase in the insert sentence and in the matrix sentence of each of the following.

a. INSERT: The boys attend the nursery school.⎤ ⇒
   MATRIX: Mrs. Flox spanked the boys.   ⎦
   RESULT: Mrs. Flox spanked the boys that attend the nursery school.
b. INSERT: The boys attend the nursery school.⎤ ⇒
   MATRIX: The nursery school burned down.   ⎦
   RESULT: The nursery school that the boys attend burned down.

c. INSERT: Jack took the girl to the dance. ⎤
  MATRIX: I argued with the girl.   ⎦ ⟹
  RESULT: I argued with the girl Jack took to the dance.

Review the steps once more. First, find in the matrix sentence the noun phrase repeated from the insert:

INSERT: *The girl* plays the piano.
MATRIX: Jack brought *the girl*.

Next, make an expanded noun phrase from the insert in which the repeated noun phrase is modified by a relative clause:

INSERT: *The girl* plays the piano. ⟹
    the girl who plays the piano

Finally, substitute this expanded noun phrase for the appropriate noun phrase in the matrix:

MATRIX: Jack brought *the girl*.
RESULT: Jack brought *the girl who plays the piano*.

Write result sentences from the following.

4. INSERT: Mr. Wilks bought the house.
  MATRIX: The house is on Wimpole Street.
5. INSERT: The house burned down.
  MATRIX: I used to live in the house.
6. INSERT: Several of those thirty little boys attend the nursery school.
  MATRIX: Several of those thirty little boys have the mumps.
7. INSERT: The nursery school is located at the end of the street.
  MATRIX: Several of those thirty little boys who attend the nursery school have the mumps.
8. INSERT: We live on the street.
  MATRIX: Several of those thirty little boys who attend the nursery school which is located at the end of the street have the mumps.

Syntax

Recursiveness

The result sentence for 8 above should be approximately the example we began with on page 177. Sentences 6–8 above illustrate a very important characteristic of grammar: *recursiveness*.

Recur means to happen again, and a grammatical rule is recursive if it can be applied more than once in a single sentence. Now the relative clause rule is recursive, because it may put into the matrix sentence a *new* noun phrase to which the transformation may be applied again:

INSERT: The boys attend the school. ⎤
MATRIX: The boys have the mumps.   ⎦ ⇒
RESULT: The boys who attend the school have the mumps.

What noun phrase does the result sentence contain that the matrix did not? This result sentence can now become the matrix for another transformation:

INSERT: The school is located on the street.   ⎤
MATRIX: The boys who attend the school have the mumps. ⎦ ⇒
RESULT: The boys who attend the school that is located on the street have the mumps.

What new noun phrase has been put in now? Again the result can become the matrix in another transformation:

INSERT: We live on the street.   ⎤
MATRIX: The boys who attend the school that is located on the ⎬ ⇒
          street have the mumps.   ⎦
RESULT: The boys who attend the school that is located on the street on which we live have the mumps.

The last transformation didn't put in a new noun phrase, so we can't keep going in that direction. However, there is another noun phrase that we haven't touched yet: *the mumps*. We can now take off from *the mumps* and keep adding so long as each addition puts in a new noun phrase:

The boys who attend the school that is located on the street on which we live have the mumps that they got from a visitor who works for a farmer who has children that get all the diseases that anyone ever heard of.

This last is a *grammatical* sentence, which doesn't necessarily mean that it's a good one. Indeed, it's a monstrosity. (Remember that we have not said that grammatical is the same as good or that ungrammatical is the same as bad.) From the point of view of style or intelligibility there are limits to how often we actually apply recursive transformations. For this sentence we were about at the stylistic limit when we began from *the mumps*. Further additions began to give the sentence what is sometimes called the "house that Jack built" quality.

But though there are limits of style and intelligibility to the application of a recursive transformation, there are no *grammatical* limits. No rule in the grammar says that it can be applied only once or twice or ten times. It can be applied a million times provided that each application puts in the necessary ingredient for the next one, in this case an NP to serve as the NP of X + NP + Y.

This is important because it is part of the explanation of the fact that the grammar is finite but the language produced by the grammar is infinite. There are only a limited number of grammatical rules, but there is an unlimited amount of language producible by those rules — an infinite number of possible sentences.

Here is a harder exercise. Work out the transformational buildup for each of the following sentences as shown in the example of recursiveness on page 188. For each you will have three sets of insert, matrix, and result sentences. The result of the first set will become the matrix of the second, and the result of the second will become the matrix of the third. Your first matrix will be "The man insulted Mr. Danby."

1. The man who brought the box that contained the plugs Harry wanted insulted Mr. Danby.
2. I know a fellow who attended a school that has a computer which really works.
3. This is the dog that worried the cat that killed the rat that ate the malt.

History of English

Borrowings from Latin

For the last thousand years, English has been a greedy borrower of words from other languages. In recent times it has been paying back because of the dominance of England and America in everything from science to sports. Mexicans now speak of *el beisbol* and Frenchmen of *le weekend*. But in earlier times words flowed the other way as the English came in contact with the ways and ideas of more highly civilized peoples on the continent of Europe.

Even before the Norman Conquest of England in 1066, English had borrowed many words, particularly from Latin and Old Scandinavian.

It borrowed from Latin because the Angles and Saxons — the Germanic tribes who spoke what was to become English — while they were still wandering on the continent of Europe, encountered Roman traders who told them about things like butter and kettles, cheese and churches, and gave them the words to go with them. Later, after the Angles and Saxons had invaded and settled England, they were converted to Christianity and acquired many words, as well as the Latin alphabet, from those who converted them. They borrowed from Old Scandinavian because the Vikings, who spoke that language, invaded England in the ninth century, got control of much of the eastern part of the country, and settled down to live with the natives.

But the real flood of borrowed words did not begin until a considerable time after 1066, the date when William the Conqueror, who spoke Norman French, achieved the last successful foreign invasion of England. For many centuries, the French civilization and the French language were considered by Englishmen to be far superior to their own. Though the mass of Englishmen didn't learn to speak French, they borrowed great numbers of French words — words for food, clothes, furniture, architecture, jewelry, recreation, religion, government, law, and many other aspects of human life.

This large embrace of French got speakers of English in the habit of borrowing and, with the coming of the Renaissance in the sixteenth century and the renewed interest in the old civilizations of Greece and Rome, large numbers of Latin and Greek words were borrowed. Later, as travel increased and communication improved, English lapped up words from Italian, Spanish, German, Russian, Persian, Hindi, and many others, including American Indian languages.

To get a notion of the diversity of the backgrounds of English words, look up the etymologies of the following in a dictionary and tell what languages they come from:

chair	umbrella	street	hoosegow
ugly	taboo	bungalow	slogan
moose	tea	deck	kindergarten

But by far the most generous lender of words to English has been Latin. About thirty-five percent of all the words in a dictionary with about 120,000 main entries are borrowings from Latin. This compares with only about fifteen percent for native English words. It is unlikely that you will write a sentence of any length without using at least one word from Latin, such as *insist, refer, apply, control, missile, tractor.*

Morphology
The Suffix –*ate*

We have borrowed so many words from Latin that we have taken over a number of Latin affixes too and used them as our own. In addition to such native English prefixes as *over–* in *overdo, mis–* in *misaddress, up–* in *upgrade, be–* in *belittle,* we have prefixes from Latin like the *ex–* of both *exclude* and *ex-wrestler* and the *re–* of both *recover* and *re-cover.* Two of the derivational morphemes already studied — **ment** and **able** — come from Latin. We borrowed so many words like *variabilis* and *tolerabilis* that the ending itself came to have a meaning for us, addable to any verb at all, whether a verb from Latin or not: *hearable, doable, get-at-able.*

One of the most common of the Latin suffixes in English words is the verb ending –*ate.* This suffix occurs in over a thousand words borrowed from Latin. Most of these are verbs, like *eliminate.* Some are adjectives, like *delicate.* Some are nouns, like *directorate.* A number are used in more than one word class. For instance, *degenerate* is used in all three:

NOUN:　He's a degenerate.
VERB:　He degenerated.
ADJ.:　　He's very degenerate.

Tell what class or classes the following are used in. Use them in sentences that will make the word class clear.

exaggerate	protectorate	considerate	subordinate
compensate	adequate	irritate	irrigate
predicate	syndicate	separate	sophisticate

Make a list of ten other words ending in –*ate.* Tell what word class or classes they belong to — noun, verb, or adjective.

A number of suffixes have an effect on the placement of the stress in the words to which they are attached, and –*ate* is one of them. All words of more than two syllables ending in –*ate* have the first stress on the syllable that is third from the end:

cómpensate	séparate	írrigate
exággerate	subórdinate	consíderate

Copy the following and put the mark ´ over the vowel of the syllable in each that has loudest stress.

emancipate	illegitimate	doctorate	articulate

The syllable *–ate* is pronounced differently according to whether the word is a verb on the one hand or an adjective or noun on the other. Say these sentences aloud, and listen to the difference in the pronunciation of *subordinate:*

NOUN: He's a subordinate.
VERB: We'll subordinate it.
ADJ.:   It's subordinate.

As verbs, the *–ate* words have third degree of stress on the *–ate* syllable with the vowel sound /ā/: /səbórdənàt/. As adjectives, and usually as nouns, they have weak stress and schwa in the *–ate* syllable: /səbórdənət/.

Write two sentences for each *–ate* word, using it as a verb in the first and as an adjective or a noun in the second.

estimate   duplicate   appropriate

Morphology

The Noun-forming Suffix *–ion*

Virtually all verbs ending in *–ate* can be made into nouns by the addition of the suffix *–ion:*

estimate/estimation   appropriate/appropriation

This suffix also comes to us from Latin in words like *invitationis* and *conditionis.* It is so familiar to us in the *–ate* words that we easily go forward and back. That is, if you know the verb *appropriate,* you can easily make *appropriation* without ever having seen it; if you know *appropriation,* you can make *appropriate.*

Make nouns with the morpheme **ion** from the following, and use each one in a sentence:

regulate   syncopate   deviate
indoctrinate   lubricate   anticipate

Use the verbs underlying the following in sentences:

education   violation   elucidation

The suffixes *–ate* and *–ion* combine in so many words to make *–ation* that *–ation* itself has been felt as a morpheme meaning "the doing of something," and it has been added to native English words, as in *starvation.* It also occurs with verbs from Latin that do not end in *–ate.* An example is *reformation,* in which the underlying verb is not *reformate but reform. Give the verbs underlying the following nouns in –ation:

degradation	recommendation	embarkation
variation	compilation	resignation

Apart from –ation, what consonant sound occurs in *resignation* that does not occur in the underlying verb?

About fifteen hundred English nouns end in the spelling –ation, but there are hundreds more in which **ion** appears instead in words spelled –tion or –sion. These are, first of all, nouns made by adding **ion** to verbs ending in a /t/ or /s/ sound. Tell what verbs underlie the following:

profession	suppression	convulsion
contraction	ejection	invention

Sound changes take place when **ion** is added, but the spelling preserves the identity of the morphemes. Which of these has a /t/ sound in it — *eject* or *ejection?* Which has a /k/ sound? Which of these has an /s/ sound — *profess* or *profession?* Which has a /ʃ/ sound?

We saw that certain verbs change both sound and spelling when adding the morpheme **able**:

permit → permissible   divide → divisible

Many of the same changes take place in the addition of **ion** to these verbs: *permission, division.* Make nouns in **ion** from the following:

admit	commit	evade	seclude
collide	extend	explode	comprehend

Various other form changes take place when **ion** is added to other verbs. Give the verbs underlying these:

consumption	compulsion	expansion	transcription
erosion	explosion	succession	absolution
procession	intercession	abolition	admonition

The morpheme **ion** also makes nouns from adjectives. Tell what adjectives underlie the following, how they are pronounced, and what they mean:

erudition	precision	tension
profusion	discretion	distinction

Like **ate**, **ion** has a particular effect on the stress pattern of the words to which it is attached. Pronounce these pairs:

regulate/regulation   anticipate/anticipation
abolish/abolition   execute/execution

Assuming that it always works this way (and it does), where does **ion** put the loudest stress?

SUMMARY OF RULES

T-relative

$$X + NP + Y \Rrightarrow NP + \begin{Bmatrix} who \\ that \\ which \end{Bmatrix} + X + Y$$

This is only the first part of the transformation — that part which converts an insert sentence into a noun phrase modified by a relative clause. This expanded noun phrase must then be used in a noun phrase function in a matrix sentence, as shown briefly in this chapter. The complete process is shown in more detail in the next chapter.

T-relative, preposition

$$X + Prep + NP + Y \Rrightarrow NP + Prep + \begin{Bmatrix} who \\ which \end{Bmatrix} + X + Y$$

In this kind of relative clause, *that* cannot be used and the relative pronoun cannot be omitted. When the noun phrase refers to a person, the form *whom* (**who** + **o**) is obligatory.

TEST

1. Transform these strings into noun phrases modified by relative clauses. Take the italicized morphemes as the NP of X + NP + Y. Illustrate all possibilities in the choice of relative pronoun — *who, that, which,* and null. When you use *who* to replace an object, write it **who** + **o.**
   a. *the + man* + past + come + to + dinner
   b. she + past + marry + a + *lawyer*
   c. we + past + have + part. + rent + a + *car*
   d. they + present + attend + a + *church* + on + Sunday
   e. *the + car* + past + be + ing + overtake + us

2. Apply T-relative, preposition to the following, switching the preposition. Write **who** + **o** when the NP refers to a person. After you write the string, write the actual expanded noun phrase.

a. he + past + be + part. + raise + by + a + aunt
b. they + present + live + in + the + mountain + plural
c. he + present + be + ing + work + with + some + man +
plural

3. Make noun phrases modified by relative clauses from the following.
Use each expanded noun phrase as subject, complement, object of a
verb, or object of a preposition in another sentence. Take the italicized
noun phrase as the NP of X + NP + Y, and use any suitable relative
pronoun.
a. Jack had mailed *the letter*.
b. *The committee* recommended the strike.
c. Billings was escorting *some ladies*.
d. He was standing on *the log*.

4. Write result sentences from the following. Use any suitable
relative pronoun.
a. INSERT: Jack built the house.
   MATRIX: The house was condemned by the inspector.
b. INSERT: The inspector saw the house.
   MATRIX: The inspector couldn't believe his eyes.
c. INSERT: A boy had been crying.
   MATRIX: Sheila encountered a boy.
d. INSERT: He was reading the book.
   MATRIX: The book was about salamanders.
e. INSERT: He had taken some pictures in Japan.
   MATRIX: He showed some pictures.

5. Write the words underlying the following nouns in **ion:**

decision   absorption   dislocation   explosion

REVIEW QUESTIONS

1. What relative pronouns are permitted in the rule which transforms a sentence into a noun phrase modified by a relative clause? In
what situations are the different relative pronouns used?
2. In formal usage, what item would be added to the string a +
boy + who + we + past + like?
3. Why is the word *whom* less common in relative clauses than
it is in *wh* questions?
4. In what circumstances may the relative pronoun be omitted
from the relative clause?

5. How does the use of relative pronouns in T-relative differ from their use in T-relative, preposition?

6. What are the two base sentences underlying the sentence "The boys who attend the school are young"?

7. What are the terms for the underlying sentences of a double-base transformation and for a sentence produced by one?

8. What is the meaning of the word *matrix*?

9. What is a *recursive rule*?

10. What do we mean when we say that a sentence has a "house that Jack built" structure?

11. There are no grammatical limits to the number of times a recursive rule may be applied. What limits are there, however?

12. What do we mean when we say that English has been a great borrower but is now paying back?

13. From what languages in particular did English borrow words before the Norman Conquest of 1066?

14. Why did English borrow so many words from French?

15. Are there more Latin words in English or more native English words?

16. In about how many English words does the ending –*ate* occur? To what word class do most of these belong? In what other word classes do we find –*ate* words?

17. What effect does –*ate* have on the stress of the words in which it occurs?

18. What is the difference between pronunciations of the –*ate* parts of *appropriate* as verb and as adjective?

19. What ending can be added to nearly all verbs ending in –*ate*? What kind of word do they become when this ending is added?

20. What is odd about the makeup of the word *starvation*?

21. What sounds do the letters *ct* stand for in *reject*? What sounds do they stand for in *rejection*?

22. What sound does *ss* stand for in *impress*? What does it stand for in *impression*?

23. What effect does **ion** have on the placement of the loudest stress?

CHAPTER 10

Syntax

The Full Relative Clause Transformation

We have so far stated by rule only that part of T-relative that converts a sentence into a relative clause:

$$X + NP + Y \Rightarrow NP + \begin{Bmatrix} \text{who} \\ \text{that} \\ \text{which} \end{Bmatrix} + X + Y$$

This will, for example, change "The Indian killed the buffalo" into *the Indian who killed the buffalo* or *the buffalo that the Indian killed.* But these are just expanded noun phrases. The process is completed by inserting the expanded noun phrases into matrix sentences to make result sentences:

> The Indian who killed the buffalo was a Shawnee.
> They cooked the buffalo that the Indian killed.

The rules for double-base transformations like T-relative are more complicated than those for single-base transformations. We won't stop in every case to work them out, but T-relative may be given in full as an illustration. This is one way to do it:

$$\left. \begin{array}{l} \text{INSERT:} \quad X~(1) - NP_1~(2) - Y~(3) \\ \text{MATRIX:} \quad Z~(4) - NP_1~(5) - W~(6) \end{array} \right\} \Rightarrow$$

$$\text{RESULT:} \quad (4) + (5) + \begin{Bmatrix} \text{who} \\ \text{which} \\ \text{that} \end{Bmatrix} + (1) + (3) + (6)$$

The numerals in parentheses merely identify the various elements so that their order can be shown in the result sentence. The subscript numeral 1 under the two NP's simply indicates that the noun phrase

197

in question must be the same in both insert and matrix. The X and Y in the insert indicate as usual what comes before and after the NP, if anything does. The letters in the matrix play the same role. We use Z and W because we have two more positions to mark.

Let us work this out in an example, concocting one in which we have X, Y, Z, and W. Here are two base strings:

INSERT: the + Indian + past + kill + the + buffalo + yesterday
MATRIX: they + past + cook + the + buffalo + this + morning

The NP_1 of the rule must be the noun phrase that occurs in both insert and matrix. What is it? Here are the other items:

X (1): the + Indian + past + kill
Y (3): yesterday
Z (4): they + past + cook
W (6): this + morning

A look at the rule will disclose that X is (1), Y is (3), Z is (4), and W is (6). We must arrange all of the items in this order: (4) + (5) + relative pronoun + (1) + (3) + (6).

Now we can arrive mechanically at the result sentence. First we write the (4), which is Z:

they + past + cook

Then the (5), the noun phrase:

they + past + cook   + the + buffalo

Then a relative pronoun:

they + past + cook + the + buffalo   + that

Then the (1), which is X:

they + past + cook + the + buffalo + that   + the + Indian + past + kill

Then the (3), which is Y:

they + past + cook + the + buffalo + that + the + Indian + past + kill   + yesterday

Then the (6), which is W:

they + past + cook + the + buffalo + that + the + Indian + past + kill + yesterday   + this + morning

What is the actual result sentence?

Here is an example with nulls:

INSERT: some + water + past + be + poisonous
MATRIX: they + past + drink + some + water

If we rewrite these with hyphens between the six parts identified by the rule and show the nulls, we get this:

INSERT: null – some + water – past + be + poisonous
MATRIX: they + past + drink – some + water – null

The NP$_1$, which occurs twice, is numbered (2) in the insert and (5) in the matrix. What is it? Here are the other items:

X (1):   null
Y (3):   past + be + poisonous
Z (4):   they + past + drink
W (6):   null

This will now roll out according to the rule:

RESULT: they + past + drink
         they + past + drink   + some + water
         they + past + drink + some + water   + that
         they + past + drink + some + water + that   + null
         they + past + drink + some + water + that + null   +
           past + be + poisonous
         they + past + drink + some + water + that + null +
           past + be + poisonous   + null

Write result strings from the following. You can probably do it by instinct, but you get a better notion of the elegance of the mechanism if you do it mechanically, keeping the letters and numbers in mind.

1. INSERT: null – the + boy – past + come + with + Ellen
   MATRIX: null – the + boy – past + enliven + the + party
2. INSERT: we + past + make – the + mistakes – yesterday
   MATRIX: null – the + mistakes – present + be + part. +
             forget + today
3. INSERT: he + past + win – the + car – in + a + raffle
   MATRIX: he + past + park – the + car – in + the + garage
4. INSERT: you + past + see – the + bird – this + morning
   MATRIX: null – the + bird + past + be + a + flicker
5. INSERT: they + past + begin – the + discussion – in + school
   MATRIX: they + past + continue – the + discussion – on + the +
             bus

Syntax

Nonrestrictive Relative Clauses

What are the relative clauses in the following sentences?

> The girl who lives upstairs keeps salamanders.
> Lucille, who lives upstairs, keeps salamanders.

Although in each sentence the same group of words makes up a relative clause, it should be clear that the two clauses play different roles in the structure of the sentences. One difference is obvious: the relative clause in the second sentence is set off by commas, and the one in the first is not. This punctuation distinction, however, reflects deeper dissimilarities.

The function of *who lives upstairs* in *The girl who lives upstairs* is to modify and identify the noun phrase *the girl*. It indicates the salamander-keeping girl. She is not the one who lives across the hall or down the block; she's the one who lives upstairs. The addition of the relative clause gives quite a different, more particular meaning to the matrix sentence, "The girl keeps salamanders." A relative clause that functions in this way, to identify or restrict the meaning of a noun phrase, is called a *restrictive* relative clause.

The clause in "Lucille, who lives upstairs, keeps salamanders" does not, however, have this identifying function. Lucille is fully identified by her proper name. It is not the case that there are several Lucilles in the picture and that the clause is used to identify the upstairs Lucille, for if that were true, we would have to use the definite article before the proper noun:

> The Lucille who lives upstairs keeps salamanders.

But without the article the relative clause does not identify Lucille. It merely adds to the matrix sentence, "Lucille keeps salamanders," the information that Lucille lives upstairs. A clause like this, which does not identify the noun phrase or restrict its meaning, is called a *nonrestrictive* clause.

The rule that generates nonrestrictive relative clauses is a little different from the one for restrictive clauses. For one thing, there is a change in the intonation pattern to be shown. Here is just the part of the rule that accounts for the expanded noun phrase which is to be inserted in a matrix sentence:

$$X + NP + Y + 2\text{-}3\text{-}1 \Rightarrow NP + 2\text{-}3\text{-}2 + \begin{Bmatrix} \text{who} \\ \text{which} \end{Bmatrix} + X + Y + 2\text{-}3\text{-}2$$

The 2-3-2 intonation patterns in the rule indicate the speech feature which is shown by commas in writing. Suppose we transform "Lucille lives upstairs" by this rule. This is the string:

Lucille + present + live + upstairs + 2-3-1

With *Lucille* as the NP, X is null and Y is **present + live + upstairs**. The rule will give us the following string:

Lucille + 2-3-2 + **who + present + live + upstairs** + 2-3-2

The 2-3-2 after **Lucille** shows that the proper noun will be pronounced like this:

Lucille

That is, one would begin as usual on the second level of pitch, rise to the third level on the syllable with first stress — the second syllable in this word — and then fall back not to 1 this time but to 2 again. This fall to 2 instead of 1 indicates a break in the sentence but indicates also that the sentence isn't finished.

The string **Lucille** + 2-3-2 + **who + present + live + upstairs** + 2-3-2 shows that there is a second 2-3-2 intonation pattern, this one applying to the words formed by **present + live + upstairs**. Again, we begin on 2, rise to 3 on the syllable that takes first stress, and then fall back to 2 again:

who lives upstairs

Once again the fall to 2 instead of 1 indicates that the sentence, though interrupted, is not finished. There is more to come. We can show the whole expanded noun phrase as follows:

Lucille who lives upstairs

The fall to 2 is shown in writing by the commas:

Lucille, who lives upstairs,

This will now be inserted in a matrix sentence such as "Lucille keeps salamanders," and the result sentence will have the following pitch pattern:

Lucille who lives upstairs keeps salamanders.

In regular orthography, this will be:

Lucille, who lives upstairs, keeps salamanders.

There are other differences between this nonrestrictive transformation and the restrictive one. One difference is that the relative pronoun *that* cannot be used. *"Lucille, that lives upstairs, keeps salamanders" is ungrammatical. This is a useful test when you are trying to decide whether a clause is restrictive or nonrestrictive. If *that* can be used, it is restrictive; if *that* can't be used, it is nonrestrictive.

Another distinction can be seen when the NP functions as object. For a restrictive clause, we can have this development:

INSERT: I met the girl.
MATRIX: The girl spoke German. } ⇛
RESULT: The girl I met spoke German.

Here the relative pronoun is omitted. Alternatively we might have had "The girl that I met spoke German" or "The girl whom I met spoke German."

But when the clause is nonrestrictive, *that* cannot be used and the pronoun cannot be omitted. *"Mabel, that I met, spoke German" is ungrammatical, and so is *"Mabel, I met, spoke German." Here *whom* is the only choice:

INSERT: I met Mabel.
MATRIX: Mabel spoke German. } ⇛
RESULT: Mabel, whom I met, spoke German.

Finally, since the nonrestrictive relative clause does not serve to identify the noun phrase, the noun phrase must be identified in some other way. One way is by being a proper noun, as in the following exercise. Convert each of the sentences into an expanded noun phrase, and use commas to mark the intonation breaks. Take the proper noun as the NP in each item and transform in this way:

John should have known better. ⇛
    John, who should have known better,
We liked John very much. ⇛
    John, whom we liked very much,

1. Allan had the key.
2. They had invited Roberta.
3. Mr. Dawson was opposed to the plan.
4. Cynthia likes olives.
5. They should have informed Mrs. Rayburn.

6. They were teasing Susie.
7. Miss Plum had never been abroad.
8. They might have comforted Mrs. Williams.
9. Ronald pitched the last three innings.
10. I spoke to Janice.

Sentence 10 might be transformed in either of two ways:

Janice, whom I spoke to,   *or*   Janice, to whom I spoke,

The preposition-shifting rule is the same for both restrictive and non-restrictive clauses except for the obligatory intonation breaks in the latter.

When the NP does not refer to a person, *which* is used:

Mount McKinley is the highest peak in North America. $\Rightarrow$
Mount McKinley, which is the highest peak in North America,

Transform the following, using *which* for nonpersons and *who* or *whom* for persons:

11. Chicago was the site of the convention.
12. They had crossed the Missouri the night before.
13. I had admired Christensen.
14. Cape Cod is crowded in the summer.
15. Angela was supposed to bring the soup.
16. They enjoyed Spain very much.
17. Nobody feared Mrs. Wilkins.
18. The United States had little interest in foreign affairs at that time.
19. Marty takes the bus to work.
20. Al Jones had never made camp bread.
21. We disliked Mr. Watkins heartily.
22. He drives on the Long Island Expressway.

In what two ways may 22 be transformed?

As we have seen, noun phrases expanded by nonrestrictive relative clauses are incorporated in matrix sentences:

INSERT: Chicago was the site of the convention. $\left.\right\}\Rightarrow$
MATRIX: Chicago had been preparing for months.
RESULT: Chicago, which was the site of the convention, had been preparing for months.

Naturally, if the nonrestrictive clause ends the sentence, its intonation pattern is 2-3-1, not 2-3-2, and a period closes it.

INSERT: Chicago was the site of the convention. ⎫
MATRIX: We bought a ticket for Chicago.   ⎬ ⇒
RESULT: We bought a ticket for Chicago, which was the site of the convention.

Write result sentences from the following:

23. INSERT: Robert had a bad cold.
     MATRIX: Robert didn't come.
24. INSERT: The Indo-Europeans were nomads.
     MATRIX: The Indo-Europeans knew little of civilization.
25. INSERT: San Luis Obispo was a thriving community.
     MATRIX: Ronald moved to San Luis Obispo.
26. INSERT: You know Mrs. Biller.
     MATRIX: This is Mrs. Biller.
27. INSERT: The Pennsylvania Railroad looked like a good investment.
     MATRIX: Mrs. Leibnitz bought the Pennsylvania Railroad.
28. INSERT: France had signed the treaty.
     MATRIX: France prepared for war.
29. INSERT: I had met Mr. Wilbermark in Kansas.
     MATRIX: I suddenly thought of Mr. Wilbermark.
30. INSERT: The Mississippi is very wide at that point.
     MATRIX: They came to the banks of the Mississippi.
31. INSERT: Albanian is an Indo-European language.
     MATRIX: Miss Witley speaks Albanian.
32. INSERT: Grandfather didn't like string beans.
     MATRIX: Grandfather dumped the dish on the floor.
33. INSERT: The Ritz Carlton is very expensive.
     MATRIX: We stayed at the Ritz Carlton.
34. INSERT: Mr. Twomey had opened a perfume shop.
     MATRIX: The ladies flocked around Mr. Twomey.
35. INSERT: He liked Mr. Whitney.
     MATRIX: Elmer worked for Mr. Whitney.

Syntax

Nonrestrictive Clauses After Other Noun Phrases

So far we have considered only those nonrestrictive clauses formed when the NP of the rule is a proper noun. We have seen that the clause will always be nonrestrictive in such a situation except when it is a matter of distinguishing between two people or places with the same name. In that case, *the* is used before the proper noun, and the clause is restrictive:

The Lucille that lives upstairs keeps salamanders.

The William Shakespeare I mean used to play for Yale.

The France that he once knew was far different from the present one.

When the NP of X + NP + Y is a personal pronoun, the clause is also generally nonrestrictive. The construction is not particularly common, but one can easily think of examples:

INSERT: You knew better.

MATRIX: You are most to blame. $\Rightarrow$

RESULT: You, who knew better, are most to blame.

When the NP is an indefinite pronoun, however, the following clause is regularly restrictive and not set off by commas:

INSERT: Everybody knows Wilkins.

MATRIX: Everybody loves him. $\Rightarrow$

RESULT: Everybody who knows Wilkins loves him.

But when the noun phrase is Det + N, a following clause may be either restrictive or nonrestrictive, depending on the meaning of the noun phrase or of the passage as a whole. For example:

INSERT: My father lives in Petaluma.

MATRIX: My father raises chickens. $\Rightarrow$

Since I have, presumably, only one father, the noun phrase *my father* cannot be further identified by a modifier, and a clause following it must be nonrestrictive:

RESULT: My father, who lives in Petaluma, raises chickens.

The clause merely gives another bit of information about *my father* — his place of residence.

But suppose we have these bases:

INSERT: My sister lives in Petaluma.

MATRIX: My sister raises chickens. $\Rightarrow$

Here the intent of the insert may be the same for *my sister* — just to tell where she lives. In that case, the clause will be nonrestrictive, and will be set off by commas:

RESULT: My sister, who lives in Petaluma, raises chickens.

But there is here another possibility. The clause may be intended to tell which particular sister I am talking about, assuming I have more than one. In that case the clause is restrictive:

My sister who lives in Petaluma raises chickens (whereas the one
who lives in Guadalajara grows orchids).

Here is a situation: Ronald is sitting in class with a girl on one
side of him and a boy on the other. Then:

INSERT: The girl sat on Ronald's left.⎫
MATRIX: The girl borrowed his pen.   ⎬ →
RESULT: The girl, who sat on Ronald's left, borrowed his pen.

There is only one girl in the picture, so the clause cannot identify
her further. It will be nonrestrictive and therefore it will be set off
with commas.

But suppose Ronald is sitting in class with a girl on either side of
him. Two girls. No boy. Then:

INSERT: The girl sat on Ronald's left.⎫
MATRIX: The girl borrowed his pen.   ⎬ →
RESULT: The girl who sat on Ronald's left borrowed his pen.

Now the clause has the function of indicating which girl is meant:
the left-hand girl, not the right-hand one. It is restrictive and is not
set off by commas.

In the following exercise, you are given a series of situations. Write
result sentences in accord with the situations.

1. Maria and three other girls are in a room.
   INSERT: The girl was washing grapes.
   MATRIX: Maria spoke to the girl.
2. Maria, one other girl, and three boys are in a room.
   INSERT: The girl was washing grapes.
   MATRIX: Maria spoke to the girl.
3. There is just one river in the vicinity.
   INSERT: The river bordered our land.
   MATRIX: The river was still and deep.
4. There are several houses on the block.
   INSERT: The house had green shutters.
   MATRIX: Gordon bought the house.
5. A pear, an apple, an orange, and a banana are in a bowl.
   INSERT: Max chose the apple.
   MATRIX: The apple was rotten.
6. The restaurant has only one waiter.
   INSERT: Sergeant Billig questioned the waiter.
   MATRIX: The waiter was sullen.

7. There are three dentists in town.
   INSERT: Mrs. Streicher goes to the dentist.
   MATRIX: The dentist doesn't use novocaine.
8. There is an old dungeon in a prison camp.
   INSERT: The dungeon was used regularly.
   MATRIX: The dungeon was not escape-proof.
9. Alice had a cat, a dog, and a parrot.
   INSERT: She called the cat Steve.
   MATRIX: Alice's favorite was the cat.
10. Several ladies are playing bridge.
    INSERT: George is engaged to the lady.
    MATRIX: The lady is dealing.

Punctuation has been left out of the following sentences, but some of them contain nonrestrictive relative clauses that should be set off by commas. Copy each sentence, and use commas to set off the clauses that you think are nonrestrictive.

11. Al Wilson who used to play football coached the team.
12. People who crossed the country in those days suffered many hardships.
13. He who had always defended Mirabelle was flabbergasted.
14. Our new car which we were very proud of was badly damaged.
15. He talked to anyone who would listen.
16. I thought of Battles whom I had known in New York.
17. King Alexander who had a bad temper destroyed the village.
18. The moon which was at the full gave us enough light.
19. The men who didn't join criticized those who did.

Phonology

Stress in Complex Sentences

We will find it useful now and then to employ the terms *simple sentence* and *complex sentence*. A *simple sentence* is any kernel sentence or any sentence made from a kernel sentence by a single-base transformation. "He was here," "Was he here?" "Where was he?" are all simple sentences. A *complex sentence* is any sentence formed by one or more double-base transformations. "The boy who was here left" and "John, who was here, left" are both complex sentences.

A simple sentence ordinarily has just one first, or heaviest, stress. This falls on the syllable at which the pitch rises to level three in the 2-3-1 and 2-3-2 pitch patterns. This will usually occur somewhere in the last word of the sentence:

He was hére.
That's a sháme.
Bert was reséntful.

But if the last word in the sentence is a personal pronoun, the first stress will ordinarily fall on a preceding word:

He doesn't líke me.
What's ín it?

Copy the following and put the mark ´ over the vowel in the syllable that has first stress in ordinary pronunciation.

1. Steve ate the cake.
2. It was an insult.
3. She insulted him.
4. Where did they put it?
5. Did they investigate?
6. What was the regulation?
7. Should we have warned them?
8. Was he just being silly?

The effect of a double-base transformation is usually to make one longer sentence of two shorter ones. This lengthening may result in the breaking up of the spoken sentence into two or more parts. Either because we are speaking slowly and carefully or because we don't have enough breath to carry through to the end in one spurt, we pause at one or more places before the conclusion of the sentence. Just before we pause, we rise to the third level of pitch and put in another first stress.

Suppose we speak the sentence "The boy who is crying is Albert Whoople." We *could* speak this sentence as one unit with one pitch rise and one first stress:

The boy who is crying is Albert | Whóople.

But we are a little more likely to let the pitch rise on *cry* also, and to have another first stress there:

The boy who is | crýing   is Albert | Whóople.

We might even, if we were speaking quite slowly, have another pause after *boy:*

The | bóy   who is | crýing   is Albert | Whóople.

However, since the clause is restrictive, none of these breaks are marked by commas in writing.

Say the following aloud, and try to pronounce them with first stress in the syllable marked.

9. The little girl who is waiting is Sally Brówn.
10. The little girl who is wáiting   is Sally Brówn.
11. The little gírl   who is wáiting   is Sally Brówn.
12. The thing that bóthered him   was the expénse.
13. He showed us a váse   that he had bought in México.
14. People who know him líke him.
15. People who knów him   líke him.

But these extra pitch rises and first stresses are optional if the clause is restrictive. With a nonrestrictive clause the situation is different. Remember the rule that transforms the insert sentence:

$$X + NP + Y + 2\text{-}3\text{-}1 \Rightarrow NP + 2\text{-}3\text{-}2 + \begin{Bmatrix} who \\ which \end{Bmatrix} + X + Y + 2\text{-}3\text{-}2$$

Lucille + present + live + upstairs + 2-3-1 $\Rightarrow$
   Lucille + 2-3-2 + who + present + live + upstairs + 2-3-2

This transformation requires the pitch rises. They are obligatory, not optional. Therefore, when the clause is inserted in the middle of the matrix sentence, there will be three obligatory pitch rises and two commas. When it comes at the end of a matrix sentence, there will be two rises and one comma.

Say the following sentences, which contain nonrestrictive relative clauses, and try to pronounce them with pitch rises that coincide with the marks showing first stress.

16. The bay hórse, which had been off its feed all wéek, began to recóver.
17. Jennifer remembered her sléd, which had been rusting in the back yard since wínter.
18. Jóhn, who liked wáffles, came down to breakfast éarly.
19. Rádio, which must compete with télevision, is still pópular.
20. Éd, whom I knew in Chicágo, has moved to Detróit.

Pronounce the following sentences, in which the first stresses are not marked, and note the obligatory pitch rises and first stresses. Then copy the sentences, punctuating them properly.

21. Marcellus who hadn't even been involved was one of those arrested.

22. We strolled down Jay Street which ends at the river.
23. Sue who will try anything ordered alligator soup.
24. This little box which weighs less than an ounce contains enormous energy.
25. We asked Jeff Davidson who knows a lot about music.
26. The other twin who was named Frieda had not spoken.
27. His next trip was on Miracle Airlines which repairs its planes with wire and scotch tape.
28. Marvin Little whom she had met at the reception was an electrical engineer.
29. He was born in Carrolton which is in southern Illinois.

Morphology

Six Related Suffixes

Students can solve a great many of their most serious spelling problems by noting relationships among words. Learning to spell English words correctly is pretty hard, but it would be nearly impossible were it not for the fact that a great many words are related to others. We do not have to retain each letter of each word as a separate memorized item. We have many clues from the sound and many from word relationships. The word *thorough* has a rather peculiar spelling, but we do know from the sound that it must begin with the letters *th* and have an *r* in the middle. Besides, if we know how to spell *thorough*, we shouldn't have any trouble with *thoroughly* or *thoroughness*, and if we should decide to break new ground and create **thoroughful*, we wouldn't hesitate about the spelling.

Two suffixes that give quite a lot of trouble are *–ant* and *–ent*. These may be considered two forms of the single morpheme **ent**, as *–able* and *–ible* are two forms of the single morpheme **able**. They are added to verbs to make adjectives and nouns:

emerge + **ent** → *emergent*   claim + **ent** → *claimant*

Most words with this morpheme are adjectives.

There are more words in the *–ent* form than in the *–ant* form, but not enough more to make the guessing odds very good. There are a few clues in the sound structure. For example, if a /k/ sound comes before the ending, the form is always *–ant: applicant, significant, vacant.* If the sound before the ending is /j/, the spelling is *–ent* except in *sergeant* and *pageant: urgent, emergent, detergent.* If the preceding sound is /g/, the spelling is *–ant: litigant, elegant, extravagant.*

If the sound is /sh/ spelled with the letters *ci*, the morpheme **ent** is spelled *–ent: proficient, efficient, sufficient.*

The **ent** words, though they usually have weak stress and /ə/ in the final syllable, *can* have third stress and /e/. One can pronounce *rodent* either /rṓdənt/ or /rṓdent/. Pronouncing such a word with /e/ a few times may help one remember the spelling. Try pronouncing the following with third stress and /e/ in the final syllable:

omnipotent   eloquent   reverent   repellent

Nearly all of these adjectives have corresponding nouns ending in the morpheme **ence**, which also has two spellings: *–ence* and *–ance.* But it has *–ence* where the underlying adjective has *–ent* and *–ance* where the adjective has *–ant:*

reverent/reverence   reluctant/reluctance

Make nouns with the proper spelling of the morpheme **ence** from the following adjectives:

insurgent	intelligent	malevolent	clairvoyant
repugnant	hesitant	negligent	dominant

Of course the relationships hold in general for meaning as well as sound. If you know what *malevolent* means, you know what *malevolence* means.

Some nouns are formed with the suffixes *–ency* or *–ancy* instead of *–ence* or *–ance.* Thus there is no word **infance*, but there is *infancy.* Here again, taking note of the relationships helps one avoid spelling errors. There is an *a* in *infancy* because there is one in *infant.*

Here are other words in *–ency* and *–ancy.* For each one write the underlying adjective or noun in *–ent* or *–ant.*

efficiency   presidency   buoyancy   flippancy

Sometimes the same base word will take either the morpheme **ence** or **ency**, with little or no difference in meaning. *Belligerence* and *belligerency* mean about the same thing, and so do *preponderance* and *preponderancy.* The meaning is not always the same in such pairs, however. *Emergence* and *emergency* don't mean the same thing.

Morphology

The Morphemes **ism**, **ist**, and **ize**

A number of sets of three words are produced by the two noun-forming morphemes **ism** and **ist** and the verb-forming morpheme **ize**, as in *communism, communist, communize.* The base word for all of these is the French word *commun,* which means "shared equally." *Communism* means the theory, *communist* one who believes in it, and *communize* making it prevail over other political systems in some country or group.

Make similar sets of three from the following, filling in the two missing members of the set:

socialism	romanticist	verbalize
catechism	vocalize	moralism
sensationalist	intellectualize	plagiarist

Not all **ism, ist,** and **ize** words belong to such sets of three, of course. For *pessimist,* there is the partner *pessimism,* but there is no **pessimize.* For *heroism* there is neither **heroist* nor **heroize.*

None of the following words belong to a full set of three. For each, tell which word or words that might occur in such a set of three do *not* occur in the normal use of English.

classicism	criticism	atheism
dentist	tourist	cyclist
apologize	tantalize	alphabetize

There are about 350 English verbs that end in *–ize,* and a large number of these have corresponding nouns that end in *–ation.* Thus the noun *legalization* is composed of the base adjective *legal* plus the verb-forming morpheme **ize** plus the noun-forming morpheme **ation.** For each of the following adjectives, write two words: first the verb that contains the morpheme **ize** and then the noun with **ize +ation.**

immortal	standard	liberal	civil
tranquil	familiar	human	national

Morphology

The Verb-forming Morpheme fy

The Latin word that meant "to make" was *facere,* in which the letter *c* represented the /k/ sound. With the passage of time, this /k/ sound ceased to be pronounced, and it does not appear in the Romance languages descended from Latin. The word in French is *faire,* in Italian *fare.*

Now this verb was used also in Latin as a morpheme added to other words to give the meaning "make." For example, the word *liquefacere* meant "make liquid." This became first *liqueficere* and then, in French, *liquefier*. When the word was borrowed from French by English, the *r* was not pronounced, and it became English *liquefy*. Many such words were borrowed, so that the morpheme and its meaning have become quite familiar to speakers of English. When we come across the word *simplify* for the first time, we probably don't reach for the dictionary. We know it means "make simple." However, many **fy** words, such as *petrify*, are not made from English words.

Most **fy** words, like *simplify* and *petrify*, have the letter *i* before the ending. In many, part of the base word has been dropped. Thus *horror* + **fy** is not **horrorfy* but *horrify*. Usually, when this happens, the base word remains identifiable, however. What is it in the following?

dignify   terrify   identify

Make verbs in **fy** with the following meanings:

make pure	make diverse	make beautiful
make false	make clear	make just
make glorious	make intense	make into a person
make specific	make null	make electric

Like **ate** and **ion,** **fy** has an effect on the placement of stress: it puts the first stress on the third syllable from the end, just as **ate** does. This effect is not always apparent, because the stress is often there to begin with, but we can see it in such a pair as *solid/solidify*. Notice in this pair that the letter *i*, which stands for /ə/ in *solid*, stands for /i/ in *solidify*. Again, noticing such relationships may help to eliminate some spelling errors.

Make verbs in **fy** from the following, and note changes in stress placement:

humid   acid   person   syllable

When verbs in **fy** are made into nouns in *–ation*, the *c* of Latin *facere* returns to the scene. The noun corresponding to *solidify* is not **solidifation* but *solidification*. Notice how the stress shifts in the set of words:

sólid   solídify   solidificátion

Make similar nouns from the following:

pacify	qualify	unify	mortify
classify	indemnify	glorify	uglify

SUMMARY OF RULES

T-relative (completed)

INSERT: X (1) – NP$_1$ (2) – Y (3)
MATRIX: Z (4) – NP$_1$ (5) – W (6) $\Rightarrow$

RESULT: (4) + (5) + $\begin{Bmatrix} who \\ that \\ which \end{Bmatrix}$ + (1) + (3) + (6)

This is given as an illustration of how a double-base transformation may be formulized. The letters are position markers, and they may of course be null. The numerals in parentheses in the result sentence show the order of the segments.

T-relative (transformation of the insert for nonrestrictive clauses)

X + NP + Y + 2-3-1 $\Rightarrow$ NP + 2-3-2 + $\begin{Bmatrix} who \\ which \end{Bmatrix}$ + X + Y + 2-3-2

When the clause is nonrestrictive, the relative pronoun cannot be *that*. Nor can it be omitted. The pitch rises are accompanied by first stresses, according to the regular phonological rule, and are reflected by commas in writing. Naturally, if the clause ends the sentence, there is only one extra pitch rise.

TEST

1. Apply the relative clause transformation to the following, writing the result strings. The six segments of the rule are separated by dashes.
   a. INSERT: null – the + lad – present + be + ing + wait
      MATRIX: null – the + lad – present + be + a + messenger
   b. INSERT: I + past + see – the + girl – this + morning
      MATRIX: Ed + past + mention – the + girl – yesterday
   c. INSERT: Mr. Marples + past + buy – the + house – null
      MATRIX: I + present + like – the + house – null
   d. INSERT: Jim + past + bring – the + girl – to + the + game
      MATRIX: null – the + girl – present + be + Jane Fairbanks

2. Write the result sentences, punctuating them correctly:
   a. INSERT: Ralph had lived in Egypt.
      MATRIX: Ralph told us about life there.

b. INSERT: The Collins Drugstore is across the street.
  MATRIX: He works in the Collins Drugstore.
c. INSERT: I knew Tom Tucker in high school.
  MATRIX: I ran into Tom Tucker last night.

3. From the following make result sentences that accord with the situations given.
  a. There are three dogs in a yard.
    INSERT: The dog had been barking.
    MATRIX: The dog ran toward us.
  b. There are three dogs and a cat in a yard.
    INSERT: The cat had been sitting in the tree.
    MATRIX: The cat jumped onto Timmy's shoulder.
  c. There was only one Walker River.
    INSERT: The Walker River flowed near our house.
    MATRIX: We often swam in the Walker River.
  d. There were two Walker Rivers.
    INSERT: The Walker River flowed near our house.
    MATRIX: The Walker River was the smaller one.

4. Copy the following sentences, and add commas to those that contain nonrestrictive relative clauses.
  a. Everyone who came had a good time.
  b. Ed Ferris who arrived early brought the sandwiches.
  c. Sue Winters brought ginger ale which we all like.

5. Copy the following and put the mark ´ over the vowels of syllables which have first stress.
  a. Mr. Gonzales, who understands horses, examined the colt.
  b. This is Sally, who goes to school with me.

6. Make nouns in **ence** or **ency** from the following:

    consequent   significant   potent   infant

7. Make sets of three words with **ism, ist,** and **ize** from the following adjectives. For example, from *social* you would make *socialism, socialist, socialize.*

      ideal   material   human   real

8. Express the following meanings with verbs in **fy:**

      make solid   make simple   make clear

REVIEW QUESTIONS

1. In the T-relative rule, the symbol NP_1 occurs in both insert and matrix sentences. What is the significance of the subscript numeral 1?

2. In this rule, what role is played by the letters X, Y, Z, and W?

3. In the rule for T-relative, what device is used to show the ordering of the elements in the result sentence?

4. How do restrictive and nonrestrictive clauses differ so far as punctuation goes?

5. How do restrictive and nonrestrictive relative clauses differ so far as relative pronouns are concerned?

6. What change in intonation is made by the rule for nonrestrictive relative clauses?

7. If the NP_1 is a proper noun, is the relative clause likely to be restrictive or nonrestrictive? If it is a personal pronoun? If it is an indefinite pronoun?

8. What is the difference in meaning between "My brother, who lives in Gary, works in a steel mill" and "My brother who lives in Gary works in a steel mill"?

9. Explain the terms *simple sentence* and *complex sentence*.

10. On what word in a simple sentence does the first stress most commonly fall? When does it not fall there?

11. How many first stresses *may* occur in "The young lady who is speaking is Miss Whipple"? How many *must* occur in that sentence?

12. How many first stresses must occur in "Miss Whipple, who is now speaking, is the program chairman"?

13. What is the relationship between first stress and pitch level?

14. To what word class do most words ending with the morpheme **ent** belong?

15. How is **ent** always spelled after the sound /k/?

16. What two morphemes are related to **ism**? To what word class do words in **ism** belong?

17. What morpheme can most verbs in **ize** add to form nouns?

18. What did *facere* mean in Latin? What part of the word ceased to be pronounced in the Romance languages?

19. On what syllable does the first stress fall in words ending in **fy**?

20. What ending is added to verbs in **fy** to make them nouns?

CHAPTER 11

Syntax

A Deletion Transformation

A very important part of the mechanism by which kernel sentences are built into complex ones is the modification of the noun phrase — the identification or description of noun phrases by structures of various kinds attached to the determiner plus common noun of the kernel. We began the discussion of noun phrase modification with the relative clause for a very good reason: the other types of noun modifiers can be derived from the relative clause.

Certain noun phrases are made up of a relative pronoun plus a form of *be* (tense + *be*) plus something else. Point out the relative pronouns and the forms of *be* in the following. Tell what the tense is in each phrase.

1. the men who were waiting for us
2. a boy that was outside
3. several of the men who are in the car
4. most of the milk that is delivered by Mr. Wilkins

A very general deletion rule says that in any construction consisting of a noun phrase, a relative pronoun, a tense, a *be*, and anything else after the *be*, the sequence relative pronoun + tense + *be* can be deleted. Here is a statement of this rule:

$$NP + relative\ pronoun + tense + be + X \Rrightarrow NP + X$$

What does X stand for in the rule?

We can call this *the deletion transformation for the relative clause* and abbreviate it T-relative, deletion. Here is an example:

$$a + boy + that + past + be + outside \Rrightarrow$$
$$a + boy + outside$$

What three morphemes have been deleted from the first string of morphemes to form the second? The first noun phrase, of course, has been derived from a kernel sentence:

a + boy + past + be + outside ⇉ *(by T-relative)*
a + boy + that + past + be + outside ⇉ *(by T-relative, deletion)*
a + boy + outside

What kind of structure is the word *outside* — a noun phrase, an adjective, or an adverbial of place? Notice that it bears the same meaning relationship to the noun phrase *a boy* throughout the transformational development.

> A boy was outside. ⇉
> a boy that was outside ⇉
> a boy outside

Suppose we start with this string of morphemes:

the + man + plural + who + past + be + ing + wait + for + us

What morphemes in the string constitute the NP of the deletion rule stated on page 217? What is the relative pronoun? the tense? the X? What morphemes may be deleted? Deleting these morphemes, we have the following string:

> **the + man + plural + ing + wait + for + us**

To what morphemes in this string will the affix transformation apply? What will the actual phrase be?

A construction like *waiting for us* in *the men waiting for us* can be called an *ing phrase*. We now have seen three constructions, in addition to the determiner, that may modify noun phrases:

RELATIVE CLAUSE: a boy *that was outside*
ADVERBIAL OF PLACE: a boy *outside*
ing PHRASE: the men *waiting for us*

Here is another type produced by this deletion transformation:

most + of + the + milk + that + present + be + part. + deliver + by + Mr. Wilkins ⇉
most + of + the + milk + part. + deliver + by + Mr. Wilkins

Again the affix transformation will apply to put **part.** after **deliver.** What is the expanded noun phrase represented by the string?

Actually an extra step is needed to produce this noun phrase, because first an active kernel sentence with a transitive verb must be made passive.

Here are all of the steps needed to produce the noun phrase *most of the milk delivered by Mr. Wilkins:*

Mr. Wilkins delivers most of the milk. $\Rrightarrow$ (*by T-passive*)
Most of the milk is delivered by Mr. Wilkins. $\Rrightarrow$ (*by T-relative*)
most of the milk that is delivered by Mr. Wilkins $\Rrightarrow$ (*by T-relative, deletion*)
most of the milk delivered by Mr. Wilkins

Such a structure contains a participle. What word is the participle? What transformation put in the participle morpheme? In this kind of construction, the group of words *delivered by Mr. Wilkins* is called a *participle phrase.* This gives us a fourth kind of noun modifier — the participle phrase. Three of the four, *participle phrase, adverbial of place,* and *ing phrase,* derive from the other kind — *the relative clause.*

Syntax

Insertion of Expanded Noun Phrases in Matrix Sentences

Like the relative clauses from which they derive, the structures you have just studied are not sentences in themselves. They must be inserted into matrix sentences. The expanded noun phrase so inserted may function as subject, object of a verb, object of a preposition, or complement. Notice what kind of noun modifier appears in the expanded noun phrase of each result sentence:

INSERT: A boy was outside. $\Big\} \Rightarrow$
MATRIX: A boy was shouting.
RESULT: A boy outside was shouting.   (*adverbial of place*)

INSERT: The men were waiting for us. $\Big\} \Rightarrow$
MATRIX: Those were the men.
RESULT: Those were the men waiting for us.   (*ing phrase*)

INSERT: Most of the milk is delivered by Mr. Wilkins. $\Big\} \Rightarrow$
MATRIX: Most of the milk is sweet.
RESULT: Most of the milk delivered by Mr. Wilkins is sweet.
          (*participle phrase*)

Make result sentences from the following, leaving out the relative pronoun and form of *be*. Tell whether the modifier in the expanded noun phrase is an adverbial of place, an *ing* phrase, or a participle phrase.

1. INSERT: Several of the men were in the cars.
   MATRIX: We spoke to several of the men.
2. INSERT: The man was pacing the floor.
   MATRIX: The man is Mr. Parish.
3. INSERT: The cake was made by Mother.
   MATRIX: The cake was inedible.
4. INSERT: The play was praised by all the papers.
   MATRIX: The class gave a play.
5. INSERT: The people are upstairs.
   MATRIX: The people complain about the noise.
6. INSERT: A snake was swimming in the pool.
   MATRIX: A snake startled Leroy.

Style

Use of T-relative, deletion

The deletion transformation we have been examining is an optional one: both "A boy who was outside was shouting" and "A boy outside was shouting" are grammatical English sentences. But one of them is better than the other: the second one. It's better because it means the same thing and it's shorter.

The nature of language is such that we can often say the same thing in two different ways. It isn't always true that the shorter way is the better, but it usually is. The principle of economy — say it in the shortest way possible — is a good one to apply when in doubt. Our tendency is to be too long-winded.

Rewrite the following sentences, deleting all sequences of relative pronoun + tense + *be*.

1. The girl who is sitting over there is Maggie Hoskins.
2. This is the letter that was left by the messenger.
3. The tenants who were complaining about the heat showed the landlord their chilblains.
4. Randy recognized a man who was in the crowd.
5. The rabbits that were in the hutches were just as contented as the ones that were in the fields.
6. The plan that was proposed by Trumplemeyer was idiotic.
7. The book that was lying there was a dictionary.
8. He is a worker who is serving without pay.

9. The girls who were sweeping the porch glanced at the planes that were flying overhead.
10. The children that are here know all about it.
11. The farmer brought a block of salt for the cattle that were in the pasture.

In order for the deletion to apply, the relative clause must contain the sequence relative pronoun + tense + *be*. A structure like *the girls that swept the porch* cannot be shortened in this way because it doesn't contain this sequence.

Write result sentences from the following. If the expanded noun phrase to be derived from the insert would contain relative pronoun + tense + *be*, delete this part and use the short form. Otherwise use the full relative clause.

12. INSERT: The telephone was on the desk.
    MATRIX: The telephone started ringing.
13. INSERT: Jim picked up the phone.
    MATRIX: The phone was the wrong one.
14. INSERT: The dentist was pulling the tooth.
    MATRIX: The dentist felt a little nervous.
15. INSERT: The man is behind the gun.
    MATRIX: The man is Uncle Louie.
16. INSERT: The grasshopper struggled on the surface.
    MATRIX: The trout grabbed the grasshopper.
17. INSERT: The engineer was in the cab.
    MATRIX: The boy waved to the engineer.
18. INSERT: The plumber repaired the sink.
    MATRIX: The plumber sent a bill.
19. INSERT: The plumber repaired the sink.
    MATRIX: The sink has started leaking again.
20. INSERT: The plumber is asking for the money.
    MATRIX: The sink that the plumber repaired has started leaking again.
21. INSERT: The money is owed to him by the tenant.
    MATRIX: The sink that the plumber asking for the money repaired has started leaking again.
22. INSERT: The tenant forgot to pay.
    MATRIX: The sink that the plumber asking for the money owed to him by the tenant repaired has started leaking again.

Items 19–22 illustrate the recursive application of T-relative and T-relative, deletion. These transformations can be applied indefinitely, so long as there are noun phrases that can be modified. We should note again, however, that while there are no grammatical limits there are limits of good style and intelligibility.

Semantics

A Possible Ambiguity

Sometimes a single noun phrase can be modified by two different modifiers. If we start with "The rabbit was in the hutch," we get *the rabbit that was in the hutch* by T-relative, and then *the rabbit in the hutch* by T-relative, deletion. This might be inserted in a matrix to give a result like "Jack was feeding the rabbit in the hutch." Now we can start again with this sentence and make another expanded noun phrase of it, taking *the rabbit in the hutch* as the NP of X + NP + Y:

the rabbit in the hutch that Jack was feeding

Now this is a slightly complicated construction, because there are two noun phrases before the relative clause *that Jack was feeding*. One is *the rabbit in the hutch* and one is just *the hutch*. We must know which the relative clause applies its meaning to. Was Jack feeding the rabbit in the hutch or was he feeding the hutch? Obviously the rabbit in the hutch. Why? Because you feed rabbits in hutches but you don't feed hutches. We are not puzzled by this construction because there is no such base sentence as * "Jack was feeding the hutch."

Suppose, however, that we start with "Jack was washing the rabbit in the hutch." T-relative will give this:

the rabbit in the hutch that Jack was washing

But now there is trouble, because you can wash not only rabbits in hutches but also hutches. That is, in addition to the base sentence that we started with, there exists the perfectly grammatical sentence "Jack was washing the hutch."

A phrase like *the rabbit in the hutch that Jack was washing* is ambiguous. This means that it has two possible meanings. It has two meanings because it can be derived from either of two base sentences:

Jack was washing the rabbit in the hutch.
Jack was washing the hutch.

Whenever a construction can be derived from either of two different base sentences, it will be ambiguous. Naturally we try to avoid ambiguity in our writing. The more heavily transformed a sentence is — that is, the more kernel sentences it has embedded in it — the greater the likelihood of ambiguity. This doesn't mean that we should avoid the danger by sticking to simple sentences. It means that when a sentence builds up through a series of transformations we have to be a little careful that the meaning still comes through unambiguously.

Each of the following noun phrases is ambiguous. For each, write the two different base sentences that may underlie it, as we wrote "Jack was washing the rabbit in the hutch" and "Jack was washing the hutch" for *the rabbit in the hutch that Jack was washing.*

1. a tree in the orchard that Bill was pruning
2. a letter in a box that had been opened
3. some people with a child who needed help
4. a magician in a show that Jenny spoke about
5. the rocks on the beach that the children play on
6. the oil inside the engine which had frozen
7. an actor on a stage that had seen better days

Semantics

Some Signals That Prevent Ambiguity

Suppose that in place of Number 7 above we had this:

an actor on a stage who had seen better days

The construction is no longer ambiguous. It is true that there is such a sentence as "A stage had seen better days," but this can't be transformed into *a stage who had seen better days.* Why can't it?

The fact that we use the relative pronoun *who* for persons but not for nonpersons and that one of the noun phrases before the relative clause refers to a person and the other to a nonperson keeps this particular construction clear. It is not ambiguous. Neither is this:

an actor on a stage which had seen better days

Why is that expanded noun phrase unambiguous?

That may be used when the NP is either a person or a nonperson, and so it won't pick out one or the other. Copy each of the following twice, once with *who* (or *whom*) and once with *which,* and note how the ambiguity clears up.

1. the child in the crib that needed attention
2. a dress on a model that we all admired
3. a dentist with pliers that terrified her

4. some travelers in cars that were frozen
5. a message for a man that had been lost
6. some children on the ice that looked thin
7. a song by the singer that everybody disliked
8. a teacher with patience that seemed unusual

Another signal that may dissolve ambiguity is agreement of just one of the noun phrases with the tense-bearing word in the relative clause. The following is unambiguous:

some trees in an orchard that were in full bloom

There is no such grammatical sentence as * "An orchard were in full bloom," so the base sentence must be "Some trees in an orchard were in full bloom." Tell what the base sentence for the following must be:

some trees in an orchard that was in full bloom

For each of these write the base sentence from which the relative clause must be derived.

9. some men in the car that were frozen
10. some men in the car that was frozen
11. rabbits in the hutch that were being washed
12. a mother with children who annoy us
13. a lady interviewed by the policemen who writes novels
14. some actors on a stage that has seen better days
15. some plans for a project that are being reviewed

We saw that *the rabbit in the hutch that Jack was feeding* is not ambiguous. The signal here is the contrast between an animate noun phrase, *the rabbit in the hutch,* and an inanimate one, *the hutch.* In general, we feed animate beings, like rabbits, but not inanimate ones, like hutches. The following are all unambiguous for this or similar reasons. Write the base sentence that underlies the relative clause of each.

16. a baby in the crib that was smiling
17. a baby in the crib that needed paint
18. a letter for a man that had been mailed in Boston
19. some people with an appointment that needed advice
20. a remark to a lady he intended to marry

Such signals, however, are somewhat weaker than contrasts like *who/which* or *was/were.* Sometimes we are not quite sure whether one of the possible base sentences can be ruled out or not. In Number 17, conceivably it's the baby, and not the crib, that needs paint. Perhaps it is a precocious baby that paints pictures and has run out of materials. Sometimes we may know perfectly well what is intended and yet, as we read, be struck by another possibility:

> a passenger in a limousine that was sleek and gaudy

It may be that we are sure that the writer means that the limousine, not the passenger, is sleek and gaudy, but the other, more ludicrous, possibility might occur to us. Then much of the writer's intended effect is lost, and he looks a bit silly. It would be better to avoid the trap in one way or another:

> a passenger in a limousine which was sleek and gaudy
> a passenger in a sleek and gaudy limousine

Syntax

T-noun modifier

We have seen the transformations that lead to *ing* phrases and participle phrases used as noun modifiers:

> A snake was swimming in the pool. $\Rightarrow$
> a snake that was swimming in the pool $\Rightarrow$
> a snake swimming in the pool

This will now be used in a matrix to give a result like "A snake swimming in the pool startled Leroy." Similarly, from the insert "A house was abandoned by its owner" and the matrix "Mr. Lubin bought a house," we get the result "Mr. Lubin bought a house abandoned by its owner."

But suppose we begin with the kernel "A snake was swimming." Then we will have this development:

INSERT: A snake was swimming. $\Rightarrow$
          a snake that was swimming $\Rightarrow$
          a snake swimming $\Bigg\} \Rightarrow$
MATRIX: A snake startled Leroy.
RESULT: *A snake swimming startled Leroy.

But this is hardly grammatical. We would expect rather "A swimming snake startled Leroy," with the word *swimming* coming between the determiner and the noun.

This is a reflection of a general rule. When the deletion transformation leaves a single-word *ing* verb or participle as the modifier of a noun phrase, the word is shifted to a position between the determiner and the noun:

$$Det + N + modifier \Rightarrow Det + modifier + N$$

We call this the *noun phrase modifier transformation* and abbreviate it T-noun modifier.

Here is an example of T-noun modifier in which a participle is shifted:

> Someone hunted a man. $\Rightarrow$
> A man was hunted. $\Rightarrow$
> a man hunted $\Rightarrow$
> a hunted man

Write similar developments for the following sentences. Notice that in the first transformation, T-passive, you omit the optional *by* + NP$_1$.

1. Something haunted a house.
2. Someone ruined the book.
3. The wind drove the snow.
4. Someone tore the page.
5. Something interrupted a meeting.

Write result sentences for the following. In each one, you will use an *ing* verb or a participle from the insert sentence between determiner and noun. For example, from "A snake was swimming" and "A snake startled Leroy," you would write "A swimming snake startled Leroy."

6. INSERT: The wind drove the snow.
   MATRIX: The snow piled up.
7. INSERT: Some children were laughing.
   MATRIX: We met some children.
8. INSERT: Something frightened a child.
   MATRIX: A child ran up to Frances.
9. INSERT: The snow was melting.
   MATRIX: The snow swelled the streams.
10. INSERT: Someone hid the gun.
    MATRIX: We found the gun.

Syntax

Adjectives as Noun Phrase Modifiers

We have so far studied adjectives only in the verb phrase after *be* and *seem*-type verbs, such as *timid* in "A lady is timid" or "A lady seemed timid." Such adjectives may sometimes be modified by prepositional phrases, as in "A lady is timid about mice." Now such a kernel sentence may be an insert and develop just as sentences with *ing* verbs and participles do:

INSERT: A lady is timid about mice. $\Rightarrow$
             a lady that is timid about mice $\Rightarrow$
             a lady timid about mice $\Big\}\Rightarrow$
MATRIX: A lady should buy a cat.
RESULT: A lady timid about mice should buy a cat.

If, however, we begin with "A lady is timid," we will arrive at *a lady timid*. Now T-noun modifier will apply:

$$\text{Det} + \text{N} + \text{modifier} \Rightarrow \text{Det} + \text{modifier} + \text{N}$$
$$\textbf{a} + \textbf{lady} + \textbf{timid} \Rightarrow \textbf{a} + \textbf{timid} + \textbf{lady}$$

With the application of T-noun modifier to adjectives just as to *ing* verbs and participles, we have this set of transformations:

A lady is timid. $\Rightarrow$
a lady who is timid $\Rightarrow$
a lady timid $\Rightarrow$
a timid lady

Write similar sets for the following.

1. A remark was silly.
2. The man was angry.
3. Some children were quiet.
4. An apple was rotten.
5. A statement was absurd.

Suppose we start with "Girls are funny." This will take us through *girls who are funny* to **girls funny*. Since *girls* here consists of the null nondefinite article plus a plural noun, there is still a determiner, and the rule applies without elaboration:

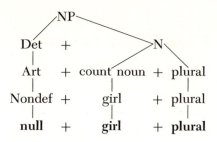

Then, adding the adjective *funny* and applying T-noun modifier, we get the following:

null + girl + plural + funny ⇉ null + funny + girl + plural

Write result sentences from the following, with the adjective between determiner and noun. Tell what the determiner is in each sentence.

    6. INSERT: Clothes were expensive.
      MATRIX: He wore clothes.
    7. INSERT: Some rabbits were hungry.
      MATRIX: He fed some rabbits.
    8. INSERT: The desk was new.
      MATRIX: The desk was delivered.
    9. INSERT: Hands are clean.
      MATRIX: Gerald has hands.
  10. INSERT: Most of the water was drinkable.
      MATRIX: Most of the water had been drunk.
  11. INSERT: Several players are good.
      MATRIX: The team has several players.
  12. INSERT: This coat is warm.
      MATRIX: Try this coat.
  13. INSERT: Angels are helpful.
      MATRIX: Angels hover over his bed at night.

Each of the following is a result sentence with one or two insert sentences embedded in it. Write the kernel insert sentence or sentences for each one. For example, if the sentence were "Curious children explored the haunted house," you would write "Children were curious" and "Something (or someone) haunted the house." You would not write "The house was haunted," because that isn't a kernel sentence.

  14. Angry men displayed the ruined books.
  15. Buckley has a new motorcycle.
  16. A smiling girl entered the little room.

17. The escaping prisoners were caught.
18. There was a lovely ring on the thin finger.
19. Hidden treasure was mentioned in the notebook.

Syntax

T-noun modifier Applied to Adverbs of Place

The noun phrase modifier transformation, which places a single-word modifier between determiner and noun, is obligatory when the modifier is an adjective. *"Girls funny entertained us" is clearly ungrammatical and must become "Funny girls entertained us." It is usually obligatory also for *ing* verbs and participles: *the faucet dripping* ⇾ *the dripping faucet, the house haunted* ⇾ *the haunted house.*

But the single-word modifier may also be an adverb of place, and here the situation is somewhat different. We might start with "The room is upstairs" and have this development:

> The room is upstairs. ⇾
> the room that is upstairs ⇾
> the room upstairs

This phrase is grammatical, and we could have a result sentence like "Mr. Weebles lodges in the room upstairs." But *the upstairs room* is also grammatical, and the sentence could be "Mr. Weebles lodges in the upstairs room."

T-noun modifier is never obligatory for adverbs of place, but it is optional for some of them. It isn't for all: *the men there,* as in "The men there knew about it," doesn't become *the there men.* But it may be applied to some adverbs of place. Rewrite the following result sentences, applying T-noun modifier.

1. He uses the entrance downstairs.
2. The thermometer outside registers eight above zero.
3. A store nearby sells sporting equipment.
4. He turned on the lamp overhead.
5. A door inside was locked.

Sometimes adverbs of place that have been thus transposed develop special meanings in the position between determiner and noun. *An inside man* doesn't usually mean the same thing as *a man inside.* Can you explain the difference?

With some adverbs of place, practice differs. Some writers use expressions like *the above paragraph* without any qualms. Others feel that this is slightly ungrammatical, that T-noun modifier should not apply when the adverb of place is *above*.

Morphology

The Adjective-forming Morpheme ic

The morpheme **ic** regularly puts the first stress on the syllable immediately preceding it. If this syllable has weak stress in the base word, the vowel there will be schwa, which gives no clue to the spelling. The stress shift brings out the vowel sound. We might say that *Byron* has the basic pronunciation /bīron/, though the vowel of the second syllable is reduced to schwa when the syllable is unstressed, so that the actual pronunciation is /bīrən/.

The morpheme **ic** is much used in English. Over a thousand words end with it. Its most common function is to make adjectives from nouns, as in these:

angel + **ic** → *angelic*   seraph + **ic** → *seraphic*

If you were asked to give a word that rhymes with the syllable before the **ic** in *angelic*, you might give *bell* or *tell*. For *seraphic*, you might give *staff* or *laugh*.

Make adjectives in **ic** from the following, and for each write another word that contains the same syllable or a rhyming syllable before the **ic**:

ocean	German	meteor	acrobat
magnet	diplomat	poet	idiot
chauvinist	Homer	Satan	alcohol

A final *e* which does not represent a final vowel sound drops before **ic** according to the regular rule: *telescope* + **ic** → *telescopic*. But letters that indicate final vowel sounds drop too, along with the sounds they indicate:

harmony + **ic** → *harmonic*   volcano + **ic** → *volcanic*

The stress shifts according to the regular rule to the syllable before the **ic**, if it isn't there already. In both *volcano* and *volcanic* the stress is on the *an*, but the vowel sound is not the same in these words. Which has /a/ and which /ā/? The vowel letter dropped in these combinations is commonly *y*, which itself sometimes stands for a morpheme.

Add **ic** to the following, making the other necessary changes:

dynamo	economy	biography	lethargy
nostalgia	rhapsody	geology	liturgy
catastrophe	panorama	hygiene	history
symmetry	parasite	geometry	satire

Some nouns add a similar morpheme **atic** instead of **ic**, sometimes with other changes as well:

> axiom + **atic** → *axiomatic*   idiom + **atic** → *idiomatic*

The same stress rule holds, and the first stress is on the *at*. Pronounce the following and give the noun on which each is built:

dogmatic	asiatic	dramatic
emblematic	enigmatic	traumatic
ecstatic	climactic	syntactic

The **ic** morpheme is also used for chemical terms, such as *sulphuric, chloric, nitric.*

Ic and **atic** are also used in a number of words which were once adjectives but are now always or usually nouns. Thus *lunatic* is made from *luna,* the Latin word for moon. It meant something like moon-struck, or, literally, moony. Since an insane person was often thought to have been affected by the moon, *lunatic* came to mean insane. Now we are more likely to use the word as a noun ("He's a lunatic") than as an adjective ("He's lunatic"). Notice that this word is an exception to the stress rule — the stress has shifted back to the first syllable.

Use each of the following in a sentence as a noun with a nondefinite article:

classic	magic	colic	hypodermic
Catholic	epidemic	mechanic	antiseptic

A number of nouns have been formed by adding *s* to adjectives in **ic**, thus producing the ending *–ics*, as in *economics, physics, semantics, ethics, civics, statistics.* Most such words, like the ones given in this list, are the names of sciences or other fields of study. But the ending occurs also in some words referring to other activities: *politics, gymnastics, athletics, tactics, logistics.*

A small problem posed by these words is whether they are to be taken as singular or plural. When they name fields of study, they are regularly singular. We say "Mathematics is difficult."

When *–ics* words do not name fields of study, they may be either singular or plural, depending on the meaning, though they are usually singular. They are plural only when they refer to personal behavior of some sort. Here are some examples:

> Politics makes an interesting career.
> His politics make me wonder about him.

> Tactics was his main interest.
> The tactics were all wrong.

When you are in doubt, singular is the best bet.

Morphology

Adverbs Made from Adjectives in ic

As you know, adverbs of manner are made by adding the morpheme **ly** to adjectives: *sweet* + **ly** → *sweetly*. Usually the morpheme **ly** simply has the shape *–ly,* as in this example.

However, when this morpheme is added to adjectives ending in *–ic,* it generally has the form *–ally:*

> tragic + **ly** → *tragically*
> chauvinistic + **ly** → *chauvinistically*

Make adverbs of manner from the following adjectives:

scientific	nostalgic	graphic
angelic	symbolic	dynamic
organic	puritanic	harmonic
heroic	generic	academic

There is only one common exception to the rule that **ly** has the form *–ally* after *–ic.* This is the word *publicly.*

Morphology

Adjectives Ending in *–ical*

A number of adjectives have the ending *–ical* instead of *–ic.* This is true first of some adjectives made from nouns ending in *–ic.* For example, *logic* is a noun, not an adjective. We make it into an adjective by adding *–al:* "That's logical." Make similar adjectives from the following:

clinic	rhetoric
music	critic

Other adjectives simply have the ending *–ical*, rather than *–ic*. They might have had *–ic*, but they don't. For example, we don't say *"They were identic" but "They were identical." Here are other examples of such words:

farcical	biblical	chemical
categorical	surgical	technical
inimical	oratorical	whimsical
grammatical	practical	vertical
nautical	lexical	numerical

There are many pairs of words, one ending in *–ic* and the other in *–ical*, which have little or no difference in meaning. *Episodic* and *episodical* are such a pair. One might say "The book had an episodic quality" or "The book had an episodical quality" and mean approximately the same thing. *Satiric/satirical, comic/comical, ironic/ironical* are other such pairs. Sometimes one member of the pair is more common than the other. One would be a good deal more likely to say "That was a tragic occurrence" than "That was a tragical occurrence."

Sometimes, however, members of *–ic/–ical* pairs differ importantly in meaning. Study the following pairs, and then make a sentence of your own with each word in *–ic* and *–ical*.

1. Mrs. Webster was a very *economical* housewife.
   The government's *economic* policy forbade a rise in wages.
2. The novel has *historic* importance.
   Grubworthy wrote a *historical* novel.
3. The *electric* current failed.
   Peter is an *electrical* engineer.

SUMMARY OF RULES

T-relative, deletion

   NP + relative pronoun + tense + be + X ⇒ NP + X

The relative pronoun and tense-*be* of an expanded noun phrase can be deleted, no matter what the source of the *be*. The *be* can come from the original rule for VP, from the auxiliary in the *be + ing* combination, or from T-passive in the *be + part.* combination. This deletion rule is the main source of the various kinds of noun phrase modifiers.

T-noun modifier

$$\text{Det} + \text{N} + \text{modifier} \Rightarrow \text{Det} + \text{modifier} + \text{N}$$

This transformation applies obligatorily when the modifier is a single-word adjective and usually when it is a single-word *ing* verb or a participle. It applies optionally when the modifier is one of certain adverbs of place.

TEST

1. Make result sentences from the following pairs of insert and matrix sentences. Use the full relative clause in the result sentence if you have to, but delete relative pronoun + tense + *be* if that sequence occurs.

    a. INSERT: The children are in the pool.
       MATRIX: The children are neighbors of ours.
    b. INSERT: Billy found the letter.
       MATRIX: The letter had been written in 1823.
    c. INSERT: Some people were waiting for a bus.
       MATRIX: We noticed some people.
    d. INSERT: A letter was opened by mistake.
       MATRIX: Jimson returned a letter.
    e. INSERT: A man was optimistic about the future.
       MATRIX: Carruthers was a man.
    f. INSERT: The table needed a coat of paint.
       MATRIX: I showed him the table.
    g. INSERT: Mother had baked the cake.
       MATRIX: The cake was delicious.
    h. INSERT: The cake was baked by Mother.
       MATRIX: The cake was delicious.

2. Rewrite the following, deleting all sequences of relative pronoun + tense + *be*.

    a. The man who is playing the violin is Edwin's father.
    b. That is the plan that was suggested by Mr. Morrison.
    c. People who are in the way will be asked to move.
    d. Give it to the girls who are outside.
    e. The birds that are sitting on the fence are ravens.

3. Each of the following noun phrases is ambiguous. For each one, write the two base sentences that might underlie it. For example, for *the fountain in the garden that they liked,* you would write "They liked the fountain in the garden" and "They liked the garden."

a. an actor in a play that everyone was enthusiastic about
b. a cupboard in a kitchen that had to be repainted
c. a mother with a child who wouldn't keep quiet
d. the worm in the apple that he was eating
e. a man with a cough that was very annoying
f. a room in a motel which had not been inspected

4. Each of the following is unambiguous. Write the base sentence that underlies each one.
   a. an actor in a play whom everybody was enthusiastic about
   b. some dishes in the kitchen that were very old
   c. a mother with some children who were whining
   d. the man in the car who was frozen
   e. the man in the car which was frozen

5. Write result sentences from the following. In each you will use an *ing* verb, a participle, or an adjective between a determiner and a noun in the matrix. Write *ing* after your sentence if the modifier is an *ing* verb, part. if it is a participle, Adj if it is an adjective.
   a. INSERT: The girls were laughing.
      MATRIX: The teacher admonished the girls.
   b. INSERT: Someone deflated the football.
      MATRIX: There was a football on the table.
   c. INSERT: The windows were soapy.
      MATRIX: The windows had to be cleaned.
   d. INSERT: Someone forgot a man.
      MATRIX: A man rang the bell.
   e. INSERT: People are forgetful.
      MATRIX: People should keep notes.
   f. INSERT: The bells were ringing.
      MATRIX: The bells kept him awake.

6. Rewrite the following sentences, applying T-noun modifier.
a. There was a window upstairs.
b. There was a stairway inside.
c. The drugstore nearby has a lunch counter.
d. We had a lot of trouble with the maid downstairs.
e. They watched the projector overhead.

7. Make words from the following:

ocean + **ic**   Homer + **ic**
economy + **ic**   lethargy + **ic**
nostalgia + **ic**   idiom + **atic**
enigma + **atic**   syntax + **atic**

tragic + **ly**   heroic + **ly**
catastrophic + **ly**   energetic + **ly**

8. Copy the following sentences, completing them with the proper past tense form of *be*.

   a. The mathematics _____ very involved.
   b. Physics _____ little studied in those days.
   c. The tactics of the army _____ badly conceived.
   d. Politics _____ an interesting profession then.
   e. His politics _____ our chief concern.

REVIEW QUESTIONS

   1. Why does the discussion of noun modification begin with the relative clause?

   2. What items are deleted in T-relative, deletion?

   3. What is the term for a construction like *waiting for us?* What is the term for a construction like *delivered by Mr. Wilkins?*

   4. Why might "A boy outside was shouting" be considered a better sentence than "A boy who was outside was shouting"?

   5. What does *ambiguous* mean?

   6. Explain the ambiguity in *the rabbit in the hutch that Jack was washing.*

   7. What keeps *an actor on a stage which had seen better days* from being ambiguous? What would be the effect if *which* were changed to *who?*

   8. What keeps *actors on a stage that were rather poor* from being ambiguous?

   9. What keeps *a baby in the crib that was smiling* from being ambiguous?

   10. What possible ambiguity is there in *a baby in the crib that needed paint?*

   11. To what kinds of words does T-noun modifier apply obligatorily? To what kind does it apply optionally?

   12. What kernel sentence underlies *hunted* in the noun phrase *a hunted man?*

   13. What kernel sentence underlies *expensive* in "She wore an expensive ring"?

   14. What effect does **ic** have on the placement of stress?

   15. What happens to a word like *harmony* when **ic** is added? What is the general rule?

   16. How are the nouns *axiom* and *idiom* made into adjectives?

17. What is the literal meaning of *lunatic?*

18. What sort of activities do most nouns ending in *–ics* stand for?

19. When may nouns in *–ics* be taken as plural?

20. How do adjectives in **ic** form adverbs of manner? What is an exception to this rule?

21. What adjective may be made from the noun *logic?*

22. *Comic* and *comical* have about the same meaning. How about *economic* and *economical?*

CHAPTER 12

Syntax

The Effect of Deletion on Nonrestrictive Clauses

We have considered this deletion rule for relative clauses:

NP + relative pronoun + tense + be + X $\Rightarrow$ NP + X

the men who were outside $\Rightarrow$ the men outside
the man who was fixing it $\Rightarrow$ the man fixing it
the men who were questioned by the police $\Rightarrow$
the men questioned by the police
the man who was angry $\Rightarrow$ the man angry

What further change must take place in the last example?

Suppose now that we apply this transformation to a nonrestrictive clause. You recall that a clause is nonrestrictive when it does not serve to specify the NP, which is specified in some other way. The NP may be a proper noun or the only one of its kind under consideration: *the girl* when there is just one girl in the room. What intonation changes take place obligatorily when the clause is nonrestrictive? What punctuation marks in writing reflect such changes?

Thus we can have this development:

INSERT: John was feeling a little better. $\Rightarrow$
John, who was feeling a little better,⎫ $\Rightarrow$
MATRIX: John came down to lunch. ⎭
RESULT: John, who was feeling a little better, came down to lunch.

This relative clause contains the sequence relative pronoun + tense + *be*. What is the relative pronoun? What word contains past tense and *be*? According to the rule, these items can be deleted to give us this result instead:

John, feeling a little better, came down to lunch.

238

Notice that we still have the intonation breaks in speech and the commas in writing.

Write similar developments for the following. You begin by turning the insert into an NP followed by a relative clause. Remember the intonation pattern and the punctuation.

1. INSERT:　Mr. Peters was reading the letter.
　　MATRIX:　Mr. Peters gasped in dismay.
2. INSERT:　The wind was blowing through the trees.
　　MATRIX:　The wind made a whistling sound.
3. INSERT:　Chicago was eager to have the convention.
　　MATRIX:　Chicago made a good offer.
4. INSERT:　Bill was up in the tree.
　　MATRIX:　Bill saw the ship's sails.
5. INSERT:　Arthur was eating peanuts.
　　MATRIX:　Arthur wanted a drink of water.
6. INSERT:　The moon was rising.
　　MATRIX:　The moon dimmed the stars.
7. INSERT:　Edgar was sorry for the child.
　　MATRIX:　Edgar bought her another ice cream cone.
8. INSERT:　Maxwell was singing in the tub.
　　MATRIX:　Maxwell had a rather strident tenor.
9. INSERT:　The captain was on the bridge at the time.
　　MATRIX:　The captain spotted the iceberg.

Here is an example in which the insert sentence is first transformed into a passive sentence, and then the deletion of relative pronoun + tense + *be* results in a participle phrase:

INSERT:　The remark offended Mary. ⇉
　　　　　Mary was offended by the remark. ⇉
　　　　　Mary, who was offended by the remark, ⇉
　　　　　Mary, offended by the remark, ⎫
MATRIX:　Mary said nothing.　　　　　　　⎬ ⇉
RESULT:　Mary, offended by the remark, said nothing.

Write similar developments for the following. You must begin by making the insert passive.

10. INSERT:　The blood alarmed Martha.
　　MATRIX:　Martha called a doctor.
11. INSERT:　A bullet wounded General Highfield.
　　MATRIX:　General Highfield could give no orders.
12. INSERT:　The explosion ruined the hotel.
　　MATRIX:　The hotel had to be evacuated.

13. INSERT: The police questioned Mr. Appleby.
    MATRIX: Mr. Appleby confessed everything.
14. INSERT: The invitation pleased Hubert.
    MATRIX: Hubert decided to buy a new suit.
15. INSERT: Mr. Whitside ordered the furniture.
    MATRIX: The furniture came to us by mistake.
16. INSERT: A mule kicked the driver.
    MATRIX: The driver went to the hospital.
17. INSERT: The quarrel spoiled the party.
    MATRIX: The party broke up early.

Syntax

T-relative, deletion, ing

Some *ing* phrases used as modifiers cannot be derived simply by
deletion of relative pronoun + tense + *be* because the verb does not
occur in the kernel sentence in the *ing* form. For example, the modifier in "John, knowing all about it, explained everything" cannot be
derived this way. There is no such kernel sentence as *"John was
knowing all about it," therefore no such relative clause as *who was
knowing all about it*, and therefore no way of deriving *knowing all
about it* by deletion of *who was*.

Such modifiers can be accounted for by a slightly different deletion
transformation, one in which the relative pronoun is deleted and tense
is replaced by *ing*. We can abbreviate this transformation T-relative,
deletion, ing:

$$\text{NP + relative pronoun + tense + X} \Rightarrow \text{NP + ing + X}$$

Here is an example with the morphemes of the sentence given
above:

INSERT: **John + past + know + all + about + it + 2-3-1** $\Rightarrow$
          **John + 2-3-2 + who + past + know + all + about +
          it + 2-3-2** $\Rightarrow$
          **John + 2-3-2 + ing + know + all + about +
          it + 2-3-2**

MATRIX: **John + past + explain + everything + 2-3-1** $\Big\} \Rightarrow$

RESULT: **John + 2-3-2 + ing + know + all + about + it +
          2-3-2 + past + explain + everything + 2-3-1**

The affix transformation applies automatically to switch not only
past + explain but also **ing + know**. The actual result sentence will
be "John, knowing all about it, explained everything."

Write the actual result sentences that can be made from the following with the application of T-relative, deletion, ing.

1. INSERT: John saw his chance.
   MATRIX: John leaped for the door.
2. INSERT: Alice had a bad headache.
   MATRIX: Alice lay down for a while.
3. INSERT: Witherwood jumped to his feet.
   MATRIX: Witherwood protested violently.
4. INSERT: Mrs. Albemarle realized the danger.
   MATRIX: Mrs. Albemarle intervened.
5. INSERT: Sergeant Smathey understood Private Juke.
   MATRIX: Sergeant Smathey spoke to him alone.

Syntax

Sentence Modifiers

We have so far distinguished the different functions of the *ing* phrase in "John, knowing all about it, explained" and "Anyone knowing all about it should explain" by saying that it is nonrestrictive in the first and restrictive in the second. In the *John* sentence it doesn't tell which John is meant but merely adds another idea to the sentence as a whole. In the *anyone* sentence, however, it restricts the meaning of *anyone*. The subject doesn't mean "anyone at all" but "anyone who knows all about it."

We have also used the term *noun phrase modifier* for the function of clauses that are restrictive and of structures resulting from such clauses by deletion. But we haven't used that term for nonrestrictive structures, and we won't. We will say instead that nonrestrictive structures function as *sentence modifiers*. In "John, knowing all about it, explained" we will say that the *ing* phrase doesn't modify *John*, though, as we shall see more precisely later on, it has a close grammatical relationship with *John*. We shall say instead that its function is to modify the whole matrix sentence "John explained." It tells not only who explained but why he did or how he was able to.

Each of the following sentences contains one sentence modifier or one noun phrase modifier. Point out the modifier, and tell which it is.

1. Marjorie, feeling ill, went to bed.
2. It was a very small oyster.
3. He has a friend who lives in Albuquerque.
4. She lives in Morro Bay, which is near San Luis Obispo.
5. Ralph, who knew horses, raised the bid.

6. People who owned property were worried.
7. Mr. Bicycles is a forgotten man.
8. Lucille, pleased by the compliment, fished for another.
9. The picture on the piano looked familiar.
10. They filled the bags with coal, which is rather heavy.

Syntax

T-sentence modifier

We have seen that when what is left of a restrictive relative clause after the deletion of relative pronoun + tense + *be* is a single-word *ing* verb or participle or adjective, the word is obligatorily shifted to a position between determiner and noun. We called this transformation T-noun modifier:

Det + N + modifier $\Rightarrow$ Det + modifier + N

a man smiling $\Rightarrow$ a smiling man
a man forgotten $\Rightarrow$ a forgotten man
a man angry $\Rightarrow$ an angry man

But when the relative clause is nonrestrictive — is what we have called a sentence modifier — the situation is a bit different. Suppose we begin with "John, who was smiling, answered the question." If we delete relative pronoun + tense + *be*, we have this:

John, smiling, answered the question.

If the modifier *smiling* had resulted from deletion from a restrictive relative clause, we would now have to apply T-noun modifier and put *smiling* between the determiner and the noun. But T-noun modifier cannot apply to a structure where the NP is *John*, because *John*, being a proper noun, has no determiner. And in fact we can leave *smiling* where it is. "John, smiling, answered the question" is quite grammatical.

The *ing* verb doesn't have to shift, and neither does a participle or an adjective, if it derives from a nonrestrictive clause:

John, who was forgotten, wandered off by himself.
John, forgotten, wandered off by himself.
John, who was angry, refused to answer.
John, angry, refused to answer.

You have seen that a nonrestrictive modifier does not have to shift when the NP is a proper noun. But what if the NP is a Det + N structure? Can the sentence modifier be moved to a position between determiner and noun? Consider the following situation. Suppose there are three boys and one girl in a room. In such a situation, we might have this sentence:

> The girl, who was laughing, moved away.

Since there is only one girl, the relative clause cannot serve to tell which girl is meant. It is nonrestrictive and a sentence modifier. It can be reduced by deletion:

> The girl, laughing, moved away.

But this will now not transform into "The laughing girl moved away," because then the *ing* verb would have become restrictive, telling which girl was meant: "The laughing girl moved away, while the weeping one stayed put." But that is not its function here, since there is only one girl in the room.

A sentence modifier will not move to the position between determiner and noun and remain a sentence modifier. However, it will move to a position before the whole noun phrase. The following sentences have the same meaning:

> The girl, laughing, moved away.
> Laughing, the girl moved away.

Notice that the comma representing the 2-3-2 intonation break moves too. In speech, there is a pitch rise on *laughing* followed by a drop to pitch level 2 and a pause, and this must be shown in writing by a comma. *"Laughing the girl moved away" is ungrammatical.

We will call this transformation, which switches a sentence modifier to a position before the whole noun phrase, T-sentence modifier and formulate it thus:

> NP + 2-3-2 + modifier $\Rightarrow$ modifier + 2-3-2 + NP

The 2-3-2 identifies the modifier as a sentence modifier, not a noun phrase modifier.

The transformation applies to the various noun phrase types that are followed by sentence modifiers:

> John, smiling, answered the question. $\Rightarrow$
>   Smiling, John answered the question.
> John, forgotten, wandered off by himself. $\Rightarrow$
>   Forgotten, John wandered off by himself.
> I, hurrying, opened the door. $\Rightarrow$
>   Hurrying, I opened the door.

When the NP is a personal pronoun, as in the last example, the transformation is virtually obligatory.

The comma between the sentence modifier and the matrix sentence is always obligatory in constructions of this sort. Expressions like *smiling John* or *angry John* may occur, but when they do, we are aware that there is something special or peculiar — in short, ungrammatical — about them.

Rewrite the following, applying T-sentence modifier.

1. Wilbur, insulted, left the room.
2. Mrs. Jensen, screaming, fell to the floor.
3. The car, skidding, hit a tree.
4. He, indignant, walked away.
5. Carstairs, applauding, rose to his feet.
6. The ship, damaged, radioed for help.
7. Agnes, alarmed, turned off the gas.
8. She, fainting, collapsed on the sofa.

Syntax

T-sentence modifier Applied to Phrases

It is a condition of T-noun modifier that it apply only to single words: *ing* verbs, participles, adjectives, and, optionally, some adverbs of place. It does not apply to phrases deriving from restrictive relative clauses. *The girl smiling at Harry* does not become **the smiling at Harry girl*. *A child eager to help* does not become **an eager to help child*.

There is no such restriction on T-sentence modifier. Phrases as well as single words can switch to the position before the NP, becoming separated from it by the 2-3-2 of speech and the comma of writing:

> John, smiling, answered the question. ⇉
>> Smiling, John answered the question.
> John, smiling at Mr. Simms, answered the question. ⇉
>> Smiling at Mr. Simms, John answered the question.
> The child, eager to help, climbed onto the roof. ⇉
>> Eager to help, the child climbed onto the roof.

Rewrite the following, applying T-sentence modifier.

1. Miss Perkins, lifting the lid, peered into the barrel.
2. Alvin, encouraged by the result, continued the experiment.

3. Chicago, determined to have the convention, made new concessions.
4. My father, hearing the news, ran into the street.
5. I, being only a small boy at the time, didn't understand the difficulty.
6. Ginger, annoyed at the disturbance, went to the door.
7. Miss Sweet, famished, ate seven sandwiches.
8. The poodle, needing a haircut, had to be taken to the barber shop.
9. Irma, anxious about Gwen, picked up the telephone.
10. The director, watching the play, smiled his approval.

Syntax

Dangling Modifiers

In "Smiling, John explained," *John* is in the subject relationship to both *smiling* and *explained*. This is a necessary consequence of the sequence of transformations, since *John* must be here the subject of both insert and matrix sentence:

INSERT: John was smiling. $\Rightarrow$
               John, who was smiling, $\Rightarrow$
               John, smiling, $\Rightarrow$
               Smiling, John $\left.\right\} \Rightarrow$
MATRIX: John explained.
RESULT: Smiling, John explained.

Now consider *"Smiling, an explanation was offered." This can only go back to an ungrammatical insert sentence:

INSERT: *An explanation was smiling. $\Rightarrow$
               *an explanation, which was smiling, $\Rightarrow$
               *an explanation, smiling, $\Rightarrow$
               *smiling, an explanation $\left.\right\} \Rightarrow$
MATRIX: An explanation was offered.
RESULT: *Smiling, an explanation was offered.

We are now getting into the area of the grammar in which ungrammaticality is fairly likely even for people who speak English as a native language. For such people grammatical mistakes occur mostly not in simple sentences but in complex ones — those resulting from one or more double-base transformations. In building up the complex sentence, the speaker or writer is apt to lose track of the underlying relationships and build with base sentences that are ungrammatical.

Nobody would make a simple sentence like *"An explanation was smiling." But in the series of transformations leading to *"Smiling, an explanation was offered," we lose control of the grammar and put the smile on the face of the explanation.

This particular error is common enough to have a name: *dangling modifier.* It is a general rule that the insert sentence supplying a sentence modifier must have the same subject as the matrix. John was smiling and John explained: "Smiling, John explained." Similarly:

INSERT: Ginger was annoyed at the disturbance.⎫ →
MATRIX: Ginger went to the door.   ⎬ ⇒
RESULT: Annoyed at the disturbance, Ginger went to the door.

INSERT: My father heard the news.   ⎫ →
MATRIX: My father ran into the street. ⎬ ⇒
RESULT: Hearing the news, my father ran into the street.

When the insert sentence has a different subject, the sentence modifier dangles; it isn't grammatically connected to the matrix. Here are some other examples, with the ungrammatical insert sentences given in parentheses:

* Seeing the results, a shout went up. (*A shout saw the results.)
* Having plenty of time, a movie was suggested. (*A movie had plenty of time.)
* Injured in action, San Diego planned a welcome-home party for Sergeant Smith. (*San Diego was injured in action.)

Write the ungrammatical insert sentences that underlie the following.

1. *Peeping into the rain barrel, a gasp escaped Miss Perkins.
2. *Marooned on the island, no hope remained.
3. *Hungry as a wolf, seven sandwiches didn't seem too much.
4. *Anxious to get home early, the report had to wait.
5. *Telephoning the garage, a car was ordered.
6. *Being only four years old, my mother forgave me.
7. *Written by a great artist, Lucille enjoyed the novel.
8. *Dipping a spoon into the ice cream, the restaurant began to shake.
9. *Thinking about other things, the canary was forgotten.
10. *Being a grandfather himself, the baby looked pretty cute to Witherspoon.

Syntax

A Cause of Dangling Modifiers

We have observed that dangling modifiers result when the writer
or speaker loses track of the simple sentences underlying the complex ones and produces result sentences that imply impossible inserts
— or, at least, unintended inserts. "Looking into her eyes, Mirabelle
was adored by John" contains the apparent insert sentence "Mirabelle
looked into her eyes." This is grammatical enough, but it presumably
isn't what is intended. It was probably not Mirabelle's looking into
her eyes that made John adore her, but his doing so.

This example illustrates a common cause of dangling modifiers.
The sentence would be all right if the matrix sentence were active:

> Looking into her eyes, John adored Mirabelle.

This identifies John as both the looker and the adorer. But if the
writer starts out with something like this in mind and for some reason
makes the matrix passive, the relationships become confused. This
doesn't mean that the sentence modifier always dangles when the
matrix is passive. The following sentence is grammatical:

> Looking into her eyes, Mirabelle was alarmed by their condition.

One must be careful with a passive matrix to see that it supplies
the insert with the proper subject. Also the switch from the active
to the passive will often weaken the sentence as well as make it
ungrammatical.

Repair the following by making the matrix active, thus expressing
the NP of *by* + NP as the subject of the matrix.

1. *Walking across the street, an accident was seen by Lucy.
2. *Flying into a rage, my hat was handed to me by Ellen's
   father.
3. *Astonished at the accusation, an explanation was offered by
   Mr. Pirbright.
4. *Believing the child had a fever, Dr. Summers was called by
   Mrs. Neville.
5. *Feeling a little foolish, the lid was lifted by Miss Perkins.

The street runs both ways of course. Sometimes the passive is what
is wanted. Repair these by making the matrix passive.

6. *Charging up the hill, a bullet struck Sergeant Davis.
7. *Having a violent temper, few people liked Lorinda.

8. *Waiting for a bus, a coughing spell overcame Ernest.
9. *Being very important, Mr. Winthrop himself answered the letter.
10. *Angry at the delay, the apology only irked Davidson.

Verbs of the *seem* class sometimes have the same effect as the passive: they put the intended subject into the predicate. For example, we might have this:

*Looking into her eyes, Mirabelle seemed adorable to John.

This could be corrected in various ways, but if the sentence modifier is retained, *John* must return to the subject position:

Looking into her eyes, John found Mirabelle adorable.

Correct the following by changing the matrix in whatever way seems best. Keep the sentence modifier as it is. In 14 and 15 you must supply a subject.

11. *Listening carefully, the explanation sounded convincing to Henry.
12. *Taking a large bite, the pie tasted delicious to Evelyn.
13. *Knowing Albert, the plan seemed foolish to us.
14. *Uncertain about the outcome, the idea appeared dangerous.
15. *Being very hungry, the food smelled wonderful.

Syntax

Sentence Modifiers After the Matrix

Sentence modifiers of the type we have been considering occur most commonly within the matrix sentence or before it. But they can occur after it too. All of these are grammatical:

> John, smiling, explained.
> Smiling, John explained.
> John explained, smiling.

For a particular sentence, one position might be less likely than the others, but all are grammatical. Remember that in all positions the 2-3-2 of speech and the comma of writing travel with the sentence modifier.

Write two sentences for each of the following, putting the sentence modifier before the matrix in the first and after it in the second.

1. Mrs. Beaver, thinking it a joke, didn't reply.

2. Alice, hoping for rescue, held on grimly.
3. William, insulted by the suggestion, declined firmly.
4. The young lady, feeling a little faint, had gone upstairs.
5. General Merrymount, not knowing what else to do, retreated.
6. Mr. Wheeler, hurt by the unexpected attack, refused to debate further.
7. The lioness, hidden in the tall grass, waited patiently.

A possible complication arises when the predicate of the matrix sentence contains a noun phrase. Compare these sentences:

> John met his future wife, waiting for a bus.
> John met his future wife waiting for a bus.

In the first sentence it is John who is waiting for the bus, in the second his future wife, and only the comma distinguishes the meanings.

It might be pointed out that in the second sentence the *ing* phrase is not a restrictive noun phrase modifier. In the normal expectation, John has only one future wife, so *waiting for a bus* cannot serve to tell which one he met. Neither is it the result of deletion of relative pronoun + tense + *be*, for the relative clause would have the intonation break and the comma in that case:

> John met his future wife, who was waiting for a bus.

The *ing* phrase here is part of a somewhat complicated transitive construction explained later.

Syntax

Appositives

We may notice one more kind of sentence modifier resulting from T-relative, deletion. The X of the sequence NP + 2-3-2 + relative pronoun + tense + *be* + X may be a noun phrase, from the predicate of an insert sentence like "John was the leader" or "The hotel was a firetrap." The sentence modifier develops in the usual way:

INSERT: John was the leader. $\Rightarrow$
             John, who was the leader, $\Rightarrow$
             John, the leader,   }
MATRIX: John made the decision. } $\Rightarrow$
RESULT: John, the leader, made the decision.
                    or:

INSERT: The hotel was a firetrap. ⇒
              the hotel, which was a firetrap, ⇒
              the hotel, a firetrap,   }
MATRIX: Nobody had inspected the hotel.   } ⇒
RESULT: Nobody had inspected the hotel, a firetrap.

Such a noun phrase functioning as a sentence modifier in this way
has a special name; it is called an *appositive*. *Appositive* is a word
from Latin meaning "put along side." In the result sentence "John,
the leader, made the decision," the transformation has put the noun
phrase *the leader* alongside the subject of the matrix, *John*. It is said
to be *in apposition* to *John*. The punctuation rules are the same as
those for the other sentence modifiers we have examined: two commas
if the appositive comes in the middle of the matrix, one if it comes at
the end.

Point out the appositives in the following, and give the insert sentence that each derives from.

1. Mabel, the cook, orders the groceries.
2. Mr. Hamilton, a friend of Father's, gave me a job.
3. She showed us the new dress, a cotton print.
4. The soldiers, Hessians from Germany, had been hired to fight
   the colonists.
5. Margaret introduced us to her sister, a pretty girl.
6. His uncle, a razor-blade manufacturer, lives in the southern
   part of Idaho.
7. He was very fond of the dog, an appealing mongrel.
8. Miracle Airlines, a prosperous firm, doesn't spend much on
   upkeep.

Make result sentences from the following. Use an appositive from
the insert sentence in each.

9. INSERT: The colt was a beautiful animal.
   MATRIX: Gonzales bought the colt.
10. INSERT: His new pencil sharpener is a Wilkinson X32.
    MATRIX: His new pencil sharpener cost a lot of money.
11. INSERT: Sally's aunt is a Scandinavian.
    MATRIX: Sally's aunt speaks seven languages.
12. INSERT: My piano teacher was Miss Biagini.
    MATRIX: My piano teacher wants to play concerts.
13. INSERT: His new car was a blue job with yellow wheels.
    MATRIX: Untermeyer arrived in his new car.
14. INSERT: His grandfather is an old grammarian.

MATRIX: Chris gets help from his grandfather.
15. INSERT: The book was a novel by Peabody Keane.
    MATRIX: The book didn't hold my attention.
16. INSERT: The tooth was a decayed molar.
    MATRIX: The dentist pulled the tooth.

The sentence modifier transformation is not so common for appositives as it is for other structures, but it occurs:

> Carstairs, a man of his word, brought the papers.
> A man of his word, Carstairs brought the papers.

Apply T-sentence modifier to the following.

17. His new car, a six-thousand-dollar bomb, impressed everyone.
18. Her husband, a handsome man of thirty, seemed perfectly charming.
19. Meatball, a mongrel of uncertain parentage, was much loved by the children.
20. The lunch, a rabbit stew of some sort, proved almost inedible.
21. The dentist, a rather unhappy person, looked into my mouth.

Both of the following are possible sentences:

> A rather unhappy person, the dentist looked into my mouth.
> A rather unhappy person, the dentist, looked into my mouth.

There is a difference between the structures, however. In the first, *a rather unhappy person* is the appositive, with its position switched by the sentence modifier transformation, and the matrix sentence is "The dentist looked into my mouth." In the second, *the dentist* is the appositive, and the matrix sentence is "A rather unhappy person looked into my mouth."

Morphology

The Morpheme ity

Another stress-shifting morpheme is **ity**, which makes nouns out of adjectives: *solid/solidity*. Which syllable has the principal stress in *solid?* Which has it in *solidity?* What is the vowel sound of the second syllable in *solid?* What is it in *solidity?* The spelling of the schwa vowel in adjectives like *solid* presents no problem if one thinks of the corresponding noun in **ity**.

Make nouns in **ity** from the following adjectives, and use the mark to show the syllable that has the first stress, like this: *solídity*.

rapid	fluid	timid	valid
total	local	frugal	genial
real	logical	essential	artificial
human	urban	Christian	uniform
solemn	modern	Latin	feminine
familiar	similar	popular	polar
civil	agile	senior	prior
active	passive	objective	festive

The vowel sounds of *bite, Pete, mate, duke,* and *rope* may be called the *vowel-consonant –e,* or VCe vowels, because they are commonly rendered by a vowel letter followed by a consonant letter and then final *e.* Their dictionary symbols are /ī/, /ē/, /ā/, /ū/, and /ō/. When the final syllable of an adjective has any of these vowels except /ū/, it changes to a simple vowel sound when **ity** is added:

/ī/ → /i/:   asinine/asininity
/ē/ → /e/:   serene/serenity
/ā/ → /a/:   profane/profanity
/ō/ → /o/:   verbose/verbosity

Add **ity** to the following, and note the change in the vowel sound in the syllable before the suffix. If you are uncertain of the pronunciation, consult a dictionary.

jocose	severe	extreme	sublime
inane	benign	mediocre	austere

What consonant sound besides /t/ occurs in *benignity* but not in *benign?*

A number of adjectives ending in *–ile,* like *futile,* are pronounced in either of two ways. *Futile* may be pronounced with schwa in the second syllable — /fyutəl/ — or with /ī/ — /fyutīl/. The former is the more common American pronunciation, the latter the more common British one. Pronounce the following with /ī/ in the second syllables, and then add **ity:**

puerile	sterile	hostile	facile
docile	juvenile	virile	volatile

We have noted **able** as a morpheme added to verbs to make adjectives: *change* + **able** → *changeable.* These adjectives may then add **ity** to become abstract nouns, but the ending is not *–*ablity* but *–ability: changeable* + **ity** → *changeability.* Make nouns by adding **ity** to the following:

reliable	probable	venerable
vulnerable	questionable	endurable
notable	accountable	inscrutable

When the adjective ends in the –*ible* form of **able,** the noun ending is –*ibility*. Unfortunately there is still no sound clue to the spelling; both the *a* of –*ability* and the first *i* of –*ibility* are usually pronounced schwa. Make **ity** nouns of the following:

credible	accessible	plausible
audible	intelligible	reversible
tangible	infallible	admissible

Some words undergo other sound and spelling changes when **ity** is added. For instance, *profound* + **ity** is not **profoundity* but *profundity*. Write the adjective underlying each of the following:

| clarity | humility | religiosity |
| curiosity | generosity | perpetuity |

Morphology

The Morpheme ous

English has over a thousand adjectives ending in the morpheme **ous.** Most of these adjectives are unusual words, many of them scientific: *marmoraceous, diadelphous, testudinarious*. But a number of them are quite common: *dangerous, vivacious, scandalous*. Some adjectives in **ous** are taken directly from Latin or made with Latin roots. Others are made by adding the morpheme to an English noun: *scandal* + **ous** → *scandalous*. The adjective in **ous** means pertaining to or having the quality of the noun.

Make adjectives by adding **ous** to the following:

peril	study	harmony	envy
grace	outrage	malice	courage
venom	miracle	ruin	ulcer

That **ous** has some effect on the placement of stress can be seen by noting pairs like *harmony/harmonious, miracle/miraculous, courage/courageous*, but the situation is a little complicated. *Harmonious*, for instance, has the first stress on the third syllable from the end, but *courageous* on the second syllable from the end.

The basic effect of **ous** is to place the main stress two syllables back from it — that is, on the third syllable from the end of the word. The following illustrate this effect. Give the underlying word for each, and note how the stress has shifted:

perfidious   ceremonious   felonious
industrious   injurious   homonymous

In words like *scandalous* and *dangerous*, the stress doesn't shift because it is already, in the underlying noun, two syllables back from the **ous**.

What, then, about *courageous*, which seems to be an exception to the rule? The explanation is that the single syllables now spelled *–geous*, *–cious*, and *–ceous*, as in *courageous*, *officious*, and *crustaceous*, were once two syllables. The letters *e* and *i*, which with *c* indicate the sound /sh/ in *officious* and *crustaceous*, and the letter *e*, which with *g* makes the sound /j/ in *courageous*, once stood for separate vowel sounds. Therefore each word had one more syllable than it does today. When this was true, these words followed the general rule, with the first stress two syllables back from the **ous**.

Make adjectives in **ous** from the following:

advantage   vice   avarice

Many adjectives in **ous** are related to nouns in **ion** or **ity**, especially **ity**. We have pairs like *capacious/capacity* and *suspicious/suspicion*. As these examples show, we do not usually add the noun ending to the **ous** adjective; we do not say *suspiciousion* or *capaciosity*. The noun ending just replaces the **ous**. The vowel changes that we noted for pairs like *asinine/asininity* and *profane/profanity* take place here too. What two different vowel sounds are represented by the second *a* in *capacious* and *capacity*?

Write the related noun ending in **ion** for each of the following adjectives:

cautious   contagious   rebellious
seditious   gumptious   contentious

Write related nouns in **ity** for the following. Point out changes in vowel sound.

audacious   pugnacious   tenacious
vivacious   ferocious   commodious
contemporaneous   spontaneous   incredulous
barbarous   promiscuous   incongruous

Morphology

The Adjective Morpheme ly

Of the two morphemes commonly spelled *–ly*, the more common is the one used to make adverbs of manner from adjectives: *rapid/ rapidly, superfluous/superfluously*. This is the one that Huckleberry Finn doesn't ordinarily bother with.

The other **ly** morpheme is used to make adjectives of nouns:

friend + **ly** → *friendly*   cost + **ly** → *costly*

This is of course only one way of making adjectives from nouns, and it is commonly added to only a few dozen nouns.

Make adjectives in **ly** from the following nouns, and use each adjective in a noun phrase after *very* and before a noun. For example, for *friendly* you might write *a very friendly person;* for *costly* you might write *very costly material.*

lord	world	coward	prince
beggar	scholar	time	leisure
home	queen	man	woman

Because of the *–ly* ending, these adjectives are sometimes construed and used as adverbs of manner: "They drove leisurely," "He spoke very friendly." People who are conservative in their use of English frown on this usage, however, and avoid it. One cannot avoid it by adding the other **ly** morpheme; **friendlily* and **leisurelily* are scarcely grammatical. Instead, one contrives to express the idea in a noun phrase or a *be* predicate:

They had a leisurely drive.
Their drive was leisurely.
He spoke in a friendly way.

SUMMARY OF RULES

T-relative, deletion, ing

NP + relative pronoun + tense + X $\Rightarrow$ NP + ing + X

This accounts for *ing* verbs and phrases used as noun phrase modifiers or sentence modifiers when the *ing* form cannot occur in the insert sentence. The rule as given is for noun phrase modifiers. It is the same for sentence modifiers except that 2-3-2 is added after the NP and the X on both sides of the arrow.

T-sentence modifier

NP + 2-3-2 + modifier ⇉ modifier + 2-3-2 + NP

The 2-3-2 identifies the modifier as a sentence modifier. The transformation is similar to T-noun modifier except that it puts the modifier before the whole noun phrase instead of between determiner and noun, it is not obligatory for single words, and it applies optionally for phrases as well as for single words.

TEST

1. Rewrite the following, applying T-relative, deletion or T-relative, deletion, ing.
    a. Abe, who was watching the horses, didn't see the car.
    b. Colonel Stone, who knew that a spaceship was due, had ordered the mooring crew to their stations.
    c. My roommate, who was indignant about the interruption, flounced out of the room.
    d. John, who understood the consequences, backed down.
    e. Marcia, who had a slight cold, stayed in bed.

2. Each of the following contains one noun phrase modifier or one sentence modifier. Point out the modifier, and tell which it is.
    a. We saw a goat that looked hungry.
    b. Barney, raising his voice, called the cattle home.
    c. It was a staggering blow.
    d. People owning property must pay taxes.
    e. The Captain, a Scandinavian, kept to himself.
    f. She lives in Chicago, which is north of Joliet.
    g. Mr. Fretwill has a beautiful home.
    h. Anna nodded her head, frowning slightly.

3. Rewrite the following, applying T-sentence modifier.
    a. Alvin, clearing his throat, entered the conversation.
    b. Mrs. Dartley, upset by the news, sat down on the sofa.

4. Make result sentences of the following, with the application of T-relative, deletion and T-sentence modifier. Write just the result sentence.
    a. INSERT: Angelo was beloved by everyone.
       MATRIX: Angelo was always welcome.
    b. INSERT: Ralph was thinking hard.
       MATRIX: Ralph hit on a solution.

c. INSERT: Corporal Flannery was a brave man.
   MATRIX: Corporal Flannery refused to retreat.
d. INSERT: We were uncertain about the weather.
   MATRIX: We postponed the trip.

5. Write the ungrammatical insert sentences embedded in the following.
   a. *Knowing Felix, an idea occurred to Harriet.
   b. *Fresh from the oven, Mrs. Abernathy served us a delicious cake.
   c. *Posted without stamps, Nelda never got the letter.

6. Correct the following by changing the matrix from passive to active or from active to passive.
   a. *Dipping into the barrel, an apple was taken by Henry.
   b. *Having a violent temper, nobody liked him.
   c. *Using all his skill, the child was saved by Dr. Bentley.

7. Write nouns in **ity** from the following adjectives:

similar	hostile	essential	extreme
benign	reliable	profound	clear

8. Make adjectives in **ous** from the following:

outrage	harmony	capacity	miracle
audacity	sedition	promiscuity	spontaneity

REVIEW QUESTIONS

1. What items are deleted in T-relative, deletion?
2. What is the kernel insert sentence embedded in "Mr. Appleby, questioned by the police, confessed everything"?
3. The *ing* phrase in "John, knowing all about it, confessed everything" cannot be derived by the simple deletion transformation. Why not?
4. In T-relative, deletion, ing, what does the morpheme **ing** take the place of?
5. Is a restrictive relative clause a noun phrase modifier or a sentence modifier?
6. T-noun modifier puts a modifier between a determiner and a noun. Where does T-sentence modifier put it?
7. Does T-sentence modifier apply to restrictive or nonrestrictive structures?
8. Is T-sentence modifier an obligatory transformation?

9. What is ungrammatical, or at least unusual, about "Smiling Ralph answered the question"?

10. What is the apparent insert sentence of *"Having plenty of time, a movie was suggested"? What is the term for a grammatical error of this sort?

11. What connection is there between the use of the passive and dangling modifiers?

12. What subclass of verbs sometimes has the same effect in relation to dangling modifiers as the passive?

13. Give an example of a sentence modifier occurring after the matrix sentence.

14. What is the literal meaning of *appositive*?

15. From what kind of kernel verb phrase does the appositive derive?

16. Explain the structural difference between "A mongrel of uncertain parentage, Meatball was loved by the children" and "A mongrel of uncertain parentage, Meatball, was loved by the children."

17. What is the effect of the morpheme **ity** on stress?

18. What is a VCe vowel?

19. What are two possible pronunciations of *juvenile*?

20. What change takes place in the morpheme **able** when **ity** is added?

21. What is the usual stress effect of the morpheme **ous**? What is the explanation of *courageous* as an exception to this stress effect?

22. What are the different functions of the two morphemes commonly spelled –*ly*?

CHAPTER 13

Syntax

Sentences Used in NP Functions

Any sentence at all can be transformed and used in a noun phrase function — subject, complement, object of a verb — by simply having the word *that* put at the beginning of it. It doesn't matter how long and complex the sentence is:

I knew that they had the mumps.

I knew that several of those thirty little boys who attend the school which is located at the end of the street on which I live had the mumps.

Here the simple sentence "They had the mumps" and the complex one beginning with *Several of* and ending with *had the mumps* are used in the predicates of the matrix sentences as objects of the verb *knew.*

The transformation that readies the insert sentence for such use is very simple:

$$S \Rrightarrow \text{Sub} + S$$

Sub is an abbreviation of the word *subordinator,* which means literally "that which puts something in a lower rank." Here it makes a sentence into a part of a sentence. The most common subordinator by far is the word *that,* but there are others, such as *whether, if, although, unless.* A structure transformed by a subordinator is called a *subordinate clause.* We call the transformation the *subordinating transformation,* or T-subordinate clause.

A relative clause is subordinate too, in the general sense of the word: it expresses tense, but it is only part of a sentence. However, it differs in structure from that to which we give the technical term *subordinate clause.* Considered apart from the noun phrase or sentence that it modifies, the relative pronoun has a noun phrase function — subject, object, etc. For instance, in the expanded noun phrase *the boy who made the speech,* the relative clause is *who made the speech,* and the relative pronoun is *who.* The relative pronoun *who* appears in the subject function like *the boy* in the kernel sentence "The boy made the speech." If we remove *who* from *who made the speech,* we have left just the verb phrase *made the speech.*

Tell what the relative clause is in each of these noun phrases. Tell what would be left of the relative clause if the relative pronoun were omitted.

> the road which had been repaired
> the house that burned down

In *the house that he bought,* the relative clause is *that he bought.* Here if we remove the relative pronoun, what is left is *he bought.* This has a subject and a verb, but it isn't a kernel sentence, because the verb phrase isn't complete. *Buy* is transitive and must have an object. We don't just buy, we buy *something.*

Thus when the relative pronoun is removed from a relative clause, what is left is not a complete insert sentence. But since the transformation that makes subordinate clauses is simply S $\Rightarrow$ Sub + S, if we take away the Sub we have our original sentence. Consider "I think that he bought the house." The subordinate clause is *that he bought the house,* and we know that it is subordinate, not relative, because if we take off the *that,* we have the full insert sentence: "He bought the house."

Each of the following sentences contains either a relative clause or a subordinate clause. Point out each clause and tell which it is. In these examples, if you can remove the word *that* and still have a grammatical insert sentence, the clause is subordinate, not relative.

1. I think that Harry has left.
2. The man that was here has left.
3. He's the one that I meant.
4. That Gertrude knew all about it was obvious.
5. He found that it couldn't be done.
6. Is this the colt that he bought?
7. This is the girl that you were speaking to.
8. I'm sure that Mrs. Perkins lifted the lid.
9. That Sam might forget his speech was our greatest worry.
10. We guessed that the hikers were lost.

Relative clauses and subordinate clauses cannot be distinguished solely by their functions. All of the relative clauses that we have considered so far have functioned as noun phrase modifiers or as sentence modifiers, but we will see that they can have NP functions too — as subject, object, etc. We will for the present consider subordinate clauses only in NP functions, but we will see later that they may also occur as noun phrase or sentence modifiers.

The description of the insertion of the subordinate clause into the matrix sentence differs a little bit from the description of double-base transformations considered so far. Here one noun phrase position in the matrix sentence is simply marked as NP; it doesn't contain actual words. The insert sentence with a subordinator prefixed to it fills that position:

INSERT: John was there. $\Big\}\Rightarrow$
MATRIX: I discovered + NP.
RESULT: I discovered + that + John was there.

INSERT: John was there. $\Big\}\Rightarrow$
MATRIX: NP + was not generally known.
RESULT: That + John was there + was not generally known.

INSERT: John was there. $\Big\}\Rightarrow$
MATRIX: The truth is + NP.
RESULT: The truth is + that + John was there.

Tell whether the subordinate clause in each result sentence above functions as subject, object of a verb, or complement.

Subordinate clauses with *that* do not commonly function as objects of prepositions. However, they have another function which is not common for ordinary noun phrases. They may occur after certain adjectives in what we may call an *adjective complement* function.

INSERT: Mrs. Perkins lifted the lid. $\Big\}\Rightarrow$
MATRIX: I'm sure + NP.
RESULT: I'm sure + that + Mrs. Perkins lifted the lid.

Write result sentences from the following, using *that* as the subordinator. Tell the function of each subordinate clause.

11. INSERT: David speaks German.
    MATRIX: I think + NP.
12. INSERT: Sally had to leave early.
    MATRIX: NP + was a pity.
13. INSERT: He had fixed it the last time.
    MATRIX: His argument was + NP.
14. INSERT: The box had been moved.

MATRIX: Mrs. Lee was certain + NP.
15. INSERT: I was somewhat to blame.
    MATRIX: NP + was perfectly true.
16. INSERT: Allan would win.
    MATRIX: We were confident + NP.
17. INSERT: Mrs. Swaray didn't know anything about it.
    MATRIX: Captain Swink's belief is + NP.
18. INSERT: There was no point in arguing.
    MATRIX: I saw + NP.

Though a sentence like the result of Number 12 — "That Sally had to leave early was a pity" — is perfectly grammatical, it is much more likely that the sentence will take a slightly different form: "It was a pity that Sally had to leave early." We insert *it* as the subject of the matrix sentence and put the subordinate clause at the end. The transformation can be called T-subordinate clause, it:

$$\text{subordinate clause} + \text{Aux} + \text{X} \Rightarrow$$
$$\text{it} + \text{Aux} + \text{X} + \text{subordinate clause}$$

Apply the transformation to the following.

19. That the presents weren't delivered was a shame.
20. That Tom hadn't seen the letter himself was quite true.
21. That Alison was Polish was not known.
22. That an agreement could be reached was not clear.
23. That he had never read the book was interesting.

Syntax

Other Subordinators

Though *that* is the most common subordinator, others are used for special meanings. The word *whether* expresses a doubt of some sort. When *whether* is used, the matrix sentence is often negative:

INSERT: Harold will come. ⎫
MATRIX: I don't know + NP. ⎬ ⇒
RESULT: I don't know + whether + Harold will come.

Commonly *or not* is added either after the *whether* or at the end of the insert:

I don't know whether or not Harold will come.
I don't know whether Harold will come or not.

Make result sentences from the following using *whether* and *or not*.

1. INSERT: He knew about it.
   MATRIX: He didn't say + NP.
2. INSERT: Nelda delivered the message.
   MATRIX: I'm not sure + NP.
3. INSERT: She agrees.
   MATRIX: NP + isn't important.

The *it* transformation can be applied to the last result sentence:

> It isn't important whether she agrees or not.

The subordinator *if* is used in sentences with similar meanings:

INSERT: He knows about it. ⎫
MATRIX: I wonder + NP.   ⎬ ⟹
RESULT: I wonder + if + he knows about it.

Write result sentences from the following using *if*.

4. INSERT: You heard the story.
   MATRIX: I don't know + NP.
5. INSERT: He can join us.
   MATRIX: Jack didn't say + NP.

Syntax

Subordinate Clauses as Noun Phrase Modifiers

Like relative clauses, subordinate clauses can function as modifiers of noun phrases, though this function isn't so common for subordinate clauses:

INSERT: Jack knew about it. ⎫
MATRIX: The idea is absurd. ⎬ ⟹
RESULT: The idea that Jack knew about it is absurd.

In this result sentence, *that Jack knew about it* is a subordinate, not a relative, clause, because *that* has no function within the clause. The insert sentence is exactly as it was, with the subordinator *that* added. If *that* is removed, what remains of the clause is a grammatical sentence: "Jack knew about it." Compare the following sentence:

> The idea that Jack had was a good one.

Here the matrix is "The idea was a good one," and the relative clause *that Jack had* modifies the noun phrase *the idea*. If we remove

the relative pronoun *that* from the relative clause, what remains of
the clause, **Jack had,* is not a grammatical sentence.

Each of the following sentences contains a relative clause or a
subordinate clause. Point out each clause and tell which it is. If what
follows *that* in the clause can be a sentence by itself, the clause is
subordinate; if not, it's a relative clause.

1. His suggestion that we should leave early was a good one.
2. The suggestion that was offered next was a foolish one.
3. The neckties that Bob bought were rather flashy.
4. My feeling that Father Reilly was worried about something kept
   growing.
5. That's like the lie that Hitler wasn't interested in conquest.
6. The fear that men from Mars were landing caused panic in a
   number of cities.
7. The fear that caused the panic resulted from a radio play.

When the subordinate clause functions as an object, the subordinator *that* may be omitted:

> I knew that he was worried.
> I knew he was worried.

But when the clause functions as subject or as a noun phrase
modifier, the *that* cannot be omitted. Both **"He was worried was
obvious"* and **"The idea Jack knew about it is absurd"* are ungrammatical, though the second is less so than the first.

Syntax

Relative Clauses as Substitutes for Noun Phrases

So far we have seen relative clauses functioning only as noun
phrase modifiers and sentence modifiers, with this transformation of
the insert for the restrictive type:

$$X + NP + Y \Rightarrow NP + \begin{Bmatrix} who \\ that \\ which \end{Bmatrix} + X + Y$$

For certain meanings, *where* and *when* can replace adverbials of
place and time in the insert to form relative clauses modifying noun
phrases. In such use, *where* and *when* can be called *relative adverbs.*
The insert part of the transformation is like that for T-wh, adverbial

of place and T-wh, adverbial of time, except that it does not apply to a morpheme string resulting from the question transformation T-yes/no.

Here are examples of the transformation of the insert with the relative adverbs *where* and *when:*

INSERT: He was born in the town. ⇾
            the town where he was born ⎫ →
MATRIX: The town is now famous.   ⎭ ⇾
RESULT: The town where he was born is now famous.

INSERT: He might have spoken at the time. ⇾
            the time when he might have spoken ⎫ →
MATRIX: The time had passed.   ⎭ ⇾
RESULT: The time when he might have spoken had passed.

Such clauses are also used in the functions of noun phrases:

INSERT: He bought it somewhere. ⎫ →
MATRIX: I don't know + NP.   ⎭ ⇾
RESULT: I don't know where he bought it.

INSERT: It happened then.   ⎫ →
MATRIX: NP + is a mystery. ⎭ ⇾
RESULT: When it happened is a mystery.

Make result sentences from the following, using *where* or *when* according to whether the insert contains an adverbial of place or an adverbial of time.

   1. INSERT: He lives here.
      MATRIX: This is + NP.
   2. INSERT: Ronald left last month.
      MATRIX: Do you remember + NP?
   3. INSERT: The plane will arrive sometime.
      MATRIX: NP + will be announced later.
   4. INSERT: The notebook is on the shelf.
      MATRIX: I'm not certain + NP.
   5. INSERT: Aunt Kathryn was going home.
      MATRIX: We wondered + NP.
   6. INSERT: We should wake him later.
      MATRIX: NP + was a problem.

When these clauses occur in the subject function, the *it* transformation can be applied:

Where he lives is not known. $\Rightarrow$
It is not known where he lives.

When the element replaced in the insert is a noun phrase, and when the relative clause has a noun phrase function in the result, the transformation is like the relative clause transformation studied earlier, but *that* does not occur. *Who,* or its object form *whom,* does:

INSERT: John was there. $\Big\}\rightarrow$
MATRIX: I wonder + NP.
RESULT: I wonder who was there.

INSERT: You saw John. $\Big\}\rightarrow$
MATRIX: I wonder + NP.
RESULT: I wonder whom you saw.

In conversation one would probably say "I wonder who you saw." But *"I wonder that you saw" is impossible.

Make result sentences from the following, replacing the italicized NP of the insert with *who* if it is a subject and with *whom* if it is an object.

  7. INSERT: They invited *Mr. Wimple.*
     MATRIX: Do you know + NP?
  8. INSERT: *Jane* was bringing the sandwiches.
     MATRIX: I forgot + NP.
  9. INSERT: *Arnold* gave the story to the newspapers.
     MATRIX: Ralph told me + NP.
10. INSERT: He had married *Gertrude Spivin.*
     MATRIX: I wasn't certain + NP.
11. INSERT: David worked with *Mr. Anderson.*
     MATRIX: Do you remember + NP?
12. INSERT: *Harold* broke the news to Mr. Smith.
     MATRIX: The teacher asked + NP.
13. INSERT: The majority voted for *Ellen.*
     MATRIX: The report told + NP.
14. INSERT: *George* promised us a surprise.
     MATRIX: I knew + NP.

What is not used as a relative pronoun in standard English when the clause modifies a noun phrase. *"The boy what brings the groceries wants his money" is substandard. However, *what* is used when the clause has a noun phrase function and the replaced element does not refer to a person:

INSERT: *Something* hit him.
MATRIX: He didn't know + NP. $\Big\}\rightarrow$
RESULT: He didn't know what hit him.

INSERT: Abe wanted *a letter of introduction.*
MATRIX: Did you find out + NP? $\Big\}\rightarrow$
RESULT: Did you find out what Abe wanted?

Make result sentences from the following. Use *what* if the italicized noun phrase does not refer to a person, *who* or *whom* if it does.

15. INSERT: Ralph needed *some paper.*
    MATRIX: I asked Mary + NP.
16. INSERT: *Bert* threw the switch.
    MATRIX: The superintendent wanted to know + NP.
17. INSERT: Max tied up the dog with *a necktie.*
    MATRIX: I wonder + NP.
18. INSERT: Mabel is visiting *an aunt.*
    MATRIX: Do you recall + NP?
19. INSERT: Benny had *a monkey* in the bag.
    MATRIX: I discovered + NP.
20. INSERT: George is helping *someone.*
    MATRIX: Does anybody know + NP?

Which is also used in clauses with NP functions, but *which* contrasts in meaning with *what*. *What* refers to something in general, but *which* refers to one of two or more things. Compare the following:

> I don't know what he wanted.
> I don't know which he wanted.

The *which* implies something like "which of those three books" or "which of those eight lampshades."
   Which in these clauses may also refer to people:

> I wonder whom he invited.
> I wonder which he invited, Ed or Bill?

We didn't include *which* in the rule for *wh* questions, but we may note now that it occurs in them, with the same contrast with *who* and *what:*

> Whom do you want?
> What do you want?
> Which do you want?

Syntax

Relative Pronouns with *-ever*

The relative pronouns that we have considered, and also the relative adverbs, occur also with the morpheme **ever** attached: *whoever, whatever, wherever,* etc. The **ever** has a kind of "of all" meaning — "who of all people," "where of all places."

Write result sentences from the following, replacing the italicized item with the proper word in *-ever*. The first one is done for you.

1. INSERT: You invite *someone.*
   MATRIX: NP + is all right with me. } ⟹
   RESULT: Whomever you invite is all right with me.
2. INSERT: *Someone* shows up.
   MATRIX: NP + will be welcome.
3. INSERT: You like *the first one.*
   MATRIX: Take + NP.
4. INSERT: John does *things.*
   MATRIX: NP + is done well.
5. INSERT: He lives *somewhere.*
   MATRIX: NP + is home to him.
6. INSERT: He can come *sometime.*
   MATRIX: NP + will be all right.

Syntax

Inner and Outer Structure

You will have noted that we have to specify two things about clauses that function as NP's: (1) What is the nature of the relative clause itself and, in particular, what kind of function does the relative word have in the insert sentence; (2) what is the function of the clause in the result sentence — subject, object, complement, adjective complement. This two-fold consideration makes the structure somewhat complex and sometimes causes us to get mixed up about what relative word should be used.

Take for example the sentence "I wonder who called her." This must have the following development:

INSERT: Someone called her. } ⟹
MATRIX: I wonder + NP.
RESULT: I wonder who called her.

The choice of *who* instead of *whom* or *what* depends on what we may call the inner structure of the clause — the makeup of the insert sentence. We use *who* instead of *whom* because the relative pronoun replaces the subject of the insert, *someone,* not the object. We use *who* instead of *what* because *someone* refers to a person. But the choice of *who* instead of *that* depends on the outer structure of the clause — its relation to the other items in the result sentence. Had the clause been a noun phrase modifier, we might have used *that:* "This is the man that called her." But since it functions as object in the result, we can't: * "I wonder that called her" is ungrammatical.

Suppose now we have this:

INSERT: *Someone* wants to come.
MATRIX: Send an invitation to + NP.

What will the result sentence be?

If you said "Send an invitation to whoever wants to come," you were correct. The relative pronoun must be *whoever* and not *whatever* because of the inner structure: *someone* refers to a person. But also it must be *whoever* and not *whomever* because of the inner structure: the replaced NP functions as a subject, not an object. There is a tendency here to let the outer structure take over and govern the choice of *whoever/whomever.* That is, we may tend to write * "Send an invitation to whomever wants to come," because the relative pronoun looks like the object of the preposition *to.* But the relative *clause,* not the pronoun, is the object of *to.* The pronoun is the subject of the relative clause, and so *whomever* is here ungrammatical.

Make result sentences from the following, using *whoever* or *whomever* according to the function of the italicized noun phrase in the insert.

1. INSERT: He liked *someone.*
   MATRIX: Albert brought + NP.
2. INSERT: *Someone* liked Albert.
   MATRIX: Geraldine liked + NP.
3. INSERT: *Someone* wins the contest.
   MATRIX: Mrs. Baxter will pin the ribbon on + NP.
4. INSERT: Steve sends *someone.*
   MATRIX: We will talk with + NP.
5. INSERT: *Someone* has room for him.
   MATRIX: Billy will go with + NP.
6. INSERT: *People* came along.
   MATRIX: Mr. Appleby talked to + NP.

7. INSERT: You need *helpers.*
   MATRIX: Call on Captain Larsen for + NP.
8. INSERT: She praised *people.*
   MATRIX: He would praise + NP.

An even more complicated situation arises in a sentence like this one:

Whoever you think will fit in will be all right with me.

Since the relative pronoun is immediately followed by *you think,* it is easy to construe the pronoun, wrongly, as the object of *think* and to use the form *whomever.* There is no such insert sentence as *"You think someone" and therefore no such clause as *whomever you think.* The pronoun is the subject of the clause *whoever will fit in,* going back to an insert like "Someone will fit in." The development is something like this:

INSERT: Someone will fit in.⎤ →
MATRIX: You think + NP.   ⎦ ⇒
RESULT: You think (that) someone will fit in.
NEW INSERT: You think *someone* will fit in. ⎤ →
NEW MATRIX: NP + will be all right with me. ⎦ ⇒
FINAL RESULT: Whoever you think will fit in will be all right with
                me.

On the other hand, "Whomever you think Jack should invite will be all right" is correct, because the clause is *whomever Jack should invite,* going back to the first insert "Jack should invite someone."
   Write the first inserts — like "Someone will fit in" and "Jack should invite someone" — for the following.

9. Whoever he thought had criticized him was his enemy.
10. Whomever they believe John dislikes has their sympathy.
11. Whoever he finds has studied hard gets a passing mark.
12. Whomever you think George was talking to should be found immediately.
13. Whoever you feel needs help will get it as soon as possible.
14. Whomever you think the class elected, you're wrong.

When you're in doubt about which pronoun to use in this construction (and nearly everyone is in doubt about it sometimes) and when you can't figure it out, it's a good deal safer to take a chance on *whoever.* Not only are the averages with you but both *who* and *whoever* are commonly used against the rule.

Syntax

Gender

English noun phrases have three genders — masculine, feminine, and neuter. This is so because we have the three third person singular personal pronouns *he, she,* and *it.*

Whenever we use one of the pronouns *he, she,* and *it* to refer to a noun phrase occurring earlier, we have to make up our mind whether that noun phrase is masculine, feminine, or neuter:

> Ernest lifted it. He was very strong.
> Ernestine lifted it. She was very strong.
> The wind lifted it. It was very strong.

By and large, masculine noun phrases are those referring to males, feminine those referring to females, and neuter those referring to lifeless things. However, the correspondence isn't exact; the grammar doesn't always march with the biology. A notable distinction is that ships, though lifeless, are considered feminine:

The *Pride of Boston* is overdue. She should have arrived yesterday.

This usage is often carried over, somewhat informally, to machines and devices of all sorts:

The car was missing yesterday, but she's running all right now.

Many beings that are either male or female biologically are neuter grammatically. This is generally true of beings about whose sex we are ignorant or incurious:

> I slapped at the mosquito, but it got away.
> The kitten couldn't open the box, but it kept trying.
> The baby is learning to walk, but it is still unsteady.

We often make human babies neuter, particularly when we are called on by their parents to admire them but can't remember whether they are he's or she's: "Isn't it cute!"

Still, English gender is closer to biology than that of most languages. In the Romance languages, there are only two genders, masculine and feminine, and sticks and stones, cotton and wool, must be one or the other. An Italian orange is feminine, while an orange tree is masculine. German has a neuter gender, as English does, but it uses its genders with considerable caprice: male German mice are feminine, and German young ladies are grammatically neuter.

English has a problem in that is has no common gender. It has no singular pronoun which can mean either masculine or feminine. Therefore, we have some uncertainty about what pronoun to use in referring to a word like *people* or *everyone* when these designate both women and men or boys and girls. The most awkward solution is to use both the masculine and the feminine pronoun:

Everyone should raise his (or her) hand when he (or she) is ready.

We usually try to avoid this by following the convention that, grammatically, men are more important than women. For reference to mixed groups, we use just the pronoun *he:*

Everyone should raise his hand when he is ready.

Naturally, if only girls are involved, we use the forms of *she:*

Everyone should raise her hand when she is ready.

Sometimes we avoid the issue by pluralizing the noun phrase to which the pronoun refers:

All the boys and girls should raise their hands when they are ready.

Fortunately the third person plural pronoun, *they,* does not make gender distinctions.

Morphology

Feminine Morphemes

English has some feminine suffixes which abet the personal pronouns in maintaining the masculine-feminine distinction. The most important is the morpheme **ess.** This is sometimes added directly to nouns to give the meaning "female": *lion* + **ess** → *lioness.* Sometimes it is added instead of **er** to nouns such as *murder* to give a definitely feminine meaning: *murder* + **ess** → *murderess.*

More often it is added to nouns which have the **er,** "one who does," morpheme. The *–er* or *–or* then collapses to *r:*

actor + **ess** → *actress*   waiter + **ess** → *waitress*

Add **ess** to the following. What is the feminine of *duke?*

tiger	god	steward	shepherd
duke	baron	govern	sorcery
heir	mayor	instructor	ambassador

A few other suffixes are used spottily to indicate feminine gender. The ending *–ette* occurs in *suffragette,* which meant a woman working for women's suffrage, or voting rights. This is also used in proper names: *George/Georgette.* The ending *–enne* occurs in words like *tragedienne,* a female tragedian, or actor in tragedies. Another feminine ending occasionally used is *–ix,* as in the words *executrix, administratrix,* and *progenetrix.* It is somewhat more common simply to use the suffix *–woman,* just as the suffix *–man* is used: *laundryman/laundrywoman.*

Names of animals often occur in masculine-feminine pairs — like *buck* and *doe* for deer. But as most people become more removed from wild or rural life, these vocabulary distinctions come less readily, and when we need to make the distinction, we are likely merely to prefix *he* or *she* and speak of, for example, a *he-goat* or a *she-goat* instead of a *billy* or a *nanny.*

Morphology

Diminutives

Most languages have morphemes that express a meaning of littleness. These are sometimes used in affection, sometimes in contempt. Such morphemes are called *diminutives,* from the Latin word meaning to make little. English has some diminutives, though it doesn't use them as freely as most languages use theirs.

One diminutive is the ending spelled *–ie* or *–y.* This is quite commonly attached to proper names: *John/Johnny, David/Davie.*

Sometimes the ending *–ie* or *–y* is added to common nouns: *bird/birdie, aunt/aunty, lad/laddie.* Of course one uses such words as *aunty* or *laddie* only in familiar situations, as in talking in one's family, with close friends, or to children.

Another diminutive morpheme is **kin,** as in *lambkin,* "a little lamb." *Tummykin* is a double diminutive: *stomach* + **ie** + **kin.** The ending *–kin* occurs in a number of words in which the notion of littleness has been forgotten: *manikin, napkin, bumpkin, pumpkin.*

The diminutive morpheme **ling** is also used in English, again rather sparingly: *prince* + **ling** → *princeling,* "a little prince." Other examples are *seedling* and *duckling.* Find the etymologies of the following:

      darling   fledgling   foundling   gosling

Still another diminutive morpheme is **let:** *brook* + **let** → *brooklet,*

"a little brook." This occurs somewhat more commonly than **kin**
or **ling.**

Finally, we have the ending –*ette*. We noticed that this is used
occasionally as a feminine ending. It is also used as a diminutive. A
cigarette is a little cigar. Other examples are *maisonette, novelette,*
and *wagonette.*

The normal effect of –*ette* is to take the first stress itself: *briquétte,*
pipétte. In some words, there is variation, however. *Etiquette* has the
stress on the first syllable, and *cigarette* is pronounced *cigarétte* by
some people and *cígarette* by others.

But where many languages, such as Russian and Italian, clap a
diminutive on almost every other noun, English uses its diminutives
with much reserve. An American mother is more likely to express
affection to her offspring with the word *little* than with diminutive
suffixes. Instead of saying "Come, sweetling, let's get off our clothes-
kins and have a nice naplet," she says "Come, little sweet, let's get
off our little clothes and have a nice little nap." Well, of course, she
might say "little sweetie."

SUMMARY OF RULES

T-subordinate clause

$$S \Rightarrow Sub + S$$

Any sentence can be equipped for use in a noun phrase function by
having a subordinator put before it.

T-subordinate clause, it

$$subordinate\ clause + Aux + X \Rightarrow$$
$$it + Aux + X + subordinate\ clause$$

A subordinate clause functioning as subject may give place to *it* and
appear instead at the end of the matrix sentence.

This chapter describes various relative clause types in addition to
the ones studied earlier. The rules are not formulated for these, but
they are essentially the same as the T-relative rule already given,
with different relative pronouns (*what, whoever,* etc.) or with the
relative adverbs *where* and *when* in clauses deriving from insert
sentences with adverbials of place and time.

TEST

1. Copy each clause and tell what kind it is.
a. I believe that Miss Wilson is joining us.
b. This is the chess set that I was telling you about.
c. The notion that he had was a pretty good one.
d. The notion that Tom had lost the game was silly.
e. Where is the book that I was reading?
f. I'm afraid that you'll have to go now.

2. Make result sentences from the following, using *where* or *when* according to whether the insert contains an adverbial of place or one of time.
  a. INSERT: I left it somewhere.
     MATRIX: I can't remember + NP.
  b. INSERT: He will arrive some time.
     MATRIX: Nobody knows + NP.
  c. INSERT: Bob lives in Boston.
     MATRIX: Can you tell me + NP?
  d. INSERT: Alison heard about it earlier.
     MATRIX: I wonder + NP.

3. Write result sentences from the following. After each write a numeral to tell whether the subordinate clause functions as (1) subject, (2) complement, (3) object of a verb, or (4) adjective complement.
  a. INSERT: You are Polish.
     MATRIX: Steve thinks + NP.
  b. INSERT: Maxwell would betray me.
     MATRIX: NP + never crossed my mind.
  c. INSERT: I left it here.
     MATRIX: I'm certain + NP.
  d. INSERT: Marriage was a mistake.
     MATRIX: Mr. Weller felt + NP.
  e. INSERT: We would leave first.
     MATRIX: The idea was + NP.

4. Apply T-subordinate clause, it to each of the following sentences.
a. That Chuck had written the letter never crossed my mind.
b. That we were going to have some rain was obvious.
c. That you could join us is splendid.
d. That we were in the way was plain.
e. Whether she finds it or not doesn't matter.

5. Make result sentences from the following, using the relative pronoun appropriate for the italicized noun phrase.

a. INSERT: We needed *some ribbons.*
   MATRIX: The salesgirl asked + NP.
b. INSERT: *Bob* found the wallet.
   MATRIX: Does anyone know + NP?
c. INSERT: I told *someone.*
   MATRIX: I don't remember + NP.
d. INSERT: Susan is staying with *Mrs. Felix.*
   MATRIX: Do you recall + NP?
e. INSERT: He had *something* in the basket.
   MATRIX: We couldn't guess + NP.
f. INSERT: *Mr. Tompkins* will bring the cucumbers.
   MATRIX: Please find out + NP.

6. Make feminine nouns by adding a feminine suffix to each of the following:

    tiger   comedian   executor   duke   gentle

7. Make diminutives by adding one of the diminutive suffixes studied to each of the following:

    John   aunt   lamb   novel
    seed   lord   book   cigar

8. Write result sentences from the following, replacing the italicized item with the proper relative pronoun in *–ever.*

a. INSERT: I did *various things.*
   MATRIX: NP + turned out badly.
b. INSERT: You can get here *later.*
   MATRIX: NP + will be all right.
c. INSERT: *Somebody* wants it.
   MATRIX: NP + can have it.
d. INSERT: You like *someone.*
   MATRIX: Bring + NP.
e. INSERT: *Somebody* wins the essay contest.
   MATRIX: Mr. Hassel will present the award to + NP.
f. INSERT: *Someone* needs it.
   MATRIX: Leave it for + NP.
g. INSERT: You think *someone* can use it.
   MATRIX: NP + ought to have it.

REVIEW QUESTIONS

1. What is the most common subordinator? What are some others?
2. How does a subordinate clause differ from a relative clause?
3. What is the term for the function of the subordinate clause in "I'm sure that he was here"?
4. How is one more likely to express a sentence like "That Benny was hiding is true"?
5. What expression is often used along with *whether* in subordinate clauses?
6. What is the function of the subordinate clause in "The idea that Jack knew about it is absurd"?
7. When can the subordinator *that* not be omitted?
8. What is the term for the word *where* in "The place where he left it has not been found"? What kind of clause is *where he left it?*
9. What relative pronoun does not occur when the relative clause functions as a noun phrase rather than as a modifier of a noun phrase?
10. What is ungrammatical about *"The boy what brings the groceries wants his money"?
11. What is the difference between *what* and *which* in relative clauses functioning as noun phrases?
12. What morpheme is sometimes added to the relative pronoun when the clause functions as a noun phrase?
13. What is meant by inner and outer structure, so far as a relative clause is concerned?
14. Why do we say *whoever* instead of *whomever* in "Send an invitation to whoever wants to come"? Is the choice dictated by inner or outer structure?
15. Why do we say *whoever* instead of *whomever* in "Whoever you think could use it can have it"? What is the insert sentence underlying the relative clause?
16. What are the three genders of English? What words indicate the gender of English noun phrases?
17. When is *it* likely to be used to refer to male or female beings?
18. When is *she* used to refer to lifeless things?
19. What problem does English have in regard to gender? How does one get around the difficulty?
20. What is the most common feminine morpheme? What are some others?
21. Give an example of a use of **ess** that might be offensive to the female concerned.
22. What is a *vixen?*

23. What might one call a male goat besides a billy?

24. What is the literal meaning of *diminutive?* What are some of the diminutives of English?

25. How do speakers of English often express endearment other than by using diminutive suffixes?

CHAPTER 14

Syntax

The Possessive Transformation

One of the eight inflectional morphemes of English is **possessive**. This has the same form in speech as the regular plural of nouns and the *s* form of the present tense of verbs, consisting of one of three sounds depending on the final sound of the noun to which it is attached:

/əz/:	/juj/-/jujəz/	(judge-judge's)
/s/:	/mak/-/maks/	(Mac-Mac's)
/z/:	/boi/-/boiz/	(boy-boy's)

In writing, the possessive is written *apostrophe-s*, except when the noun ends in the regular *s* plural; in that case, it is represented by just the apostrophe:

the boy/the boy's   the men/the men's
the boys/the boys'

The most common meaning of the possessive is "having," and we can show this meaning by deriving the possessive from insert sentences containing the verb *have*. The subject of such a sentence takes the possessive morpheme and replaces a definite article in a matrix sentence:

INSERT: Mr. Smith had a problem. ⎫ ⇒
MATRIX: The problem was using will and shall. ⎭
RESULT: Mr. Smith's problem was using will and shall.

Here is another example, this time written in morpheme strings. The morpheme **possessive** is abbreviated **poss.**

INSERT: **Jack + present + have + a + bride** ⎫ ⇒
MATRIX: **the + bride + present + be + Lydia** ⎭
RESULT: **Jack + poss. + bride + present + be + Lydia**

What two morphemes have replaced the definite article of the matrix?
What is the actual result sentence?

Of course the definite article to be replaced can occur anywhere
in the matrix sentence:

> INSERT: **Jack + present + have + a + bride** ⎫ →
> MATRIX: **Lydia + present + be + the + bride** ⎭
> RESULT: **Lydia + present + be + Jack + poss. + bride**

What is the actual result sentence?

When the subject of the insert sentence is a personal pronoun,
special phonological rules give the form of the possessive noun phrase:
I + **poss.** → *my*, *he* + **poss.** → *his*. What are *she* + **poss.**, *we* +
poss., *they* + **poss.**, *you* + **poss.**, *it* + **poss.**?

Write result sentences from these. Write both the strings of morphemes and the actual result sentences.

> 1. INSERT: **Gloria + past + have + a + headache**
>   MATRIX: **the + headache + past + be + worse**
> 2. INSERT: **he + present + have + a + pony**
>   MATRIX: **the + pony + present + be + at + the + ranch**
> 3. INSERT: **everyone + past + have + a + trip**
>   MATRIX: **the + trip + past + be + part. + ruin**
> 4. INSERT: **a + man + present + have + a + home**
>   MATRIX: **the + home + present + be + the + castle**
> 5. INSERT: **he + present + have + a + castle**
>   MATRIX: **a + man + poss. + home + present + be + the +
>   castle**
> 6. INSERT: **we + past + have + a + boat**
>   MATRIX: **we + past + sell + the + boat**

Syntax

Recursiveness in T-possessive

Like most double-base transformations, T-possessive is recursive. It
can keep occurring in the same sentence so long as there is a definite
article for the subject of the insert and the possessive morpheme to
replace. Suppose we start with the following development:

> INSERT: **the + boy + present + have + a + uncle** ⎫ →
> MATRIX: **the + uncle + present + be + Mr. Williams** ⎭
> RESULT: **the + boy + poss. + uncle + present + be +
>   Mr. Williams**

The result has a new definite article in the noun phrase **the + boy.** This result sentence can therefore become the matrix of a new transformation:

INSERT: **she + present + have + a + boy**
MATRIX: **the + boy + poss. + uncle + present + be + Mr.** $\Big\rbrace \Rightarrow$
              Williams
RESULT: **she + poss. + boy + poss. + uncle + present + be +**
              Mr. Williams

What will the final result sentence be? This cannot become a new matrix for still another possessive transformation, because the last one didn't put in the word *the.* But there is no grammatical rule that says the transformation can be performed only twice or only any particular number of times.

Apply the possessive transformation recursively as follows. Make a result sentence from the first insert and matrix. Then use that result as the matrix for the second insert. Then use that result as the matrix for the third insert, and so on. Write the sentences, not the strings.

FIRST INSERT: The child has a wagon.
FIRST MATRIX: The wagon is broken.
SECOND INSERT: The employer has a child.
THIRD INSERT: The father has an employer.
FOURTH INSERT: The brother has a father.
FIFTH INSERT: The friend has a brother.
SIXTH INSERT: I have a friend.

Could the transformation be repeated a seventh time?

Remember that grammatical is not the same as good. The final result sentence that you came out with is quite all right grammatically but it is quite poor stylistically. One ordinarily avoids letting a particular transformation recur as often as this one does.

Syntax

The Possessive Transformation for Inanimate Noun Phrases

All of the subjects of the insert sentences used so far to illustrate the possessive transformation have referred to animate beings: *Mr. Smith, Gloria, I, everyone, the boy, the employer,* etc. The possessive morpheme is mostly used when the subject of the *have* sentence is animate. When the subject is inanimate, it is most common to use a variation in which the morpheme **of** appears before the noun phrase from the insert and both come after a noun phrase in the matrix:

INSERT: **the + table + present + have + a + top** $\Big\}\Rightarrow$
MATRIX: **the + top + present + be + dirty**
RESULT: **the + top + of + the + table + present + be + dirty**

Make similar result sentences from the following.

1. INSERT: **the + house + present + have + a + roof**
   MATRIX: **the + roof + present + need + repair + plural**
2. INSERT: **the + trouble + past + have + a + start**
   MATRIX: **that + past + be + the + start**
3. INSERT: **the + city + past + have + light + plural**
   MATRIX: **we + past + see + the + light + plural**
4. INSERT: **the + room + past + have + a + corner**
   MATRIX: **it + past + be + in + the + corner**
5. INSERT: **the + book + that + I + past + be + ing + read + past + have + illustration + plural**
   MATRIX: **the + illustration + plural + past + be + beautiful**

The rule that we use the possessive morpheme with animate noun phrases and **of** with inanimate ones is not very rigid. The possessive is used sometimes with inanimate noun phrases:

The course's requirements were severe.

And sometimes the *of* form is used with animate noun phrases:

The hind leg of the cat had to be amputated.

But ordinarily the rule is adhered to. We say "John's leg," not *"the leg of John," and "the leg of the table," not *"the table's leg."

Make result sentences from the following. Use the possessive morpheme if the subject of the insert sentence is animate, the *of* form if it isn't. Write the sentences, not the strings.

6. INSERT: Gabriel had a complaint.
   MATRIX: The complaint was justified.
7. INSERT: The car had a windshield.
   MATRIX: The windshield had to be replaced.
8. INSERT: The street has an end.
   MATRIX: Our house is at the end.
9. INSERT: A boy has trust.
   MATRIX: The trust should not be betrayed.

10. INSERT: The desk had drawers.
    MATRIX: We looked in the drawers.
11. INSERT: The dog has a dish.
    MATRIX: The dish was empty.

Semantics

Meanings of the Possessive Morpheme

The morpheme that we call *possessive*, **poss.**, does not always mean simple possession. It does in something like *John's hat*, which we could derive from an insert sentence indicating possession with the verb *own:* "John owns a hat." But we could not derive *John's mother* from * "John owns a mother." Both of these meanings, however, are included in the more general meaning of *have* and can be derived from "John has a hat" and "John has a mother."

But there are some meanings of the possessive that cannot be derived from *have* inserts either. *Sheridan's plays* will not derive from "Sheridan had plays" unless we mean something like *Shakespeare's plays that Sheridan owned*. If we mean plays that Sheridan wrote, we must derive the noun phrase as follows:

INSERT: Sheridan wrote plays. $\Big\} \Rightarrow$
MATRIX: The plays are interesting.
RESULT: Sheridan's plays are interesting.

Write result sentences from the following.

1. INSERT: Mark told stories.
   MATRIX: We listened to the stories.
2. INSERT: Talenti made a speech.
   MATRIX: The speech was very persuasive.
3. INSERT: Dickens wrote novels.
   MATRIX: Sam Weller is a character in one of the novels.

For the last sentence you wrote either *Dickens's novels* or *Dickens' novels*. Either is correct for a proper noun ending in a sound spelled *s*.

Another use of the possessive is to give a measurement, usually of time, as in *a week's delay*. Obviously the insert sentence cannot be * "The week has a delay" but must be something like "The delay lasted a week."

Other examples of the use of the possessive to give a measurement are: *a moment's notice, a day's work, a dollar's worth*. What others can you think of?

In another meaning, the noun forming the possessive is the subject of a verb in the insert related to the noun modified in the result. This may be a noun with the same form as the verb, like *reply* in the following:

INSERT: **Bob + past + reply**
MATRIX: **the + reply + past + be + inaudible** $\Big\} \rightarrow$
RESULT: **Bob + poss. + reply + past + be + inaudible**

What is the actual result sentence?

Or the word modified by the noun in the possessive may be the insert verb plus a noun-forming morpheme:

INSERT: **Bob + past + produce + something**
MATRIX: **the + produce + ion + past + be + large** $\Big\} \rightarrow$
RESULT: **Bob + poss. + produce + ion + past + be + large**

What is that result sentence?

Make up sentences using the subjects of the sentences below in the possessive to modify nouns related to the verbs. For example, if the sentence were "Bob hoped for the best" you might write "Bob's hope was forlorn." If it were "Bob insisted," you might write "We were surprised by Bob's insistence." You will need to add noun-forming morphemes.

4. Margaret answered.
5. Pedro embarked.
6. Allen waited.
7. Phoebe resented it.
8. Stuyvesant resisted.
9. Witherwood fascinated people.
10. Triphammer started well.
11. Montford confessed all.

Sometimes the word taking the possessive morpheme is the object of a transitive verb in the insert sentence:

INSERT: **someone + past + humiliate + Don**
MATRIX: **the + humiliate + ion + past + be + complete** $\Big\} \rightarrow$
RESULT: **Don + poss. + humiliate + ion + past + be + complete**

Make up result sentences from the following, using the possessive with the object of the verb to modify a noun related to the verb. For "Some people pursued Ralph," you could write "Ralph's pursuers were gaining."

12. The voters defeated Senator Grube.
13. Wealth corrupted Uncle Louie.
14. The problem confused Morgan.
15. The captors tormented Ferguson.
16. Miss Wilson punished Susie.
17. The incident mortified Mr. Rumbold.

Sometimes the noun in the possessive form modifies a noun related to an adjective:

INSERT: He was tolerant.
MATRIX: He was known for the tolerance. } ⇒
RESULT: He was known for his tolerance.

Of what two morphemes is *his* composed in the result sentence?

Make up result sentences from the following, using the subject in the possessive form to modify a noun related to the adjective. For "Martin is curious" you might write something like "Martin's curiosity gets him into trouble."

18. Bella is faithful.
19. Philip is persistent.
20. Maxine is hostile.
21. Gerald is weak.
22. Louise is agile.

For some adjectives the noun-forming morpheme of the transformation is **ty**:

The country is safe.
The country's safety is our prime concern.

Make up similar sentences with the possessive from the following.

23. Helen is loyal.
24. The soldiers were cruel.
25. The woman was frail.

The *of* form has some special meanings too. One is called the *appositive* meaning because it is somewhat similar to the appositive construction. An example is *the city of Denver*. This is like *the city, Denver* except that *of* is used instead of the intonation break. Other examples are *the state of New York, an accusation of bribery, the month of June.*

Another kind is called the *partitive* because the modified noun names a part and the *of* phrase names the whole from which the part is taken. *A cup of tea, a pound of coffee, a regiment of soldiers* are examples. Give others.

Syntax

Another Kind of Relative Clause

Review the major rule for T-relative in the summary on page 194. If this rule is applied to a string which contains the possessive morpheme, we get a development like this:

INSERT: the + girl + poss. + mother + past + be + here ⇉
          the + girl + who + poss. + mother + past + be +⎫
              here   ⎬⇉
MATRIX: the + girl + present + be + Edna   ⎭
RESULT: the + girl + who + poss. + mother + past + be +
              here + present + be + Edna

Then the phonological part of the grammar contains this rule:

who + **poss.** → *whose*

So what will be the actual result sentence in the example above? Write result sentences from the following.

1. INSERT: The man's dog died.
   MATRIX: The man asked for an investigation.
2. INSERT: The boy's books were stolen.
   MATRIX: Arnold is the boy.
3. INSERT: The children's nurse abandoned them.
   MATRIX: The police found the children.
4. INSERT: The teacher's classes went on the field trip.
   MATRIX: The student talked to the teacher.
5. INSERT: You like the artist's work.
   MATRIX: Mr. Digby is the artist.
6. INSERT: He saved the man's life.
   MATRIX: He got no thanks from the man.
7. INSERT: She bandaged the dog's wound.
   MATRIX: She was bitten by the dog.

We have seen that in the relative clause transformation we use *who* for persons and *which* for nonpersons: *the man who came, the package which came.* (We can use *that* for either, of course.) Similarly we use the possessive morpheme for animate nouns and *of* for inanimates: *John's head, the head of the table.* When an insert sentence with *of* undergoes T-relative, there is some uncertainty about what to do. One way is to replace the NP after *of* with *which*. This transformation is called T-relative, of which. In this transformation, the NP before *of* remains there, and the X and Y take their usual places.

The rule for T-relative, of which might be written as follows:

$$X + NP_1 + of + NP_2 + Y \Rrightarrow NP_2 + NP_1 + of + which + X + Y$$

As you can see, the rule for T-relative, of which is a little complicated, and for that reason the construction is sometimes felt as awkward and is often avoided. Still you should command it. Here is an example with the segments labeled:

INSERT: he had played on (X) + the streets (NP$_1$) + of + a city
              (NP$_2$) + as a boy (Y) $\Rrightarrow$
              a city (NP$_2$) + the streets (NP$_1$) + of + which + he
              had played on (X) + as a boy (Y) $\Big\}\Rrightarrow$
MATRIX: He drove through a city.
RESULT: He drove through a city the streets of which he had
              played on as a boy.

Here is another example. In this one X is null.

INSERT: null (X) + the cover (NP$_1$) + of + a book (NP$_2$) + was
              stained $\Rrightarrow$
              a book (NP$_2$) + the cover (NP$_1$) + of + which + null
              (X) + was stained (Y) $\Big\}\Rrightarrow$
MATRIX: A book lay on the table.
RESULT: A book the cover of which was stained lay on the table.

Write result sentences from the following, using T-relative, of which in the manner illustrated.

   8. INSERT: We had heard a part of the poem the night before.
      MATRIX: Mrs. Lacey recited the poem.
   9. INSERT: The leaves of a tree were falling.
      MATRIX: They sat under a tree.
10. INSERT: The end of a quarrel is not in sight.
      MATRIX: The incident started a quarrel.
11. INSERT: Mark had painted the ceiling of a room yesterday.
      MATRIX: I showed Mrs. Wilson a room.
12. INSERT: The windshield of a car was cracked.
      MATRIX: Ronald was driving a car.
13. INSERT: I had pruned the branches of a tree severely in the
              winter.
      MATRIX: I examined a tree.
14. INSERT: The legs of a chair gave way.
      MATRIX: Belinda sat down on a chair.

Because of the complexity of the *of which* construction, there is a tendency to use instead *who* + **poss.**, even though this breaks the rule of not using *who* for nonpersons and that of not using the possessive morpheme for inanimates.

We can substitute *who* + **poss.** for *of which* in the sentence "Belinda sat down on a chair the legs of which gave way." This substitution gives us the following:

Belinda sat down on a chair whose legs gave way.

Write result sentences from the following, using *whose* instead of the *of which* construction.

15. INSERT: The door of a hutch needed fixing.
    MATRIX: The rabbit was in a hutch.
16. INSERT: The ending of a movie disappointed us.
    MATRIX: We went to a movie.
17. INSERT: The motor of a car had been souped up.
    MATRIX: Molly bought a car.
18. INSERT: Bert was telling me about the plot of the novel.
    MATRIX: This is the novel.
19. INSERT: The characters of the story seemed very real.
    MATRIX: Mildred was reading a story.
20. INSERT: The roof of a house leaked.
    MATRIX: We stayed in a house.

Semantics

Other Meanings of the Possessive

Nouns with the possessive morpheme sometimes serve to characterize or describe the nouns they modify. An example is *a girls' school.* This is clearly quite different in structure from *a girl's school.* In *a girls' school, girls* is plural, as the placement of the apostrophe shows. Therefore the nondefinite article *a* cannot go with *girls;* it must go with the combination *girls' school.* But in *a girl's school,* the *a* goes with *girl's,* just as it does in *a girl's dresses. A girl's school* means a school that a particular girl attends. It might even mean a school that a girl owns, having inherited it from her rich uncle. *A girls' school,* in contrast, means a school for girls, not one for boys.

Similarly *a man's store* might mean a store that a particular man owns or manages; the *a* goes with *man's.* But *a men's store* must mean a store for men; the *a* goes with *men's store.* Furthermore, if *a man's store* means a store owned by a particular man, the principal stress falls on *store: a man's stóre.* In *a men's store* the principal stress falls on *men's: a mén's store.*

Say the following out loud as naturally as you can, and note the difference in stress:

> The owner of Togland is a man, so it's a man's store.
> Togland sells only clothes for men, so it's a men's store.

Where does the first stress fall in *a girl's school?* Where does it fall in *a girls' school?*

The noun in the possessive form doesn't have to be plural in this descriptive or characterizing meaning. *A driver's license* ordinarily means a license for a driver, not a license owned by some particular driver. Sometimes such a phrase can have two meanings. *A carpenter's hammer* might mean the kind of hammer that carpenters use or a hammer belonging to a particular carpenter. It would normally have the principal stress on *carpenter's* in the first meaning, on *hammer* in the second.

If *a cárpenter's hammer* means the kind of hammer carpenters use and *a gírls' school* means a school for girls, what do the following mean?

a chíld's game	a dáncer's shoes
a déntist's chair	a políceman's whistle
a wómen's college	a dóg's life

When a plural noun modifies another noun, as in *a teachers' college,* there is a tendency to drop the apostrophe and treat *teachers* not as a possessive noun but simply as a noun modifying another noun: *a teachers college.* This is possible because it is very common in English for nouns, apart from possessive nouns, to modify other nouns. For example, in *a book cover,* the noun *book* modifies *cover.* *Book* cannot be an adjective here, because the modifier cannot derive from an insert sentence *"A cover is book." It must derive from something like "A cover is for a book" or "A cover is that of a book," where *book* is clearly seen to be a noun.

The stress contrast that we saw between *a girl's schóol* and *a gírls' school* reappears here. When an adjective modifies a noun, the first stress is normally on the modified noun: *an old cóver.* But when a noun modifies another noun, the first stress is normally on the modifying noun: *a bóok cover.* Say the following aloud and note the contrast:

> I found an interesting cover.
> I found a book cover.

When we want to specify the grammatical meaning of structures in transforms, we can usually do so by going back to the underlying sentences of which the transforms are made.

By going back to the underlying sentences, we can say that *an old cover* means a cover that is old, whereas *a book cover* means a cover for a book. Turning it around, we can point out that *an old cover* does not mean *"a cover for an old" and *a book cover* does not mean *"a cover that is book."

Nouns modifying other nouns convey quite a variety of grammatical meanings; that is, they derive from a variety of insert sentences. Thus *a picture gallery* could be derived from "A gallery displays pictures"; *a coffee cup* from "A cup holds coffee"; *a necktie salesman* from "Someone sells neckties"; *a dinner gong* from "A gong summons people to dinner." What all of these modifiers have in common is that they express noun meaning, rather than adjective, verb, or adverb meaning.

Suggest underlying sentences to show the meaning of the modifiers in the following:

a country boy	a floor lamp
a drugstore clerk	a supermarket cart
a theater aisle	a steam engine
an insect exterminator	a college professor
a ceiling light	a flower girl

Though the normal stress pattern in such phrases has the heaviest stress on the modifying noun, there are some phrases in which the modified noun takes the heaviest stress. Here are some examples: *a city emplóyee, a dollar bíll, a kitchen sínk, a college président.*

Orthography

The Spelling of Phrases with Nouns Modifying Other Nouns

When a noun modifies another noun, we have to decide whether to write the nouns separately, as in *steam engine;* or with a hyphen between them, as in *man-hour;* or solid, as in *streetcar.* About the only general advice that can be given is that if the two nouns have been used together frequently for a long time, they are likely to be written solid; if the union is less frequent or more recent, they may be written with a hyphen; and if the acquaintance is a casual one, they will probably be written separately. But even this generalization has a lot of leaks. Steam engines have been around for a long time, but the words are still written separately.

It might be said also that the hyphen type is the least common one. Guessing, one does best to go for either the *steam engine* spelling or the *streetcar* one, not *man-hour*.

In any case, most of us have to consult the dictionary a good deal to know when to write noun-noun combinations separately, hyphenated, or solid. Consult yours for the following, all of which are printed with a diagonal line between the nouns to obscure the issue. Find the proper spelling and use each phrase in a sentence.

steam/roller	staff/officer
meal/ticket	lotus/eater
life/time	life/line
crow's/nest	dream/land

Syntax

Recursiveness in Noun Modifiers

You have seen that the relative clause transformation is recursive. We can keep piling up relative clauses as long as there is a new noun phrase in the result sentence. The result sentence can then become the matrix for the next round.

As a matter of fact, all of the transformations that put modifiers into noun phrases are recursive. We can pile up as many adjectives as we have breath, ink, or ingenuity for:

Wilkins was noted for his clear, pungent, interesting, trenchant, witty, grammatical style.

Similarly, we can keep adding *ing* verbs:

a howling, shrieking, murdering, pillaging mob

Or we can add participles indefinitely:

a dispirited, winded, broken, dejected nag

Nouns can pile up in the noun phrase too, though in a somewhat different way. Usually the first noun modifies the one that follows, the two together modify the next one, and so on. Suppose we begin with the unit *Christmas tree.* Here the noun *Christmas* modifies the noun *tree;* the meaning is a tree for Christmas. Etymologically *Christmas* itself is composed of two nouns and means the mass of Christ.

Now the unit *Christmas tree* can function as a modifier of another noun:

Christmas tree ornament

Christmas tree ornament means an ornament for a Christmas tree. This group may now apply its meaning to another noun:

Christmas tree ornament salesmen

These are people who sell Christmas tree ornaments. This can go with still another noun:

Christmas tree ornament salesmen convention

This is a convention of Christmas tree ornament salesmen. Such a convention would probably have a chairman:

Christmas tree ornament salesmen convention chairman

And there might be a problem of choosing chairmen:

Christmas tree ornament salesmen convention chairman selection

So perhaps there should be a committee to do the choosing:

Christmas tree ornament salesmen convention chairman selection committee

A committee has to have a meeting:

Christmas tree ornament salesmen convention chairman selection committee meeting

Meetings must be planned:

Christmas tree ornament salesmen convention chairman selection committee meeting planners

And so on. There is no cut-off rule in the grammar. Obviously, the phrase had become awkward, hard to understand, and ludicrous well before we got to *planners,* but it hadn't become ungrammatical.

This piling up of nouns in the noun phrase is a mark of a particular sort of bad style, one often associated with the writing in government offices, in the Army, and in similar institutions with lots of bureaucracy and paper work. A good writer tries to avoid it, perhaps by not saying everything in one sentence, perhaps by expressing some of the ideas in the base structures instead of transforming them into the noun phrase. One might get by with *Christmas tree ornament salesmen,* but instead of *Christmas tree ornament salesmen convention* it would probably be better to use *convention of Christmas tree ornament salesmen.* And *chairman of a convention of Christmas tree ornament salesmen* would be better than *Christmas tree ornament salesmen convention chairman.*

The phrase *a pencil company sales promotion order* could be rewritten thus: *an order concerning the promotion of sales in a company that manufactures pencils.* Notice that in this version the order of the nouns is reversed; the word *order* comes first, then *promotion, sales, company, pencils.* Rewrite the following in a similar way, reversing the order of the nouns and using prepositions or other structures to show the relationships of meaning.

1. a tiger hunters gathering reception committee
2. a book binder apprentices grievance spokesman
3. a river control board policy meeting
4. a teacher trainer program administrators announcement
5. a city sewer investigation report editor
6. a compass reader instructors policy consultation

Morphology

The Morpheme ory

Many adjectives are formed from verbs by the addition of the morpheme **ory**. Thus *prepare* + **ory** is *preparatory*. Often there is a change in sound and spelling in the verb part: *inflame* + **ory** is *inflammatory; satisfy* + **ory** is *satisfactory*. Name the verbs that underlie each of the following adjectives:

explanatory	conciliatory	exclamatory
anticipatory	introductory	recommendatory

A number of words in **ory** are nouns rather than adjectives:

laboratory	category	territory	inventory

Most of these and some of the **ory** adjectives are taken directly from Latin and have no underlying English verbs.

The morpheme **ory** has a complicated effect on the placement of stress. In some **ory** words the stress is on the first syllable before the **ory**: *compúlsory;* in others it is two syllables back: *obsérvatory;* in still others it is three syllables back: *retáliatory;* and in a very few it is four syllables from the **ory**: *módificatory.*

Because of this diversity in the stress assignment and because many of the **ory** words are somewhat uncommon, the group presents a pronunciation as well as a spelling problem. We may often be in doubt how to stress an **ory** word, and there are some, indeed, that are stressed now one way and now another. However, it isn't all memory work. Though there are some irregularities, there are also some rules to guide us to the pronunciation.

The words in the group that have the principal stress on the syllable just before the ending are of two sorts: those in which an /s/ or a /z/ sound immediately precedes the ending and those in which two or more consonant sounds do. Here are the common words that have /s/ or /z/ before the ending. Pronounce them as they are marked, and find the meanings of any that are unfamiliar to you:

advísory	derísory	supervísory
elúsory	accéssory	intercéssory

In those with two or more consonant sounds, the usual combinations are those spelled with the letters *ct, st, ls, rs, nct,* or *mpt.* Pronounce the following as marked:

fáctory	satisfáctory	refráctory
trajéctory	diréctory	contradíctory
valedíctory	perfúnctory	introdúctory
compúlsory	precúrsory	perémptory

The largest group of **ory** words consists of those that have the main stress two syllables before the **ory**. Most of these end in *–atory,* and many are related to verbs in **ate**. Pronounce the following as marked:

állegory	cátegory	prómissory
prédatory	mándatory	comméndatory
recomméndatory	láudatory	préfatory
derógatory	interrógatory	púrgatory
depréciatory	appréciatory	ámatory
exclámatory	crématory	inflámmatory
refórmatory	explánatory	sígnatory
mígratory	óratory	explóratory
compúlsatory	compénsatory	hórtatory
lávatory	retríbutory	óffertory
obsérvatory	presérvatory	prohíbitory
áuditory	dórmitory	admónitory
térritory	repósitory	expósitory
désultory	ínventory	contríbutory
státutory	répertory	interlócutory

Notice that a few words in this group — *promissory, offertory, desultory, inventory* — meet the requirements of the first group that puts the first stress on the syllable before **ory**. However, they regularly have the stress two syllables back.

The third group, containing words with the first stress three syllables before the **ory,** is also quite large. Naturally these must all be words of five syllables or more. They all end in *–atory.* Included in this group are the adjectives which are related to nouns like *pacification,* which end in *–cation.* Pronounce the following as marked:

déprecatory	dédicatory	índicatory
pacíficatory	commúnicatory	recíprocatory
elúcidatory	delíneatory	denúnciatory
médiatory	retáliatory	concíliatory
ámbulatory	círculatory	ósculatory
ádulatory	congrátulatory	expóstulatory
discríminatory	antícipatory	emáncipatory
revérberatory	láboratory	corróboratory

The words *módificatory* and *quálificatory* are pronounced with the stress four syllables from *–ory. Classificatory* is sometimes pronounced that way too, but probably it is more often *classíficatory.* Other words with different stress placement are *óbligatory/obligatory* and *réspiratory/respíratory.* You can take your choice on these. *Prepáratory* is sometimes *préparatory* and *perémptory* sometimes *péremptory.*

Morphology

The Morpheme ish

Another adjective-forming morpheme is **ish,** as in *Danish, babyish, bookish.* Its earliest use was to make adjectives relating to names of people: *Dane* + **ish** → *Danish, Angle* + **ish** → *English.* Other examples of this use are *Spanish* and *Turkish.* Can you think of more?

Later, **ish** was added to common nouns to make adjectives meaning "having the quality of" the noun. *Babyish* means like a baby, *bookish* having to do with books. Add **ish** to the following, and use each adjective in a sentence:

boy	shrew	style	owl
ghoul	fever	coquette	nightmare
slave	devil	fool	sheep

The meaning of **ish** is similar to that of **ly** in pairs like *womanly/womanish.* There is this difference, however, that **ly** in such pairs has a good sense and **ish** a bad one. *Womanly* is applied to women but *womanish* to men who have the qualities of women. *Manly* and *mannish* have the same distinction.

In recent times **ish** has been used very commonly with adjectives to add to them the meaning "somewhat." Thus *sweetish* means not really sweet, just somewhat sweet. Other examples are:

darkish	bluish	heavyish	softish
dampish	oldish	longish	weakish

Give other examples of words made up of adjective plus **ish**.

Finally, **ish** is often added to numbers to give the meaning "approximately." If we say of someone that he's *fiftyish* we mean that he's about fifty years old. This usage is somewhat informal, involving such forms as:

thirtyish   one-thirtyish   fivish

Morphology

The Morpheme some

A morpheme having a meaning similar to that of **ish** is **some**, as in such words as *lonesome, wearisome, awesome.* This is added both to adjectives (*lone, weary*) and to nouns (*awe*). It is not used so freely to make new words as **ish** is. Most of the words with **some** have been in the English language for a long time.

In a number of words in **some** the form or meaning of the base word is forgotten. The word *hand* is apparent in *handsome,* but the adjective originally meant "easy to handle." The base of *winsome* is *wyn,* an Old English word meaning joy. *Winsome* earlier meant full of joy; now it means pretty or pleasing or attractive.

The meanings of the adjective *fulsome* are quite mixed up, as is its etymology. It may be composed of *full* + **some** or of *foul* + **some.** That is, it may have originally meant very full or full of foulness. It is often used with something suggestive of the latter meaning. Thus *fulsome flattery* is likely to mean flattery that is insincere and oily and unwelcome as well as abundant. To many people, however, *fulsome praise* means just a lot of praise.

SUMMARY OF RULES

T-possessive

The subject of a sentence with the verb *have* takes the possessive morpheme and replaces a definite article somewhere in the matrix sentence:

INSERT: Mrs. White had a geranium.

MATRIX: The painter dropped the geranium. $\Big\} \Rightarrow$

RESULT: The painter dropped Mrs. White's geranium.

This accounts only for some of the uses of the possessive morpheme, those in which it expresses the meaning of "having." Structures like *Sheridan's plays, the country's safety, a week's delay* have different insert structures, though all contain a noun or noun base which with the possessive morpheme replaces *the* in the matrix.

The possessive morpheme is used chiefly with animate nouns. With inanimate nouns, the morpheme **of** usually appears before the NP from the insert, and both follow an NP in the matrix:

INSERT: The barn has a roof.

MATRIX: The roof leaks. $\Big\} \Rightarrow$

RESULT: The roof of the barn leaks.

T-relative, possessive

This is just a variation of T-relative in which the relative pronoun *who* is inserted in a matrix sentence before the possessive morpheme. Then, by a phonological rule, *who* + **poss.** $\rightarrow$ *whose.*

T-relative, of which

$$X + NP_1 + of + NP_2 + Y \Rrightarrow NP_2 + NP_1 + of + which + X + Y$$

This is the part of the rule which transforms the insert:

INSERT: he had played on (X) + the streets (NP$_1$) + of + a city (NP$_2$) + as a boy (Y) $\Rrightarrow$
a city (NP$_2$) + the streets (NP$_1$) + of + which + he had played on (X) + as a boy (Y)

This transform can be inserted in a matrix like "He drove through a city" to give "He drove through a city the streets of which he had played on as a boy." Often *whose* is used instead: *a city whose streets he had played on as a boy.*

TEST

1. Write the sentences resulting from the application of the possessive transformation to the following.
   a. INSERT: Susie has a sister.
      MATRIX: The sister is seven years old.
   b. INSERT: Somebody has books.

MATRIX: These must be the books.
c. INSERT: She has a cold.
MATRIX: The cold is much better.
d. INSERT: They had a car.
MATRIX: We rode in the car.
e. INSERT: The children have parents.
MATRIX: The parents kept them home.

2. Apply T-possessive recursively to the following, using the first result as the matrix for the second insert, the second result as the matrix for the third, etc.

FIRST INSERT: The kittens had a ball.
FIRST MATRIX: The ball was lost.
SECOND INSERT: The cat had kittens.
THIRD INSERT: The sister had a cat.
FOURTH INSERT: The friend had a sister.
FIFTH INSERT: We had a friend.

3. Make result sentences from the following. Use the possessive morpheme if the subject of the insert sentence is animate. Use the *of* form if it is inanimate.
a. INSERT: The street had an end.
MATRIX: The end was blocked.
b. INSERT: He has brains.
MATRIX: John doesn't use the brains.
c. INSERT: The tree had leaves.
MATRIX: The leaves covered the lawn.
d. INSERT: The barrel had a lid.
MATRIX: We couldn't find the lid.
e. INSERT: The horse has a blanket.
MATRIX: Gonzales folded the blanket.

4. Make up sentences using the possessive of the proper nouns in each of the following to modify nouns related to the verbs.
a. Margaret answered.
b. They attacked Jim.
c. Doug refused.
d. Peter insisted.
e. It humiliated Anne.
f. They'll arrest Mr. Bean.
g. Bob repudiated it.
h. She punished Ernest.

5. Make up sentences from the following, using the subject in the possessive to modify a noun related to the adjective.

a. Jenny was ill.
b. Dean is courageous.
c. Allen was cruel.
d. Martha was frail.
e. The land is fertile.
f. The girls were indignant.

6. Make result sentences in *whose* or *of which* from the following. Use *whose* if the insert contains the possessive morpheme, *of which* if it contains *of*.

a. INSERT: The top of a barrel was missing.
   MATRIX: We found a barrel.
b. INSERT: A man's son was ill.
   MATRIX: A man was talking to the principal.
c. INSERT: Alfred married the woman's daughter.
   MATRIX: Mrs. Jenkins is the woman.
d. INSERT: The beginning of a poem was fairly interesting.
   MATRIX: She recited a poem.
e. INSERT: Nobody had checked the motor of a plane.
   MATRIX: We boarded a plane.

7. The phrase *a pencil company sales promotion order* could be rewritten *an order concerning the promotion of sales in a company that manufactures pencils*. Rewrite the following similarly.

a. a duck farm barnyard water pump
b. a government employee salary reduction committee

8. Copy the following and put the mark ′ over the vowel of the syllable that has the heaviest stress:

category	elusory	desultory	ambulatory
advisory	valedictory	conciliatory	accessory

REVIEW QUESTIONS

1. What is the most common meaning of **poss.**?
2. What word in the matrix is replaced by NP + **poss.**?
3. There are three insert sentences embedded in the phrase *my friend's brother's bicycle*. What are they?
4. Why cannot still another possessive be embedded in *my friend's brother's bicycle*?
5. Why does one generally avoid letting a transformation recur often in a single sentence?

6. When in general is *of* used instead of the possessive morpheme?

7. A phrase like *Wilson's novels* is ambiguous. What two insert sentences might underlie it?

8. What insert sentence underlies *a week's work?*

9. In terms of subject-verb-object, what is the difference between *Margaret's answer* and *Margaret's defeat?*

10. From what kind of insert sentence is *Margaret's safety* derived?

11. Why is the meaning of the *of* phrase in a construction like *the city of Denver* called *appositive?*

12. What is the term for the meaning of a construction like *a cup of tea* or *a pound of butter?*

13. What is the likely difference in meaning between *a man's store* and *a men's store?*

14. What is the difference in meaning between *a cárpenter's hammer* and *a carpenter's hámmer?*

15. In what other way might *a teachers' college* be written?

16. How do the combinations adjective-noun and noun-noun usually differ so far as stress is concerned?

17. How does the insert sentence embedded in *a book cover* differ from that embedded in *an old cover?*

18. Which of the following has the least common spelling pattern: *steam engine, man-hour, streetcar?*

19. When is such a combination most likely to be written solid, as in *streetcar?*

20. Give an example of recursiveness in nouns modifying other nouns.

21. To what word class do most words with the morpheme **ory** belong?

22. Words with **ory** may have the first stress on the first, second, third, or fourth syllable before the **ory**. Which two of these stress placements are most common?

23. What is true of words that have the stress on the first syllable before **ory?**

24. *Turkish, roguish, mannish, sweetish,* and *fortyish* represent five different uses of **ish**. What are the differences?

25. What kind of words are formed with the morpheme **some?**

CHAPTER 15

Syntax

The Comparative Transformation

The two inflectional morphemes not yet studied are the **comparative** and the **superlative**. The comparative morpheme is regularly pronounced /ər/ and spelled *–er*. It is added to many adjectives and a few adverbs. The adjectives that take the comparative morpheme are the following:

1. Nearly all one-syllable adjectives: *sweet/sweeter, fine/finer, sad/sadder*.

2. A number of two-syllable adjectives, particularly those ending in *–y: dirty/dirtier, happy/happier*, also *friendly/friendlier, narrow/narrower, pleasant/pleasanter*, etc.

3. Three-syllable adjectives made by adding the prefix *un–* to words of the second group: *unhappy/unhappier, unfriendly/unfriendlier*.

In the comparative transformation, two sentences, each with the same adjective or adverb in the predicate, are put together with the comparative morpheme, spelled *–er*, and the word *than* to form a result sentence, in this fashion:

INSERT: John is young. ⎫ →
MATRIX: Bill is young. ⎭
RESULT: Bill is young + er + than + John is young.

This would of course yield the ungrammatical sentence *"Bill is younger than John is young." An obligatory deletion must now cut off the adjective of the insert to give this:

Bill is younger than John is.

301

Then an optional deletion can remove the second *is:*

> Bill is younger than John.

If we know who is being talked about, we also have the option of deleting *than John:*

> Bill is younger.

Write result sentences for the following, including the obligatory deletion. That is, given the insert "John is young" and the matrix "Bill is young," you would write "Bill is younger than John is."

1. INSERT: Sugar is sweet.
   MATRIX: Honey is sweet.
2. INSERT: The boys are wise.
   MATRIX: The girls are wise.
3. INSERT: The play was funny.
   MATRIX: The movie was funny.
4. INSERT: He is brave.
   MATRIX: You are brave.
5. INSERT: A horse is fast.
   MATRIX: A rabbit is fast.
6. INSERT: I am unhappy.
   MATRIX: David is unhappy.
7. INSERT: The lady was kind.
   MATRIX: The man was kind.
8. INSERT: The dog was quick.
   MATRIX: The rabbit was quick.
9. INSERT: The bus was slow.
   MATRIX: The boat was slow.
10. INSERT: Mr. Jones is old.
    MATRIX: Mr. Winter is old.
11. INSERT: Bob is handsome.
    MATRIX: John is handsome.
12. INSERT: Sally is pretty.
    MATRIX: Mary is pretty.

An adverb of manner which does not end in *–ly* may have the comparative morpheme. The development goes like this:

INSERT: Horses can run fast. $\Big\} \Rightarrow$
MATRIX: Rabbits can run fast.
RESULT: Rabbits can run faster than horses can run fast.

Then the adverb and verb of the insert must be deleted:

Rabbits can run faster than horses can.

If the insert and matrix predicates begin with a verb instead of a modal, *have,* or *be,* then *do* is used in the embedded sentence, just as it is in T-yes/no and T-negative:

INSERT: Horses run fast. $\left.\right\}\rightarrow$
MATRIX: Rabbits run fast.

RESULT: Horses run faster than rabbits run fast. $\Rightarrow$
          Horses run faster than rabbits do.

Write result sentences, deleting the adverb from the insert sentence and substituting *do* if the insert contains a verb.

13. INSERT: Maurice can shoot straight.
    MATRIX: Philip can shoot straight.
14. INSERT: Alice works hard.
    MATRIX: Betty works hard.
15. INSERT: The mothers may do the work fast.
    MATRIX: The fathers may do the work fast.
16. INSERT: I drew it straight.
    MATRIX: Jim drew it straight.

There are only a few adjectives and adverbs that form the comparative irregularly.

$$\text{good} + -er \rightarrow better \qquad \text{bad} + -er \rightarrow worse$$
$$\text{well} + -er \rightarrow better \qquad \text{badly} + -er \rightarrow worse$$
$$\text{little} + -er \rightarrow less$$

Write result sentences from the following.

17. INSERT: The roast is good.
    MATRIX: The potatoes are good.
18. INSERT: John looks well.
    MATRIX: Felix looks well.
19. INSERT: The women worked little.
    MATRIX: The men worked little.
20. INSERT: Jennifer behaved badly.
    MATRIX: David behaved badly.
21. INSERT: The lodging was bad.
    MATRIX: The food was bad.

When the *than* and the whole of the insert of this transformation have been deleted, the comparative adjective can behave just like any other adjective. For instance, we might have this kind of development:

FIRST INSERT: Some boys are big.⎫ ⇒
FIRST MATRIX: The boys are big. ⎭
FIRST RESULT: The boys are bigger than some boys are big. ⇒
                    The boys are bigger than some boys are. ⇒
                    The boys are bigger than some boys. ⇒
                    The boys are bigger.
SECOND INSERT: The boys are bigger. ⇒
                    the boys that are bigger ⇒
                    the boys bigger ⇒
                    the bigger boys   ⎫ ⇒
SECOND MATRIX: The boys ought to carry the suitcases. ⎭
SECOND RESULT: The bigger boys ought to carry the suitcases.

Syntax

The Comparative with *more*

For adjectives that do not add the comparative morpheme with
the spelling –*er,* the comparative meaning is expressed with the
word *more.* The situation is similar to that of the possessive of nouns,
where animate nouns express the meaning with the possessive morpheme and the inanimate ones mostly with the word *of: John's leg,
the leg of the table.* For most adjectives of two syllables and all of
more than two except the *un*– type, *more* must be used instead of
–*er.* We say *more hopeful* instead of **hopefuller:*

INSERT: Joan is hopeful. ⎫ ⇒
MATRIX: Anne is hopeful. ⎭
RESULT: Anne is + more + hopeful + than + Joan is
               hopeful. ⇒
          Anne is + more + hopeful + than + Joan is.

Write result sentences from the following.

1. INSERT: The sky was beautiful.
   MATRIX: The bridge was beautiful.
2. INSERT: Mortimer was villainous.
   MATRIX: Kenworthy was villainous.
3. INSERT: The forwards were agile.
   MATRIX: The guards were agile.
4. INSERT: Mr. Lumpkin is eccentric.
   MATRIX: Mrs. Lumpkin is eccentric.
5. INSERT: The movie is boring.
   MATRIX: The book is boring.

Adverbs of manner ending in –*ly* also express the comparative meaning with *more* rather than –*er*. We say "She wrote more neatly than Jane did," not *"She wrote neatlier than Jane did." Write result sentences from the following.

6. INSERT: Her mother watched anxiously.
   MATRIX: Betty watched anxiously.
7. INSERT: The sergeant examined the room carefully.
   MATRIX: The lieutenant examined the room carefully.
8. INSERT: I spoke nervously.
   MATRIX: Willie spoke nervously.
9. INSERT: Davidson reacted angrily.
   MATRIX: Johnson reacted angrily.

Most adjectives which express the comparative meaning with –*er* may alternatively express it with *more*. That is, we can say either *sweeter* or *more sweet, angrier* or *more angry*. But we can't do both at once in standard modern English. We don't say *more sweeter* or *more angrier*. This is what is called a double comparative. It was still used in serious writing in Shakespeare's time, but it isn't any more. For most of the adjectives that can express the comparative meaning either way, –*er* is the more common.

Syntax

The Superlative Transformation

Adjectives and adverbs that express the comparative meaning with –*er* express the superlative (*most*) meaning with –*est:*

sweet/sweetest	dirty/dirtiest
narrow/narrowest	unhappy/unhappiest

The superlative transformation is more complicated than the comparative transformation. In the superlative, the word *the* is inserted before the adjective or adverb, which is then followed by the superlative morpheme, spelled –*est*, the word *of*, and the subject of the insert sentence:

INSERT: All of them were wise. ⎫
MATRIX: Albert was wise.   ⎬ ⇒
RESULT: Albert was + the + wise + est + of + all of them. ⎭

Write similar result sentences from the following, omitting the plus signs and writing the actual words.

1. INSERT: The boys were tall.
   MATRIX: Lenny was tall.
2. INSERT: All the girls were brave.
   MATRIX: Marcella was brave.
3. INSERT: The rooms in the house were dirty.
   MATRIX: The kitchen was dirty.
4. INSERT: The ships of the line were fast.
   MATRIX: The *Indomitable* was fast.
5. INSERT: The children in the family were friendly.
   MATRIX: Raymond was friendly.

Adjectives and adverbs that express the comparative meaning with *more* express the superlative with *most*. *The* and *most* are placed before the adjective, and *of* after it:

INSERT: The girls were beautiful.⎫ ⇉
MATRIX: Sally was beautiful.   ⎭
RESULT: Sally was the most beautiful of the girls.

Write result sentences from the following.

 6. INSERT: The boys were courageous.
    MATRIX: Abe was courageous.
 7. INSERT: All of the speeches were inspiring.
    MATRIX: Mr. Flim's talk was inspiring.
 8. INSERT: The players were insolent.
    MATRIX: The quarterback was insolent.
 9. INSERT: The books were interesting.
    MATRIX: *Lost Harbor* was interesting.
10. INSERT: All of the students worked carefully.
    MATRIX: Evelyn worked carefully.
11. INSERT: All of the boys that Mr. Maxim coached were
              successful.
    MATRIX: Fred was successful.

The result sentence that you made for Number 11 can go through various deletions:

Fred was the most successful of all the boys that Mr. Maxim
    coached. ⇉
Fred was the most successful of the boys that Mr. Maxim coached. ⇉
Fred was the most successful that Mr. Maxim coached.

Adjectives and adverbs that have irregular forms for the *–er* comparative also have irregular forms for the *–est* superlative:

$$\text{good} + \textit{-est} \rightarrow \textit{best} \qquad \text{bad} + \textit{-est} \rightarrow \textit{worst}$$
$$\text{well} + \textit{-est} \rightarrow \textit{best} \qquad \text{badly} + \textit{-est} \rightarrow \textit{worst}$$
$$\text{little} + \textit{-est} \rightarrow \textit{least}$$

Write result sentences from the following.

12. INSERT: The children were good.
    MATRIX: Samuel was good.
13. INSERT: All worked well.
    MATRIX: Georgeanne worked well.
14. INSERT: All of the food tasted bad.
    MATRIX: The desserts tasted bad.
15. INSERT: The children recited badly.
    MATRIX: Edith recited badly.
16. INSERT: All found little.
    MATRIX: Albert found little.

The comparative suffix –er, or *more*, sometimes is used in a transformation similar to the superlative transformation:

INSERT: The two boys are small. $\Big\} \rightarrow$
MATRIX: Ernest is small.
RESULT: Ernest is + the + small + er + of + the two boys.

INSERT: The two are expensive. $\Big\} \rightarrow$
MATRIX: This dress is expensive.
RESULT: This dress is + the + more + expensive + of + the two.

These examples show the considered usage of standard English: comparative for two people or things, superlative for more than two. We say "the better of the two" but "the best of the three," "the more patiently of the two" but "the most patiently of the three."

The rule that the comparative is used for two people or things, the superlative for more than two, isn't always adhered to, even by educated people. One often hears the superlative used even when only two persons or things are involved. However, practice the rule as given by writing result sentences from the following.

17. INSERT: The five men were tough.
    MATRIX: Reilly was tough.
18. INSERT: The two were good.
    MATRIX: Flaxon's plan was good.
19. INSERT: The two sisters are young.
    MATRIX: Janice is young.
20. INSERT: The boys in the class are studious.

MATRIX:	Peter Young is studious.
21. INSERT:	The two ideas seemed dangerous.
MATRIX:	Ralph's seemed dangerous.
22. INSERT:	The two worked hard.
MATRIX:	Frank worked hard.
23. INSERT:	The ten stories are lively.
MATRIX:	*The Smiling Eel* is lively.
24. INSERT:	The two are bad.
MATRIX:	Mine is bad.

Naturally an individual can be compared with the remainder of a group:

> John is brighter than any other boy in his class.

There is a tendency for the *other* to drop out here, giving "John is brighter than any boy in his class." Some would argue that this is ungrammatical, or at least illogical, since, assuming that John is a boy, it seems to say that he is brighter than himself, among others. "John is brighter than any girl in his class" is, of course, all right.

Clearly ungrammatical is the use of the superlative with an "other" noun phrase:

> *John is the brightest of all the other boys.

Syntax

Clauses with *as . . . as*

When we want to say that two people or things are the same in some way, with no idea of more or most, we do it in a transformation that puts the word *as* before the adjective or adverb of the matrix and another *as* after it, followed by the insert sentence:

INSERT:	John is bright. $\Big\} \Rightarrow$
MATRIX:	Mary is bright.
RESULT:	Mary is + as + bright + as + John is bright. $\Rrightarrow$
	(*obligatorily*) Mary is as bright as John is. $\Rrightarrow$
	(*optionally*) Mary is as bright as John.

The transformation is quite parallel to the comparative transformation. It works in the same way for adverbs of manner, with a form of *do* replacing a verb in the insert sentence after the deletion:

INSERT:	John plays brilliantly. $\Big\} \Rightarrow$
MATRIX:	Mary plays brilliantly.

RESULT: Mary plays as brilliantly as John plays brilliantly. ⇒
Mary plays as brilliantly as John does. ⇒
Mary plays as brilliantly as John.

Write result sentences like "Mary is as bright as John is" or "Mary plays as brilliantly as John does" for the following.

1. INSERT: Stephen is tall.
   MATRIX: Larry is tall.
2. INSERT: The boys are clever.
   MATRIX: Maxine is clever.
3. INSERT: Her brother worked hard.
   MATRIX: Barbara worked hard.
4. INSERT: I was frightened.
   MATRIX: My father was frightened.
5. INSERT: The first string played well.
   MATRIX: The second string played well.
6. INSERT: Mr. Dodson made money rapidly.
   MATRIX: Mr. Fogg made money rapidly.
7. INSERT: He was cruel.
   MATRIX: Mrs. Hairshirt was cruel.

Syntax

more . . . than in Noun Phrases

The combination *more . . . than* can be used with noncount and plural count nouns in the expansion of noun phrases:

INSERT: Mr. Dodson made money. ⎫
MATRIX: Mr. Fogg made money. ⎭ ⇒
RESULT: Mr. Fogg made + more + money + than + Mr. Dodson made money. ⇒
Mr. Fogg made more money than Mr. Dodson did.

Write result sentences similar to the preceding one for the following.

1. INSERT: Rabbits eat hat.
   MATRIX: Elephants eat hay.
2. INSERT: I knew girls.
   MATRIX: My brother knew girls.
3. INSERT: Babs wrote words.
   MATRIX: Carol wrote words.
4. INSERT: Hans goes to parties.
   MATRIX: Fran goes to parties.

5. INSERT: The vegetable garden needs water.
   MATRIX: The lawn needs water.

When the noun is a singular count noun, the *more* goes before the article:

INSERT: John is a hero. } →
MATRIX: Bill is a hero.

RESULT: Bill is + more + a hero + than + John is a hero. ⇉
           Bill is more a hero than John is.

Write result sentences for the following.

6. INSERT: A monkey is a clown.
   MATRIX: An otter is a clown.
7. INSERT: Mr. Dodson was a speculator.
   MATRIX: Mr. Fogg was a speculator.
8. INSERT: The boys were a nuisance.
   MATRIX: The girls were a nuisance.

Sometimes the deletion in *more . . . than* sentences is a little more complicated. Consider this:

INSERT: There was food in the kitchen. } →
MATRIX: There was dirt in the kitchen.

RESULT: There was + more + dirt + in the kitchen + than +
           there was food in the kitchen.

As the result sentence now stands, we would get the ungrammatical sentence *"There was more dirt in the kitchen than there was food in the kitchen." Most repeated portions of sentences are deleted or deletable. Here it is obligatory to delete at least the repeated adverbial of place:

There was more dirt in the kitchen than there was food.

But we still have a repeated part: *there was*. This may be deleted optionally:

There was more dirt in the kitchen than food.

Here is another example of a somewhat complicated deletion in a result sentence of this kind:

INSERT: He had cows on his ranch. } →
MATRIX: He had sheep on his ranch.

RESULT: He had + more + sheep + on his ranch + than +
           he had cows on his ranch. ⇉

(*obligatorily*) He had more sheep on his ranch than he had cows. $\rightrightarrows$

(*optionally*) He had more sheep on his ranch than cows.

Alternatively, the adverbial of place could have been deleted in its first occurrence to give these:

He had more sheep than he had cows on his ranch.
He had more sheep than cows on his ranch.

Write result sentences containing just the obligatory deletion from these.

9. INSERT: There were oranges in the basket.
   MATRIX: There were bananas in the basket.
10. INSERT: There was sand on the floor.
    MATRIX: There was straw on the floor.
11. INSERT: There were girls in the class.
    MATRIX: There were boys in the class.
12. INSERT: She had money in her purse.
    MATRIX: She had junk in her purse.
13. INSERT: He had brains in his head.
    MATRIX: He had dreams in his head.
14. INSERT: There was water in the sink.
    MATRIX: There was water on the floor.
15. INSERT: I saw deer in the forest.
    MATRIX: I saw deer in the fields.

Syntax

as much (many) . . . as in Noun Phrases

When we want to say that two nouns stand for the same quantity or number we use *as much . . . as* or *as many . . . as* in a transformation parallel to that for *more . . . than.*

Much is used with noncount nouns:

INSERT: Elephants eat hay. $\Big\rbrace \rightrightarrows$
MATRIX: Cows eat hay.
RESULT: Cows eat + as much + hay + as + elephants eat hay. $\rightrightarrows$
           Cows eat as much hay as elephants do.

The construction is used with plural count nouns as shown in the following transformation:

INSERT: Ellen has friends. ⎫
MATRIX: Peter has friends. ⎭ ⇉

RESULT: Peter has + as many + friends + as + Ellen has
         friends. ⇉

         Peter has as many friends as Ellen has.

Make result sentences from the following using *as much . . . as* or *as many . . . as*.

1. INSERT: Mr. Dodson has money.
   MATRIX: Mr. Fogg has money.
2. INSERT: Keats wrote poems.
   MATRIX: Shelley wrote poems.
3. INSERT: Bab's composition contained words.
   MATRIX: Fran's composition contained words.
4. INSERT: The Armenians experienced misery.
   MATRIX: The Albanians experienced misery.
5. INSERT: Cortez found gold.
   MATRIX: Pizarro found gold.
6. INSERT: Pedro can eat ice cream.
   MATRIX: Buster can eat ice cream.
7. INSERT: You have faith.
   MATRIX: I have faith.
8. INSERT: Ruth has foreign stamps.
   MATRIX: Jenny has foreign stamps.
9. INSERT: Their cat has kittens.
   MATRIX: Our cat has kittens.

Because of the double nature of *have* in Numbers 1 and 7 (it's a verb in these sentences besides being a *have*), you could form either of two result sentences. The result sentence for 7, for example, could be either "I have as much faith as you have" or "I have as much faith as you do." What are the two possible result sentences for Number 1?

Syntax

A Possible Ambiguity

Deletions in the transformations you have been studying can make possible identical result sentences from two different sources. When that happens, the result sentences will be ambiguous; one can't tell what their insert and matrix sentences are. Here is an example:

INSERT: Sally likes Scott. ⎫
MATRIX: Ellen likes Scott. ⎬ →
RESULT: Ellen likes Scott as much as Sally likes Scott. ⇉
             Ellen likes Scott as much as Sally does. ⇉
             Ellen likes Scott as much as Sally.
INSERT: Ellen likes Sally. ⎫
MATRIX: Ellen likes Scott. ⎬ →
RESULT: Ellen likes Scott as much as Ellen likes Sally. ⇉
             Ellen likes Scott as much as Sally.

In the first transformation, *Sally* is the subject of *likes,* in the second, the object. This is seen in the insert sentences and in the results before the deletions. But after the deletions there is no way of telling. One sometimes has to be careful that sentences are not so heavily deleted as to produce ambiguity.

Here is another ambiguous result sentence:

> Cats kill more birds than mice.

The insert sentence could be either "Cats kill birds" or "Mice kill birds." The second possibility could be made clear by restoration of the last deletion:

> Cats kill more birds than mice do.

The first possibility could not be made clear by restoring "Cats kill," for this would give an ungrammatical sentence:

> *Cats kill more birds than cats kill mice.

By a regular rule that a repeated noun phrase is represented by a personal pronoun, we have *they* in place of the second *cats:*

> Cats kill more birds than they kill mice.

Then, as in so many other similar situations, *do* replaces the repeated verb:

> Cats kill more birds than they do mice.

For each of the following, write two sentences like "Cats kill more birds than mice do" and "Cats kill more birds than they do mice" to make clear the two meanings.

1. Horace hates Herbert more than Henry.
2. Elephants tolerate crocodiles as much as rhinos.
3. Mr. Dodson needed money more than Mr. Fogg.
4. The girls enjoyed the movie more than their escorts.

5. Mabel turned to Eloise more quickly than Sylvia.
6. The cannibals liked the apple pie more than the missionaries.
7. Girls like concerts more than boys.

Of course there would be other ways to express most of these sentences without ambiguity. Neither of the following is ambiguous:

> The cannibals liked the apple pie, but the missionaries didn't care
> too much for it.
> The cannibals preferred the apple pie to the missionaries.

Morphology

The y Morphemes

It has been mentioned that a large number of the two-syllable adjectives that may take the comparative morpheme with the spelling *–er* instead of the words *more . . . than* are those ending in *–y: dirty/ dirtier.* Most of these words are adjectives that are made from nouns by the addition of the morpheme y. Add the morpheme y to the following nouns and use each adjective in a sentence in the comparative form:

sand	room	fluff	grime
gab	greed	mud	need

In a number of adjectives ending in *–y*, the ending is no longer felt as a morpheme. It isn't in *happy,* for example, because we aren't aware of any underlying noun **hap*. There was once such a noun in English, with the meaning luck, but it has gone out of use, although we still have the word *hapless*, which means having no luck.

Find the etymologies of the following adjectives and tell what nouns, now obsolete, once underlay them:

>   shabby   spiffy   soggy   tidy

In a few adjectives made from nouns, y appears in the spelling *–ky:*

>   panic + y → *panicky*   garlic + y → *garlicky*

Why do you think these words are spelled thus instead of **panicy, *garlicy?*

In some words, y has been added to other adjectives, perhaps to make them seem more like adjectives. An example is *chilly,* which is made of the adjective *chill* plus **y**. Make similar adjectives from the following words:

lank   yellow

In a word like *yellowy*, the morpheme **y** has something like the meaning of **ish** in *yellowish:* "somewhat."

Sometimes the morpheme **y** is added to verbs: *jump* + **y** → *jumpy*. Make similar adjectives from the following, and use each in a sentence:

stick   drowse   quaver   blow

Turning things about, as it were, we have another **y** morpheme which makes nouns from adjectives or from other nouns. Thus *honest* + **y** → *honesty*. Most nouns so made, like *honesty*, are noncount nouns with abstract meanings, but some are count nouns: *felon* + **y** → *felony*.

Make nouns by adding **y** to the following:

jealous	victor	baron	synonym
beggar	modest	orthodox	armor

In some words **y** has an effect on stress. Compare *sýnonym* and *synónymy*. In these words, the first stress is placed on the syllable two syllables before the final **y**. Another example is *télegraph/telégraphy*. Count the syllables back from the **y** in *telegraphy*. Make nouns ending in –*y* from the following, and put the mark ´ over the syllable that has the first stress:

homophone   phonograph   photograph

Many words that end in the letter *y* have no English underlying nouns, but the stress pattern is the same. For example, there is no word **geograph*. If there were, we would stress it this way: **géograph*. But there is, of course, the word *geography*, which we stress this way: *geógraphy*.

Note that in each of the following words the heaviest stress comes two syllables before the letter *y*.

calligraphy	lexicography	choreography
Egyptology	etymology	entymology
polygamy	monogamy	bigamy
physiognomy	economy	gastronomy
cosmogony	telephony	cacophony
philanthropy	microscopy	fluoroscopy

Morphology

The Morpheme ery

A goodly number of English nouns are made from other words by the addition of the morpheme **ery.** For example *mock* + **ery** gives *mockery.*

Add **ery** to the following words:

witch	bribe	savage	forge	fine
debauch	fish	bake	jewel	can
droll	fool	scene	refine	buffoon

It is sometimes difficult to know whether a word ending in *–ery* is a case of "base + **ery**" or a case of "base + **er** + **y.**" *Witchery* is clearly a case of the former, because there is no noun **witcher* that could be made into another noun by adding **y.** But there is a noun *baker,* so *bakery* might be felt as being composed of *bake* + **er** → *baker* + **y** → *bakery.* Or it might be *bake* + **ery** → *bakery* − **y** → *baker.* As users of the language, we may arrive at word meanings by routes that do not reflect the actual histories of the words. It doesn't matter.

Give two words related to each of the following, as *bake* and *baker* are related to *bakery:*

forgery   brewery   bindery

Many words in **ery,** like *bakery* and *bindery,* are names of businesses. Here are some other, less common, ones:

ironmongery	haberdashery	curriery
vintnery	drapery	pottery

Other words in **ery** signify places where certain animals or plants are kept. A *piggery* is a place where pigs are kept. However, a *battery* is not an abode of bats. It comes from the verb *batter,* in the sense of beat or pound. Find the etymology of the following nouns:

cutlery   buttery   chicanery   rookery

When the morpheme **ery** is attached to a word ending in *–e,* like *scene,* of course only the letters *ry* are added: *scenery.* Just *–ry* is added in certain other cases too, particularly those in which the base word ends in the letter *d, l, n,* or *t.* Make nouns by adding **ery** in the spelling *–ry* to the following:

d:	herald	wizard	husband
l:	rival	revel	devil
n:	falcon	yeoman	mason
t:	dentist	gallant	forest

A few words may be acceptably spelled either *–ery* or *–ry*. Perhaps the most common example of these is *jewelry*, which is also spelled *jewellery*.

Morphology

The Morpheme ary

Lest we begin to think that life and English spelling are simple, we must note that we also have a morpheme **ary**, pronounced just like **ery** but spelled with *a* rather than *e*. One difference is that, whereas **ery** makes only nouns, **ary** makes both nouns and adjectives. If it's an adjective, it is spelled *–ary*, not *–ery*. Make adjectives by adding **ary** to the following:

element	imagine	sanguine	reaction
caution	honor	planet	parliament

Many adjectives in **ary** have come to us directly from Latin and have no underlying English word. Some of these are:

subsidiary	fiduciary	pecuniary
tutelary	primary	tertiary
epistolary	centenary	preliminary
estuary	seminary	itinerary

SUMMARY OF RULES

T-comparative

a. INSERT: $\left. \begin{array}{l} NP_1 + Aux + be + Adj \\ NP_2 + Aux + be + Adj \end{array} \right\} \Rightarrow$

  MATRIX:

  RESULT: $NP_2 + Aux + be + Adj + er + than + NP_1 + Aux + be + Adj$

b. INSERT: $\left. \begin{array}{l} NP_1 + Aux + be + Adj \\ NP_2 + Aux + be + Adj \end{array} \right\} \Rightarrow$

  MATRIX:

  RESULT: $NP_2 + Aux + be + more + Adj + than + NP_1 + Aux + be + Adj$

These generate sentences of the type "Marjorie is prettier than Lucille is" or "Lucille is more beautiful than Marjorie is," with obligatory deletion of the second adjective, and, with slight variations, other comparisons, like "Peter works harder than Stephen does" or "Peter can talk more persuasively than Stephen can."

T-superlative

a. INSERT: NP$_1$ + Aux + be + Adj $\rceil$ $\Rightarrow$
   MATRIX: NP$_2$ + Aux + be + Adj $\rfloor$
   RESULT: NP$_2$ + Aux + be + the + Adj + est + of + NP$_1$
b. INSERT: NP$_1$ + Aux + be + Adj $\rceil$ $\Rightarrow$
   MATRIX: NP$_1$ + Aux + be + Adj $\rfloor$
   RESULT: NP$_2$ + Aux + be + the + most + Adj + of + NP$_1$

These generate sentences like "Marjorie is the prettiest of them all" or "Lucille is the most beautiful of them all," depending on the adjective. Slight variations will take care of adverbials of manner in the superlative. Conservative usage requires that the NP$_1$ refer to a group of more than two: "Lucille is the prettiest of the three." Otherwise the comparative is used.

T-as . . . as

INSERT: NP$_1$ + Aux + be + Adj $\rceil$ $\Rightarrow$
MATRIX: NP$_2$ + Aux + be + Adj $\rfloor$
RESULT: NP$_2$ + Aux + be + as + Adj + as + NP$_1$ + Aux + be + Adj

With the second adjective obligatorily deleted, this will yield sentences like "Mary is as bright as John is." Variations will give sentences like "Mary works as hard as John does."

TEST

1. Make comparative result sentences from the following. Use the ending –er whenever it is grammatical to do so. Otherwise use *more*. Make just the obligatory deletion.

a. INSERT: Fred is wise.
   MATRIX: Buck is wise.
b. INSERT: Sylvia is gorgeous.
   MATRIX: Maxine is gorgeous.
c. INSERT: I was frightened.
   MATRIX: Billy was frightened.

d. INSERT: The girls were studious.
  MATRIX: The boys were studious.
e. INSERT: This book looks interesting.
  MATRIX: That book looks interesting.

2. Make superlative result sentences from the following. Use –*est* where it is grammatical to do so. Otherwise use *most*.

a. INSERT: All of them were big.
  MATRIX: The log Dick carried was big.
b. INSERT: The parents were indignant.
  MATRIX: Mrs. Gardner was indignant.
c. INSERT: The plays were complicated.
  MATRIX: Play number 17 was complicated.
d. INSERT: The men in the office were considerate.
  MATRIX: Stan was considerate.
e. INSERT: The summer months are warm.
  MATRIX: August is warm.

3. Make result sentences with the comparative or the superlative according to the rule given.

a. INSERT: The five girls were pretty.
  MATRIX: Lucille was pretty.
b. INSERT: The two men were rich.
  MATRIX: Mr. Fogg was rich.
c. INSERT: The two novels are interesting.
  MATRIX: *Lost Gate* is interesting.

4. Make result sentences with *as . . . as* from the following. Make only the obligatory deletion.

a. INSERT: Hans is handsome.
  MATRIX: Jeff is handsome.
b. INSERT: The parents work hard.
  MATRIX: The children work hard.

5. Make result sentences with *more . . . than* from the following.

a. INSERT: Cats catch mice.
  MATRIX: Hawks catch mice.
b. INSERT: The patient needed attention.
  MATRIX: The doctor needed attention.
c. INSERT: Patricia knows boys.
  MATRIX: Melissa knows boys.
d. INSERT: The corporal was a coward.
  MATRIX: The sergeant was a coward.

6. Make result sentences with *as much . . . as* or *as many . . . as* from the following.

  a. INSERT: The Malaysians eat rice.
     MATRIX: The Indonesians eat rice.
  b. INSERT: Donald has relatives.
     MATRIX: Ronald has relatives.
  c. INSERT: Helen goes to dances.
     MATRIX: Elaine goes to dances.
  d. INSERT: Bert is in trouble.
     MATRIX: Herb is in trouble.

7. Each of the following is ambiguous. Expand each sentence in two ways to make the two meanings clear. For example, for "Cats kill more birds than mice" you would write "Cats kill more birds than mice do" and "Cats kill more birds than they do mice."

  a. Betty likes Diana more than Eloise.
  b. The manager praises the players as much as the coach.
  c. She needs pity more than her husband.
  d. We saw the Williamses more than Bob.

8. Make words by adding the morpheme y to the following, and after each write N or A to show whether the word you have made is usually a noun or an adjective:

        greed   honest   drowse   fun   jealous

9. Copy the following, and make the mark ′ over the vowel of the syllable that has the first stress:

      geography   telegraphy   etymology   philanthropy

10. Use each of the following words in a sentence that gives some idea of its meaning:

      drollery   wizardry   sanguinary   piggery
      cutlery   tutelary   yeomanry   antiquary

REVIEW QUESTIONS

1. How is the comparative morpheme spelled?
2. What sort of three-syllable adjectives add the comparative morpheme?
3. What adverbials of manner add it?
4. What obligatory deletion must apply to "Bill is younger than John is young"? What optional deletion may apply?

5. What obligatory change takes place in "Horses run faster than rabbits run"?

6. What words are represented by *good + –er, bad + –er,* and *little + –er?*

7. What is a double comparative?

8. How do adjectives and adverbs which express the comparative meaning with *more* express the superlative meaning?

9. What is peculiar about a sentence like "Lucille is prettier than any girl in her class"?

10. After the obligatory deletion of the second *faith* in "I have as much faith as you have faith," what two forms may the sentence have?

11. "Ellen likes Scott as much as Sally" is ambiguous. What are the two possible insert sentences?

12. What derivational morpheme do most two-syllable adjectives have that take *–er* in the comparative transformation?

13. On what syllables does the first stress come in the words *synonym* and *synonymy?*

14. What class of words is made with the derivational morpheme **ery?**

15. The most common form of **ery** is *–ery.* What other form does it sometimes have?

16. What two classes of words are made with the derivational morpheme **ary?**

CHAPTER 16

Syntax

More Sentence Modifiers

We have seen sentence modifiers resulting from nonrestrictive relative clauses. The modifiers do not restrict or identify any particular noun phrase but apply their meaning to the matrix sentence as a whole. Thus we can have this development:

INSERT: John felt bad about it. $\Rightarrow$
John, who felt bad about it, $\left.\right\} \Rightarrow$
MATRIX: John apologized.
RESULT: John, who felt bad about it, apologized.

Remember that nonrestrictive relative clauses, and also the structures that derive from them by deletion, are set off from the matrix sentence by commas.

The preceding result sentence can be shortened by T-deletion, ing, in which the relative pronoun is deleted and *ing* is substituted for the tense:

John, who felt bad about it, apologized. $\Rightarrow$
John, feeling bad about it, apologized.

Now T-sentence modifier can apply to put the *ing* phrase before the whole matrix sentence:

Feeling bad about it, John apologized.

Or the *ing* phrase can go at the end of the matrix:

John apologized, feeling bad about it.

In all of these changes, a comma or commas continue to separate the sentence modifier from the matrix.

Throughout this construction, there is a condition that the subject of the insert sentence and the subject of the matrix must be identical. If this condition is not met, we get a dangling modifier, like this:

*Feeling bad about it, an apology seemed to be in order.

A somewhat simpler transformation produces a sentence modifier of a different kind. We have seen that insert sentences may be transformed into subordinate clauses that serve in noun phrase functions, such as subject or object. Thus "John felt bad about it" can receive the subordinator *that* and function as a noun phrase in a matrix sentence:

That John felt bad about it was obvious.
I knew that John felt bad about it.

In this use the most common subordinator is *that,* although others, such as *whether* and *if,* also occur.

Subordinate clauses may also function as sentence modifiers. In this transformation a subordinator is merely prefixed to an insert sentence, and the subordinate clause is placed before or after a matrix. The subordinator *that* does not occur in this transformation. Several others do. Here is an example:

INSERT: John felt bad about it.   ⎫
MATRIX: Something had to be done.   ⎬ ⇛
RESULT: Because John felt bad about it, something had to be
          done.

Notice that in this transformation, the insert and matrix do not have to have the same subject. The insert is a full clause and contains its own subject and predicate.

If both the insert and matrix sentence in this transformation have the same subject, the appropriate pronoun appears in the result sentence as follows:

INSERT: John felt bad about it. ⎫
MATRIX: John apologized.   ⎬ ⇛
RESULT: Because John felt bad about it, he apologized.

Or one could say "Because he felt bad about it, John apologized."

So far as the insert sentence is concerned, the transformation is the same simple one that produces subordinate clauses that replace noun phrases, T-subordinate clause:

$$S \Rrightarrow Sub + S$$

Subordinators used in subordinate clauses that function as sentence modifiers include *because, unless, if, although, since, while, inasmuch as, whereas*. Use one of these in forming a result sentence from each of the following. Use the one that seems to make best sense. Put the subordinate clause at the beginning of the matrix. Separate the clause from the matrix with a comma.

1. INSERT: Andy knew nothing about it.
   MATRIX: He didn't say anything.
2. INSERT: The day was cloudy.
   MATRIX: We decided to stay home.
3. INSERT: You have nothing better to do.
   MATRIX: We might practice the duet.
4. INSERT: They get there before ten.
   MATRIX: They won't see Mr. Robinson.
5. INSERT: Dan showed you the letter.
   MATRIX: You should know what the facts are.
6. INSERT: We were waiting for the ferry.
   MATRIX: A windstorm blew up.
7. INSERT: Mr. Sawyer was only five feet two.
   MATRIX: Mr. Allen was over six feet tall.
8. INSERT: There was only one way to clear the walk.
   MATRIX: Mrs. Kevane picked up the snow shovel.
9. INSERT: She couldn't approve of their conduct.
   MATRIX: Miss Wilkins felt sorry for the boys.
10. INSERT: They start work at once.
    MATRIX: They will be too late.

When the sentence modifier is a subordinate clause at the beginning of the sentence, the rule for separating it from the matrix with a comma is not so strictly adhered to as when it is a phrase resulting from a nonrestrictive relative clause. Still, most writers punctuate that way.

The situation is more complicated when the subordinate clause follows the matrix. Here the comma is frequently omitted:

> We'll be late if we don't hurry.
> He'll be here on time unless he has trouble.

The use of the comma in this position depends partly on the particular subordinator employed. The comma is generally used when the subordinator is *although, though, whereas*, and *provided (that)*. Make result sentences from the following, using a different one of these subordinators for each. Put the subordinate clause after the matrix, and use a comma.

11. INSERT: He was very tired.
    MATRIX: Callahan kept plugging away.
12. INSERT: He was a brooding type.
    MATRIX: Rob was always polite enough.
13. INSERT: His sister had a sunny disposition.
    MATRIX: Rob was a brooding type.
14. INSERT: He sends a written apology.
    MATRIX: Mr. Snowbound is willing to forgive Rob.

A clause with *since* may have either a time meaning or a cause meaning. There is usually a comma before it if it has a cause meaning, but not if it means time:

He hasn't been to the house since he quarrelled with Harry.
He never comes to the house, since he can't stand Harry.

Clauses in the end position with other subordinators do not usually have a comma before them. Make result sentences of the following, using *if, unless, while, before, after,* or *because.* Put the insert sentence after the matrix, and use no comma.

15. INSERT: He needs help.
    MATRIX: We'll help him.
16. INSERT: It was raining.
    MATRIX: They stayed home.
17. INSERT: Mr. Betrix watered the lawn.
    MATRIX: Malcolm pruned the almond tree.
18. INSERT: They realized what was happening.
    MATRIX: They quietly tiptoed away.
19. INSERT: I get some more money.
    MATRIX: I can't buy the picture.
20. INSERT: He knew what the trouble was.
    MATRIX: The police arrested him.

A sentence with such a subordinator will have a comma when the clause is felt to be an afterthought:

There is really no excuse for Ed's behavior, unless perhaps we didn't get the whole story.

You must use your ear in deciding how to punctuate these.

Syntax

Relative Clauses as Sentence Modifiers

We have seen that relative clauses may be used in noun phrase functions:

INSERT: He left at noon.
MATRIX: I knew + NP. $\Rightarrow$
RESULT: I knew when he left.

Such clauses can also function as sentence modifiers, as in the following example:

INSERT: He left at noon.
MATRIX: We went to the station to see him off. $\Rightarrow$
RESULT: When he left, we went to the station to see him off.

Note the comma in the result sentence above.

Make similar sentences with *when* from these.

1. INSERT: I found out about it later.
   MATRIX: I protested to Mrs. Appletree.
2. INSERT: They heard the news yesterday.
   MATRIX: They boarded a plane for Kansas City.
3. INSERT: The team came on the field.
   MATRIX: The crowd cheered.

As is sometimes used to replace an adverbial of time in the insert. Make sentences with *as* from the following. Remember the comma.

4. INSERT: He was getting out of the car then.
   MATRIX: He twisted his ankle.
5. INSERT: They walked out of the building at five o'clock.
   MATRIX: The sirens began to wail.

An adverbial of place in the insert sentence may be replaced by *where* or *wherever*. The relative clause that results may be used as a sentence modifier.

INSERT: Roderick traveled to many countries.
MATRIX: He thought about Melinda. $\Rightarrow$
RESULT: Wherever Roderick traveled, he thought about Melinda.

Make result sentences with *where* or *wherever* from the following pairs of insert and matrix sentences.

6. INSERT: The ground is stony there.
   MATRIX: The crops do poorly.
7. INSERT: Berkman lived in many cities.
   MATRIX: He always found a good job.
8. INSERT: Mary went everywhere.
   MATRIX: The lamb followed her.

Syntax

Deletion in Subordinate and Relative Clauses

It is often possible in either a subordinate or a relative clause to drop out the subject and a following form of *be* according to this deletion transformation:

$$\left\{ \begin{array}{l} \text{subordinator} \\ \text{relative adverb} \end{array} \right\} + \text{NP} + \text{tense} + \text{be} + \text{X} \rightrightarrows \left\{ \begin{array}{l} \text{subordinator} \\ \text{relative adverb} \end{array} \right\} + \text{X}$$

Suppose we have the relative clause *when Joe is in Boston.* This consists of the following morphemes:

when + Joe + present + be + in + Boston

What is the relative adverb? What is the tense? What is the X? According to the rule, this can be rewritten as follows:

when + in + Boston

The deleted NP will be made clear by the subject of the matrix sentence:

When Joe is in Boston, Joe does as the Bostonians do. $\rightrightarrows$
When in Boston, Joe does as the Bostonians do.

It is clear that Joe is the one in Boston and that the insert sentence is something like "Joe is in Boston occasionally."

Rewrite the following, deleting NP + tense + *be* from the subordinate or relative clause.

1. When Steindorf was visiting relatives, Steindorf always brought his own food.
2. When I was hungry, I would get food at the delicatessen.
3. Although Rob was polite, Rob was a brooding person.
4. If you are late, you can eat in the kitchen.
5. While Mark was in class, Mark used standard English.

The subject *it* is frequently deleted even if the subject of the matrix is different:

> When it was necessary, Mr. Wynn could be very stern. ⇉
> When necessary, Mr. Wynn could be very stern.

One has to be careful to avoid ambiguity in deleting the subject *it*. For example, "When cold, Mr. Wynn wore his overcoat" might be a deletion of *when it was cold,* but on the other hand it might be a deletion of *when he was cold.* The following is an error rather like a dangling modifier:

> *When hungry, Mr. Wynn gave the cat some food.

Who's hungry?

Other deletions are optional or obligatory in relative clauses on the general principle that major structures in the matrix are not repeated in the insert. In particular, structures after tense-modal, tense-*have,* and tense-*be* are commonly omitted, and when what follows tense in the verb phrase is a verbal, the verbal is deleted and *do* is provided to carry the tense. The mechanism is just like that of T-yes/no or T-negative:

INSERT: You can understand it.⎫
MATRIX: I can understand it.   ⎬ ⇉
RESULT: I can understand it if you can understand it. ⇉
          I can understand it if you can.

INSERT: He heard the noise. ⎫
MATRIX: She heard the noise. ⎬ ⇉
RESULT: She heard the noise before he heard the noise. ⇉
          She heard the noise before he did.

Make similar deletions from the following.

6. Jack will get to the gym before you will get to the gym.
7. Jack gets to the gym before you get to the gym.
8. The boys are reciting after the girls are reciting.
9. Sam has time to discuss it if Tim has time to discuss it.
10. I took the examination when Peter took the examination.
11. I can dive from the high board if you can dive from the high board.

Syntax

Nominative Absolutes

A *nominative absolute* is a construction like *Mark being sick* in the sentence "Mark being sick, the performance had to be postponed." The term *nominative absolute* is a very old traditional one, going back to the influence of Latin grammar. We could just as well use another term; we could call it X or 007 if we wanted. It is just another kind of sentence modifier. But tradition is important and should be kept when possible, so we will use the traditional term.

This is the transformation that transforms an insert sentence into a nominative absolute:

$$\text{NP + tense + X} \Rightarrow \text{NP + ing + X}$$

If we begin with "Mark was absent," we have this string:

Mark + past + be + absent

Mark is the NP of the rule. What is the tense? What is the X? The transformation goes thus:

Mark + past + be + absent $\Rightarrow$ Mark + ing + be + absent

This, then, is used with a matrix sentence like "The performance had to be postponed," to give the result sentence, "Mark being absent, the performance had to be postponed."

Notice that in this transformation the subject of the insert does not have to be the same as the subject of the matrix. In our example, the subject of the insert is *Mark* and that of the matrix, *the performance.*

Make result sentences with nominative absolutes from the following. Remove the tense of the insert sentence, and use the *ing* form of whatever the tense was attached to.

1. INSERT: Marcella was sick.
   MATRIX: Vivian took her place.
2. INSERT: The chest was locked.
   MATRIX: They had to pry it open.
3. INSERT: Edna's plane had been delayed.
   MATRIX: They had a long wait at the airport.
4. INSERT: Mr. Jarvis had pointed out the difficulty.
   MATRIX: The group debated what they should do next.

5. INSERT: The day was a very clear one.
   MATRIX: We had a fine view of the city.
6. INSERT: The troops had been given their orders.
   MATRIX: There was nothing to do but wait.
7. INSERT: All signs were favorable.
   MATRIX: We decided to take the canoe trip.
8. INSERT: What he wanted was power.
   MATRIX: He couldn't be tempted by money.

What kind of structure is the subject of the insert of 8? In a variation, the tense and *be* may simply be deleted:

INSERT: The job was finished.
MATRIX: Mr. Grimshaw lighted his pipe. } ⇒
RESULT: The job finished, Mr. Grimshaw lighted his pipe.

Make result sentences from the following by simply deleting the tense and *be*.

 9. INSERT: The dinner was ready.
    MATRIX: Silverbrace sounded the gong.
10. INSERT: Jack was already overburdened with work.
    MATRIX: Miss Whiffle made Dick chairman.
11. INSERT: Everything was in order.
    MATRIX: We saw no objection to going ahead.
12. INSERT: They were reassured.
    MATRIX: No obstacle remained.

The last result sentence, "They reassured, no obstacle remained," is a pretty unlikely one, but we bring it in to explain the source of the term *nominative absolute*. As you know, five of the personal pronouns and *who* have different forms according to whether they function as subjects or objects: *they/them, he/him, who/whom,* etc. The subject forms are sometimes called *nominative* forms and the object forms *accusative* forms. These terms come from Latin grammar. When the subject of the insert sentence in this transformation is a personal pronoun, it keeps the nominative form: *they,* not *them.* The *absolute* part of the term derives from the fact that the insert and the matrix sentence do not have to have the same subject. The sentence modifier is independent, as it were, of the matrix, so far as its subject is concerned, and *absolute* is here a kind of synonym for *independent.*

Morphology

The Subjunctive

The nominative-accusative contrast is vestigial in English. That is, we have now just a remnant, or vestige, of what was once a much larger system. At one time all noun phrases showed a contrast between subject and object forms, as most do in Latin and Greek and modern Russian. Now this contrast is limited to just the pronouns mentioned.

Another vestige of what was once a large system is what is called the *subjunctive mood.* At one time our verbs, and also *be,* had quite different forms according to the speaker's attitude toward the content of the sentence — for example, whether it was true or not, whether it was likely, whether it was desirable. The word *mood* is a variant of *mode,* which has the adjective form *modal,* and in fact most of these feelings are now expressed in the modals of the auxiliary. But a few vestiges of the old system remain.

Compare the subordinate clauses in these two sentences:

> I hope that he comes.
> I asked that he come.

In both sentences, *come* is present tense. But whereas in the first it has the *s* form after *he,* according to the usual rule, in the second it has the simple form. A morphological rule says that a verb must have the simple form, no matter what the subject, in certain conditions — particularly, when it occurs in a subordinate clause functioning as object of verbs like *ask, urge, insist. Be* has the form *be:*

> I asked that he *be* here.

The same morphological rule operates when the clause serves as complement of certain adjectives:

> It is important that he come.
> It is important that he be here.

These forms of the verb and *be* are what remain of the subjunctive mood in English, so far as the present tense goes.

Make result sentences from the following, using the subjunctive mood.

  1. INSERT: She leaves.
     MATRIX: I asked + NP.

2. INSERT: Mr. Burroughs is invited.
   MATRIX: Mr. Damron insisted + NP.
3. INSERT: Everyone hands in the paper by Friday.
   MATRIX: Mr. Baxter urged + NP.
4. INSERT: The book is read.
   MATRIX: It was required + NP.
5. INSERT: David drinks more milk.
   MATRIX: The doctor suggested + NP.
6. INSERT: The colonel is awakened.
   MATRIX: General Axworthy ordered + NP.
7. INSERT: Each applicant is given an oral interview.
   MATRIX: It is necessary + NP.
8. INSERT: Angela talks to Bruce first.
   MATRIX: It was imperative + NP.
9. INSERT: I am up by six.
   MATRIX: The job required + NP.
10. INSERT: Miss Durkin is there.
    MATRIX: Mr. Meadows wished + NP.

Now compare the following sentences and notice what form of *be* is used in each:

> Mr. Meadows wished that Miss Durkin be there.
> Mr. Meadows wished that Miss Durkin were there.

In the first sentence, with *be*, *wished* has something of the meaning of *requested* or *suggested*. Mr. Meadows expressed the wish, and Miss Durkin turned up. But in the second sentence, with *were*, Mr. Meadows is wishing for something that didn't happen. Miss Durkin wasn't there, but Mr. Meadows wished she were.

But the only formal difference in the two sentences is that between *be* and *were*. In the first sentence, *be* is the subjunctive form of *be* for the present tense, in the use already discussed, in a clause following a verb with the meaning of *ask*. In the second, *were* is the subjunctive form of *be* for the past tense. *Were* is the subjunctive past tense form whatever the subject. We don't say *"Miss Durkin were here," but we do say "I wish Miss Durkin were here."

Only *be* has a special form for the subjunctive in the past. For verbs we use either the regular past form ("I wish Miss Durkin cooked") or a modal ("I wish Miss Durkin could cook"). The past subjunctive of *be* is used in clauses that express things that aren't so. (Miss Durkin wasn't there. He wished that she *were*.) In clauses in noun phrase functions, it occurs mostly after the verb *wish*. Use it in the results of the following.

11. INSERT: It was sunny.
    MATRIX: I wish + NP.
12. INSERT: Harold was on our side.
    MATRIX: We wished + NP.
13. INSERT: School was over.
    MATRIX: Georgette wished + NP.
14. INSERT: The weather was warm.
    MATRIX: We all wished + NP.

The past subjunctive of *be* — which is *were* for all subjects —
occurs also in clauses that function as sentence modifiers. Here also
the clause expresses something that isn't so. The subordinator in
such clauses is commonly *if*, and the matrix usually contains a modal:

INSERT: George was chairman.
MATRIX: He would get things done. }⇒
RESULT: If George were chairman, he would get things done.

Make similar result sentences from the following. Don't forget the
comma.

15. INSERT: I was in charge.
    MATRIX: There would be some changes made.
16. INSERT: Sally was helping us.
    MATRIX: We would get through in no time.
17. INSERT: It was a little warmer.
    MATRIX: I wouldn't wear my coat.
18. INSERT: The store was near his house.
    MATRIX: Bert could pick up the package.
19. INSERT: Father was here.
    MATRIX: Things would quiet down.
20. INSERT: I was rich.
    MATRIX: I could travel around the world.
21. INSERT: Charley was willing.
    MATRIX: We could use his canoe.
22. INSERT: Wishes were horses.
    MATRIX: Beggars could ride.

When the subject of the insert is plural, as in the last sentence,
the subjunctive is not different in form, and the meaning of unreality
is carried by the *if*.

The past subjunctive is used also in clauses functioning as adverbials of manner. These clauses are mostly introduced by *as if* or *as
though*:

INSERT: He was chairman.
MATRIX: George acted + Adv-m. $\Big\} \Rightarrow$
RESULT: George acted as if he were chairman.

Make result sentences from the following, using either *as if* or *as though*, whichever sounds better to you. There is no comma punctuation in these sentences.

23. INSERT: She was sick.
    MATRIX: Ellen acted + Adv-m.
24. INSERT: There was all the time in the world.
    MATRIX: Judy behaved + Adv-m.
25. INSERT: It was a complete shock to him.
    MATRIX: Maxwell looked + Adv-m.
26. INSERT: He was asleep on his feet.
    MATRIX: He weaved about + Adv-m.
27. INSERT: She was unhappy.
    MATRIX: She talked + Adv-m.
28. INSERT: They were unsure of themselves.
    MATRIX: The boys stammered + Adv-m.

Morphology

The Morpheme al

We have already noticed the morpheme **al** as a part of adjectives and adverbs of manner made on base words ending in –*ic:*

music/musical/musically
heroic/heroically
enthusiastic/enthusiastically

This ending is used with many other base words too. In fact, nearly two thousand English words end with a syllable spelled –*al.* This morpheme comes to us from Latin, and most of the bases to which it is added also come from Latin.

The morpheme **al** is used to make adjectives from nouns. The adjective means pertaining to or relating to whatever the noun means. Thus *tribe* + **al** is *tribal,* which means pertaining to a tribe. **Al** adjectives may also be made from the following nouns:

tide	norm	form
faction	emotion	season
rent	brute	person
nation	structure	anecdote

This morpheme often has an effect on the stress. Whether or not the morpheme affects the stress depends on the sounds with which the base word ends. When the morpheme does have an effect, it is to put the first stress on the syllable just before the **al.** The following adjectives are pronounced as marked:

developméntal	homicídal	monárchal
baptísmal	orchéstral	oriéntal
paréntal	anecdótal	sepúlchral

A number of **al** words were used, even in Latin, as nouns as well as or instead of adjectives, and many are used this way in English too. An example is *principal.* The basic meaning is "chief," as in *the principal reason,* but we use the word as a noun in the sense *principal of a school,* where it means the chief person of the school. Each of the following may be used as an adjective or as a noun:

original	diagonal
principal	professional

For some **al** words, the noun use is the most important. *Animal* is an example. This was made in Latin from the noun *anima,* which meant breath or life. An "animal being," or, for short, an animal, was one with life in it. Other **al** words from Latin include:

hymnal	decimal	journal	corporal

We have a number of noun-adjective pairs in English of which the noun is of native English origin and the adjective is borrowed from Latin. An example is *nose/nasal.* It is true that we have an adjective *nosy,* but when we mean not "inquisitive" but "pertaining to the nose," we use *nasal,* not *nosy:* "He had trouble with his nasal passages." Each of the following **al** adjectives refers to a part of the body:

dental	oral	aural	lingual
labial	cerebral	digital	dorsal

Find the etymologies of the following words:

matinal	nominal	coronal
fraternal	cathedral	lateral
austral	saggital	rival

Why do you suppose Australia was so named?

The morpheme **al** is also used to make nouns from verbs, as in *arrive/arrival.* Such nouns mean the act of doing whatever the verbs mean. Nouns may be made from the following verbs by adding *–al:*

betray	dispose	revive
rehearse	renew	portray
propose	reverse	bestow
dismiss	acquit	survive

Morphology

The *–ial* Form of al

Many adjectives in Latin had an *i* before *–al,* and these words have come into English with the morpheme **al** written *–ial.* Make adjectives of the following by adding *–ial:*

adverb   face   editor   part

The *–ial* form of **al** has a regular effect on stress. It puts the first stress on the syllable immediately before the *–ial* if it isn't there already in the base word: *éditor/editórial.* This can be useful in spelling. If you are in doubt about whether *editor* should end in *–or* or *–er, editorial* tells you.

Pronounce the following words in *–ial* together with the base words that underlie them, and note the shifting of the stress:

gladiatorial	senatorial	tutorial
participial	presidential	residential
sacrificial	proverbial	microbial
differential	oratorial	managerial

Nouns ending in *–y* drop the *y* before *–ial: ceremony/ceremonial.* (One could also say that they change *y* to *i* before *–al;* it comes to the same thing.) Make *–ial* adjectives from the following, and note again the shift in stress:

matrimony	custody	colony
testimony	glossary	secretary
monastery	memory	observatory

Words in the *–ial* form of **al,** like those in the *–al* form, often come directly from Latin and have no underlying English word, as in the following:

| connubial | terrestrial | celestial |
| septennial | primordial | parochial |

A relatively few words with the **al** meaning end in the spelling
–*eal*. The following are the most important of them:

laryngeal	lineal	cereal
sidereal	ethereal	funereal
corporeal	arboreal	empyreal

Morphology

The Morpheme ular

Another adjective-forming morpheme is **ular,** in words like *spec-
tacular.* This also comes from Latin and was used with nouns which
in Latin had a diminutive morpheme spelled –*ul.* Some of the **ular**
words in English are very common: *regular, circular, singular.* Others
are much less common and may be found only in rather special
writing, scientific and the like.

This morpheme has a very regular effect on stress. It puts the
first stress on the syllable immediately preceding it. Pronounce the
following with the first stress as marked:

spectácular	vehícular	perpendícular
rectángular	penínsular	tubércular

Quite a number of **ular** words are related to nouns ending in the
spelling –*le: spectacle/spectacular.* Note the spelling relationships.
The –*le* of the noun becomes the –*ul–* of the adjective. Remember
this rule in making adjectives of the following nouns:

circle	oracle	angle	gland
cell	valve	muscle	particle

Find out the meaning of the following less common **ular** words.
Tell if you can the meaning of the underlying Latin word.

avuncular	pedicular	vernacular
funicular	reticular	homuncular

Some adjectives end in –*ar* instead of –*ular: pole/polar.* Find the
meaning of the Latin word underlying each of the following:

lunar	solar	molar	stellar

A very few adjectives end in –*iar,* the only common ones being
peculiar and *familiar.*

Morphology

The Morpheme an

Still another adjective-forming morpheme is **an,** which is spelled *–an* in some words and *–ian* in others. It is used first of all with names of places: *American, African, Russian.* These can mostly be used as nouns as well as adjectives:

ADJ.:   He's American.
NOUN: He's an American.

Make **an** words from these place names:

Nebraska   California   South Dakota

With some formations there are other changes: *Texas/Texan.*
When **an** has the form *–ian,* the first stress goes on the syllable immediately before the suffix: *Bóston/Bostónian.* Add *–ian* to the following, and note where the stress falls:

Canada   Corinth   Mongol
reptile   Hungary   grammar

This morpheme is commonly added to names of people to make adjectives of them. Thus *Shakespearian* means pertaining to Shakespeare. The *–ian* form is the most common, and it has the effect on stress already noted. Add it to the following:

Bacon   Johnson   Mendel   Edward   Smith

SUMMARY OF RULES

T-subordinate clause

The transformation that produces subordinate clauses for use in noun phrase functions also produces them for use as sentence modifiers:

$$S \Rrightarrow Sub + S$$

The subordinators used include such words as *because, if, although, whereas, since, unless, until.*

Clauses produced by the relative clause transformations are also used as sentence modifiers. They are introduced by such relative adverbs as *when, as, where, wherever.*

T-deletion for subordinate and relative clauses

$$\left\{ \begin{array}{l} \text{subordinator} \\ \text{relative adverb} \end{array} \right\} + \text{NP} + \text{tense} + \text{be} + \text{X} \Rightarrow \left\{ \begin{array}{l} \text{subordinator} \\ \text{relative adverb} \end{array} \right\} + \text{X}$$

For example, *when he was in Boston* may become *when in Boston.* When this deletion takes place, the subject of the insert sentence and the matrix sentence is usually the same. After the matrix sentence, a part of the insert sentence predicate that is identical with that of the matrix sentence will usually be deleted, leaving a modal, *have, be,* or *do.*

T-nominative absolute

$$\text{NP} + \text{tense} + \text{X} \Rightarrow \text{NP} + \text{ing} + \text{X}$$

The morpheme **ing** is substituted for tense to produce what is called a nominative absolute, like *Mark being absent.* In a variation of this, both tense and a following *be* are deleted: *Mark absent.*

Subjunctive Mood

In certain constructions a phonological rule produces what is called the subjunctive mood. In this, verbs have the simple form with all subjects in the present tense, and *be* has the form *be.* In the past tense, *be* has the form *were* for all subjects: "I asked that he come," "I asked that he be here," "I wish that he were here."

TEST

1. Make result sentences of the type "Since he didn't want to make trouble, Bert kept quiet" from the following. Use any subordinator that makes good sense.
   - a. INSERT: He was only a little boy.
   - MATRIX: He seemed to understand a great deal.
   - b. INSERT: The fever goes down soon.
   - MATRIX: You should call a doctor.
   - c. INSERT: He had to get up at five.
   - MATRIX: Smithfield went to bed early.
   - d. INSERT: It used to take many days to get there.
   - MATRIX: Europe is now only a few hours away.

2. Make a relative clause with *when, whenever, as, where,* or *wherever* from the insert and use it as a sentence modifier before the matrix.

   a. INSERT: Montrose left town yesterday.
     MATRIX: He didn't know where he was going.
   b. INSERT: Clarice gets a good idea sometimes.
     MATRIX: She jots it down in her notebook.
   c. INSERT: He was coming in then.
     MATRIX: He bumped into Colonel Proud.
   d. INSERT: There is warm weather in Southern California.
     MATRIX: Avocados may be grown.
   e. INSERT: She stopped here and there.
     MATRIX: She sent us a postcard.

3. Rewrite the following, making the possible deletions from the sentence modifier.

   a. When Ellen is in Texas, Ellen does as the Texans do.
   b. When he is ill with a cold, he stays in bed.
   c. If you are interested, you should send for a free booklet.
   d. While he was waiting for a bus, David saw a red Cadillac.

4. Make result sentences from the following, using the insert sentence in the form of a nominative absolute.

   a. INSERT: The revolver was empty.
     MATRIX: Sternworthy picked up an axe.
   b. INSERT: The sun had set.
     MATRIX: We began to think about dinner.
   c. INSERT: Al was a friend of mine.
     MATRIX: I felt I could speak frankly.
   d. INSERT: The children had been got off to bed.
     MATRIX: Mrs. Humble flopped into a chair.

5. Make result sentences from the following, using the subjunctive form of the verb or *be* in the subordinate clause.

   a. INSERT: She leaves the document with me.
     MATRIX: I asked + NP.
   b. INSERT: Mark is a little more polite.
     MATRIX: Mr. Feebleton suggested + NP.
   c. INSERT: The radio is turned down.
     MATRIX: The neighbors requested + NP.
   d. INSERT: He finds fault with everything.
     MATRIX: Is it necessary + NP?
   e. INSERT: The paper is written on a typewriter.
     MATRIX: It was required + NP.

6. From the following, make result sentences containing subordinate clauses with *if* and the past subjunctive of *be*.

a. INSERT: Danny was with us.
   MATRIX: We wouldn't have to worry about him.
b. INSERT: Anyone was home.
   MATRIX: There would be a light on.
c. INSERT: I was you.
   MATRIX: I'd call a doctor.
d. INSERT: Sue was a little older.
   MATRIX: She could go by herself.
e. INSERT: The weather was better.
   MATRIX: We could eat outside.

7. Make result sentences with *as if* or *as though* and the past subjunctive from the following.

a. INSERT: He was ill.
   MATRIX: Benny looked + Adv-m.
b. INSERT: Her foot was hurting her.
   MATRIX: Barbara walked + Adv-m.
c. INSERT: He wasn't interested.
   MATRIX: Jim acted + Adv-m.

8. Make words from the following by adding the morpheme **al**. Some have the *–al* form and some the *–ial* form.

emotion   brute   tutor   parent   adverb

9. Make adjectives by adding **ular** to the following:

circle   rectangle   muscle   particle

10. Make adjectives by adding **an** to the following. Some have the morpheme in the form *–an* and some in *–ian.*

Canada   Nebraska   Hungary   grammar   Nevada

REVIEW QUESTIONS

1. Subordinate clauses and relative clauses may function as noun phrases and as noun phrase modifiers. How else may they function?

2. What is the general punctuation rule when a sentence modifier comes before the matrix sentence?

3. Name five words used as subordinators.

4. Name two subordinators that usually have commas before them even when the clause comes after the matrix.

5. What are the two meanings of *since?*

6. Name two relative adverbs.

7. What may be deleted in the sentence "When Bill is eating, Bill never reads"?

8. What is a nominative absolute, and why is it so called?

9. What do we mean when we say that the nominative-accusative contrast is vestigial in English?

10. How does the present tense form of a verb in the subjunctive mood differ from the usual present tense form?

11. What is the present tense form of *be* in the subjunctive mood? What is the past tense form?

12. After verbs with what kind of meaning does a subordinate clause have the present subjunctive of verbs or *be*?

13. What is the difference in meaning between "He wished that she be there" and "He wished that she were there"?

14. From what kind of words does **al** make adjectives?

15. What kind of word is made by verb + **al**?

16. What is a *principal*? a *principle*?

17. What is the difference between *nosy* and *nasal*?

18. Name two adjectives from Latin other than *nasal* that refer to parts of the body.

19. When **al** has the form –*ial*, what is the effect on stress?

20. What effect does **ular** have on stress? What kind of words are made by the addition of **ular** to nouns?

21. To what kind of nouns is the morpheme **an** added?

22. When **an** has the form –*ian*, what is the effect on stress?

CHAPTER 17

Syntax

T-for . . . to

Earlier it was shown that one way to embed an insert sentence in a matrix is to transform the insert by this rule:

$$S \rightrightarrows Sub + S$$

After the insert has been transformed by the rule for T-subordinate clause, it is used in an NP position in the matrix:

INSERT: Steve raised pigeons.
MATRIX: NP + was widely known. $\Big\} \Rightarrow$
RESULT: That Steve raised pigeons was widely known.

The *it* transformation can then put the word *it* in the subject position and transpose the embedded sentence to a position after the matrix:

It was widely known that Steve raised pigeons.

The subordinate clause can occur in functions other than that of subject:

INSERT: The word had been abolished.
MATRIX: The Party members knew + NP. $\Big\} \Rightarrow$
RESULT: The Party members knew that the word had been abolished.

What is the function of the subordinate clause above?

Another way in which an insert sentence can be embedded in a matrix is by the use of the words *for* and *to:*

For the Party to abolish the word was necessary.

What group of words make up the subject of this result sentence? What noun phrase stands in the subject relationship to *abolish* in the *for . . . to* result sentence?

We can show the development of the example in this way:

INSERT: The Party + tense + abolish the word. ⎫ →
MATRIX: NP + was necessary.   ⎭ ⇉
RESULT: For + the Party + to + abolish the word + was
          necessary.

What words occur in both the insert sentence and the result sentence? What element occurring in the insert sentence is deleted in the result sentence? What two morphemes not in the insert sentence are added in the result sentence?

The part of T-for . . . to that transforms the insert is this:

$$NP + tense + X \rightrightarrows for + NP + to + X$$

To replaces the tense, and *for* is used before the NP subject. The NP is in the subject relation to the verbal or *be* construction in the result as it is in the insert.

Here is another example:

INSERT: Max + tense + be late. ⎫ →
MATRIX: NP + was unheard of. ⎭ ⇉
RESULT: For + Max + to + be late + was unheard of. ⇉
          For Max to be late was unheard of.

Write results for the following, as shown in the preceding example. That is, for each insert and result pair given, write a line showing the key elements of the result sentence between plus signs, and then write the actual result sentence.

1. INSERT: Marline + tense + disobey.
   MATRIX: NP + was surprising.
2. INSERT: Mr. Cresap + tense + try to fix it himself.
   MATRIX: NP + was foolish.
3. INSERT: The girls + tense + complain about it.
   MATRIX: NP + was natural.
4. INSERT: Mrs. Wood + tense + be here by seven.
   MATRIX: NP + would require that she get up at five.
5. INSERT: The rabbits + tense + refuse the alfalfa.
   MATRIX: NP + was very annoying.

When the subject of the insert is a personal pronoun, the object form is used in the result:

INSERT: He + tense + learn to drive. ⎫
MATRIX: NP + took a lot of time.   ⎬ ⇒
RESULT: For him to learn to drive took a lot of time.

Write similar result sentences for the following.

6. INSERT: She + tense + refuse ice cream.
   MATRIX: NP + was something new.
7. INSERT: They + tense + interfere.
   MATRIX: NP + is ridiculous.
8. INSERT: I + tense + understand that.
   MATRIX: NP + is rather difficult.
9. INSERT: He + tense + say that to Minnabelle.
   MATRIX: NP + was inexcusable.
10. INSERT: We + tense + be there by eight.
    MATRIX: NP + is impossible.

The *it* transformation that puts *it* at the beginning of the sentence and a subordinate clause subject at the end is now familiar (for example, "That he will be here tomorrow is understood" ⇒ "It is understood that he will be here tomorrow"). This transformation operates also for the *for . . . to* construction:

> For us to be there by eight is impossible. ⇒
> It is impossible for us to be there by eight.

The transformation is not obligatory. Both of the sentences in the example are grammatical. But the *it* transform is clearly the more common, the more natural.

Apply the *it* transformation to the following *for . . . to* result sentences.

11. For Frank to talk to Sheila was hard.
12. For them to help us is unnecessary.
13. For George to repair the television took a lot of time.
14. For anyone to try to convince Susie was hopeless.
15. For someone to point out the error required courage.

Syntax

T-for . . . to, deletion

When the insert sentence has a vague subject, like 14 and 15 in the preceding exercise — that is, when it doesn't matter much what the subject of the insert is — a deletion transformation commonly takes place. One simply leaves out the word *for* and the subject of the insert. The deletion occurs also when the subject matters, but is known. Thus we might have these shortenings:

> For anyone to try to convince Susie was hopeless. $\Rightarrow$
> To try to convince Susie was hopeless.
> For me to be there at eight is impossible. $\Rightarrow$
> To be there at eight is impossible.

This is the transformation:

$$\text{for} + \text{NP} + \text{to} + \text{X} \Rightarrow \text{to} + \text{X}$$

Rewrite the following, deleting *for* + NP.

1. For someone to learn mathematics requires patience.
2. For Samuel to antagonize Lucy was a mistake.
3. For people to argue about politics is frustrating.
4. For anyone to dislike Minnabelle is impossible.
5. For me to finish the paper should be easy.
6. For somebody to convince Ralph is unlikely.
7. For you to win me over would be difficult.

The *it* transformation works on these deleted structures too:

> To finish the paper should be easy. $\Rightarrow$
> It should be easy to finish the paper.

Transform the following in the same way.

8. To find a solution was necessary.
9. To dislike Virginia was impossible.
10. To enlist Alicia's help was important.
11. To oppose Mr. Haywagon took courage.
12. To be editor of a dictionary is a thankless task.
13. To predict the outcome is futile.
14. To be cheerful is hard sometimes.

Syntax

The *for . . . to* Construction in the Complement Function

Insert sentences transformed to *for . . . to* sometimes occur as complements after *be:*

INSERT: His son + tense + be a senator. $\left.\begin{array}{c} \\ \end{array}\right\} \Rightarrow$
MATRIX: Mr. Burnwater's aim was + NP.

RESULT: Mr. Burnwater's aim was for his son to be a senator.

Make similar result sentences from the following.

   1. INSERT: Tom + tense + play the part of Julius Caesar.
      MATRIX: My notion was + NP.
   2. INSERT: Edna + tense + come a few minutes early.
      MATRIX: The plan is + NP.
   3. INSERT: Allan + tense + accompany Mrs. Heartness.
      MATRIX: The solution was + NP.
   4. INSERT: The children + tense + play quietly outside.
      MATRIX: Their intention was + NP.
   5. INSERT: Mr. Dixie + tense + win the prize.
      MATRIX: Mr. Dixie's hope was + NP.

The last sentence you wrote, if you did it according to directions, was ungrammatical: *"Mr. Dixie's hope was for Mr. Dixie to win the prize." In such a sentence, in which the subject of the insert repeats that of the matrix, the deletion of *for* + NP is generally obligatory:

     Mr. Dixie's hope was for Mr. Dixie to win the prize. ⇉
       Mr. Dixie's hope was to win the prize.

Deletion also may take place when the subject of the insert is clear from the context or doesn't matter very much:

     The object was for us to have a good time. ⇉
      The object was to have a good time.

This deletion would not take place if there were some special emphasis on the subject of the insert, some contrast with something else: "The object was for *us* to have a good time, not those other people."

Rewrite the following, deleting *for* + NP. In some sentences the deletion is obligatory, in others optional.

   6. John's ambition was for John to be rich.
   7. The problem was for us to find a way to open the safe.
   8. His difficulty is for him to get home after the meeting.
   9. My suggestion is for everyone to think it over for a while.
  10. Their intention was for them to float down the river on a raft.

Sometimes we have *for . . . to* constructions in both subject and complement functions:

   INSERT: John + tense + say something. ⎱ ⇉
   MATRIX: NP + is + NP. ⎰
   RESULT: For John to say something is + NP.

SECOND INSERT: Emily + tense + disagree.
SECOND MATRIX: For John to say something is + NP. $\Bigg\} \Rightarrow$
SECOND RESULT: For John to say something is for Emily to dis-
                  agree.

Make sentences like the second result above with the following insert sentences. Use the first as the subject of *is* and the second as the complement.

11. Albert + tense + come into a room.
    Mark + tense + leave.
12. Spring + tense + come.
    The swallows + tense + return to Capistrano.
13. Mr. Dodson + tense + have an idea.
    Mr. Fogg + tense + go into action.

When the subject of the two inserts is the same and known from the context or not important, the *for* + NP of both are usually deleted:

For anyone to know Billings is not necessarily for anyone to know
    Montana. $\Rightarrow$
To know Billings is not necessarily to know Montana.

Write similar sentences from the following.

14. For John to think was for John to act.
15. For someone to become Prime Minister was for someone to
    be in considerable peril.
16. For anyone to know Selma was for anyone to like her.
17. For Mr. Dallas to hear a sparrow was for Mr. Dallas to know
    that spring had come.
18. For them to hear of a problem was for them to organize a
    committee.
19. For us to know about need was for us to give help.

Syntax

T-poss. + ing

Another transformation produces constructions with meanings very similar to those produced by T-for . . . to but with a different pair of morphemes. These are constructions such as the subject of the following sentence:

Anne's misusing a word was unusual.

In "Anne's misusing a word was unusual," *Anne* is in the subject relation to *misuse* and tense is omitted, but now the subject is in the possessive form and the verb is in the *ing* form. The development goes like this:

INSERT: Anne + tense + misuse a word. $\left.\right\} \Rightarrow$
MATRIX: NP + was unusual.
RESULT: Anne + poss. + ing + misuse a word + was unusual.

The phonological rule we have discussed earlier converts *Anne +* **poss.** to *Anne's* and the **ing** goes on the end of *misuse* to give *misusing*. This is the insert part of the transformation, which we can call T-poss. + ing:

$$NP + tense + X \Rightarrow NP + poss. + ing + X$$

Here is another example:

INSERT: Max + tense + be late. $\left.\right\} \Rightarrow$
MATRIX: NP + was unheard of.
RESULT: Max + poss. + ing + be late + was unheard of. $\Rightarrow$
          Max's being late was unheard of.

Write results for the following like those of the example above. First write a line showing the key elements divided by plus signs. Then write the actual result sentence.

1. INSERT: Jim + tense + complain.
    MATRIX: NP + bothered us.
2. INSERT: Virginia + tense + tell on Mario.
    MATRIX: NP + was reprehensible.
3. INSERT: The rabbit + tense + go to sleep.
    MATRIX: NP + gave the tortoise the race.
4. INSERT: The store + tense + be closed.
    MATRIX: NP + never entered my mind.
5. INSERT: The children + tense + get something to eat.
    MATRIX: NP + was the important thing.
6. INSERT: The girls + tense + clean house.
    MATRIX: NP + must have destroyed the fingerprints.
7. INSERT: Their parents + tense + refuse to let them go.
    MATRIX: NP + spoiled everything.

When the subject of the insert is a personal pronoun, the special morphological rules for forming the possessive apply; for example, *we* + **poss.** → *our*.

INSERT: We + tense + win the money. ⎫
MATRIX: NP + changed everything.   ⎬ ⇒
RESULT: Our winning the money changed everything.

Write just the actual result sentences of the following, using T-poss. + ing.

8. INSERT: He + tense + speak up to Mr. Brady.
   MATRIX: NP + required courage.
9. INSERT: She + tense + play the drums.
   MATRIX: NP + kept the baby awake.
10. INSERT: You + tense + get sarcastic.
    MATRIX: NP + was what spoiled our chances.
11. INSERT: They + tense + have moved away.
    MATRIX: NP + interrupted a fine friendship.
12. INSERT: I + tense + be a lexicographer.
    MATRIX: NP + was a social disadvantage.

Syntax

The poss. + *ing* Construction in Other Functions

The construction produced in T-poss. + ing has a wider range of occurrence than the *for . . . to* construction. It can occur in all the NP functions:

OBJECT OF A VERB: I can understand *John's wanting to go.*
OBJECT OF A PREPOSITION: We were confused by *John's insisting.*
COMPLEMENT: The difficulty was *our having to get home.*

Write result sentences from the following, and be prepared to tell the function of the poss. + *ing* construction in each sentence you write.

1. INSERT: We + tense + leave early.
   MATRIX: Everybody noticed + NP.
2. INSERT: Diana + tense + be seen.
   MATRIX: The danger was + NP.
3. INSERT: Bill + tense + report late.
   MATRIX: There was an argument over + NP.
4. INSERT: The soldiers + tense + charge with bayonets.
   MATRIX: General Merrymount insisted on + NP.
5. INSERT: Edna + tense + burst into tears.
   MATRIX: The crisis was + NP.
6. INSERT: The children + tense + have to lie about it.
   MATRIX: She hated + NP.

7. INSERT: They + tense + claim a foul.
   MATRIX: We were confused by + NP.
8. INSERT: He + tense + steal the lunches.
   MATRIX: Johnson reported + NP.

Syntax

T-poss. + ing, deletion

We have noticed the possible deletion of *for* + NP in the *for . . .
to* construction:

> For anyone to believe the story was pretty hard. $\Rightarrow$
>   To believe the story was pretty hard.

Similarly, NP + poss. can often be deleted in the poss. + *ing* construction. As with *for . . . to,* the deletion ordinarily takes place
when the subject of the insert sentence is clear from the context or
doesn't matter:

> Anyone's believing the story was pretty hard. $\Rightarrow$
>   Believing the story was pretty hard.

This produces an *ing* phrase, just as deletion of personal pronoun +
tense + *be* from a relative clause may:

> People who are feeding the animals will be arrested. $\Rightarrow$
>   People feeding the animals will be arrested.

Thus a phrase like *feeding the animals* may have three different
sources. It may be generated by kernel rules — a verbal plus *ing*
from the auxiliary:

> John is feeding the animals.

Or it may come from deletion after T-relative:

> The boy feeding the animals is John.

Or it may come from deletion after T-poss. + ing:

> Feeding the animals is against the law.

The last sentence comes from something like *John's feeding the
animals,* which comes from the insert "John + tense + feed the
animals."

Rewrite the following sentences, deleting any occurrence of NP +
poss. Some of the deletions are obligatory.

1. Jeff's teasing Julie was a mistake.
2. Dirk was annoyed at Dirk's having to go to class.
3. Mr. Riverton hated anyone's talking at the table.
4. People's throwing canned tuna to the seals is forbidden.
5. I was aware of someone's singing in the living room.
6. Mrs. Treehouse was awakened by someone's screaming outside.
7. My upsetting the ink infuriated Miss Twistleton.
8. Anyone's understanding Billings is anyone's understanding Montana.
9. Cathy regretted Cathy's swallowing the cleaning fluid.
10. I admitted to my having seen the fight.
11. He was confused by his staring into the headlights.

Syntax

Constructions with *for . . . to* Used as Sentence Modifiers

English frequently uses *to* phrases as sentence modifiers. An example is the first part of "To go to San Diego, you turn right at the next stoplight." This results from obligatory deletion of a fuller sentence:

For you to go to San Diego, you turn right at the next stoplight.

This looks just like the *for . . . to* constructions we have seen used in such sentences as "For you to go to San Diego is a mistake." But there is a difference. The sentence modifier, in a still fuller sentence, can begin with the words *in order:*

In order for you to go to San Diego, you turn right at the next stoplight.

Now since the insert and the matrix have the same subject, the subject of the insert is obligatorily deleted:

In order to go to San Diego, you turn right at the next stoplight.

Then the *in order* may be optionally deleted:

To go to San Diego, you turn right at the next stoplight.

Here is another example:

INSERT: John + tense + understand science. $\Big\}\rightarrow$
MATRIX: John had to study mathematics.
RESULT: In order for John to understand science, John had to study mathematics. $\rightrightarrows$

(*obligatorily*) In order to understand science, John had to study mathematics. ⇉

(*optionally*) To understand science, John had to study mathematics.

If the subject of the insert sentence is different from that of the matrix, the *for* + NP is not deleted:

INSERT: John + tense + study mathematics. ⎫
MATRIX: His parents had to make sacrifices. ⎬ ⇉
RESULT: In order for John to study mathematics, his parents had to make sacrifices.

If we here deleted *for John* we would get "In order to study mathematics, his parents had to make sacrifices," and if our meaning is that John is the student, the deleted version of the sentence would be an error similar to the dangling modifier — we would have had to start with the insert "His parents + tense + study mathematics," and this is not what was intended.

Make result sentences beginning *in order* from the following. Delete the subject of the insert if it is the same as that of the matrix; otherwise don't. Don't delete the *in order*. Separate the sentence modifier from the matrix with a comma.

1. INSERT: Mary + tense + see better.
   MATRIX: Mary leaned over the rail.
2. INSERT: David + tense + make the trip.
   MATRIX: We had to lend him money.
3. INSERT: The British + tense + encourage the others to do better work.
   MATRIX: The British occasionally hanged an admiral.
4. INSERT: Fish + tense + get up the stream.
   MATRIX: Water had to be released from the dam.

Sentence modifiers of this type may occur after the matrix, as well as before it:

Water had to be released from the dam, in order for fish to get up the stream.

The comma is sometimes used when the sentence modifier is in this position and sometimes not. Make result sentences from the following, putting the sentence modifier after the matrix and punctuating as your ear instructs you.

5. INSERT: Ralph + tense + get ready for the ball.
   MATRIX: Ralph had to hurry home.
6. INSERT: Mr. Danby + tense + give the painters a chance
               to work.
   MATRIX: Mr. Danby moved out of the house.
7. INSERT: The others + tense + have a chance.
   MATRIX: Miss Maloney spoke very briefly.
8. INSERT: Dan + tense + become a veterinary surgeon.
   MATRIX: The Williamses made enormous sacrifices.

Syntax

Adverbials in the Sentence Modifier Position

Adverbials of various kinds can occur at the beginning of a sentence. For the most part these are generated in the kernel sentence by the kernel rules already given. They shift position by a simple single-base transformation:

$$X + verbal + Adv \Rightarrow Adv + X + verbal$$

According to the rule, the shift takes place as follows:

John + past + examine the books + in the meantime. $\Rightarrow$
       In the meantime + John + past + examine the books.

What is the verbal in this example? the X? the Adv?

There is no very large agreement on the part of writers and editors on how adverbials in this position should be punctuated. Some use a comma, and some don't:

In the meantime, John examined the books.
In the meantime John examined the books.

A comma is always used, however, when it is possible that the adverbial will wrongly scoop up a following structure. Suppose that we make the following transformation and that we omit the comma:

The house needed paint outside. $\Rightarrow$
       Outside the house needed paint.

One is likely to read the first three words wrongly as a prepositional phrase. To prevent this, one punctuates:

Outside, the house needed paint.

Transform the following and use the comma. Not all writers would punctuate in all of the sentences, but use the comma anyway to become familiar with its availability.

1. The house needed repairs underneath.
2. Streams of refugees blocked traffic on the roads.
3. Faint signs of morning could be seen in the east.
4. Richard read the letter with a choked voice.
5. They played pinochle after lunch.
6. The new arrivals were settling in upstairs.
7. The farmer had planted evergreens alongside.
8. Duncan was back with the coffee in no time.
9. Renfrew explained his plan afterwards.
10. An orchestra was playing outside.
11. The cider was cooling in the springhouse.
12. The refreshments were served at midnight.
13. The apples ripened in the sun.
14. The apples ripened slowly.

When the base sentence has a predicate consisting of *be* + Adv-p, a further change takes place. The subject and tense + *be* are transposed:

> An orchestra was inside. $\Rightarrow$ Inside was an orchestra.
> The map was on the table. $\Rightarrow$ On the table was the map.

Transform the following by transposing the subject and tense + *be*, as well as changing the position of the adverbial.

15. An angry crowd was in the street.
16. A scarecrow was in the middle of the cornfield.
17. A wrecked dory was on the beach.
18. A flagpole was outside the embassy.
19. A half-starved stowaway was in the lifeboat.
20. A huge chandelier was overhead.

You may note that these sentences satisfy the conditions for T-there. The last one, for example, could also be transformed into "There was a huge chandelier overhead." Or the two transformations can be combined:

> Overhead there was a huge chandelier.

Intransitive verbs followed by adverbials of place take part in a similar transformation:

> The promise of a better future lay beyond. $\Rightarrow$
> Beyond lay the promise of a better future.

Transpose the following similarly.

21. A large grey overcoat hung on the hook.
22. A beady-eyed official sat at the desk.
23. Denunciations of the dictionary appeared in the papers.
24. A slight breeze came from the ocean.
25. A swarthy sailor stood by the gun.

Morphology

The Adjective-forming Morpheme ive

The morpheme **ive,** which comes to us from Latin, is added mostly to verbs to make adjectives of them. Its meaning is "having a tendency toward" whatever the verb means. Thus *disrupt* + **ive** → *disruptive*, having a tendency to disrupt. Make adjectives by adding **ive** to each of the following:

prohibit	assert	act	attract
restrict	elect	possess	abuse

The addition of **ive** to many verbs involves other sound and spelling changes in patterns already familiar to you:

submit + **ive** → *submissive*   expend + **ive** → *expensive*

destroy + **ive** → *destructive*

Write the words represented by the following:

permit + **ive**	extend + **ive**	corrode + **ive**
repulse + **ive**	decide + **ive**	cohere + **ive**
expand + **ive**	explode + **ive**	deduce + **ive**

This morpheme is frequently added to verbs in **ate:**

manipulate + **ive** → *manipulative*

The stress generally, but not always, stays the same. In the following words the principal stress is marked:

remúnerative	cúmulative	commúnicative
interrógative	demónstrative	spéculative

In two of the six words above, the principal stress is not where it would be in the underlying **ate** verb. Which two?

We have observed that **ion** has been so often added to **ate** verbs that the combination **ation** has come itself to be felt as a morpheme, as in *starvation.* The same thing has happened with **ate + ive.** A new morpheme **ative** has come into being to be added directly to verbs. An example is *talkative*. This cannot be made up of **talkate* + **ive**, since there is no verb **talkate*. It is composed rather of *talk* + **ative**. Add **ative** to the following:

affirm	form	determine	prepare
explore	cure	calm	inform

A number of adjectives in **ive** have no underlying English verbs. The adjectives have been taken directly and by themselves from Latin. Find the meaning of each Latin verb embedded in the following:

adjective	cursive	fricative	sedative
purgative	amative	sanative	imperative

Morphology

The Noun-forming Morpheme ee

You are familiar with the morpheme **er**, which means doer of an action, as in *helper, employer, doctor*. Another morpheme, **ee**, which also makes nouns from verbs, has the meaning receiver of an action. Thus an *employer* is one who employs; an *employee* is one who is employed. In serious use, the **ee** words are mostly legal terms, in origin at least, as *grantor/grantee*.

The stress effect of **ee** is to put the principal stress on the *–ee* itself: *grantée*. In words in common use, however, the stress often shifts back to where it is in the underlying verb. One can say *employée*, but one is more likely to say *emplóyee*. Make an **ee** noun from each of the following, and let the principal stress fall on the *–ee:*

pay	divorce	escape	refer	trust	address

Sometimes **ee** is used to make a playful contrast with an **er** noun, the **ee** noun being coined for the moment:

"Are you the waiter?"   "No, I'm not. I'm a waitee."

Make a similar dialogue with **ee** words corresponding to the following: *driver, washer, murderer, teacher*.

Some words ending in the spelling *–ee* are made on different principles and do not have underlying verbs or corresponding nouns in **er**. Among them are:

perigee	apogee	refugee	filigree
repartee	chimpanzee	marquee	grandee

The morpheme **ee** comes from French, in which it is pronounced with the vowel /ā/ as in *may,* not with /ē/, as in *me.* It is still usually pronounced that way in *negligee* and *fiancee.*

Morphology

The Noun-forming Morphemes hood and ship

It might seem at first look that all of our derivational morphemes come to us from other languages, particularly Latin. But of course this is not so. The morpheme **er** is a native English one, as are a number of others. Among them is **hood,** which is added to concrete nouns to make abstract ones: *baby +* **hood** → *babyhood. Babyhood* means the condition or state of being a baby.

Make nouns in **hood** from the following:

priest	child	brother	girl
man	father	neighbor	parent
saint	boy	knight	widow

Hood is also added to a few adjectives to make nouns. Make nouns in **hood** from the following:

likely   hardy   lively

Like **ee, hood** is sometimes used playfully to coin new words: "Fido felt that the essence of doghood was to bite people." Such coinages hardly ever stick, of course, but they may relieve the tedium of the moment. Coin **hood** words from the following:

doctor   pupil   waiter   sibling

Another noun-forming morpheme coming down to us from Old English is **ship,** as in *friendship.* This has a meaning quite similar to that of **hood.** However, there are subtle differences. If we coin the word *authorhood* and ask ourselves whether it means the same thing as *authorship,* we would probably answer, not quite. *Authorhood* would mean the condition of being an author. But *authorship* would point more to the fact of having written something. We could say "Coughlin acknowledged the authorship of the novel" but hardly *"Coughlin acknowledged the authorhood of the novel."

Make **ship** nouns from these:

general	marksman	penman	citizen
kin	scholar	leader	partner
fellow	judge	seaman	sportsman

Like **hood, ship** can be used playfully in the coining of new words. There is a book by Stephen Potter called *Gamesmanship,* the science of winning games without actually cheating. The word is a takeoff on *sportsmanship* and led to other coinages, like *guestmanship, lifeman-ship,* and *one-upmanship.* All of these, like *sportsman,* have the morpheme **man,** which comes before the **ship.**

A few **ship** words are formed in other ways. *Hardship* has **ship** added to an adjective. In *worship,* the *wor–* part is a reduced form of the word *worth.*

Another morpheme from Old English used to make abstract nouns is **dom,** as in *kingdom.* The meaning is similar to that of **hood** and **ship,** but usually with some difference. *Kingdom* means the country, while *kinghood* means the condition of being a king.

Make nouns by adding **dom** to the following:

martyr   free   bore   official

Dom is also used quite a bit, playfully or otherwise, to coin new words. Such words are often used just once, or for the nonce, so they are called *nonce words.* Make a nonce word with **dom** from each of the following:

school   baseball   business   book

SUMMARY OF RULES

T-for . . . to

$$NP + tense + X \Rightarrow for + NP + to + X$$

This turns an insert sentence into a *for . . . to* construction, like *for John to forget about it.*

T-for . . . to, deletion

$$for + NP + to + X \Rightarrow to + X$$

The *for* and the NP may be deleted when the subject of the insert is clear from the context or doesn't matter.

T-poss. + ing

$$NP + tense + X \Rightarrow NP + poss. + ing + X$$

Again, this is just the insert part of the transformation, producing constructions like *John's forgetting about it.*

T-poss. + ing, deletion

$$NP + poss. + ing + X \rightrightarrows ing + X$$

The NP and the possessive morpheme may be deleted when the subject of the insert is clear or doesn't matter.

T-in order to

$$NP + tense + X \rightrightarrows in\ order\ for + NP + to + X$$

This produces something like *in order for John to forget about it,* which will be used as modifier of a matrix sentence.

T-in order to, deletion

a. in order for + NP + to + X $\rightrightarrows$ in order + to + X
b. in order for + NP + to + X $\rightrightarrows$ for + NP + to + X

The *a* part is obligatory when insert and matrix have the same subject. The *b* part is optional. Both the *in order* in *a* and the *for* + NP in *b* may be deleted, leaving *to* + X.

T-adverbial

$$X + verbal + Adv \rightrightarrows Adv + X + verbal$$

When the base sentence contains *be* + Adv-p in the predicate, there is a variation. A similar shift takes place in structures containing intransitive verbs and adverbials of place.

$$NP + tense + be + Adv\text{-}p \rightrightarrows Adv\text{-}p + tense + be + NP$$

TEST

1. Write a result sentence with a *for . . . to* construction from each of the following.

a. INSERT: Everyone + tense + be a little tense.
   MATRIX: NP + was natural.
b. INSERT: Maurice + tense + study Swedish.
   MATRIX: Mrs. Mulligan's dream was + NP.
c. INSERT: She + tense + arrive before nine.
   MATRIX: NP + is undesirable.
d. INSERT: The fullback + tense + pretend to be dead.
   MATRIX: The plan was + NP.
e. INSERT: I + past + complain to the teacher.
   MATRIX: NP + would be a bad mistake.

2. Rewrite the following, applying T-subordinate clause, it.

a. For Lou to get another coat was necessary.

b. For them to make a fuss is unusual.

c. For a few of the boys to forget their books is normal.

d. For Emmanuel to say a thing like that is unforgivable.

3. Write a result sentence with a poss. + ing construction for each of the following.

a. INSERT: Nelda + tense + catch a cold.
   MATRIX: NP + changed all our plans.

b. INSERT: He + tense + be an Arab.
   MATRIX: NP + has nothing to do with it.

c. INSERT: They + tense + want to come with us.
   MATRIX: We forgot about + NP.

d. INSERT: Mr. Parker + tense + ride on the hood.
   MATRIX: Mrs. Wilson objected to + NP.

e. INSERT: She + tense + have to go home after class.
   MATRIX: The difficulty was + NP.

f. INSERT: I + tense + be right all the time.
   MATRIX: Sally hated + NP.

g. INSERT: Parish + tense + come along.
   MATRIX: Payne insisted on + NP.

4. Rewrite the following, deleting each occurrence of NP + poss.

a. Anyone's speaking about it won't help.

b. We all regretted our having done it.

c. The problem was someone's having to explain it to Marilyn.

d. Mr. Butler was annoyed at his having to clean the fish.

5. Write a result sentence for each of these. Make the insert into a construction of the *in order for* NP *to* type. Leave out the *for* + NP if the deletion of it is obligatory. Put the sentence modifier before the matrix, and punctuate according to the rule given.

a. INSERT: John + tense + get home by midnight.
   MATRIX: John had to leave at eleven.

b. INSERT: Maxine + tense + be able to come.
   MATRIX: We had the party on Friday.

c. INSERT: The jam + tense + be cleared.
   MATRIX: The men had to dynamite the logs.

d. INSERT: Everyone + tense + have a chance to speak.
   MATRIX: The chairman limited each person to three minutes.

e. INSERT: We + tense + keep the animals from freezing.
   MATRIX: We put electric heaters in the barn.

6. Transpose the adverbials in the following sentences, and make any other changes necessary. Punctuate as recommended.

a. Mrs. Delphos was knitting a sweater in the corner.
b. We found a small boy outside.
c. Small onions were in the soup.
d. Grandma sat on the front porch.
e. Witherwood wrote a strange symbol on the envelope.
f. An enraged bear was in front of him.
g. The gates of Hercules lay behind him.
h. An escaped prisoner was in the trunk of the car.

7. Make adjectives in **ive** or **ative,** whichever is correct, from the following:

possess	destroy	submit	interrogate
affirm	respond	calm	attract
decide	determine	inform	explode

8. For each of the following sentences with an **er** noun, write a question with an **ee** one. For example, for "John was the employer," you would write "Who was the employee?"

a. John was the payer.
b. John was the endorser.
c. John was the addresser.

9. Write a plausible sentence using each of the following nonce words:

pupildom   garagemanship   waiterhood

REVIEW QUESTIONS

1. When *for* and *to* are added to the insert in T-for . . . to, what drops out?

2. How may a sentence like "For Anne to misuse a word was unusual" be further transformed?

3. When the NP of T-for . . . to is a personal pronoun, what form does it have in the result sentence?

4. Under what circumstances may the *for* and the NP of a *for . . . to* construction be deleted?

5. What is ungrammatical about "Mr. Dixie's hope was for Mr. Dixie to win the prize"?

6. In what NP functions may constructions produced by T-poss. + ing be used?

7. What morphemes may sometimes be deleted from a construction like *John's forgetting about it?*

8. From what three different sources may a phrase like *feeding the animals* come?

9. How do constructions with *in order to* function?

10. In "In order for John to see better, John leaned forward," what must be deleted, and what may be?

11. How may "The house needed paint outside" be transformed?

12. Why does "Outside the house needed paint" need a comma?

13. How may "The head of a deer hung on the wall" be transformed?

14. What kind of words are made by the addition of the morpheme **ive?**

15. In what way are *talkative* and *starvation* morphologically similar?

16. What kind of words are formed by the morpheme **ee?**

17. What is the effect on stress of the morpheme **ee?**

18. What kind of nouns are made by the morphemes **hood, ship,** and **dom?**

19. What is a *nonce word?*

CHAPTER 18

Syntax

T-conjunction

English has seven words called conjunctions: *and, or, but, for, yet, so,* and *nor.* Sometimes these words are called *coordinating conjunctions.* This is done when words like *that, because, whether, if* are called *subordinating conjunctions* and a distinguishing term is needed. Since we have called the *that, because* group simply *subordinators,* we can call *and, or, but, for, yet, so, nor* simply *conjunctions,* without confusion.

One function of conjunctions is simply to join base sentences. The transformation in which this is done is called T-conjunction. When a conjunction is used for this purpose, it is preceded by a comma. This punctuation rule is not universally followed, but it is common, and we shall assume it in this book.

Tell which conjunctions join base sentences in the following.

1. Ralph mowed the lawn, and Hank pruned the tree.
2. That's a Devonshire Warbler, or I am mistaken.
3. The mail had come, but there weren't any letters.
4. We started early, for we wanted to get to Wichita by six.
5. He had excellent manners, yet everyone distrusted him.
6. The pigs had all been sold, so we got rid of the sty.

When two sentences are joined by *nor,* the second is transformed according to a pattern we have seen operating in T-yes/no and elsewhere:

Mabel mustn't know about it, nor should anyone tell Edna.
Mabel never comes to meetings, nor has Edna been to one in a
    long while.
Mabel liked the idea, nor was Edna completely opposed to it.

Mabel never thought of it, nor did it occur to Edna.

A tense-modal, tense-*have*, or tense-*be* reverses with the subject after *nor*. If there is no modal, *have*, or *be*, just tense reverses, and *do* is added to express the tense. The *nor* takes the place of a *not* in an underlying base sentence:

Mabel never thought of it. ⎫ →
It did not occur to Edna. ⎭
Mabel never thought of it, nor did it occur to Edna.

Combine the following base sentences with the conjunction *nor*. Don't forget the comma.

   7. Bill didn't like the plan. Tom wasn't very keen on it.
   8. Mr. Dodson is always busy. Mr. Fogg hasn't much free time.
   9. The girls were very attentive. The boys weren't as noisy as usual.
  10. The coaches hadn't brought a football. It hadn't occurred to the players to do so.
  11. Lorna was willing to go swimming. Donna didn't object.
  12. Alfred was eager to go. Mac didn't have to be coaxed.

Put the following together with one of the six other conjunctions — *and, or, but, for, yet, so*. Try to use the one that makes the best sense. Don't use any one conjunction more than three times.

  13. Murphy showed up. There was no sign of Fiedler.
  14. Mr. Summers was feeling a little chilly. He spoke to the landlord about the heat.
  15. Alfred played the piano beautifully. Herbert was a marvel on the trombone.
  16. We were getting a little worried. None of us had heard from Mother for three years.
  17. Keep well buttoned up. You will come down with pneumonia.
  18. The job seemed almost impossible. Flaxman never allowed himself to get discouraged.
  19. The show was interrupted. The announcer warned all citizens to remain in their homes.
  20. I decided to make an appointment with the dentist. That pesky molar was bothering me again.
  21. Everything seemed to be all right. She couldn't get rid of a vague feeling of nervousness.
  22. Jason will do as I tell him. I'll know the reason why.
  23. I'm going to tell you a secret. You must promise to keep it to yourself.

24. It was still early afternoon. Mrs. Barton decided to stroll over to the museum.
25. Miss Hedgerow didn't want to marry Mr. Reilly. She couldn't bear to hurt his feelings.
26. He has to pay up by the afternoon. They will take away the furniture.
27. We supposed it was morning. The roosters were making a lot of fuss.

We have made the general rule that a conjunction connecting two sentences has a comma before it. Professional writers often omit the comma, particularly when the sentences are short, but you might as well stick to the rule if you have no reason for breaking it. Punctuation rules applied automatically are useful because they leave us time for other activities, like thinking.

We might perhaps have said more precisely that in such constructions there is *at least* a comma before the conjunction. There may also be a semicolon or a period:

The mail had come; but there weren't any letters for Mildred.
The mail had come. But there weren't any letters for Mildred.

The semicolon would be a bit unusual in a construction as short as this. It is more often used when one or both of the connecting sentences is long and contains commas within it:

The mail, which we had been waiting for since early dawn, had come; but there weren't any letters for Mildred.

The period is fairly common before a conjunction, however, even when both sentences are short. It has the effect of making the reader pause and of throwing a greater emphasis on the second sentence. There is a feeling among some people that it is wrong to use a period before *and* and other conjunctions, but this punctuation is used intentionally by most of our very best writers.

Use any conjunction that makes good sense between the following. Leave the period at the end of the first sentence.

28. Mary was going for another of her long walks. The lamb decided to stay home.
29. I did my best to reason with David. It seemed to me that he was making a dreadful mistake.
30. David was making a dreadful mistake. I felt it my duty to tell him so.

31. Marjorie certainly told a very convincing story. We couldn't rid ourselves of a nagging doubt.
32. Mr. Wiggins got a company to ship the boxes back to New Jersey. That's all there was to it.

Syntax

T-conjunction, deletion

When two sentences are joined by *and* and when parts of the two sentences are the same, one of the repeated parts can be deleted. This leaves the different parts joined by *and*. The different parts must, however, be the same sort of structure — for example, two noun phrases, two verb phrases, two adjectives, two relative clauses. Here is an example of this transformation, which is called T-conjunction, deletion:

> John saw a thrush, and John heard a whippoorwill. $\Rightarrow$
> John saw a thrush and heard a whippoorwill.

The subject of each sentence connected by *and* is identical, and so it is written only once. This leaves two verb phrases connected by the conjunction. This deletion, if not obligatory, is usually advisable, on the principle of saying things as economically as possible. If the second subject isn't deleted, of course, it must become the personal pronoun *he*.

Notice that the comma drops out too.

Here is an example with identical predicates:

> Mary saw a thrush, and Elena saw a thrush. $\Rightarrow$
> Mary and Elena saw a thrush.

T-conjunction, deletion can be stated in a fairly simple rule:

> X + A + Y, + conjunction + X + B + Y $\Rightarrow$
> X + A + conjunction + B + Y

In this illustration neither X nor Y is null:

Yesterday Mary saw a thrush, and yesterday Elena saw a thrush.

The A and B are the parts that are different in the two sentences. These are the words *Mary* and *Elena*. They are both noun phrases, so they can be combined. The X's are the two occurrences of *yesterday*, and the Y's are the two occurrences of *saw a thrush*. So we write first an X:

Yesterday

Then the A:

Yesterday   Mary

Then *and,* omitting the comma before it:

Yesterday Mary   and

Then the B:

Yesterday Mary and   Elena

Then the Y:

Yesterday Mary and Elena   saw a thrush.

Usually the X's or the Y's are nulls. Here the X's are nulls:

> Mary saw a thrush, and Elena saw a thrush. ⇒
> Mary and Elena saw a thrush.

What are A, B, and Y in the result sentence?
In this one, the Y's are null:

> Mary saw a thrush, and Mary heard a mockingbird. ⇒
> Mary saw a thrush and heard a mockingbird.

What are the X, A, and B in the result?
Here *Felix felt* is X, *healthy* is A, *gay* is B, and Y is null:

> Felix felt healthy, and Felix felt gay.

The result is, of course, "Felix felt healthy and gay."
Combine the structures in 1–9 below that are expressed in different words, using the X's and Y's only once. Omit the commas.

   1. Edna was hungry, and Edna felt miserable.
   2. Edna felt hungry, and Judith felt hungry.
   3. Edna felt miserable, and Edna looked miserable.
   4. She had a book, and she had some pens.
   5. She left a book in the car, and she left the pens in the car.
   6. They ran in the meadow, and they played in the meadow.
   7. Julian opened the door, and Julian peered inside.
   8. Ed waited at the station, and Tom waited at the station.
   9. Ed looked in the closet, and Ed looked under the bed.

Now apply T-conjunction, deletion to the following.

   10. Steve walked with me in the park, and Steve told his story in
       the park.

For Sentence 10 you should have got "Steve walked with me and told his story in the park." In this result sentence it is clear that Steve told his story in the park and that he walked with me, but it is not clear that he and I did our walking in the park. In a structure of this kind, where neither X nor Y is null, you have to be a little careful that the Y clearly goes with both the A and the B — in this case, that *in the park* applies both to *walked with me* and to *told his story* — or else that it clearly doesn't.

In a sentence like "George had lunch and visited some friends in the afternoon," it isn't clear whether he just visited friends in the afternoon or also had lunch then. There are two possible analyses of the pre-deletion sentence:

a. George (X) + had lunch (A) + in the afternoon (Y), and + George (X) + visited friends (B) + in the afternoon (Y).
b. George (X) + had lunch (A) + null (Y), and + George (X) + visited friends in the afternoon + null (Y).

Either meaning could be made clear in various ways:

a. In the afternoon, George had lunch and visited friends.
b. George had lunch and then, in the afternoon, visited friends.
c. George had lunch at twelve and visited friends in the afternoon.

The following are similarly ambiguous. Rewrite each twice, contriving sentences that make each meaning unmistakable.

11. Steve walked with me and told his story in the park.
12. Ellen flew to Chicago and talked to Mr. Young last evening.
13. They have goats and cows that give milk.
14. He could write his name and read a newspaper with difficulty.

Deletion does not usually occur when the conjunction is *for, yet, so,* or *nor*. But it does with *or* and *but*:

> Mabel will help us, or Edna will help us. ⇉
> Mabel or Edna will help us.
> Mabel was tired, but Mabel was contented. ⇉
> Mabel was tired but contented.

The shortened structure does not occur with *but* when A and B are subjects. That is, there is no such grammatical sentence as *"Mabel but Edna is tired." The reason is that there is no such long construction as *"Mabel was tired, but Edna was tired." This is an *and,* not a *but,* relationship.

Rewrite the following, deleting an X or a Y or both. Omit the comma.

15. They told stories, or they sang songs.
16. Martha must have known about it, or Alison must have known about it.
17. Mr. Bloodfire worked hard, but Mr. Bloodfire didn't make much money.
18. The pie was tart, but the pie was delicious.
19. They usually played chess in the evenings, or they usually watched television in the evenings.
20. He was useful on the job, but he was unreliable on the job.

When the A and B are subjects followed by a form of *be* or the present tense of a verb, *and* and *or* have a different effect. *And* makes two singular subjects plural, while *or* leaves them singular:

> George and Tom were there.
> George or Tom was there.
>
> Beatrice and Sylvia milk the cows.
> Beatrice or Sylvia milks the cows.

Apply T-conjunction, deletion to the following.

21. Al is going to help me, and Bert is going to help me.
22. Al is going to help me, or Bert is going to help me.
23. A man comes every day, or a boy comes every day.
24. A man comes every day, and a boy comes every day.

When, in such a construction with *or*, one subject is singular and the other plural, the second one governs the predicate as shown in these examples:

> A man or some boys come every morning.
> Some boys or a man comes every morning.

But such constructions are awkward, and it is usually better to avoid them in some way: "Some boys come every morning, or else a man does."

All of the more complicated structures that we have seen derived by transformation — relative clauses, subordinate clauses, *ing* phrases, *for . . . to* constructions, etc. — may serve as A's and B's in T-conjunction, deletion.

Rewrite the following, making the possible deletions and noting the structures that serve as A's and B's.

25. John said that he was tired, and John said that he wanted to go to bed.

26. The people who live upstairs are named Wilkins, and the people who complained about the noise are named Wilkins.
27. It was difficult for Hans to speak English, and it was difficult for Betty to understand German.
28. When the chores were done, we had supper, and when the sun had set, we had supper.
29. Seeing the little boy, Mr. Grancord tried to help, and wondering what was wrong, Mr. Grancord tried to help.
30. The cat teased by the boys had a miserable life, and the cat chased by the girls had a miserable life.

Syntax

Correlative Conjunctions

The words *both, not, either,* and *neither* can join with *and, but, or,* and *nor,* respectively, to form pairs called *correlative conjunctions: both . . . and, not . . . but, either . . . or, neither . . . nor:*

> Both John and Bill are here.
> Not John but Bill is here.
> Either John or Bill is here.
> Neither John nor Bill is here.

In the correlative constructions *but* and *nor* can join subjects, which they can't do alone. The *not* and the *neither* replace negatives from earlier stages in the transformation:

> John is not here, but Bill is here. ⇒
>   Not John but Bill is here.

> John is not here, and Bill is not here. ⇒
> John is not here, nor is Bill here. ⇒
>   Neither John nor Bill is here.

Rewrite the following, deleting the X's and Y's and coupling *both, not, either,* or *neither* with its partner.

1. John works hard, and Bill works hard.
2. John did not help us, but Bill helped us.
3. John will bring the ice cream, or Bill will bring the ice cream.
4. John didn't take the book, nor did Bill take the book.
5. John is lazy, and John is careless.
6. John is not lazy, but John is careless.
7. John is lazy, or John is careless.

8. John is not lazy, nor is John careless.
9. Nell designed the pattern, and Nell made the dress.
10. Pedro did not like grapes, nor did Pedro like plums.
11. She is disturbed by it, or she wants to make trouble.
12. It was not in the closet, nor was it under the sofa.
13. The people at fault were not the girls, but the people at fault were the boys.
14. Mr. Opulake was master, and Mr. Opulake was slave.
15. She did not love the child wisely, but she loved the child too well.
16. The parents who disciplined the child are to blame, or the grandparents who spoiled her are to blame.
17. Melissa used *infer* incorrectly, and Eliza used *infer* incorrectly.
18. The stories she told were always dull, or the stories she told were always incomprehensible.
19. Frank was not a liar, nor was Frank a thief.
20. Sir Humboldt did not slay the dragon, but Sir Lacey de Mers slew the dragon.

Sometimes instead of *not . . . but* we have the correlatives *not only . . . but also*. The meaning of this pair is approximately that of *both . . . and:*

Both Sir Humboldt and Sir Lacey de Mers slew the dragon.
Not only Sir Humboldt but also Sir Lacey de Mers slew the dragon.

We have noted that constructions joined by conjunctions must be the same type: two noun phrases, two adjectives, two relative clauses, etc. This is called the rule of *parallelism*. When two unlike structures are joined, the error is one of faulty parallelism. Here is an example:

*John is a patriot and who longs to fight for his country.

This is an error because it would have to derive from the following, in which the second sentence pattern is ungrammatical:

*John is a patriot, and John is who longs to fight for his country.

Instead, the development must go like this:

John is a patriot, and John is a man who longs to fight for his country. ⇒
John is a patriot and a man who longs to fight for his country.

The rule of parallelism holds also for constructions with correlative conjunctions. *"Either John is lazy or careless" is not parallel, since the *either* is followed by a sentence, "John is lazy," and the *or* by an adjective. The sentence should be either of the following:

> John is either lazy or careless.
> Either John is lazy, or he is careless.

The first would usually be the better because it is shorter.

Syntax

Series

A group of three or more base sentences can be reduced by deletion to a *series* — a set of three or more like structures, such as noun phrases, adjectives, adverbials, relative clauses:

> John is lazy, and John is careless, and John is useless. $\Rightarrow$
> John is lazy, careless, and useless.

Note that here the commas do not drop out. A comma separates the first two adjectives and another separates the second from the *and*. This "A, B, and C" punctuation rule is not always used. Some writers and editors prefer "A, B and C" with no comma before the *and:*

> John is lazy, careless and useless.

However, in the exercises that follow, punctuate "A, B, and C."
Here is an example with verb phrases as "A, B, and C":

John worked hard, and John saved money, and John bought a house. $\Rightarrow$
John worked hard, saved money, and bought a house.

Here is one with noun phrases in the subject function:

John worked hard, and Bill worked hard, and Tom worked hard. $\Rightarrow$
John, Bill, and Tom worked hard.

Reduce the following similarly, producing sentences with series and punctuating as directed.

1. Gloria agreed, and Alison agreed, and Minette agreed.
2. Jeff studied hard, and Jeff took the examination, and Jeff passed with honors.
3. The quarterback played skillfully, and the quarterback played cautiously, and the quarterback played well.
4. Mrs. Warfield bought a squash, and Mrs. Warfield bought a goose, and Mrs. Warfield bought some potatoes.
5. Mr. Grancord was a man who loved his country, and Mr. Grancord was a man who was willing to make sacrifices, and Mr. Grancord was a man who was utterly without fear.

6. A lion was there, and a lamb was there, and a mongoose was there.
7. They saw a thrush that morning, and they saw a crow that morning, and they saw a whippoorwill that morning.
8. He ate peanuts in the morning, and he ate peanuts in the afternoon, and he ate peanuts at night.
9. It was hard to like Raymond, or it was hard to dislike him, or it was hard to ignore him.
10. Each child was responsible for the chickens, or each child was responsible for the goats, or each child was responsible for the sheep.
11. Bert had read all of the books on the subject, and Bert had read all of the articles on the subject, and Bert had read all of the speeches on the subject.
12. He had a sharp ear for the syntax, and he had a sharp ear for the vocabulary, and he had a sharp ear for the rhythm.

Deletion is obligatory for all twelve items above — even Number 12 could hardly stand as it is. However, the deletion can be of different degrees. All of the following would be possible for Number 12:

a. He had a sharp ear for the syntax, for the vocabulary, and for the rhythm.
b. He had a sharp ear for the syntax, the vocabulary, and the rhythm.
c. He had a sharp ear for the syntax, vocabulary, and rhythm.

The c form is of course the most economical; it's shorter than either of the others. But it is not necessarily the best, since much depends on the intent of the writer. The a and b forms are both more emphatic and might be what was wanted. Reduce each of the following in two sentences. In the first make the most economical series possible, and in the second write a less economical but possibly more emphatic construction.

13. Albert had a horse, and Albert had a goat, and Albert had a parrot.
14. The boys did their best, and the girls did their best, and the parents did their best.
15. Some handkerchiefs were always lying on the table, or some gloves were always lying on the table, or some lipsticks were always lying on the table.

Whichever element one decides to put into series, one must be consistent. The following is inconsistent and is an instance of faulty parallelism:

> John decided to study, and John decided to save his money, and
> John decided to improve himself generally. ⇾
> *John decided to study, save his money, and to improve himself
> generally.

This contains a series that is not parallel: *to study, save his money, and to improve himself generally.* Either a *to* must be kept before *save,* or the *to* before *improve* must be deleted. The following are parallel:

> John decided to study, save his money, and improve himself
> generally.
> John decided to study, to save his money, and to improve himself
> generally.

Rewrite the following, making each construction parallel by either adding a word or leaving one out.

16. *To do his best at all times, live in harmony with his fellows, and to return library books promptly is all the school asks of any student.
17. *Reynolds knew that the message was important, it had to be delivered, and that it was up to him to deliver it.
18. *Veronica was a girl who wore jewels well, had a great many of them, and who wanted as many more as she could get.

Syntax

Series of Adjectives

Adjectives can occur either in the kernel position after *be* or a V-s, or, through the relative clause and deletion transformations, within a noun phrase:

> The boy was lazy. The boy seemed lazy.
> The lazy boy did nothing.

In the last position, two or more adjectives may occur in series without any conjunction, but with a comma or commas separating them.

> The lazy boy did nothing, and the careless boy did nothing. ⇾
> The lazy, careless boy did nothing.

Julia is a pretty girl, and Julia is an intelligent girl, and Julia is a
kind girl. $\Rightarrow$
Julia is a pretty, intelligent, kind girl.

Reduce the following similarly, punctuating them in the way shown
in the models.

1. It was an old house, and it was a lovely house, and it was a
   comfortable house.
2. A wet rabbit stared at us, and a frightened rabbit stared at us.
3. They had to read dull books, and they had to read long books,
   and they had to read uninteresting books.
4. Mitford was an elderly man, and Mitford was a kindly man.

Now compare the last sentence you made with this one:

Mitford was a nice old man.

The constructions are different. *An elderly, kindly man* comes from
a man who was elderly and kindly. But *a nice old man* comes from
an old man who was nice. In the first, *elderly* and *kindly* modify *man*;
in the second, *nice* modifies the unit *old man*. This explains the difference in punctuation.

Make expanded noun phrases from Sentences 5–12 below, and use
them in sentences of your own as in the following examples:

A house was enormous and lovely.
They lived in an enormous, lovely house.

A little house was funny.
It was a funny little house.

5. A little girl was shy.
6. A girl was shy and frightened.
7. A bear was huge and dangerous.
8. A little bear was friendly.
9. A green meadow was beautiful.
10. A reply was bitter and vindictive.
11. An old man was foolish.
12. Young children were innocent.

Morphology

Latin Prefixes and Roots

So many words have been borrowed by English from Latin that as
speakers of English we have some sort of familiarity with their parts.
In some sense, the parts have achieved morpheme status for us. Take

the word *conceive*. We may not be able to say what the *–ceive* part means, but we know that whatever it means it is the same *–ceive* that we have in *deceive, receive,* and *perceive.*

Moreover, if we can spell and pronounce *–ceive* in one word, we can spell and pronounce it in all.

We recognize the *con–* of *conceive* turning up in *concur, conform, conduce.* We may not know what *conduce* means, but we know that it has some relationship to *conceive* and to *reduce.* Furthermore, knowing about *conceive/conception,* we are not surprised to find *deception, reception,* and *perception* trailing after *deceive, receive,* and *perceive.* All these are systems that we work with in learning and using our language.

The words we have borrowed from Latin are mostly based on verbs. Generally they can be made into nouns (*conceive/conception*) and into other word classes (*conceptual, conceptually*), but the verb is usually the base. The verb, in turn, is typically made up of a prefix like *con–* or *re–* and a root like *–ceive* or *–duce.* The prefix had an adverbial or prepositional meaning in Latin; *con–* meant with, and *re–* meant again or back. The root had a simple verb meaning; *–ceive* came from *capere,* which meant take, and *–duce* came from *ducere,* which meant lead. So *conceive* has the literal meaning "take with" and *reduce* has the literal meaning "lead back." What literal meanings then do *conduce* and *receive* have?

We seldom use these words in their literal meanings. We don't say "He conceived his marbles" to mean "He took his marbles with him." Most of these verbs have developed meanings slightly or greatly different from the literal ones. However, their literal meanings are buried in them.

Here are some Latin prefixes with their literal meanings:

ad–	to, toward	*con–*	with
de–	down	*dis–*	away
ex–	out of	*in–*	into
in–	not	*inter–*	between
ob–	against	*pre–*	before
pro–	for, forward	*re–*	again, back
se–	apart	*sub–*	under
super–	above	*trans–*	across

There are two **in** morphemes from Latin. One has the meaning "into," as in *induce,* and one the meaning "not," as in *indecent.*

Following are some common Latin verbs whose roots are used in English. You are given first the Latin verb, then the form it usually has in English, and then the literal meaning:

caedere	–cide	cut	*cedere*	–cede or –ceed	go
claudere	–clude	close	*clinare*	–cline	lean
currere	–cur	run	*ferre*	–fer	carry
fidere	–fide	trust	*mandare*	–mand	order
mittere	–mit	send	*mutare*	–mute	change
pellere	–pel	drive	*pendere*	–pend	hang
petere	–pet	seek	*plicare*	–ply	fold
portare	–port	carry	*scandere*	–scend	climb
scribere	–scribe	write	*sedere*	–sede	sit
tendere	–tend	strive	*tenere*	–tain	hold

Now, using the lists, write the literal meanings of each of the following verbs. For instance, for *deceive* you would write "take down," for *conduce* you would write "lead with."

confide	depend	remand	obtain	transcribe
intercede	subscribe	descend	proceed	submit
expel	incline	contend	supersede	seduce
decide	infer	preclude	transmute	reply
recede	dispel	export	recur	concede

Latin verbs have key forms called *principal parts*. Thus the verb *portare*, "carry," has these principal parts:

$$porto \quad portare \quad portavi \quad portatus$$

These can be translated, in order, "I carry," "to carry," "I have carried," and "carried." Latin verbs are usually cited in the second, or infinitive, form — *portare*, "to carry." This is the form that is given in the list above.

However, in many Latin verbs it is the participle that has been used in English, along with, or instead of, the infinitive form. Here are the principal parts of *ferre*:

$$fero \quad ferre \quad tuli \quad latus$$

We have made some verbs from the infinitive: *defer;* some from the fourth principal part, the participle: *relate.*

The infinitive and participle forms of the following Latin verbs are given, together with the form the root takes in English and the meaning:

flare	*flatus*	–flate	blow
gradi	*gressus*	–gress	walk
jacere	*jactus*	–ject	throw
legere	*lectus*	–lect	choose
movere	*motus*	–mote	move
ponere	*positus*	–pose	put
trahere	*tractus*	–tract	drag

Using the list of infinitive and participle forms of Latin verbs and referring as necessary to the table of prefixes, write the literal meanings of the following English verbs:

subtract	demote	depose	inject
select	regress	inflate	promote

Phonology

Assimilation

The prefixes that are attached to forms of Latin verbs are in certain circumstances slightly disguised by the process known as assimilation. This is a tendency for sounds to adapt themselves to neighboring sounds. For example, we don't say *inlegal,* as one might expect, but *illegal.* The /n/ of the prefix has become /l/ to match the first sound of the root.

Sometimes the sound of the prefix becomes not the same as that of the root but similar. For instance, *con–* + *–pose* does not become *coppose* but *compose.* The nasal /n/ of *con–* changes to the nasal sound most like /p/, the labial nasal /m/.

English speech does not have long, or double, consonants. Therefore, the word *illegal* is not pronounced with an /ll/ sound after the *i,* but just with an /l/ sound, as in *elect.* Since the pronunciation gives no clue to the double *l,* there is some tendency to spell such words with a single consonant letter: *ilegal.* This error can be avoided if one thinks of what the word is composed of and keeps assimilation in mind. There must be one *l* for the prefix and one for the root.

All of the following undergo assimilation of one sort or another:

con + lect	ad + pend	ob + pose
con + pel	sub + pose	in + pel
ad + tend	con + mute	con + late
sub + port	sub + fer	con + mit
ob + clude	ad + tract	sub + ply
in + regular	in + possible	in + material

The prefixes *ex–*, *ob–*, and *dis–* drop their final consonants before certain roots:

elect   omit   digress

SUMMARY OF RULES

T-conjunction

$$S_1. + S_2. \rightrightarrows S_1, + \text{conjunction} + S_2.$$

Conjunction: *and, or, but, for, yet, so, nor*

Two sentences may be put together with one of the conjunctions named between them. The general rule is that a comma precedes the conjunction, but sometimes a semicolon or period does instead. When the conjunction is *nor*, a change like that of T-yes/no takes place in the second sentence: the subject reverses with a following tense-modal, tense-*have*, tense-*be*, or, if there is a verb, with just tense. In this case, *do* is added.

T-conjunction, deletion

$$X + A + Y, + \text{conjunction} + X + B + Y \rightrightarrows$$
$$X + A + \text{conjunction} + B + Y$$

When parts of two sentences joined by a conjunction are identical, the identical parts need not be, and usually should not be, repeated. One of them drops out, along with the comma, and the conjunction then joins sentence parts smaller than sentences. These parts (the A and B), though not alike as words, must be alike as structures: two noun phrases, two verb phrases, two relative clauses, etc. This deletion takes place only when the conjunction is *and, or,* or *but*.

The words *both, not, either,* and *neither* team with *and, but, or,* and *nor* to produce pairs of *correlative conjunctions*.

TEST

1. Put the following together with one of the conjunctions *and, or, but, for, yet,* or *so.* Don't use any conjunction more than once.
    a. Mrs. Peters wanted an oval swimming pool. Her husband insisted on a rectangular one.
    b. The evening was balmy. We decided to drive to the beach.
    c. The rabbits were increasingly peckish about their food. The appetite of the chickens left much to be desired.

2. Combine the following sentences with the conjunction *nor,* and punctuate according to the recommendation given.
  a. Tom didn't want to have a picnic. Dick wasn't very enthusiastic.
  b. Dick doesn't have a car. Harry hasn't any way to get there.
  c. The heat was awful. It wasn't much better at night.
  d. Mr. Dodson agreed to go ahead with it. Mr. Fogg didn't have any objections.
  e. The students didn't want the meeting to end. The teachers didn't insist on going home.

3. Rewrite the following the most economical way, deleting repeated X's and Y's.
  a. Georgette was beautiful, and Georgette was kind.
  b. Wilbur didn't like the plan, and Samuel didn't like the plan.
  c. Mary asked us to pardon Al, and Mary asked us to pardon Bert.
  d. She kept her books in the study, and she kept her books on a shelf in her bedroom.
  e. Jenny found wild strawberries, and John found a lump of chalk.
  f. They played cards in the evening, and they told stories in the evening.
  g. He likes to play the organ, or he likes to play the saxophone.
  h. Mr. Campbell read the book, but Mr. Campbell didn't understand it.
  i. Susie will play the recorder, or Taffy will play the recorder.
  j. Jim is going to be here, and Dirk is going to be here.
  k. Jim is going to be here, or Dirk is going to be here.
  l. Geroge said that the river was full of crocodiles, and George said that they were hungry.
  m. Stooping down, Mr. Metz wondered what he should do, and tying his shoelace, Mr. Metz wondered what he should do.

4. The following are ambiguous. Rewrite each twice in such a way as to make the two meanings clear.
  a. Mabel stuffed a turkey and served it last night.
  b. They have a daughter and a son who can play the cello.
  c. He would read the report and sign his name carelessly.

5. Rewrite the following, deleting repeated parts and using *both, not, either,* or *neither* to form correlatives with *and, but, or,* or *nor.*
  a. Edna seemed to approve, and Virginia seemed to approve.
  b. We can eat the chicken, or we can eat the goose.
  c. Benjie didn't agree, nor did Benjie disagree.
  d. King Filibreck was not a gentleman, nor was King Filibreck a scholar.

e. Bertrand did not write the poem, but James wrote the poem.

6. Apply the deletion transformation to the following, punctuating as recommended in the chapter.
   a. Every Tom did it, and every Dick did it, and every Harry did it.
   b. They swam, and they played tennis, and they had a good time.
   c. She was beautiful, and she was clever, and she was kind.

7. Rewrite these as sentences containing series of adjectives.
   a. She is a beautiful girl, and she is a clever girl, and she is a kind girl.
   b. They lived in a new house, and they lived in an expensive house.
   c. He wrote a long paper, and he wrote a lively paper, and he wrote an interesting paper.

8. Write the literal meanings of the following words. For example, for *conduce* you would write "lead with"; for *import,* you would write "carry into."

concur	admit	transpose	preclude
collate	depend	supersede	retain

9. Write the words represented by the following, all of which involve assimilation.

ad + tend   con + mit   in + pel   ob + clude   in + licit

REVIEW QUESTIONS

1. What are the seven conjunctions of English?
2. What convention of punctuation is usually followed when conjunctions join whole sentences?
3. What takes place in the second sentence when two sentences are joined by *nor?*
4. What punctuation marks may be used in structures of the type S, + conjunction + S in place of the comma? For what reasons would these other marks be used?
5. When X + A + Y, *and* X + B + Y is transformed by deletion, what drops out in addition to an X and a Y?
6. What is ambiguous about "George had lunch and visited friends in the afternoon"?
7. When *and* and *or* connect two singular subjects, what different effects do they have?

8. What words combine with *and, but, or,* and *nor* to form correlative conjunctions?

9. What is the rule of parallelism?

10. When the rule of parallelism is broken, what is the error called?

11. What is wrong with *"Either John is lazy or is careless"? How might the sentence be corrected?

12. What is a series?

13. What is the rule recommended in this book for the punctuation of a series of three?

14. What is wrong with the sentence *"John decided to study, save his money, and to improve himself generally"? In what two ways might it be corrected?

15. What is the difference in word relationship between the following: *an elderly, kindly man; a nice old man?*

16. What is meant by the statement that some Latin roots have morpheme status in English?

17. Of what is an English verb borrowed from Latin typically composed?

18. What are the meanings of the two **in** morphemes from Latin?

19. What is the literal meaning of *conduce?*

20. What are the key forms of a Latin verb called?

21. In borrowing verbs from Latin, we sometimes use the infinitive form, like *portare* or *ferre.* What other form do we sometimes use?

22. What is meant by assimilation?

CHAPTER 19

Sentence Connectors

We have examined several small groups of words that serve to put sentences together in one way or another. One group, the simplest, is the set of conjunctions: *and, or, but, for, yet, so, nor*. These just stand between sentences or parts of sentences and show a meaning relationship of some sort for them.

Another group is the subordinators — *that, whether, if, unless, until,* etc. — which embed an insert sentence in a matrix, letting it serve in a noun phrase function or as a noun phrase modifier or as a sentence modifier. Still another is the set of relatives, of which there are two kinds: relative pronouns — *who, that, which, what, whoever,* etc. — which replace noun phrases of the insert sentence; and relative adverbs — *when, where, wherever,* etc. — which replace adverbials of the insert. The relative clauses produced with these words also function as modifiers of noun phrases or of sentences or take noun phrase positions in the matrix.

Finally, there is a set which we will call *sentence connectors*. These are words like *therefore, however, nevertheless*. These are frequently confused with either conjunctions or subordinators. They must be kept separated, however, because different conventions of punctuation apply to them.

The most important point is that when two sentences are joined by a sentence connector, a semicolon or a period — not a comma — must come at the end of the first sentence:

Something had to be done immediately; therefore we formed a committee.

Something had to be done immediately. Therefore we formed a committee.

Either of these is correct, and there is no particular difference between them, except perhaps that the period makes the following sentence a trifle more emphatic.

But a comma in the position before the sentence connector is an error commonly called a *comma fault* or a *comma splice* or a *run-on sentence:*

> *Something had to be done immediately, therefore we formed a committee.

It is an error also, of course, to use a comma between two sentences that have no connecting word between them:

*Gerald is a good boy, he always does what people tell him to do.

Put Sentences 1–4 together with the sentence connectors *therefore, however, moreover, nevertheless.* Use the one that makes the best sense, and use each one only once. Use a semicolon. This transformation is called T-sentence connector.

1. Gerald is a good boy. He gets into a little trouble now and then.
2. It was rather late to start out for the beach. The papers had predicted rain.
3. Mrs. Hill knew that she had very little control over Lambert. She kept trying to help him.
4. If the line were broken at that point, the whole front would give way. General Merrymount threw in the Twelfth Division.

Put the following together with one of the sentence connectors *thus, hence, consequently, accordingly,* using the one that makes the best sense. Use each only once.

5. Derivational morphemes serve to put words into different word classes. The morpheme **ity** makes a noun from the adjective *solid.*
6. They knew that they had to get along with one another. Each tried to avoid making irritating remarks.
7. Midnight was the hour set for the attack. The Twelfth Division began moving forward.
8. They couldn't tell which cans of tomatoes were poisonous. The whole lot had to be destroyed.

Put the following together with one of the sentence connectors *nonetheless, besides, likewise, indeed.* Use each only once. Use a semicolon at the end of the first sentence.

9. We really had to invite Mr. Ernest to the party. We all enjoyed his company very much.
10. We all enjoyed Mr. Ernest's company. We hesitated to invite
him to the party.
11. We all enjoyed Mr. Ernest's company. A party was hardly complete without him.
12. We really had to invite Mr. Ernest to the party. Miss Lamberton
could hardly be left out.

Correct each run-on sentence by punctuating it properly.

13. *Roger was late, however he made up the lost time.
14. *The wind died down, consequently we went fishing.
15. *Nobody wanted to leave at the end of the talk, indeed we all
clustered around the speaker.

Semantics

The Meaning of the Sentence Connectors

In meaning, the various sentence connectors correspond more or
less to various conjunctions:

CONJUNCTIONS	SENTENCE CONNECTORS
and	moreover, besides, likewise, furthermore, also
but, yet	however, nevertheless, nonetheless
so	consequently, therefore, accordingly, hence, thus

It isn't true that a sentence connector can always be substituted
for an *and, but, yet,* or *so* between sentences, but one often can.
Furthermore, there are shades of difference among the different sets
of sentence connectors. The choice between conjunction and sentence
connector, however, or among several sentence connectors is often one
of style rather than meaning. Conjunctions are generally felt as simple
and informal, sentence connectors as somewhat formal and literary.
We don't use sentence connectors much in ordinary conversation, and
even in writing they may sometimes give more weight and serious-
ness to a passage than we want to convey.

Rewrite each of the following, replacing the conjunction with the
sentence connector that seems most appropriate. Remember that the
punctuation must be changed too.

1. The outside temperature was around eighty, and it was rather
muggy.
2. Sandra has sent in her contribution, but no one has heard from
Sylvia.

3. Roland studied very hard, yet he couldn't seem to get a grade higher than a B.
4. You can never have too many soldiers in a battle, so General Merrymount threw in a few more divisions.
5. The dictionary was the product of many years of scholarship, yet the reviews were highly unfavorable.
6. A citizen's committee had protested the mayor's ruling, and the governor was expected to intervene.
7. The situation was very unpleasant, but there was nothing anyone could do about it.
8. Grandma complained about having to lug the groceries home from the supermarket, so Grandpa decided to buy her a bicycle.

Here are more sentences for practice in replacing a conjunction with an appropriate sentence connector.

9. Predictions for the wheat crop had been good, but farmers were beginning to worry about the lack of rain.
10. Pythons are sometimes very affectionate pets, and they are very good at catching rats and mice.
11. The party was getting a little dull, so Burnbrooke decided to tell the one about the retarded crocodile.
12. Millicent was very quiet and shy, yet she was one of the most popular girls in the class.

Syntax

Differences Between Conjunctions and Sentence Connectors

It may be asked why, if some sentence connectors and some conjunctions have approximately the same meaning and if both are used to join sentences, they do not constitute just one word class instead of two. The answer is that the two groups have quite different grammatical behavior. In particular, their positions with respect to the sentences joined may be different. A conjunction joining two sentences must come between them:

> Stefan didn't like it, and he didn't care who knew it.
> Stefan didn't like it, yet he didn't say a word.

A sentence connector *may* come in the same position, but it may also occur at the end of the second sentence:

> Stefan didn't like it; he didn't care who knew it, moreover.
> Stefan didn't like it; he didn't say a word, however.

This is not a possible position for a conjunction:

> *Stefan didn't like it. He didn't care who knew it, and.
> *Stefan didn't like it. He didn't say a word, yet.

Or the sentence connector may occur within the second sentence:

> Stefan didn't like it. He didn't, moreover, care who knew it.
> Stefan didn't like it. He didn't, however, say a word.

This position is not permitted to conjunctions either:

> *Stefan didn't like it. He didn't, and, care who knew it.
> *Stefan didn't like it. He didn't, yet, say a word.

It is ordinarily required, as has been said, that sentences connected by sentence connectors have a semicolon or a period between them. Nothing so pleasantly simple can be said about the punctuation used after the sentence connector. Some have a comma after them and some do not; some do for some writers and not for others. The ones most commonly taking a comma after them are *moreover, besides, likewise, furthermore, consequently, accordingly, however.* The words *also, therefore, thus, hence, nevertheless, nonetheless,* take a comma less commonly.

> Birkins was useful to us. Moreover, we liked him.
> Birkins was useful to us. Also we liked him.

The same practice in punctuation is followed when the sentence connector appears at the end of the second sentence:

> He was rather silly. Everyone liked him, however.
> He was rather silly. People avoided him therefore.

When the sentence connector is used in the middle of the second sentence, the punctuation depends a good deal on where it comes — between subject and predicate, within the verb phrase, etc. At some positions it will be accompanied by principal stresses and pitch rises and in other positions not:

> John was hot-headed. He nevertheless tried to be fair.

> John was hot-headed. He nevertheless tried to be fair.

> John was hot-headed. He tried nevertheless to be fair.

> John was hot-headed. He tried, nevertheless, to be fair.

Your best bet is to listen for these breaks in the intonation and to represent them with commas when they occur.

Rewrite the following twice each. The first time put the sentence connector at the end of the second sentence and the second time within it. Such changes are called T-sentence connector, transposition. Use commas according to the suggestions given and your own best judgment, but in any case keep the semicolon or period between the two sentences.

1. Nobody wanted to mention the matter to Mr. Friendly. However, we all felt that he should know about it.
2. The river was filled with crocodiles. Moreover, they seemed to be of a particularly vicious sort.
3. Berkman didn't feel at all equal to the job. Furthermore, he had all that he could do already.
4. Felicia and Melliflua knew that their quarrel could only damage themselves and others. Accordingly, they decided to make peace.

Here are more sentences for practice. Rewrite each sentence twice, first using the sentence connector at the end of the second sentence, and then using it within the second sentence.

5. It looked as if the refreshments wouldn't last the afternoon. Therefore Mrs. Strauss suggested that everyone sing.
6. France was fearful of Germany. Besides, she was bound by a treaty to come to the aid of Russia.
7. The children were quarreling, and the ants had invaded the cake. Consequently, Mrs. Noe decided to end the picnic.
8. Seventeen divisions had been chewed up by the enemy. Nevertheless General Merrymount pluckily threw in a few more.

Syntax

The Difference Between Subordinators and Sentence Connectors

Some subordinators are very similar in meaning to some conjunctions. For instance, the conjunction *for* and the subordinator *because* are frequently interchangeable:

Robert didn't want to hurt Mrs. Wilkins, because he was a kindly lad.
Robert didn't want to hurt Mrs. Wilkins, for he was a kindly lad.

However, there is again a difference. A conjunction, as we have seen, must occur between the two sentences. A subordinator cannot, like a sentence connector, occur at the end of the second sentence. The following are ungrammatical:

*Robert didn't want to hurt Mrs. Wilkins. He was a kindly lad, because.
*Robert didn't want to hurt Mrs. Wilkins. He was, because, a kindly lad.

However, the insert sentence with a subordinator can occur at either the beginning or the end of the matrix:

Robert didn't want to hurt Mrs. Wilkins, because he was a kindly lad.
Because he was a kindly lad, Robert didn't want to hurt Mrs. Wilkins.

The second of these is not a possible position for either a conjunction or a sentence connector:

*For he was a kindly lad, Robert didn't want to hurt Mrs. Wilkins.
*However, we all felt he should know about it, nobody wanted to mention the matter to Mr. Friendly.

So conjunctions, sentence connectors, and subordinators have the following possible positions in the joining of sentences:

CONJUNCTION: S_1 conjunction S_2.
SENTENCE CONNECTOR: S_1 sentence connector S_2.
S_1 S_2 sentence connector.
S_1 S sentence connector $_2$.
SUBORDINATOR: S_1 subordinator S_2.
Subordinator S_2 S_1.

This different positional behavior is reflected in differences in punctuation in the position between two sentences that conjunctions, sentence connectors, and subordinators have in common. A conjunction in this position is preceded by a comma, a semicolon, or a period; a sentence connector by a semicolon or a period; a subordinator by a comma or nothing. If you precede a sentence connector by a comma or nothing, you have the comma fault or run-on sentence error. If you precede a subordinator by a semicolon or a period, you have the error called a fragment.

The following are all errors of punctuation. Rewrite each, changing the punctuation according to the rules given.

1. Charles was angry. Because Stewart would not help.
2. The refreshments ran out but the party was a success.
3. It was hard to get books in America at that time, therefore Franklin hit on the notion of a circulating library.
4. The children were constantly wet and cold, moreover, they were always in danger of being eaten by wolves.

5. He got an F on the paper. Although he had used no word that was not in the dictionary.
6. The Prime Minister's adherents were already gathering in the streets, consequently the Army had to move fast.
7. It was impossible to change the plan for Merrymount's forces were already in motion.
8. Mrs. Pinafore did not want to take any steps. Until she had had a reply from the bishop.
9. The little songbirds were singing in the trees and the pythons were oozing in and out of the branches.
10. Philip had a lot of homework to do, besides he felt he was coming down with a cold.

Phonology

Interrupters

We have seen that a sentence connector placed within the second sentence will sometimes interrupt the intonational flow of the sentence and sometimes not. Say these aloud:

John wasn't much interested in the project. He was nevertheless determined to do his best.
John wasn't much interested in the project. He was determined, nevertheless, to do his best.

In the first of these it would be at least possible to go through the second sentence with just one principal stress or pitch rise, on the word *best*. There is no necessary pause before and after *nevertheless*. In the second, however, there is a necessary principal stress on the *ter* of *determined*, another on the *–less* of *nevertheless*, and a pause before and after *nevertheless*. In some sentences, as in this one, the sentence connector interrupts the smooth going forward of the sentence, and the interruptions are marked with commas.

In the following also, sentence connectors interrupt the intonational flow. Rewrite each sentence, using commas before and after the interrupters.

1. John needed the job badly. He was anxious therefore to make a good impression.
2. They were still forty miles from One-Ton Camp. They knew moreover that a storm might come up at any moment.
3. Sam Weller couldn't write poetry very well. It was his intention however to compose a valentine poem.

4. News that the men were stuck on the ledge reached Fallen Leaf; the Scouts set off accordingly to effect a rescue.
5. The situation of the Second Brigade seemed desperate. There was always a chance nevertheless that help would arrive.

It would be possible to formulate syntactic rules to state in what positions the sentence connector will interrupt the intonational flow, but it is probably easier in these cases to cultivate a sensitivity to the breaks of the intonation and simply to mark them with commas.

One thing to bear firmly in mind is that when an interrupter — sentence connector or otherwise — comes in the middle of a sentence, it requires two commas, one fore and one aft. The first of the following is punctuated defensibly; the second is not:

> He knew nevertheless that there would be trouble.
> *He knew, nevertheless that there would be trouble.

It is arguable whether *nevertheless* interrupts here. But if it does interrupt, it does so on both ends and needs two commas:

> He knew, nevertheless, that there would be trouble.

Phonology

Other Constructions as Interrupters

We have noticed two positions for subordinate clauses used as sentence modifiers — before or after the matrix. In the first position, they are usually marked off by commas; in the second they sometimes are, depending somewhat on the subordinator:

> Until John spoke, we didn't dream that anyone objected.
> We didn't dream that anyone objected, until John spoke.

But such a clause can also come within the matrix. When it does, it usually effects an intonational interruption that should be marked with commas:

> We didn't dream, until John spoke, that anyone objected.

Rewrite each of the following, setting off with commas the clause that interrupts.

1. He guessed although there was little evidence that there was something fishy.
2. I firmly trusted in whereas George was dubious about Mildred's loyalty.

3. Everyone expected after the generals signed the agreement a return to normal.
4. Sally before the news was announced was very uneasy.
5. Mrs. Philibrick if the truth were known found the parties terribly boring.

A relative clause may also move out of its usual position and interrupt the flow of a matrix:

Sally knew, when she heard the announcement, that there was no more hope.

Rewrite the following, setting off the interrupting relative clauses with commas.

6. They talked whenever they met with careful courtesy.
7. Mildred suggested when her opinion was asked that the matter be put to a vote.
8. The Scouts tried whenever they got an opportunity to rescue people from ledges.
9. Mary knew from experience that wherever she went the lamb would be tagging along.
10. Arthur remembered when loud barking reminded him that he should have fed Rover.

In the following a clause as sentence modifier appears in the normal position before the matrix sentence. Rewrite each one, placing the clause within the matrix and marking it off with commas.

11. As they approached the river, they noticed a higher volume of monkey chatter.
12. Because he was a very good speaker, Richard was chosen to give the welcoming address.
13. If you look closely, you will see that the smaller mollusks have pink spots on them.
14. Before they walked out, the delegates from Upper Buq-Buq made one last try for a compromise.
15. When she heard the news, Bridget turned quite pale.
16. Though he was only seventeen, Sternsheets had already written several operas.
17. Whenever they made a mistake, the girls giggled nervously.
18. After he saw what had happened, Mr. Boundpost decided to reorganize the company.
19. Until she saw Venice, Millicent believed that Billings, Montana, was the most beautiful city in the world.

20. Unless you have something more pressing to do, you might help me wash the poodle.

Many of the other structures that we have considered — prepositional phrases, nominative absolutes, the various residues of clauses through deletion — may shift from normal positions to interrupting ones within a matrix. Then they will be marked off by intonation breaks in speech and by commas in writing:

John having gone on ahead, Bill directed the operation of breaking camp. ⇉
Bill, John having gone on ahead, directed the operation of breaking camp.

In the meantime, no one dared to look at his neighbor. ⇉
No one dared, in the meantime, to look at his neighbor.

Each of the following contains such an interrupter. Rewrite each sentence, marking the interrupter off with commas.

21. We were forced the door being closed to try a window.
22. Henry as it happened knew the whole story.
23. Maxine had in point of fact recited the poem very well.
24. The League was at that time a center of conservatism.
25. They intended most likely to try to bribe the teller.
26. It was as it were a case of excess irritation.
27. Rendahl found out to his dismay that Cresap had a tape recording of the whole conversation.
28. The chairman in making his ruling forgot that a motion to table cannot be debated.

Rewrite the following, putting the sentence modifier within the matrix and setting it off with commas.

29. As it happened, the students knew about it all along.
30. Unfortunately, David couldn't afford to pay the fee.
31. In the nick of time, the snake charmer began to play his flute.
32. After the meeting, some of the members gathered to discuss the result.
33. When in doubt, one should probably say nothing.

In the writing of dialogue and sometimes in other writing, one may indicate the name of the person being spoken to. Such a naming interrupts the intonational flow and is set off with commas:

I must ask you, Carruthers, to wipe that smile off your face.

A noun phrase like *Carruthers* in this example is said to be used in direct address. Rewrite the following, setting off each noun phrase so used.

34. It was nice of you Penelope to offer to help.
35. We must remember my friends that these are troubled times.
36. I am glad Mrs. Morrison to find you looking so well.
37. We all know Philip that you meant very well indeed.

Morphology

Morphemes from Greek

Since about 1500, English has borrowed extensively from Greek as well as Latin, but with a difference. The borrowing from Greek has contributed to a noticeably different part of our vocabulary. The Latin words are prominent in any kind of talk beyond the nursery. Such words as *permit, offend, responsible, liberal, animal* — all from Latin — are familiar to all adults who speak English, and are used by them, and many thousand more from Latin are too.

The Greek words stand on a slightly different level. Some of them, like *telephone,* have become altogether familiar. But the main contribution of Greek has been to scientific English rather than to common English. English — like other modern languages — has used Greek roots to give names to many new concepts, products, and processes developed by modern science. Most of these, of course, were unheard of in ancient Greece. Socrates never used a telephone and wouldn't have known a proton from a seismograph.

The new words formed on old Greek roots used to be known as Schenectady Greek, because so many were formed in the electrical laboratories of Schenectady, New York.

Let us begin with the word *telephone.* When that instrument was developed, a name was needed for it, and there was more than one possibility. It was an instrument by which one could speak to another person from afar, and it might have been descriptively named a *far-speaker.* Indeed, that is what was done in German, in which a telephone is called a *Fernsprecher.* But English, accustomed as it was to borrowing from the classical languages, went the Greek way. It took the Greek word *tele,* which meant far, and the Greek word *phōnē,* which meant voice, and put them together to make *telephone* — a far voice, or a voice from afar.

Use your dictionary to find the etymology of the following words. The first part in each meant far in Greek. What did the second parts mean?

telegraph	telegram	telescope
telemeter	telephoto	teletype

The last part of *telephone,* like the first, has proved useful in the production of new English words. Look up the etymology of the following and find out what their first parts meant in Greek:

microphone	megaphone	xylophone
gramophone	homophone	hydrophone

English has never been very pedantic in the use of Greek roots. That is, it has never insisted on using one Greek root only together with another one. In fact, it often puts a Greek root with a Latin one, as in *television.* Here the *vision* part comes from the participle of Latin *vidēre,* which meant to see. Find the etymology of the following:

audiphone	dictaphone	telemotor

The derivational morphemes that we have already considered can be added to Greek words too. Some of them, indeed, like **ic** and the final *y* of *synonymy,* come ultimately from Greek. These have the same stress effect on Greek words that they do on other words, the observation of which may be an aid in spelling. Pronounce the following as marked:

télegràph	tèlegráphic	telégraphỳ

In which of the three is the *leg* syllable pronounced with the vowel /e/? Make a similar set from *telephone.*

Words coined in English from Greek have generally kept Greek spellings, thus contributing to the confusion. Thus the *ph* of *telegraph* and *telephone,* which at one time in Greek stood for a /p/ sound followed by an /h/ sound, in English is just one more way of spelling /f/. Similarly, the *ch* of *character* becomes just another way of spelling initial /k/.

Two Greek roots much used in English are *gram* and *graph,* as in *telegram* and *telegraph.* As one might guess from their shapes, these are actually two forms of the same Greek root. Greek had a noun *gramma,* which meant letter, as in letter of the alphabet, or just writing in general. This noun was derived from the verb *graphein,* which meant to write. The noun gives us our word *grammar,* which originally meant the study of writing. It gives us also *glamour,* with an English dialectal change of the /r/ to /l/. Centuries ago, people who could write or study writing were considered to be like magicians and thus glamorous in the magical sense.

Look up the following *–gram* and *–graph* words, and find out what their first parts meant in Greek:

diagram	epigram	heliogram
anagram	monogram	cryptogram
autograph	polygraph	homograph
seismograph	paragraph	lithograph

We can begin in either direction with such words. Thus we can take *–graph* words, as we have done, and find the meanings of their first parts, as in *polygraph,* where the *poly–* means many. Then we can take *poly–* words and find the meanings of their second parts. Do so for the following:

polychrome	polyglot	polygon
polyhedron	polymorph	polypod
polytechnic	polygamy	polyphonic

In all of the words above except two, the principal stress is on the syllable *pol–.* How are *polygamy* and *polyphonic* pronounced? Why are they different?

One Greek root very important in the English vocabulary is *–logy.* This comes from the Greek word *logia,* which meant study of. *Logia,* in turn, was built on the noun *logos,* which meant word and was related to the verb *legein,* to speak. Look up the following words that end in *–logy* and find out what their first parts meant in Greek. Some of them you already know from other Greek words cited previously.

biology	seismology	geology
theology	archeology	etymology
entomology	cosmology	technology
chronology	hydrology	dendrology
horology	cetology	psychology

You probably won't find *chromology* in your dictionary. It is a word used rarely or not at all. But if you know the meaning of the roots of *polychrome* and *biology,* you can guess the meaning of *chromology* if you should encounter it. What would it probably mean?

Sometimes words that end in *–logy* have more the meaning of word than of study. The word *eulogy* means a speaking well of, a good saying. When one pays tribute to someone, detailing his good points, one delivers a *eulogy.* The *eu–* part meant good or well in Greek, and it is used in a number of English words. Find the meanings of the following and the Greek meaning of the parts that follow the *eu–:*

| eucalyptus | eugenic | eupepsia |
| euphemism | euphony | euphoria |

A number of our proper names come from Greek. *Eugene* is an example. It is composed of *eu–* plus *–genes,* which meant born, and so its literal meaning is well-born.

Another Greek root built on the word *logos,* which meant word, is *–logue,* as in *catalogue.* The *cata–* part comes from Greek *kata,* which had the general meaning down. You read down the items in a catalogue and choose those that interest you. *Catalogue* may also be spelled *catalog,* and this is true in general of the *logue* words. People have suggested that they be simplified by the dropping of the *–ue,* and the suggestion has sometimes been followed. Give or find the Greek meaning of the parts that precede *–logue* in the following. Some of them you have encountered already.

dialogue   epilogue   monologue

Similar to the *–logue* words in sound but different in meaning are those that end in *–gogue,* like *pedagogue.* The root *ped–* meant child in Greek, and the *–gogue* came from *agein* which meant to lead. So a pedagogue was a leader of children, or a teacher. A *demagogue* was a leader of the people; *demos* meant people. What meaning has *demagogue* taken on in modern English? A *synagogue* was a leading together. *Syn* meant together or with.

The root *syn–* has been used abundantly in the coining of English words. Find out the meaning of any of the following that are unfamiliar, and in any case find out the meaning of the Greek root that follows the *syn–:*

| synchronize | syndrome | synonym |
| synopsis | syntax | synthesis |

Like such Latin prefixes as *sub–* and *ad–, syn–* undergoes assimilation before roots with certain sounds. The *n* becomes *l* before *l,* as in *syllable.* The second part of *syllable* comes from Greek *lambanein,* which meant to take, so a syllable is literally that which is taken or pronounced together. Before *m, b,* and *p* or *ph* for /f/ the *n* of *syn–* becomes *m,* just as the *n* of Latin *con–* does in *commotion, combine, compel.*

Write the words made up of the following parts, and find the meaning of the Greek root underlying the second part:

syn + logism	syn + metry	syn + pathy
syn + bol	syn + phonic	syn + biosis
syn + posium	syn + ptom	syn + pathetic

The second part of *sympathy* comes from the verb *pathein*, which meant to feel or suffer. This root occurs in a number of other words too. Find the meaning of the following and of the Greek words that underlie their first parts. The *y* of *–pathy* has the regular effect of putting the principal stress on the syllable just before the *–pathy*.

antipathy	empathy	apathy
telepathy	osteopathy	neuropathy

The *a* of *apathy* is the Greek equivalent of the Latin prefix *in–* or the English *un–*. It gives a negative or opposite meaning to what follows: *Apathy* means literally without feeling. Before roots beginning with a vowel or with *h*, *a* has the form *an*. Give the literal meaning of the following:

atheist	amorphous	asymmetric
anarchy	anecdote	agnostic
anhydrous	anonymous	anemia

SUMMARY OF RULES

T-sentence connector

$$S_1. + S_2. \Rrightarrow S_1; + \text{sentence connector} + S_2.$$

The punctuation mark following the first sentence may be a period instead of a semicolon, but not a comma.

Sentence connector → therefore, however, furthermore, nevertheless, consequently . . .

T-sentence connector, transposition

$$S_1; + \text{sentence connector} + S_2. \Rrightarrow$$
$$S_1; + S_2 + \text{sentence connector}.$$

The sentence connector may be placed at the end of the second sentence or, alternatively, within it. This mobility distinguishes the group of sentence connectors from conjunctions.

TEST

1. Put the following sentences together with *moreover, furthermore, however,* and *consequently,* using each sentence connector only once. Use either a semicolon or a period.

   a. The fall in Chicago had been exceptionally mild. The winter
      was very cold indeed.
   b. Billy's fits of anger alarmed me. I didn't like his habit of carry-
      ing a gun.
   c. They had very similar interests. They got along very well.
   d. The new Congress was determined to revise the banking laws.
      It felt it had a mandate from the country to do so.

   2. Put the following together with *besides, nevertheless, therefore,
hence,* using each only once.
   a. They had very little in common. They seemed to get along
      together very well.
   b. Mrs. Primrose's nephew was an orphan. She felt an obligation
      to look after him.
   c. Gilmore was utterly bored with writing novels. He decided to
      try his hand at poetry.
   d. Gilmore was utterly bored with writing novels. He had never
      succeeded in getting one published.

   3. Put the following together with *likewise, nonetheless, accordingly, thus,* using each only once.
   a. Harold's flashing eyes were gazing at Millicent's laughing ones.
      We knew that the movie was nearly over.
   b. The store was threatening to take back the furniture. The gas
      and electric company was insisting on being paid.
   c. The Scouts had no idea how to get the men off the ledge. They
      were eager to try.
   d. The Scouts had no idea how to get the men off the ledge. They
      stayed in camp and practiced tying knots.

   4. Rewrite each sentence twice, using the sentence connector once
at the end of the second sentence and once within it.
   a. Howard was having trouble at his present job. Furthermore, he
      thought a change would do him good.
   b. Mrs. Balfour may have had her faults. However, there was no
      one among us who knew of any.

   5. Rewrite each of the following, correcting the punctuation according to the rules given.
   a. The rabbits and hares all go in pairs and even the bears in
      couples agree.
   b. The rabbits and hares got along all right, however the bears
      were always quarreling.
   c. Noah insisted on taking along a pair of pythons. Although his
      wife was much opposed to the idea.

d. We decided not to say anything about it; because we didn't want to get Alfred into trouble.

6. Rewrite the following, setting off the interrupters with commas.
a. We knew however that help was on the way.
b. It seemed useless consequently to try to go farther.
c. His Aunt Judith in the meantime had alerted the police.
d. The firemen when they saw that the blaze was out of control sent for another fire company.
e. It is often best when in doubt to keep quiet.
f. I am pleased my friends to see so many smiling faces.

7. Copy the following words, and after each write the meanings of the Greek roots it contains. For example, for *microphone* you would write "small sound."

telephone autograph polyglot
geology eulogy synonym

8. Make words from the following:

syn + logism   syn + phonic   syn + metry

REVIEW QUESTIONS

1. What is the term for words like *therefore, however,* and *nevertheless?*
2. What punctuation marks are used before words of this class when they join sentences?
3. What is the error called when a comma is used before a sentence connector?
4. Give sentence connectors that have meanings similar to the meanings of *and, but,* and *so.*
5. What positions can sentence connectors have that conjunctions cannot have?
6. The question of whether a sentence connector can have a comma after it or not is complicated. What is the situation?
7. How many principal stresses would ordinarily occur in the sentence "He had, furthermore, to catch a train"? On what syllables would they fall?
8. What position may a subordinator have that is not possible for a sentence connector?
9. *Because* and *for* are similar in meaning. What is the justification for assigning them to different word classes?

10. In speech, what does an interrupter interrupt?

11. How is the interruption in speech indicated in writing?

12. Which of the following contains an interrupter and should have commas: "He nevertheless tried to help," "He tried nevertheless to help"?

13. Where may a clause functioning as sentence modifier occur in addition to the positions before or after the matrix?

14. What is meant by "direct address"?

15. When did English begin borrowing extensively from Greek?

16. What general difference is there between words borrowed from Latin and those borrowed from Greek?

17. How are *telephone* and *television* morphologically different?

18. Describe the change of stress in the set *telegraph, telegraphic, telegraphy.*

CHAPTER 20

Syntax

More About V_I and V_T

The constructions that we have until now labeled just V_I for verb intransitive, and V_T for verb transitive, are among the most complicated and most interesting parts of the grammar. Therefore they have been saved for a special treat at the end.

The rule for *verbal* was elaborated up to this point:

$$\text{verbal} \rightarrow \left\{ \begin{array}{l} \left\{ \begin{array}{l} \left. \begin{array}{l} V_I \\ V_T + NP \end{array} \right\} \quad + (\text{Adv-m}) \\ V_s + Adj \\ V_b + \left\{ \begin{array}{l} NP \\ Adj \end{array} \right\} + (\text{Adv-p}) \\ V\text{-mid} + NP \end{array} \right\} + (\text{Adv-f}) + (\text{Adv-t})$$

This accounts for quite a lot of constructions in the English verb phrase, but there are many for which it will not account. For example, there is no provision for an adverbial of place after a V_I or a $V_T + NP$. That is, it doesn't describe sentences like "John walked in the garden" or "John put the papers in the desk." Nor does it account for "John wised up" (if we may admit the expression to the discussion), nor for "John looked up the word," nor for "John gave Mary the book," "John thought Mary silly," "John told Sam to sit down," "John decided to quit studying," and many more.

We can include at least some of these in the grammar by elaborating the rules for V_I and V_T. So far V_I and V_T have been identified simply by lists of simple verbs: $V_I \rightarrow$ *walk, dream, arrive* . . . ; $V_T \rightarrow$ *see, chase, find* . . . . But in fact some intransitive verbs must be followed by other structures and some may be, and this turns out to be true for transitive verbs also.

Syntax

Subdivisions of V_I

The intransitive verb *wise* cannot occur by itself in the verb phrase. We don't say *"John wised." Neither can it occur with just an adverbial of manner: *"John wised quickly." This particular verb, if it is used as a verb at all, must be followed by the word *up:* "John wised up," "John wised up quickly."

The word *up* in this use is called a *particle.* Other words used as particles include *down, in, over, away, out, off, by.* Many of these words, not all, are used also as prepositions.

Here are some other examples of intransitive verbs used with particles: "John glanced up," "John stepped down," "John dropped in," "John came over," "John stayed away," "John walked out," "John goofed off," "John stood by." This is a fairly modern construction, and many of the combinations, like *wise up* and *goof off* have a marked colloquial or slangy aspect. But many others, like *glance up* and *drop in,* are beyond any reproach.

Copy the following, and in each blank use some verb not used in the examples given above:

He _____ up.   They _____ down.   Bert _____ in.
Al _____ away.   Mark _____ out.   Ed _____ by.

So we have so far two possibilities for V_I. It may be composed of just an intransitive verb, like *arrive,* or it may be an intransitive verb plus a particle, as in *wise up.* There is a third possibility. The verb *lie,* in the sense of recline or rest, doesn't occur by itself. We don't say *"John lay." It may occur with a particle: "John lay down." But it may also occur with an adverbial of place: "John lay in bed." In making the rule, we will not use the term *adverbial of place* for this third possibility but the more general term *complement,* because we will want it to embrace several other structures in the comparable rule for V_T.

You may remember that we said we capitalized the I and T of V_I and V_T because we would want to subdivide these further. Here is the rule that subdivides V_I:

$$V_I \rightarrow \begin{Bmatrix} V_{i\text{-}1} \\ V_{i\text{-}2} + \text{particle} \\ V_{i\text{-}3} + \text{complement} \end{Bmatrix}$$

The term V_I is thus a general one standing for any of three structures: an intransitive verb alone, an intransitive verb plus a particle, or an intransitive verb plus a complement. The complement of an intransitive verb will be an adverbial of place.

There are thus three kinds of intransitive verbs: V_{i-1}: *arrive*; V_{i-2}: *wise*; V_{i-3}: *lie*. However, there is enormous overlapping among the three categories, with a great many verbs occurring now in one category and now in the other. Thus *drop* is a V_{i-1} in "John dropped," a V_{i-2} in "John dropped by," and a V_{i-3} in "John dropped out of sight." Notice, however, that the meaning sometimes changes substantially as the verb moves from one category to another. *Drop, drop by,* and *drop out of sight* show a considerable semantic range in the verb *drop.*

Tell of each V_I below whether it is a V_{i-1}, a V_{i-2} + particle, or a V_{i-3} + complement.

1. Jenny stood by.
2. Jenny stood beside me.
3. Jenny stood up.
4. Jenny stood.
5. Harry went away.
6. Harry went to Chicago.
7. Harry went gladly.
8. Jane walked out.
9. Jane walked.
10. Jane walked out of the room.

Syntax

Subdivisions of V_T

The transitive verbs have as much complexity as the intransitives and a good bit more.

The V_T differs from the V_I in that the V_T is followed in the kernel sentence by a noun phrase functioning as its object. The same word may be a V_I in one sentence and a V_T in another:

V_I: drop, drop in, drop out of sight
V_T: drop the book

Note, however, that in *drop the book,* just *drop* is the V_T. The whole expression is V_T + NP. But in *drop in* and *drop out of sight* the expression as a whole is a V_I. The first is a V_{i-2} + *particle* and the second is a V_{i-3} + *complement.*

Like the V_I, the V_T may comprise just a single word, as in "*drop* the book" or "*see* the game" or "*understand* the question," though

V_T must be followed by an NP. Make sentences in which the following verbs are followed just by noun phrases, and are thus V_T's:

choose   watch   hear   make   buy   carry

But the V_T may also be composed of a transitive verb plus a particle, and some transitive verbs must be followed by particles. For
instance, we don't say *"John looked the word," but we do say "John
looked up the word." Here the V_T is composed of the words *look up.*
The noun phrase *the word* is not the object of *look* but of *look up.*
Here are other examples of transitive verb plus particle. Use each
combination in a sentence with an object after it.

put away   knock down   run down
buy off   clean up   single out

So V_T can be so far described thus:

$$V_T \rightarrow \begin{Bmatrix} V_{t\text{-}1} \\ V_{t\text{-}2} + particle \end{Bmatrix}$$

Either must be followed in the kernel sentence by an NP object.

The next thing to be noted is that in a string containing as its
verbal the items $V_{t\text{-}2}$ + particle + NP, the particle and the NP can
trade places. This transformation is called T-verb transitive. Take the
string of "John looked up the word":

John + past + look + up + the + word

What is the $V_{t\text{-}2}$ of the string? What is the particle? The V_T, then,
is *look up.* What is the NP object? Applying T-verb transitive, we
can rewrite the string thus:

John + past + look + the + word + up

What will the sentence be now?

Similarly, "John put away the books" can become "John put the
books away" and "Mary cleaned up the room" can become "Mary
cleaned the room up." Make similar transformations of the following.

1. Edith locked in the children.
2. Barbara threw away the leftovers.
3. Alice put down her knitting.
4. Henry knocked over the paint bucket.

Now suppose we take a string in which the NP object of the V_T
composed of a $V_{t\text{-}2}$ + particle is a personal pronoun:

John + past + look + up + it

If we carry this into a sentence immediately, the result will be ungrammatical: *"John looked up it." When the object of V_{t-2} + particle is a personal pronoun, T-verb transitive is obligatory. The particle and the NP must change places, in this case to give "John looked it up."

The following are all ungrammatical. Rewrite each.

    5. *Edith locked in them.
    6. *Manny bought off him.
    7. *We found out her.

Suppose, however, that we wanted to apply to such a string the passive transformation:

$$NP_1 + Aux + V_T + NP_2 \Rrightarrow$$
$$NP_2 + Aux + be + part. + V_T + (by + NP_1)$$

We must apply T-passive *before* the transposition of particle and NP:

$$\textbf{John} + \textbf{past} + \textbf{look} + \textbf{up} + \textbf{it} \Rrightarrow$$
$$\textbf{it} + \textbf{past} + \textbf{be} + \textbf{part.} + \textbf{look} + \textbf{up} + \textbf{by} + \textbf{John}$$

What sentence does this represent?

If we had first applied the transformation transposing particle and NP, T-verb transitive, we would have had this:

$$\textbf{John} + \textbf{past} + \textbf{look} + \textbf{it} + \textbf{up}$$

This is no longer a case of $NP + Aux + V_T + NP$, since the components of the V_T, *look* and *up*, have been separated. Therefore the passive transformation could not apply.

To each of the following strings apply two transformations: T-passive and T-verb transitive. Write the result strings and the actual sentences for each transformation.

    8. **Jerry + past + throw + out + the + letter**
    9. **Hazel + past + put + down + the + rebellion**
  10. **Sam + past + break + up + the + party**
  11. **Sally + past + trump + up + the + accusation**
  12. **Ed + past + eat + up + the + leftover + plural**
  13. **Joe + past + knock + over + the + wastebasket**
  14. **Mary + past + take + up + a + collection**

So far, T-verb transitive goes like this:

$$V_{t-2} + particle + NP \Rrightarrow$$
$$V_{t-2} + NP + particle$$

This is obligatory when the NP is a personal pronoun. When the NP is anything else, T-verb transitive is optional.

Syntax

V_T as V_{t-3} + complement

Just as V_I has a third possibility, consisting of V_{i-3} + complement, as in *lie in bed* or *walk in the garden*, so does V_T. As with V_{i-3}, the complement following V_{t-3} may be an adverbial of place, like *in the desk*. For example, we might fill out the string V_{t-3} + complement + NP in this fashion:

NP + Aux + V_{t-3} + complement + NP
John + past + leave + in the desk + the paper

Here *leave* is the V_{t-3}, the adverbial of place *in the desk* is the complement, and the V_T is *leave in the desk*. The NP object is *the paper*.

If we want to make this into a passive string, we do so directly from the string above, with the NP_2, *the paper*, becoming the subject:

the + paper + past + be + part. + leave + in the desk + by John

What would the actual sentence be?

If, instead of being passive, the finished sentence is an active one, T-verb transitive is obligatorily applied:

John + past + leave + in the desk + the paper $\Rightarrow$
John + past + leave + the paper + in the desk

This gives us the grammatical "John left the paper in the desk" instead of *"John left in the desk the paper."

To let T-verb transitive embrace this change, we enlarge the rule for T-verb transitive as follows:

$$V_{t-x} + \begin{Bmatrix} \text{particle} \\ \text{complement} \end{Bmatrix} + NP \Rightarrow V_{t-x} + NP \begin{Bmatrix} \text{particle} \\ \text{complement} \end{Bmatrix}$$

The symbol V_{t-x} is just a convenient way to include both V_{t-2} and V_{t-3}, for V_T is now enlarged to include V_{t-3} + complement as well as the other types:

$$V_T \rightarrow \begin{Bmatrix} V_{t-1} \\ V_{t-2} + \text{particle} \\ V_{t-3} + \text{complement} \end{Bmatrix}$$

Identify the V_T's in the following, and tell of each whether it is a V_{t-1}, a V_{t-2} + particle, or a V_{t-3} + complement.

1. **John + past + see + the + fire**
2. **Steve + past + ring + up + Melinda**
3. **We + past + hide + in + the + cupboard + the + present**
4. **Abe + past + roll + up + his + cuff + plural**
5. **They + past + find + on + the + porch + the + newspaper**
6. **George + past + buy + a + bucket + of + oil**

Some of the following are ungrammatical. Tell which require the application of T-verb transitive, and apply the transformation to those that need it.

7. Stan cleaned up it.
8. Stan cleaned up the hutch.
9. He dropped in the river his watch.
10. She placed on the table it.
11. They shoved aside them.

Apply the passive transformation to each sentence above.

Syntax

Other Complements in V_T

A number of structures other than adverbials of place may occur as complement in the combination V_{t-3} + complement. These differ, however, from the adverbials of place in a fundamental way. The adverbials of place are generated by a kernel rule, which says simply that a complement after V_{i-3} or V_{t-3} may be an adverbial of place. The other complements, however, are generated by double-base transformational rules.

Consider the sentence "John thought Mary silly." Here the relationship of *John* to *thought Mary silly* is that of subject to predicate. But the relationship of *Mary* to *silly* is a subject-predicate one also. *Mary* and *silly* are in the same connection here as they are in kernel sentences like "Mary was silly." Therefore, in "John thought Mary silly" we have one sentence embedded in another. The matrix is "John thought complement Mary," and the insert is "Mary Aux be silly":

INSERT: **Mary + Aux + be + silly**
MATRIX: **John + past + think + complement + Mary** $\Big\} \Rightarrow$
RESULT: **John + past + think + silly + Mary**

The adjective *silly* from the insert sentence fills the unspecified complement position in the matrix.

Now either of two things can happen. The passive transformation can be applied to the result string to give "Mary was thought silly by John," or T-verb transitive can be applied to give "John thought Mary silly." T-verb transitive is obligatory here, as usual in such cases, if T-passive is not applied.

Write three similar structures for each of these: the result string with plus signs; that string transformed into an actual passive sentence; the string transformed into an active sentence.

1. INSERT: **Ella + Aux + be + intelligent**
   MATRIX: **the + teacher + present + think + complement + Ella**

2. INSERT: **the + game + Aux + be + dangerous**
   MATRIX: **we + past + consider + complement + the + game**

3. INSERT: **we + Aux + be + guilty**
   MATRIX: **somebody + present + believe + complement + us**

After verbs like *think* and *consider*, the complement received from the insert can be a noun phrase instead of an adjective:

INSERT: **John + Aux + be + a + hero**
MATRIX: **Mary + past + consider + complement + John** $\Bigg\}\Rightarrow$
RESULT: **Mary + past + consider + a + hero + John** $\Rightarrow$
          John was considered a hero by Mary.   *or*
          Mary considered John a hero.

Write three similar structures for each of the following: the result string with plus signs; that string transformed into an actual passive sentence; the string transformed into an active sentence.

4. INSERT: **Phil + Aux + be + a + nuisance**
   MATRIX: **the + old + comparative + boy + plural + present + consider + complement + Phil**

5. INSERT: **June + Aux + be + a + genius**
   MATRIX: **the + teacher + present + think + complement + June**

6. INSERT: **the + revolution + Aux + be + a + threat**
   MATRIX: **they + past + believe + complement + the revolution**

7. INSERT: **the + movie + Aux + be + a + bore**
   MATRIX: **George + past + find + complement + the + movie**

8. INSERT: **Max + Aux + be + the + thief**
   MATRIX: **we + past + suppose + complement + Max**

It will be seen that there is more than one kind of $V_{t\text{-}3}$ verb. We have already studied the *consider* kind in which the complement is an adjective or a noun phrase:

> John considered silly Mary. $\rightrightarrows$
> John considered Mary silly.

Then there is the *leave* kind, in which the verb goes with an adverbial of place as the complement to make up the V$_T$:

> John put in the desk the paper. $\rightrightarrows$
> John put the paper in the desk.

Some verbs may occur in either group, but the groups as a whole are not interchangeable. We don't have *"John put Mary silly" or *"John considered the paper in the desk."

A third type of V$_{t\text{-}3}$ is that in which the verb is of the type *elect*, for which the complement can be a noun phrase but not an adjective:

INSERT: **John + Aux + be + chairman**
MATRIX: **the + class + past + elect +** complement **+ John** $\Big\} \rightarrow$
RESULT: **the + class + past + elect + chairman + John** $\rightrightarrows$
        John was elected chairman by the class.   *or*
        The class elected John chairman.

Here an adjective won't occur: we don't have *"The class elected John popular."

Write a result string and then an actual passive and an active sentence for each of the following:

9. INSERT: **Mary + Aux + be + the + pretty + superlative + girl**
   MATRIX: **they + past + vote +** complement **+ Mary**

10. INSERT: **Tom + Aux + be + we + poss. + representative**
    MATRIX: **we + past + choose +** complement **+ Tom**

11. INSERT: **O'Grady + Aux + be + spokesman**
    MATRIX: **the + miner + plural + past + elect +** complement **+ O'Grady**

12. INSERT: **Harold + Aux + be + president**
    MATRIX: **we + past + make +** complement **+ Harold**

The *leave, consider,* and *elect* groups do not exhaust the V$_{t\text{-}3}$ groups. There is, for example, the *regard* group, which must have the word *as* before the complement:

INSERT: **John + Aux + be + a + friend**
MATRIX: **Mary + past + regard +** complement **+ John** $\Big\} \rightarrow$
RESULT: **Mary + past + regard + as + a + friend + John** $\rightrightarrows$

> John was regarded as a friend by Mary.   *or*
> Mary regarded John as a friend.

Although there are minor differences, the same general mechanisms apply to all of these V_{t-3} groups.

Indirect Objects

Similar, but different enough to be listed as a separate group in the V_T complex, are verbs that are followed by two NP objects, of which one is called the direct object and the other the indirect object. We will call these verbs V_{t-4}. The most common of them is *give*, but there are several others. An example of the construction is "John gave Mary a book," in which *Mary* is the indirect object and *John* is the direct object.

There is more than one way to derive sentences of this type, but it seems simpler to do it through kernel rules rather than by means of a double-base transformation. Here is the V_T rule with V_{t-3} added:

$$V_T \rightarrow \begin{cases} V_{t-1} \\ V_{t-2} + \text{particle} \\ V_{t-3} + \text{complement} \\ V_{t-4} + \text{to} + \text{NP} \end{cases}$$

All of these must be followed by a noun phrase object.

Now for "John gave Mary a book," we can draw the following tree of derivation, with the 2-3-1 omitted:

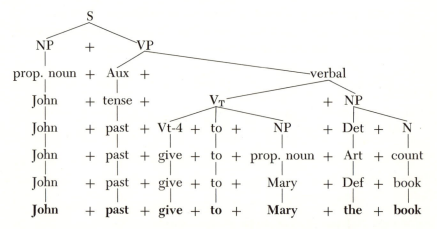

To this K-terminal string we cannot apply T-affix immediately, for that would yield the hardly grammatical *"John gave to Mary the book." We could, however, apply several other transformations to the string.

a. We can simply delete the *to:*

John + past + give + to + Mary + the + book $\Rightarrow$
John + past + give + Mary + the + book
(John gave Mary the book.)

b. Or we could apply the passive immediately:

John + past + give + to + Mary + the + book $\Rightarrow$
the + book + past + be + part. + give + to + Mary + by + John
(The book was given to Mary by John.)

c. From the last result we can delete the *to:*

(The book was given Mary by John.)

d. In the original string, we can treat the **to + Mary** as we did particles and complements and apply T-verb transitive:

John + past + give + to + Mary + the + book $\Rightarrow$
John + past + give + the + book + to + Mary
(John gave the book to Mary.)

e. Finally, we can delete *to* and treat *Mary* as an NP$_2$ in a variation on the passive transformation:

(Mary was given the book by John.)

You will agree that this construction is complicated.

From each of the following, write five grammatical sentences corresponding to those in Examples a–e.

1. **June + past + sent + to + Tom + a + letter**
2. **Al + past + lend + to + me + it**
3. **the + teacher + past + show + to + them + a + picture**
4. **Mr. Ross + past + mail + to + him + a + package**

After some verbs the word *for* is used before the indirect object instead of *to:*

the + agent + past + find + for + them + a + house $\Rightarrow$
        The agent found them a house.
        A house was found for them by the agent.
        A house was found them by the agent.

The agent found a house for them.
They were found a house by the agent.

Make five similar sentences from this:

Mother + past + save + for + Sam + some + pie

Syntax

V$_{t\text{-}5}$

The last transitive verb types that we will consider are less complicated in their machinery than the indirect object verbs, the V$_{t\text{-}4}$'s, but more prolific. That is, their transformations account for a wider variety of English sentences.

The first of these, which we will arbitrarily call V$_{t\text{-}5}$'s, are verbs like *hear* in "John heard Bill leaving the house." Again, we have a double-base situation because we have two subject-predicate relationships. One is that of *John* to *hear,* and the other that of *Bill* to *leave.* John does the hearing, and Bill does the leaving. So we can treat V$_{t\text{-}5}$'s as we did V$_{t\text{-}3}$'s:

INSERT: **Bill + Aux + leave + the + house**
MATRIX: **John + past + hear + complement + Bill** $\Big\} \Rightarrow$
RESULT: **John + past + hear + ing + leave + the + house + Bill**

The transformation inserts the morpheme **ing** between the V$_{t\text{-}5}$ and the complement. The V$_{t\text{-}5}$ is **hear,** the complement is **ing + leave + the + house,** and the V$_T$ is **here + ing + leave + the + house.**

To the result string, we can apply the passive in the usual way and get "Bill was heard leaving the house by John." Or we can apply T-verb transitive and have "John heard Bill leaving the house." In either case T-affix applies automatically to put the **ing** on the right side of **leave.**

Here is another example of V$_{t\text{-}5}$:

INSERT: **Mary + Aux + walk + to + class**
MATRIX: **we + past + see + complement + Mary** $\Big\} \Rightarrow$
RESULT: **we + past + see + ing + walk + to + class + Mary** $\Rightarrow$
          Mary was seen walking to class (by us).   *or*
          We saw Mary walking to class.

For the following write a result string with plus signs and then two actual sentences, as in the example:

1. INSERT: **Morris + Aux + study + in + the + library**
   MATRIX: **Noam + past + find + complement + Morris**
2. INSERT: **the + fisherman + plural + Aux + cast + they + poss. + net + plural**
   MATRIX: **I + past + watch + complement + the + fisherman + plural**
3. INSERT: **William + Aux + sneak + out**
   MATRIX: **mother + past + catch + complement + William**
4. INSERT: **Joe + Aux + count + the + money**
   MATRIX: **Bob + past + surprise + complement + Joe**

The insert and the matrix sentences may have the same subject. In this case, after some V_{t-5} verbs, the subject of the insert appears in the result in the reflexive, or *–self*, form:

INSERT: **she + Aux + dance + the + waltz**
MATRIX: **she + past + imagine + complement + herself** $\Rightarrow$
RESULT: She imagined herself dancing the waltz.

Write similar results from these:

5. INSERT: **he + Aux + think + about + the + old + day + plural**
   MATRIX: **he + past + find + complement + himself**
6. INSERT: **they + Aux + eat + more**
   MATRIX: **they + past + notice + complement + themselves**

After other verbs the subject of the result simply is omitted:

INSERT: **she + Aux + try + hard + comparative**
MATRIX: **she + past + begin + complement** $\Rightarrow$
RESULT: She began trying harder.

The same subject-predicate relationships obtain however: she's both the beginner and the trier.

Similarly, from the insert **she + Aux + drive + fast + comparative** and the matrix **she + past + start + complement**, we would derive the result sentence "She started to drive faster."

Syntax

V_{t-6}

Our last set of transitive verbs are those that take *to* before the complement instead of *ing*. These occur in sentences like "John urged Bill to try harder." The machinery is quite like that we have been examining for other types:

INSERT: **Bill + Aux + try + harder** $\Big\}\Rightarrow$
MATRIX: **John + past + urge + complement + Bill**
RESULT: **John + past + urge + to + try + harder + Bill**

The V_T is **urge + to + try + harder,** with **urge** what we will call a $V_{t\text{-}6}$ and the rest the complement. The passive transformation can be applied to the string:

Bill was urged to try harder (by John).

Or T-verb transitive can transpose complement and object:

John urged Bill to try harder.

Write a result string and two actual sentences for each of the following.

1. INSERT: **I + Aux + here + the + concert**
   MATRIX: **my + father + past + persuade + complement + me**
2. INSERT: **we + Aux + learn + it**
   MATRIX: **the + teacher + past + require + complement + us**
3. INSERT: **Al + Aux + appreciate + music**
   MATRIX: **Bert + past + teach + complement + Al**
4. INSERT: **the + troops + Aux + die + bravely**
   MATRIX: **General Merrymount + past + tell + complement + the + troops**

As with the $V_{t\text{-}5}$'s, an insert subject identical with that of the matrix either takes the *–self* form or is omitted:

John taught himself to be patient.
John tried to be patient.

Like other double-base transformations, those involving transitive verbs are recursive:

INSERT: **Ralph + Aux + use + bad + language** $\Big\}\Rightarrow$
MATRIX: **Ralph + past + stop + complement**
RESULT: Ralph stopped using bad language.
SECOND INSERT: **Ralph + Aux + stop + using bad language**
SECOND MATRIX: **Benny + past + persuade + complement + Ralph** $\Big\}\Rightarrow$
SECOND RESULT: Benny persuaded Ralph to stop using bad language.

Morphology

More Greek Roots

The Greek verb meaning to love was *philein,* and the noun was *philos.* We have used this root in many English words, some taken from Greek, some coined, to express the idea of loving or liking. For instance, *philosophy* is made of *philos* plus *sophos. Sophos* meant wise, and *philosophy* has the literal meaning "love of wisdom." A philosopher is one who loves wisdom.

Find out what the following mean literally:

> philanthropy   philately   philharmonic
> philodendron   philology

The last item looks as if it might have the literal meaning "study of love." But its meaning is instead "fondness for words."

The Greek word for horse was *hippos,* and the word for river was *potamos.* A *hippopotamos* was thought of as a horse of the river. The root *hippos* occurs as the last part of the proper name *Philip.* What does the name mean literally?

The root *philos* occurs also as the second part of English words in the form *–phile.* For instance an *anglophile* is literally "lover of the English," actually one who is very fond of British customs and ways of life. What do the following words with the ending *–phile* mean?

> Russophile   Francophile   Montanaphile
> dendrophile   bibliophile   gastrophile

Montanaphile is a coined word; possibly it was never used before. But the fact that it can be coined shows that *–phile,* like many other Greek roots, has morpheme status in English. If you use them, speakers of English know what you mean. A *Montanaphile* must mean someone who is fond of Montana. If the fondness centered on the city of Billings, the person would presumably be a *Billingsphile.*

Any emotion, including love, if it is carried to a certain extreme, becomes madness, and the Greek word for madness was *mania. Mania* appears in many English words. If you love England or Montana not wisely but too well, you become an *Anglomaniac* or a *Montanamaniac.* Find out, if you can, the nature of the excessive loves indicated by the following words:

> pyromania   dipsomania   bibliomania
> megalomania   cynomania   hippomania
> kleptomania   acromania   polymania

Potichomania means a craze for decorating the inside of transparent vessels, but a person who lets such a term flower in his vocabulary might be said to be suffering from megalogomania, or excessive fondness for big words.

The opposite of love is hate, and the Greek opposite of *philein* was *misein*. *Philanthropy* is literally the love of man, and *misanthropy* the hatred of man. What is a *misanthrope?* The hatred of women is *misogyny*, of marriage *misogamy*, of reason *misology*.

But the root used most commonly in opposition to *–phile* is not *misein*, but *–phobe*, from the noun *phobos*, which meant fear in the Greek language. We tend to hate what we fear, and if an *Anglophile* is a person who loves England, an *Anglophobe* is someone who fears it or hates it or both. What do the following fear or hate?

Slavophobe	hippophobe	demophobe
pedophobe	neophobe	musophobe

Excessive fear or hate, like excessive love, is a disease, and a number of diseases or disorders are named with the related root *–phobia*. This root has itself become a common noun in English, so that we say that so-and-so has a phobia about busy streets or girls with pigtails or English compositions. What do people suffering from the following fear?

acrophobia	bibliophobia	claustrophobia
agorophobia	photophobia	toxiphobia
ailurophobia	demophobia	hemophobia

The Greek words for *dog, dead body,* and *sleep* were *cynos, necros,* and *hypnos*. Make up words meaning fear of dogs, fear of dead bodies, and fear of sleep.

Demophobia, as you presumably found out, means fear of the people, with *–phobia* added to the Greek word for people, *demos*. A *demagogue* is literally a leader of the people, though nowadays it suggests one who leads them badly, stirring their emotions for his own ends. *Democracy* means literally "rule of the people." Its last part comes from Greek *kratia*, rule. A *democrat* is literally one who believes in government by the people. Tell who, in the literal meaning, rule in the following:

aristocracy	hierocracy	plutocracy
gynocracy	autocracy	bureaucracy

Bureaucracy, like *television* and *Montanaphile*, is a case of a Greek root being added to a root from another source, in this case *bureau,* a French word meaning office. It is the rule of government offices. Such a word, made up of a piece from one language and a piece from another, is called a *hybrid*.

Autocracy, which means "absolute government by an individual," is literally self-rule. *Autos* was the Greek word for self, and it is used in many English words. Find the literal meanings of the following:

> autograph   autobiography
> autonomy   autopsy
> automatic   automobile

The last word in the list, *automobile*, is another hybrid. What language does its second part come from?

A Greek root similar in meaning to *–cracy*, as in *democracy*, is *–archy*, as in *oligarchy*. (As usual in Greek words, the *ch* represents the English /k/ sound.) This root comes from *archos*, which meant ruler. The first part comes from *oligos*, few, so an *oligarchy* was a rule of the few. Who would rule in the following?

> monarchy   matriarchy
> patriarchy   squirearchy
> gynarchy   polyarchy

Which of the words in the list is a hybrid? Write sentences using three of the six *–archy* words above in such a way as to reveal their meanings.

We even use the Greek cardinal numbers in English. In fact, we use them commonly in scientific words and others with a certain elevation. The Pentagon in Washington takes its name from the Greek word for five, *pente*, plus the Greek word for angle, *gonia*. So the Pentagon is a building having five angles, and therefore five sides. Here are the Greek words for the numbers one to ten in the forms in which they are used in English:

> 1 mono   3 tri   5 pente   7 hepta   9 ennea
> 2 di   4 tessera 6 hexa   8 octo   10 deca

Now tell how many of what each of the following means:

> hexagon   monotone   triptych
> octarchy   enneahedron   heptameter
> decalogue   diphthong   pentadactyl
> heptateuch   monorail   ennead
> hexangular   decapod   tripod
> pentathlon   octopus   dimity

SUMMARY OF RULES

Subdivisions of V_I and V_T

The rule for verbal contained the items V_I and V_T + NP. V_I and V_T are now subclassified as follows:

$$V_I \rightarrow \begin{Bmatrix} V_{i\text{-}1} \\ V_{i\text{-}2} + \text{particle} \\ V_{i\text{-}3} + \text{complement} \end{Bmatrix}$$

$$\text{particle} \rightarrow \text{up, in, away} \ldots$$

The complement following a $V_{i\text{-}3}$ is ordinarily an adverbial of place. Most intransitive verbs can occur in any of the three subcategories, according to whether they are followed by nothing, by a particle, or by a complement. Some, however, can occur in only one or two of the three.

The subclassification of V_T is more complex than that of V_I:

$$V_T \rightarrow \begin{Bmatrix} V_{t\text{-}1} \\ V_{t\text{-}2} + \text{particle} \\ V_{t\text{-}3} + \text{complement} \\ V_{t\text{-}4} + \text{to} + \text{NP} \\ V_{t\text{-}5} + \text{ing} + \text{complement} \\ V_{t\text{-}6} + \text{to} + \text{complement} \end{Bmatrix}$$

For $V_{t\text{-}3}$ the complement may be an adverbial of place, an adjective, or a noun phrase, with some other variations depending on the particular type of $V_{t\text{-}3}$. The NP after the *to* following $V_{t\text{-}4}$ is an indirect object. After $V_{t\text{-}5}$ the complement is a verbal or *be* construction from an insert combining with *ing*. After $V_{t\text{-}6}$ it is such a construction combining with *to*.

T-verb transitive

$$V_{t\text{-}x} + \begin{Bmatrix} \text{particle} \\ \text{complement} \end{Bmatrix} + \text{NP} \Rrightarrow V_{t\text{-}x} + \text{NP} + \begin{Bmatrix} \text{particle} \\ \text{complement} \end{Bmatrix}$$

$V_{t\text{-}x}$ means any type of transitive verb followed by a particle or a complement: $V_{t\text{-}2}$, $V_{t\text{-}3}$, $V_{t\text{-}5}$, or $V_{t\text{-}6}$. The transformation is ordinarily obligatory when the transitive verb is followed by a complement. When it is followed by a particle, it is obligatory when the object is a personal pronoun; otherwise it is optional. The *to* + NP following the $V_{t\text{-}4}$ may participate in a similar transformation, changing places with the NP object, but in a somewhat more complicated way.

TEST

1. Each of the following sentences contains an intransitive verb. Point out each one and tell whether it is a V_{i-1}, a V_{i-2}, or a V_{i-3}.
   a. Edmund dozed.
   b. Mulligan rode on a white palfrey.
   c. Buntner stayed in bed.
   d. Whiteside looked on.
   e. Burns stared insolently.
   f. Dennis started out confidently.

2. Make sentences by using each of the following verbs as a V_{i-2} followed by a particle:

   wise   take   drop   glance

3. Apply T-verb transitive to the following, switching the particle and the object. Write *ob* after your sentence if the transformation is obligatory, *op* if it is optional.
   a. Stan cleaned out the hutch.
   b. Bert washed up them.
   c. Flem helped out us.
   d. Rube is looking over the report.
   e. Dave looked up *potichomania*.
   f. Turk found out me.

4. Point out the complement and the object in each of the following sentences.
   a. Cresap thought Abraham a dolt.
   b. We put the flowerpot on the ledge.
   c. Ralph persuaded William to confess his mistake.
   d. He found John studying in the library.
   e. Mrs. Hipshank thinks all babies cute.
   f. General Merrymount found himself outflanked.

5. For each of the following, write a result string, a passive sentence, and an active sentence. Example:

   INSERT: **John + Aux + be + a + hero** $\left.\begin{matrix} \\ \end{matrix}\right\}$
   MATRIX: **Mary + present + consider + complement + John** $\Rightarrow$
   RESULT: **Mary + present + consider + a + hero + John** $\Rightarrow$
              John is considered a hero by Mary.   *or*
              Mary considers John a hero.

In the passive sentence include the optional *by* + NP$_2$ or not, as you like.

   a. INSERT: **Jack + Aux + be + charming**
       MATRIX: **Miss Bell + past + think + complement + Jack**
   b. INSERT: **figures + Aux + be + difficult**
       MATRIX: **Mr. Ball + present + find + complement + figures**
   c. INSERT: **Ken + Aux + be + the + most + likely + to + succeed**
       MATRIX: **the + class + past + vote + complement + Ken**
   d. INSERT: **Mr. Wapish + Aux + be + our + leader**
       MATRIX: **we + past + regard + complement + Mr. Wapish**
   e. INSERT: **it + Aux + be + futile**
       MATRIX: **I + past + believe + complement + it**
   f. INSERT: **Mr. Arragh + Aux + stay + with + us**
       MATRIX: **we + past + invite + complement + Mr. Arragh**
   g. INSERT: **Howard + Aux + practice + the + cello**
       MATRIX: **Sheila + past + find + complement + Howard**
   h. INSERT: **Mr. Spence + Aux + let + him + have + a + report**
       MATRIX: **he + past + ask + complement + Mr. Spence**
   i. INSERT: **Maude + Aux + help + him + with + his + economics**
       MATRIX: **Bob + past + persuade + complement + Maude**
   j. INSERT: **Mr. Jones + Aux + be + on + his + toes**
       MATRIX: **Mr. Winter + past + tell + complement + Mr. Jones**

6. Write five sentences, all with the same meaning, from each of the following K-terminal strings.

   a. **John + past + give + to + Mary + the + book**
   b. **someone + past + send + to + Millicent + some + roses**

7. Build up a complex sentence by using each result that you get from the following as the insert of the succeeding matrix.

   INSERT: **Laura + Aux + complain**
   MATRIX: **Laura + past + stop + complement**
   SECOND MATRIX: **Annie + past + tell + complement + Laura**
   THIRD MATRIX: **Sandy + past + urge + complement + Annie**

8. Copy the following words from Greek, and after each write the literal meaning of its roots:

philanthropy	Anglophobe	pyromania
aristocracy	autobiography	patriarchy
pentagon	monologue	heptameter

9. Write a word from Greek for each of the following:

love of wisdom	river horse
hatred of mankind	fear of heights
rule of the people	something with three feet

REVIEW QUESTIONS

1. For which of these verbals does the rule for verbal account: *walk happily, walk in the garden?*

2. What are the three possible structures for V_I?

3. What sort of complement usually follows a V_{i-3}?

4. Which of these cannot be used as a V_{i-1}: *arrive, goof, lie* ("recline")?

5. What construction must follow every V_T?

6. When is the transformation V_{t-2} + particle + NP $\Rightarrow$ V_{t-2} + NP + particle obligatory?

7. What is the difference between V_{t-3}'s of the *consider* type and those of the *elect* type?

8. What word must be added to make the following sentence grammatical: *"John regards Bill his friend"?

9. What is the term for the function of the NP *Mary* in "John gave Mary the book"?

10. From "John gave the book to Mary" we can derive the passive "Mary was given the book." What other passive form could this sentence have?

11. What is the V_T in **John + past + catch + ing + loaf + Bill**? What is the V_{t-5}? What is the complement? What is the object?

12. What is the difference between a V_{t-5} and a V_{t-6}?

13. What are the two subject-predicate relationships in "Steve urged Alice to study harder"?

14. What form will the subject of the insert **he + Aux + lead + a + orchestra** take in a matrix beginning "He imagined"?

15. The Greek verb meaning hate is *misein*. What is the Greek verb meaning love?

16. What is the Greek word that means "fondness to the extent of madness"?

17. What root is most commonly used as the opposite of *–phile*, as in *Anglophile?*

18. What is the literal meaning of *democracy?*

APPENDIX

Vowel Sounds and Their Common Spellings

The charts that follow summarize the vowel sounds of English, the symbols used to represent the sounds, and common ways of spelling them.

Fourteen Vowel Sounds				
SOUNDS	/i/	/e/	/a/	/u/	/o/
SPELLINGS AND EXAMPLES	*i:* hit	*e:* red *ea:* dead	*a:* cat	*u:* but *o:* son	*o:* top *a:* far
SOUNDS	/ī/	/ē/	/ā/	/ū/	/ō/
SPELLINGS AND EXAMPLES	VCe: line *igh:* high *y:* try *ie:* die	VCe: Pete *ee:* deed *ea:* heat *e:* he *ie:* chief *ei:* deceive	VCe: lame *ai:* wait *ay:* pay *ei:* weigh	VCe: June *oo:* root *ew:* few *ue:* Sue *o:* to	VCe: lone *oa:* goat *ow:* slow *oe:* hoe *o:* no
SOUNDS	/oo/		/ou/	/oi/	/au/
SPELLINGS AND EXAMPLES	*oo:* look *u:* push		*ou:* out *ow:* cow	*oi:* oil *oy:* toy	*au:* haul *aw:* flaw *a:* ball *o:* long *ough:* fought *augh:* caught

The Vowel Sound Schwa /ə/

	i	e	ea	u	o
THE /ə/ SOUND IN ONE-SYLLABLE WORDS	stir girl	were her	learn earth	burn spur	world worse

	–er	–or	–ar
THE /ə-r/ SOUND	runner maker father	actor orator navigator	beggar liar sugar

	–al	–le	–el	–ul	–ile	–il
THE /ə-l/ SOUND	legal moral rural	steeple battle circle	camel satchel travel	beautiful useful helpful	fertile juvenile hostile	April evil council

	–en	–an	–ain	–in
THE /ə-n/ SOUND	frozen deepen oaken garden	Mexican orphan policeman fireman	captain curtain mountain certain	robin cabin basin cousin

Consonant Sounds and Their Common Spellings

This chart summarizes the consonant sounds of English, the symbols used to represent the sounds, and common ways of spelling them.

Consonant Sounds and Their Common Spellings

SOUND	AT THE BEGINNING	AT THE END
/p/	p: pie	p: rip; pe: ripe
/t/	t: ten	t: pet; te: date
/k/	k: kit; c: cold	ck: lick; ke: like
/ch/	ch: chin	tch: witch; ch: reach
/b/	b: bed	b: tub; be: tube
/d/	d: do	d: rid; de: ride
/g/	g: get	g: beg; gue: league

Consonant Sounds and Their Common Spellings (cont.)

SOUND	AT THE BEGINNING	AT THE END
/j/	*j:* jet; *g:* gentle	*dge:* budge; *ge:* cage
/f/	*f:* fun; *ph:* phrase	*ff:* stuff; *fe:* life; *f:* beef; *ph:* paragraph
/v/	*v:* very	*ve:* save
/s/	*s:* see; *c:* center	*ss:* glass; *s:* bus; *se:* case; *ce:* rice
/z/	*z:* zoo	*z:* quiz; *zz:* buzz; *se:* rose; *ze:* sneeze
/sh/	*sh:* ship	*sh:* push
/zh/	*j:* Jacques	*ge:* rouge; (in the middle) *s:* treasure
/r/	*r:* run; *wr:* wrist; *rh:* rhyme	*r:* car; *re:* care
/l/	*l:* lose	*ll:* pill; *le:* smile; *l:* fail
/m/	*m:* move	*m:* Sam; *me:* same; *mb:* tomb
/n/	*n:* nose; *gn:* gnaw; *kn:* know	*n:* pin; *ne:* pine
/ng/		*ng:* strong; *n:* trunk
/th/	*th:* thick	*th:* path
/th/	*th:* then	*th:* smooth; *the:* bathe
/y/	*y:* you; *u/y-ū/:* use	
/w/	*w:* will; *o/w-u/:* one; *qu/k-w/:* quick	
/h/	*h:* hat; *wh:* who	

Technical Terms

adjective   A descriptive word like *happy, hungry, friendly, new.* Adjectives may occur in predicates after *be* and after verbs like *seem,* as well as before nouns.

adverb   A single-word adverbial. (See next three entries.)

adverbial of manner   A word or group of words that can be replaced by *how* in questions: "John worked carelessly." → "How did John work?" Adverbs of manner are made mostly by adding the suffix *–ly* to adjectives: *careless/carelessly, soft/softly.* An adverbial of manner may be not only a single-word adverbial like *carelessly,* but also a prepositional phrase like *with close attention.*

adverbial of place   A word or group of words that can be replaced by *where* in questions. Adverbials of place occur after *be* in the predicate or after certain verbs. Single-word adverbials of place —

outside, upstairs, there — are called *adverbs*. Groups of words — *in the house, near a car* — are prepositional phrases.

adverbial of time   A word or group of words that can be replaced by *when* in questions: "The Mayor spoke yesterday." → "When did the Mayor speak?" An adverbial of time may be one word, like *yesterday,* a prepositional phrase like *in the afternoon,* or even a noun phrase like *this evening.*

affirmative sentence   A sentence that does not have a form of *not* in the predicate. An affirmative sentence says something happened or was so.

affix   Either a prefix or a suffix.

appositive   The function of the noun phrase residue which is the result of deletion from a relative clause. In the following sentence *a happy child,* which resulted by deletion from the relative clause *who was a happy child,* functions as an appositive: "Elsie, *a happy child,* recovered quickly from her disappointment."

article   The most important kind of determiner. There are two kinds of articles — definite and nondefinite. There is one definite article: the word *the.* There are three nondefinite articles: *a/an, some,* and *null.* Some nouns can occur as noun phrases with no word before them: *pie, boys.* We then say that they have the nondefinite article *null,* which has the symbol Ø. Their nondefiniteness is marked by the absence of a word.

auxiliary   A structure in the verb phrase that contains the tense a sentence has, and may also contain a modal, a *have* + part., or a *be* + *ing,* or any combination of these if the order given here is observed.

common noun   A word like *boy, teacher, school.* Not a proper noun.

complement   The function of a noun phrase used in the predicate after *be* or after a verb of the *seem* type — like *a student* in "John is a student." A complement may also be an adjective or an adverbial of place.

complex sentence   A sentence made from two simple sentences by transformation. "Helen's hat is red" is a complex sentence because it is made from the simple sentences "Helen has a hat," "The hat is red."

complex vowel   Any vowel other than those of *pit, pet, pat, putt, pot.* The complex vowels are made and spelled in more complicated ways than the five simple vowels are.

compounding   Combining two or more sentences into more complex ones by connecting the compounded structures with conjunctions. Structures which are the same — verb phrases, noun phrases, adverbials — may be compounded, or whole sentences may be compounded. When the compounded structures are whole sentences, a comma is used before the conjunction.

conjunct   The elements in a compound structure that are joined by a conjunction. For example, in the sentence "Jerry lost the set but won the match," the conjunction *but* joins the two conjuncts *lost the set* and *won the match.*

conjunction   The words *and, but, yet, so, or, for, nor* are conjunctions. They are used to join the combined structures in a compound sentence. *Correlative conjunctions* are related pairs of conjunctions: *not . . . but, either . . . or, neither . . . nor.*

consonant   A sound made by stopping the breath in some way.

consonant cluster   Two or more consonant sounds in succession in a word without intervening vowel sounds.

dangling modifier   A grammatical error that may result when the subject of an insert sentence is not the same as the subject of the matrix sentence. For example, the *ing* verb phrase *seeing land* in the sentence **"Seeing land, a shout was raised"* would have had to result from the ungrammatical insert sentence **"A shout saw land."*

deletion   A transformation in which certain optional structures in a transform are omitted. For example, "I was seen by Phil" may become by deletion "I was seen," and "The boy who was in the park is my friend" may become "The boy in the park is my friend."

demonstratives   The determiners *this, that, these, those.*

determiner   An article, with the optional addition or substitution of other words like demonstratives, numbers, quantifiers, possessives. A determiner determines something about the meaning of the noun that follows it.

dialect   A form of a language that differs from another form, but not so greatly that speakers of one form are unable to communicate with speakers of the other.

function   The use to which a word or group of words is put.

grammar   The structure of sentences.

homophone   One of two words pronounced alike but spelled differently and having different meanings: *meet/meat.*

indefinite pronoun   Any combination of *some–, every–, any–, no–,* with *–one, –body, –thing: someone, everybody, anything,* etc. The indefinite pronoun is one type of noun phrase.

ing form of verb Any verb to which the morpheme **ing** has been added: *watching, hoping, studying, running.*

insert sentence One of the underlying sentences in a double-base transformation which is transformed into a structure other than a sentence and inserted into the other sentence to create a transform.

juncture A kind of break or pause in speaking, marked by a comma in the writing system. In the following sentence, this kind of break occurs after *John* and after *ahead:* "John, who was ahead, looked back at the other runners."

kernel sentence A sentence to which no optional transformational rules have been applied. It is made up of two main parts — a noun phrase that functions as the subject, and a verb phrase that functions as the predicate.

matrix sentence One of the underlying sentences in a double-base transformation into which a structure created by changing the other sentence is inserted to create a transform.

modal One of the words *may, can, will, shall, must.* The first four of these have the past tense forms *might, could, would, should.*

modifier The function of a word or group of words used to expand a noun phrase, verb phrase, or other kernel structure. In *the man in the car,* the prepositional phrase *in the car* expands the noun phrase *the man,* and thus functions as a *noun modifier.* The nonrestrictive relative clause *who was overanxious* functions as a *sentence modifier* in the sentence "Alice, *who was overanxious,* spoke before she thought."

morpheme The smallest unit of meaning. This may be a word or a part of a word. *Car* is one word and one morpheme. *Cars* is one word made up of two morphemes: **car + plural.** A sentence is composed of a sequence, or string, of morphemes, some of which may combine to form words. Thus **the + car + plural + past + be + use + ful** is a string of morphemes showing all the units of meaning of the sentence "The cars were useful." A *base word* is a word in its simplest form and represents a single morpheme. A *derivational morpheme* is a unit of meaning like **ly** or **ness** that is added to base words to change them into other kinds of words. An *inflectional morpheme* is one of the eight units of meaning that express ideas such as "past tense," "present tense," "possessive," "plural."

morphology The study of morphemes.

noun   A word like *Jerry, Mr. Dean, boy*. Proper nouns are also noun phrases. Common nouns are parts of noun phrases. Nouns usually indicate persons, places, things. *Count nouns* refer to things which can be counted, like *boy, battle, lake*, and may take the plural. *Noncount nouns* refer to things like *water* or *sugar* which cannot normally be counted. They are singular in number. *Abstract nouns* refer to something we can know and think about apart from any real object: *capability, excitement*. A noun that is not abstract is *concrete*.

noun phrase   The word or group of words used as subject of a simple sentence and in certain functions in the predicate. *Jerry, he, everybody, the boy* are all noun phrases.

object of a preposition   A function of a noun phrase. A prepositional phrase (*near the desk*) is made up of a preposition (*near*) and a noun phrase functioning as its object (*the desk*).

object of a verb   A function of a noun phrase. In "He hit the ball," *the ball* functions as the object of the verb *hit*.

participle   The form of a verb or *be* used after the word *have* or after *be* in the passive. In *has worked, have fallen*, and *had been*, the words *worked, fallen*, and *been* are participles. Participles are formed by the combination part. + verb, when the morpheme **part.** means whatever you do to a verb to make it a participle. All regular verbs and most irregular ones have a participle form that is identical with the past tense form.

particle   Such a word as *up, down, in, out, away*, which follows a verb and changes the meaning of the verb it accompanies. For example, in "The boys *fell*" the verbal is the simple intransitive verb *fell*. But in "The boys *fell out*" it is *fell* plus the particle *out*.

passive sentence   A transform in which the object of the verb of a kernel sentence becomes the subject and is followed by a form of *be* and the participle form of the verb. Thus, "Phil saw me" becomes "I was seen by Phil."

past tense   One of the two tenses of verbs, *be*, and modals.

personal pronoun   One of the words *I, he, she, it, we, you, they*. Personal pronouns are a kind of noun phrase.

phonology   The study of sounds.

phrase   A group of words used as a unit. The term is used also in the expressions *noun phrase* and *verb phrase*, which sometimes consist of single words.

pitch   The musical tone that is produced by the vibration of voiced sounds in speaking. An English sentence usually has three levels of pitch: *middle, high,* and *low.*

predicate   The function of the second of the two main parts of a kernel sentence.

prefix   A beginning added to a word to change its meaning. For example, *re–* is a prefix in *renew.*

preposition   A word like *in, on, by, near, with.*

prepositional phrase   A construction like *in the house, to the store,* formed by a preposition and a noun phrase functioning as its object.

present tense   One of the two tenses of verbs, *be,* and modals.

principal parts   The forms of a verb which one must know in order to be able to tell what all of the other forms will be. The principal parts of English verbs are the simple form, the past tense, and the participle: *eat/ate/eaten; think/thought/thought.*

quantifier   A part of a determiner like *several of, many of, much of, a few of.*

recursive   Capable of occurring repeatedly. The relative clause transformation, for example, is recursive; that is, the sentence can be expanded again and again by adding more relative clauses.

reflexive pronoun   The form a personal pronoun used as object has when it refers to the same person as the subject. In "John hurt himself," *himself* is a reflexive pronoun. Reflexive pronouns end in *–self* or *–selves.*

relative clause   A group of words that begins with a relative pronoun and contains at least the part of the predicate that expresses tense. Though it may contain a subject and a predicate, a relative clause is not a sentence. For example, *who was there, that the car struck, whom Ed knew, which burned up* are relative clauses. *Restrictive* clauses single out, or restrict, the meaning of the noun phrase to which they are attached: "The man *who called up* didn't leave his name." *Nonrestrictive clauses* simply give additional information: "Mr. Brown, who has a deep voice, called up." A nonrestrictive clause is set off by commas.

relative pronoun   *Who, which,* or *that.* The object form of *who* is *whom,* which is used when the noun phrase the pronoun refers to functions as object in the original sentence: "The dog bit the man." → *whom the dog bit.*

result sentence   A sentence that results from the addition of an insert to a matrix sentence.

schwa /ə/   The vowel that occurs in all syllables of English words
that have weak stress. It is spelled with various vowel letters: *e* in
happen, *a* in *beggar*, *u* in *careful*. It occurs in stressed syllables
only before /r/: *sir, heard, worm*, etc.

sentence connector   A word like *therefore, moreover, however, hence,
thus, consequently, furthermore*, which is used to join sentences.
Some of these have meanings similar to certain subordinators and
conjunctions, but behave somewhat differently, and are punctuated
differently. In the following sentence, *however* functions as a sentence connector: "Bill really tried; *however*, Jack just pretended to
try." Sentence connectors have either a semicolon or a period before them. The use of a comma before a sentence connector, rather
than a semicolon or colon, produces what is called a *run-on sentence*, or *comma fault*.

sentence modifier   A structure which applies its meaning to a matrix
sentence as a whole, not to some part of it. Nonrestrictive relative
clauses and the structures which derive from them are sentence
modifiers. In the following sentence, *willing to wait*, which resulted
by deletion from the nonrestrictive relative clause *who was willing
to wait*, functions as a sentence modifier: "Irene, *willing to wait*,
sat quietly on the bench."

series   A compound containing three or more conjuncts. All but the
last conjunct, or in some styles the last two conjuncts, are followed
by a comma: "The *wild, lean, tusked*, and *dangerous* boar charged
suddenly."

s form   The present tense form of verbs that goes with singular
subjects: *eats, wins, goes*.

simple form   The form of the verb that has no additions and is used
as the present tense with *I, we, you, they*, or plural subjects: *walk,
hurry*.

simple sentence   A sentence that is not made by combining other
sentences. "The boy is here" is a simple sentence. "The boy who
is here is John" is not a simple sentence, because it is made from
"The boy is here" and "The boy is John."

simple vowel   One of the five vowels shown in the words *pit, pet,
pat, putt*, and *pot*. These are indicated by the symbols /i/, /e/,
/a/, /u/, and /o/.

stress   The degree of loudness with which a syllable in a word or
sentence is pronounced. There are four degrees of stress in English:
first or principal (loudest), second (next loudest), third (next to
softest), weak (softest).

structures   Kinds of words, like *noun, adjective, verb*, and kinds of
groups of words like *noun phrase, verb phrase, relative clause*.

subject   The first of the two main parts of a kernel sentence. Subject is one of the functions of a noun phrase. It indicates someone or something about which the predicate makes a statement.

subordinate clause   A structure introduced by a subordinator and having a subject and predicate without being in itself a sentence. In the following sentence, *until he tried* is a subordinate clause: "*Until he tried*, Ed didn't know how easy it was." A semicolon or period is not used before a subordinate clause: "Bill ran, while John only trotted." To use a semicolon or a period instead of a comma here produces an error called a *fragment.*

subordinator   A word, like *because, if, unless, until, before, after, although, while, since*, which introduces a subordinate clause. In the following sentence, *after* functions as a subordinator: "*After* he had dressed, Joe went into the garden."

suffix   An ending added to a word to change its meaning. For example, *–ly* is a suffix in *quickly.*

syllable   A word or part of a word containing one vowel sound. Words have as many syllables as they have vowel sounds. *Hope* is a one-syllable word, because it contains just the vowel sound /ō/. *Hoping* has two syllables. *Hopefully* has three.

syntax   A part of the grammar — the way in which words are put together to form sentences.

tense   A feature of verbs and *be* related to the expression of meanings of time. The two English tenses, present and past, express various time meanings, but *past tense* generally expresses past time, and *present tense* generally doesn't.

transform   A sentence that is not a kernel sentence but has been made more complicated by a change of some kind.

transformation   The process by which kernel sentences are made into more complicated ones (transforms). A *single-base transformation* affects only a single sentence. A *double-base transformation* involves changing the structure of one sentence and inserting it in another sentence.

VCe pattern   A system by which complex vowels are distinguished from simple ones by the letter *e* following a vowel (V) letter and a consonant (C) letter. Thus the vowel of *pine* (/ī/) is distinguished from that of *pin* (/i/) by the *e* at the end of *pine.*

verb   A word like *sing, teach, think, feel, inspect*. Verbs usually express action of some sort. Some verbs, like *feel* and *know*, do not. In a kernel sentence, a verb is part of the predicate which says something about a subject. A *transitive verb* must be followed by an object. An *intransitive verb* does not take an object. Both kinds of verbs may be followed by certain other structures. Verbs of the *seem* type are neither transitive nor intransitive. Unlike other verbs, they may be followed by adjectives: *seem glad, look sad.*

verbal   A verbal is one of two structures that may follow the auxiliary in the verb phrase of a kernel sentence. A verbal consists of a verb alone or a verb plus one or more following structures. The other structure that may follow the auxiliary instead of a verbal begins with a form of *be.*

verb phrase   A structure that contains the auxiliary and either a verb with or without following structures or a form of *be* with following structures.

voiced sounds   When the breath that is used to make sounds comes from the throat, it may create a vibration. This vibration makes it have a little humming or buzzing sound. A sound with this hum or buzz is a voiced sound. A sound that does not have it is voiceless. All English vowels and most of the consonants are voiced sounds. The voiceless sounds are the consonants /p/, /t/, /k/, /ch/, /f/, /th/, /s/, /sh/, /h/.

vowel   A sound made without stopping the breath. Different vowel sounds are made by changing the shape of the mouth.

word class   A classification of words like *noun, relative pronoun, preposition,* in which all the members are alike in some way. The four large word classes are *noun, verb, adjective,* and *adverb of manner.* Many words occur in more than one word class.

INDEX

Abbreviations, 12; adverbial of frequency, 104; adverbial of manner, 40; adverbial of place, 36; adverbial of time, 105; affix, 57; article, 24; auxiliary, 32; common noun, 24; middle verb, 43; noun phrase, 13; participle, 77; subordinator, 259; verb phrase, 13

Abstract nouns, 31–32

Adjectives: adverbs made from, 232; *be* +, 34; complement function of, 261; ending in *–ed*, 165–67, formed from nouns, 167–68; ending in *–ical*, 232–33; meaning of, 35–36; morphemes forming, 8, 171–72, 230–32, 255, 356–57; as noun phrase modifiers, 227–29; partial (semi-), 35; series of, 375–76; transformations making, 148–50

Adverbials: of frequency, 104–05, abbreviation for, 104, rule for, 105, transformation and, 141–42; of manner, 40–41, 103, abbreviation for, 40, transformation and, 139–41; of place, 36–37, 103–04, 404, abbreviation for, 36, *be* and, 87, rule for, 36, transformation and, 135–37; in the sentence modifier position, 354–56; of time, 105–07, abbreviation for, 105, transformation and, 137–39

Adverbs: of frequency, 111–12; made from adjectives, 232; morphemes forming, 41, 172–73; of place, 36–37, noun modifiers and, 229–30; relative, 264–65

Affixes: abbreviation for, 57; *be-*, 52; definition of, 52; derivational, 51–52; *–ed*, 51; *–ful*, 52; inflectional, 51–52, plural, 53; *–ion*, 52; *–ness*, 52; *–ous*, 52; transformation and, 57–58

Apostrophes: to mark omissions, 123; to show possession, 279

Appositives, 249–51, 285; definition of, 250

Articles: abbreviation for, 24; definite, 24–27, 98–99; determiners and, 95, 99; meaning of, 27–29; nondefinite, 24–28, 96–101, 151–53; null, 25–27, 29, 81, 96–97, 151–53; number and, 101–02; proper nouns and, 17

As . . . as, 308–09

As much (many) . . . as, 311–12

Assimilation, 379–80

Auxiliaries, 48–51, 89–90, 409–12, 414–16; abbreviation for, 32; + *be*, 33–34, 37; combinations from, 84–86; rule for, 48, 72, 86–88; tense and, 49, 72–73; verbals and, 32–33, 57

Base words, 51–52, 168

Be: + adjective, 34; adverbials and, 87, 103–04, 106; auxiliary +, 33–34, 37; + *ing,* 80–90; + noun phrase, 33–34; + tense, 60–61, 239; transformation and, 107–11, 119–20, 123, 158–59

Become class of verbs, 42

Capitalization: days of the week, 17; holidays, 17; months of the year, 17; proper nouns, 17–18

Cardinal number, 101–02

Collective nouns, 97

Comma fault (splice), 385, 390

Commas: conjunctions and, 366; nonrestrictive clauses and, 200–01; sentence connectors and, 388–90; in series, 373

Common nouns, *see* Nouns, common

Comparative transformation, 301–05; with *more,* 304–05

Complements, 404, 414–16; *for . . . to* in, 346–48; transitive verbs and, 408–12

Concrete nouns, 31–32

Conjunctions, 384, 386, 389–90; commas and, 366; coordinating, 364; correlative, 371–73; periods and, 366; sentence connectors and, 388–90; subordinating, 364; transformation and, 364–67

Connectors, *see* Sentence connectors

Consonants: doubling of, 82; sounds of, 425–26, spellings of, 425–26; voiceless, 55–56

Contractions, 76

Coordinating conjunctions, 364

Correlative conjunctions, 371–73

Count nouns, 25–27, 30–31, 55

Definite articles, 24–27, 98–99

Deletion, 159–60; conjunctions and, 367–71; *for . . . to* and, 345–46; nonrestrictive relative clauses and, 238–40; possessive + *ing*

Index

39